THE MARKET CITIZENSHIP ILLUSION: FREE MOVEMENT RIGHTS FOR ATYPICAL WORKERS

This open access book challenges the existing focus in EU citizenship scholarship which overlooks the limitations of free movement for atypical workers.

Arguing that the deliberately vague EU concept of 'work' allows for its restricted application in Member States, the book shows how many workers and economic contributors are left out of the free movement regime. It does this by taking a mixed methods approach: relying on both qualitative case studies and legal analysis of EU and UK legislation, case law, and decision maker guidance. All this leads to a significant and original argument that, if EU free movement rights are awarded on the basis of market credentials, more must be done to work towards a more contemporary, accurate and inclusive market citizenship. Provocative and thought-provoking, this book will appeal to all scholars of EU free movement law.

Volume 130 in the Series Modern Studies in European Law

Modern Studies in European Law

Recent titles in this series:

The Future of EU Constitutionalism
Edited by Matej Avbelj

The Changing Role of Citizens in EU Democratic Governance
Edited by Davor Jancic

The EU and the Baltic Sea Area
Edited by Allan Rosas and Henrik Ringbom

The Evolving Governance of EU Competition Law in a Time of Disruptions: A Constitutional Perspective
Edited by Carlo Maria Colombo, Kathryn Wright and Mariolina Eliantonio

The European Integrated Border Management: Frontex, Human Rights, and International Responsibility
Giulia Raimondo

Private Autonomy in EU Internal Market Law: Parameters of its Protection and Limitation
Rufat Babayev

Free Movement and Welfare Access in the European Union: Re-Balancing Conflicting Interests in Citizenship Jurisprudence
Victoria Hooton

EU Trade and Investment Treaty-Making Post-Lisbon: Moving Beyond Mixity
Gesa Kübek

The Normative Foundations for EU Criminal Justice: Powers, Limits and Justifications
Jacob Öberg

EU Neighbourhood Law: Wider Europe and the Extended EU's Legal Space
Alessandro Petti

The Dynamics of Powers in the European Union
Edited by Christina Eckes, Päivi Leino-Sandberg and Anna W Ghavanin

The European Convention on Human Rights and Private Law: Comparative Perspectives from South-Eastern Europe
Edited by Mateja Durovic and Cristina Poncibò

Judging Composite Decision-Making: The Transformation of European Administrative Law
Filipe Brito Bastos

EU Diplomacy in Multilateral Fora
Edited by Christine Kaddous and Frank Hoffmeister

For the complete list of titles in this series
see www.bloomsbury.com/uk/series/modern-studies-in-european-law/

The Market Citizenship Illusion: Free Movement Rights for Atypical Workers

Alice Welsh

•HART•
OXFORD • LONDON • NEW YORK • NEW DELHI • SYDNEY

HART PUBLISHING

Bloomsbury Publishing Plc

Kemp House, Chawley Park, Cumnor Hill, Oxford, OX2 9PH, UK

1385 Broadway, New York, NY 10018, USA

Bloomsbury Publishing Ireland Limited, 29 Earlsfort Terrace, Dublin 2, D02 AY28, Ireland

HART PUBLISHING, the Hart/Stag logo, BLOOMSBURY and the Diana logo are trademarks of Bloomsbury Publishing Plc

First published in Great Britain 2025

A catalogue record for this book is available from the British Library.

A catalogue record for this book is available from the Library of Congress.

Library of Congress Control Number: 2024950002

ISBN: HB: 978-1-50996-660-8
ePDF: 978-1-50996-662-2
ePub: 978-1-50996-661-5

Typeset by Compuscript Ltd, Shannon

For product safety related questions contact productsafety@bloomsbury.com

To find out more about our authors and books visit www.hartpublishing.co.uk. Here you will find extracts, author information, details of forthcoming events and the option to sign up for our newsletters.

ACKNOWLEDGEMENTS

There are so many people who have been generous with their time and help throughout the course of the research undertaken for this book. A huge and special thank you to my wonderful PhD supervisors. I am especially grateful for the guidance, inspiration and support of my supervisor, colleague and friend, Charlotte O'Brien. Thank you for always supporting and inspiring me, showing me the research ropes and making my PhD and work on the EU Rights and Brexit Hub such a rewarding and fun experience. Thank you to the amazing Nicolas Rennuy for stepping in as PhD supervisor and his continued mentorship throughout the project, sharing his invaluable knowledge, advice and kind words. Also, to Simon Lightfoot for his encouragement and for always reminding me to step back and reflect on the bigger picture. I also want to thank my PhD examiners, Michael Dougan, Niamh Nic Shuibhne and Caroline Hunter, for their feedback, suggestions and encouragement to develop the work further. Thanks are also owed to the Economic and Social Research Council for funding the initial research for my PhD and then for the funding the work of the EU Rights and Brexit Hub.

Thank you to all who contributed and collaborated on the work for this book. I am indebted to Matthew Evans and the AIRE Centre for hosting me as a caseworker and granting me access to their vital advice work for this research. I am also so thankful to Willem Maas for his generosity and insightful discussions during my research visit to Toronto. Much of the work in this book has been supported and impacted by the expertise of the project team of the EU Rights and Brexit Hub, including Charlotte O'Brien, Simon Parker, Madeleine Sumption, John Evemy, Mariña Fernández-Reino and Denis Kierans. I am also so privileged to have shared the time of my PhD studies with inspiring colleagues at PLP, the AIRE Centre and the Refugee Council. I have also had the great fortune of insight from a number of advice organisations and stakeholders working on the protection of EU citizens' rights in the UK. In the interests of keeping the casework anonymous it is not possible to name everyone here – but the book would simply not exist without referrals and evidence submissions from advice organisations and their clients. Without this it would not be possible to identify and explore the problems migrant workers experience in the UK. Thank you for showing me the importance of this research in taking a small snapshot of the vital work you do.

I have had immeasurable support from colleagues at York Law School. It is impossible to list everyone who has helped me these last 13 years, for welcoming me as an undergraduate in 2011 and giving me the necessary tools and confidence to pursue this research and career. Special thanks must be given to the late Salwa Eweis for having the answers to my endless questions and always being confident that I would 'get through it'. The casework in this book has been directly supported by the expertise, organisation and technical support of the Baroness Hale Legal Clinic, including Sara Boulton, Stephen Levett and Francess Daly. I'd like to thank Vicki Hillyard for all her help in editing this book. And thanks to the excellent Sasha Jawed for guiding me through the publishing process, and to all at Hart Publishing.

Finally, thank you to my family and friends. Thanks to my mum, dad and brother for their wisdom, support and for always keeping me humble. A very special thank you to Katie – my dearest and oldest friend – your letters, care packages and frequent pep talks mean the world to me. Last, but certainly not least, thank you to my husband, Tim, for your care and support and for always cheering the loudest.

Alice Welsh
July 2024

TABLE OF CONTENTS

LIST OF ABBREVIATIONS

ADM	Advice for decision-makers
CA	Carer's Allowance
CJEU	Court of Justice of the European Union
DMG	Decision-maker guidance
DWP	Department for Work and Pensions
ECI	European Citizens' Initiative
EEA	European Economic Area
ESA	Employment and Support Allowance
EU	European Union
EU-LFS	European Labour Force Survey
HB	Housing Benefit
HMRC	Her Majesty's Revenue and Customs
IS	Income Support
JRC	Joint Research Centre
JSA	Jobseeker's Allowance
MET	Minimum earnings threshold
NRM	National referral mechanism
SSHD	Secretary of State for the Home Department
SSWP	Secretary of State for Work and Pensions
UC	Universal Credit
UK	United Kingdom
UT	Upper Tribunal
ZHC	Zero-hours contract

TABLE OF CASES

Domestic Cases

European Cases

TABLE OF LEGISLATION

UK Legislation

Primary Legislation

Secondary Legislation

European Legislation

1

Introduction

Naomie is a citizen of the European Union (EU). She is a national of the Czech Republic and has lived in the UK since 2011 with her four-year-old son and her mother, for whom she provides full-time care. Naomie also has two jobs. For the last three years she has worked as a housekeeper for three and half hours each weekday. Alongside this, for the last four years she has worked casually, distributing mail and leaflets. Although the income from this is sporadic, it is all she can find to fit around the care she provides to her mother, who is blind, and her responsibilities as a lone parent. However, in October 2016, when Naomie became homeless and sought assistance from the welfare system, her status as an EU citizen was of no avail and she was denied equal treatment with UK nationals. Her local council rejected her application for housing assistance as it wrongly assumed that she did not earn enough for her work to be genuine and effective. Moreover, the council claimed it was not possible for her to be a worker *because* of the time she spent providing care for her mother. Naomie's five years of residence and at least four years of work counted for nothing.

Naomie's case illustrates the central goal of this research – to investigate the limits of EU citizenship and free movement through the experience of EU citizens in atypical work. The atypical worker occupies a curious space in EU law. While freedom of movement is theoretically available to all EU citizens, those who are deemed to be economically inactive have a much weaker claim to equal treatment rights and access to social welfare systems in a host Member State. The stark lines drawn between those who are entitled – the economically active – and those who are not – the economically inactive – have sometimes been rationalised as part of a trade-off in which the scope of economic activity is drawn widely, to minimise the number of migrants who fall the wrong side of the line. This book tests that rationale, adopting the atypical worker as the focal point – an EU citizen who is both economically active and a potential claimant on host Member States welfare systems.

The definition of EU migrant work for the purposes of Article 45 TFEU is not limited to standard employment. The Court of Justice of the European Union (CJEU) has acknowledged that non-standard employment, in this case specifically part-time work, 'constitutes for a large number of persons an effective means of improving their living conditions' and that the effectiveness of EU law would be jeopardised if the free movement rights of workers were 'reserved solely to persons engaged in full-time employment'.[1] However, the definition adopted at the EU level leaves the outer edges of worker status fuzzy, delegating its implementation and application to Member States. The UK's minimum earnings threshold (MET) is one such incarnation of this delegation and plays a central role in the case studies adopted in this book.

This work makes the case for the explicit inclusion of atypical work in the EU definition of worker. While other scholarship on the limitations of free movement typically focuses on the exclusion of those deemed to be economically inactive,[2] and while I position my argument in agreement with the literature that find their treatment problematic, there is little scrutiny of the exclusions *within* economic activity in this debate. How economic activity is experienced has shifted significantly away from the full-time and permanent employment that was more prevalent when free movement rules were written. The narrative that characterises the rights of free movement as a reward for engagement in the internal market can be misleading as it overlooks the treatment of work that is deemed to be outside the scope of 'economic activity'. An outdated conception of work moves the goalposts for EU citizens who are required to demonstrate, not just economic activity, but *enough* of the *right kind* of economic activity. As work is less likely to automatically denote self-sufficiency,[3] depriving atypical workers of equal access to welfare benefits could prevent them, in practice, from exercising their free movement rights. Additionally, given that already disadvantaged demographics are disproportionately represented among atypical workers, a failure to adapt or update the meaning of economic activity entrenches inequality by withholding equal treatment rights from the workers who may need it most, and in turn withholding free movement from them as a means to improve living standards.

The empirical data presented in this research provides insight into how free movement rights are experienced by atypical workers in the UK. As well as contributing to existing evidence that the test is incompatible with EU law,[4] it also illustrates the considerable discretion given to (or assumed by) Member States in the implementation of the EU concept of migrant work. The delegation of the construction of the outer edges of worker status to Member States allows it to

[1] Case 53/81 *Levin* ECLI:EU:C:1982:105, [1982] ECR 1035 [15].

[2] E Spaventa, 'Earned Citizenship – understanding Union citizenship through its scope' in D Kochenov, *EU Citizenship and Federalism: the Role of Rights* (Cambridge University Press, 2017) 207; N Nic Shuibhne, 'Limits Rising, Duties Ascending: The Changing Legal Shape of Union Citizenship' (2015) 52 *Common Market Law Review* 889; D Thym, 'The Elusive Limits of Solidarity: Residence Rights of and Social Benefits for Economically Inactive Union Citizens' (2015) 52 *Common Market Law Review* 17.

[3] N Nic Shuibhne, 'Reconnecting free movement of workers and equal treatment in an unequal Europe' (2018) 43 *European Law Review* 477; G Davies, 'Migrant Union Citizens and Social Assistance: Trying to Be Reasonable About Self-Sufficiency' (College of Europe Research Papers in Law No 2/2016) 7.

[4] C O'Brien, *Unity and Adversity: EU Citizenship, Social Justice and the Cautionary Tale of the UK* (Hart Publishing, 2017).

be co-opted as a tool for exclusion – to reject welfare claims from the most vulnerable and already marginalised workers. This analysis challenges the logic behind limiting free movement rights to the economically active. The exclusion of persons in atypical work who contribute to the internal market cannot be reconciled with pure market citizenship, and neither can it be justified by the requirement of an economic nexus. It instead represents a political value judgement to disregard some forms of economic activity or contribution to the Member State. As such, the plight of some economically active EU nationals are ignored and inequalities present in the labour market are further entrenched to placate Member States' desires to exclude, and thereby to discriminate.

1.1. Methodology

The decision to examine the rights of atypical workers in the UK was informed by the introduction of the MET in February 2014 and subsequent limitations on EU migrants rights in the UK. The MET adopts a two-tier approach. The first tier consists of a strict earnings threshold and the second tier acts as a discretionary space for decision-makers to apply the EU's test of 'genuine and effective' work. The MET has been critiqued for its potential to be used as a sweeping exclusionary tool to separate economically active EU migrants from their free movement rights.[5] It therefore provides a suitable testing ground to investigate how free movement is experienced by economically active EU nationals, while atypical workers are especially likely to be subjected to the second tier of the test, so provide appropriate cases for ascertaining just how substantive and inclusionary this second tier is. Atypical work in this research is interpreted broadly to include all work that sits outside the standard conception of full-time and permanent employment contracts. This includes work that may feature one or more of the following characteristics: part-time, temporary, fixed-term, casual, zero-hours or on-call, agency work and pay-per-gig work.

To explore atypical workers' access to welfare in the UK, this research utilises a mixed socio-legal approach.[6] The book begins with an analysis of secondary data on the changes to the labour market in the UK and the EU more broadly. It then undertakes a doctrinal analysis of the law governing the rights of EU atypical migrant workers at both the Union and Member State level in the UK[7] to identify implications for the welfare of mobile atypical workers.[8] This analysis is then paired

[5] C O'Brien, 'The pillory, the precipice and the slippery slope: the profound effects of the UK's legal reform programme targeting EU migrants' (2015) 37 *Journal of Social Welfare and Family Law* 111.

[6] F Cownie and A Bradney, 'Socio-legal studies: a challenge to the doctrinal approach' in D Watkins and M Burton (eds), *Research Methods in Law*, 2nd edn (Routledge, 2013) 36.

[7] T Hutchinson, 'Doctrinal Research: Researching the Jury' in D Watkins and M Burton (eds), *Research Methods in Law*, 2nd edn (Routledge, 2013) 13.

[8] P Chynoweth, 'Legal Research' in A Knight and L Ruddock (eds), *Advanced Research methods in the Built Environment* (Wiley-Blackwell Publishing, 2008) 31.

with an empirical examination of real case studies, drawing out specific issues with the worker status test and how it is applied to and excludes EU atypical workers. Finally, the book takes a broadly socio-legal analysis of the fundamental status of EU citizenship combining doctrinal and empirical work. Through this, the efficacy of Union citizenships ability to protect the rights of mobile market citizens is questioned, particularly for those atypical workers who are excluded from 'worker status'.

1.1.1. Case Studies of Worker Status Decisions

The empirical limb of this research consists of case studies which review the law in action for EU migrant atypical workers attempting to access welfare benefits in the UK. These case studies are drawn from a qualitative data analysis of documents (decision letters, mandatory reconsiderations and appeal documentation) and case records drawn from the advice work of the AIRE Centre and the EU Rights and Brexit Hub research project.[9] This methodological approach is necessary to gain insight into how the rights of EU citizenship and free movement are experienced and to capture the specific hurdles faced by EU nationals in atypical work.

Law at the administrative level can often be shrouded in mystery, leaving barriers to justice frequently unnoticed.[10] Document analysis provides one of the best available means to examine how UK decision-makers apply the relevant EU law and its interpretation to a variety of real cases involving atypical workers.[11] This method involved analysing case notes on the circumstances of the atypical workers and decision letters, revealing the reasoning of decision-makers, including the law and evidence on which they relied. Using real case studies provides a better understanding of how EU law is implemented than hypothetical case studies, 'microsimulation', or only having sight to the cases that make it to court appeals.

Case studies throw up some problems that are harder to predict, such as misunderstandings and mistakes by decision-makers. Where errors exist at these early stages, claimants lose confidence in the system and are put off by long, drawn-out processes and appeals.[12] Therefore, examining initial decisions, even when potentially corrected at a later stage, or with the intervention of specialist legal advice charities, can unveil processes, erroneous decisions and potentially systemic errors that can leave a lasting impact on how free movement rights are experienced in the UK.

[9] L Webley, 'Qualitative Approaches to Empirical Legal Research' in P Cane and H Kritzer (eds), *The Oxford Handbook of Empirical Legal Research* (Oxford University Press, 2010).

[10] V Lens, A Ausberger, A Hughes and T Wu, 'Choreographing Justice: Administrative law judges and the management of welfare disputes' (2013) 40 *Journal of Law and Society* 199; O'Brien (n 4).

[11] Webley (n 9).

[12] House of Commons Work and Pensions Committee, 'Decision making and appeals in the benefits system' (HC313, February 2010) Ev 1, S Howes and KM Jones, 'Computer says "No!" Stage two: challenging decisions' (Child Poverty Action Group, July 2019) 29.

The AIRE Centre is a UK-based specialist legal charity which works to ensure that people enjoy their rights under European law. Among other activities, they provide advice to individuals and caseworkers from non-specialist organisations who can contact them through a nationwide advice line.[13] The case studies were collected in partnership with the AIRE Centre, which provided access and permission to record anonymous data. The EU Rights and Brexit Hub is a legal action research project which provides free nationwide second-tier advice on EU nationals' and their family members' access to public services in the UK, including welfare benefits. The EU Rights and Brexit Hub collected cases between September 2020 and July 2023. These case studies were collected as part of the author's role as a research fellow on the project, where I worked with benefit advisers to provide the necessary advice on EU rights to ensure that cases could be appealed.[14]

As I engaged only with cases in which individuals sought help, I could not examine the experiences of EU workers who did not seek assistance. This means excluding those who did not require help, but also those who did not understand that they could challenge a decision – individuals may lack knowledge of national legal and administrative environments or struggle with language requirements.[15] Even so, there was a steady demand from individuals and organisations seeking help from the AIRE Centre and EU Rights and Brexit Hub; the current legal advice landscape in the UK and cuts to legal aid, have created an 'advice deficit', resulting in increased demand for legal advice charities.[16] Legal advice 'deserts' in specialist areas such as immigration and EU free movement law[17] mean that local advice charities may rely on specialist organisations such as the AIRE Centre or EU Rights and Brexit Hub, especially in the context of welfare for EU nationals in the UK, where the accuracy of decision-making has been found to be of a poor quality.[18]

[13] I spent three months as a legal caseworker at the AIRE Centre as part of the ESRC Company Internship Scheme. I was not involved in advising any of the AIRE Centre cases used in this research.

[14] I spent three years as a research fellow on this Governance after Brexit project funded by the Economic and Social Research Council, grant reference number ES/S007385/1. While I advised all these cases, no identifying information was recorded in the process and examination of casework documents for this book was taken after the advice had concluded in each case.

[15] See for example L Wintersteiger, 'Legal Needs, Legal Capability and the Role of Public Legal Education' (Law for Life: the Foundation for Public Legal Education, 2015); P Pleasence, NJ Balmer and C Denvir, 'How People Understand and Interact with the Law' (PPSR, 2015); Amnesty International UK, 'Cuts that hurt: The impact of legal aid cuts in England on access to justice' (October 2016).

[16] The Low Commission, 'Tackling the Advice Deficit: A strategy for access to advice and legal support on social welfare law in England and Wales' (Legal Action Group, 2014); D Morris and W Barr, 'The impact of cuts in legal aid funding on charities' (2013) 35 *Journal of Social Welfare and Family Law* 79; J Organ and J Sigafoos, 'The impact of LASPO on routes to justice' (Equality and Human Rights Commission Research report 118, September 2018).

[17] N Byrom, 'The State of the Sector: The impact of cuts to civil legal aid on practitioners and their clients' (University of Warwick, April 2013); J Wilding, 'Droughts and Deserts: A report on the immigration legal aid market' (April 2019).

[18] O'Brien (n 4) 119; J Shaw, 'Between Law and Political Truth? Member State Preferences, EU Free Movement Rules and National Immigration Law' (2015) 17 *Cambridge Yearbook of European Legal Studies* 247.

1.1.2. Identifying Cases

Both the AIRE Centre and EU Rights and Brexit Hub received a range of queries from across the country. This research aimed to identify cases where the applications of EU migrants in atypical work for welfare benefits or permanent residence depended on the worker status test. Relevant search terms were adopted to draw out any cases from the two databases that interacted with the worker status test, the MET specifically, or that mentioned atypical work. These were then manually examined for more detail. From these, cases were only selected where the above search criteria were mentioned in the decision-making process or reported by the first-tier adviser in the decision-making process. By using secondary records of cases advised by the AIRE Centre, the data collection was limited to the information recorded by the caseworker at the time. Similarly, as the EU Rights and Brexit Hub worked only on second-tier advice, the data available was contingent on what first-tier advisers could access and choose to send on. Sometimes this would mean that decision letters were missing, or specific information on income was left out. Further cases were therefore discarded where insufficient information was available concerning applicants' working conditions, the result of their application, or the reasons for a decision. After this process, 15 cases were drawn from the AIRE Centre and 19 from the case files of the EU Rights and Brexit Hub. All cases were recorded using pseudonyms and any decision letters or court documents were redacted of any identifiable information. I have also altered specific dates where they are given, although the duration of the relevant periods of time are kept the same. Nationalities have also been swapped with other Member States where possible.

Due to the nature of the data collection the case studies are varied in their level of detail. However, each provides an insight into how the worker test affects the rights of a variety of EU atypical workers to access welfare benefits and permanent residence in a host Member State. The cases all concerned the rights of EU migrants who were both resident and working in the UK. The analysis in this thesis therefore focuses on the relationship between EU citizens and the state in which they exclusively work and reside. The recorded cases cover a variety of working conditions, demographics, application type and personal circumstances. A qualitative content analysis was used to draw out emerging themes and common problems from decision letters and advice notes. These themes informed and constructed the basis of the analysis as to how decision-makers apply the test, including levels of compliance with and understanding of the relevant EU concepts.

1.2. Structure of the Book

Chapter two sets the scene by exploring the rise in and precarity of atypical work in the European labour market. It analyses secondary data on the European labour market to highlight the growing significance of atypical work, and to shed light on the demographic features of atypical workers. The precarity created by the atypical labour market is analysed, highlighting the potential barriers to free movement and further underscoring the importance of access to welfare systems to off-set the social risks of atypical work. The chapter sets the context within which the EU's concept of economic activity is tested against the reality of work in the European labour market.

The EU's definition of work and its potential to be inclusive of the variety of economic activity is explored in chapter three. The CJEU's concept of 'genuine and effective' work is identified as the pivotal point of contention. The appearance of inclusivity in this vague concept is tested by identifying aspects of atypical work that have been expressly included, as well as potential gaps. This chapter also examines the decision of EU legislators and the CJEU not to adopt more specific guidance for the definition of work, instead delegating the responsibility to Member States, who are granted the ability to distil the concept to the exclusion of atypical workers.

The next three chapters include a close examination of the how the worker status test has been adopted in the UK. Chapter four begins with a doctrinal analysis of how the UK tests whether an EU migrant worker has worker status, including the introduction of MET and how it works. This is compared with how other Member States assess worker status and potential compatibility issues with the test under EU law are raised.

Chapters five and six then turn to the empirical challenge in the research: to examine how atypical workers experience their free movement rights in practice. These chapters demonstrate the impact of the imprecise and broad definitions when left to the discretion of Member States. Chapter five identifies a number of concerns with how the MET and second-tier 'genuine and effective test' treats atypical work. These concerns relate to the use of the earnings threshold as a conclusive indicator of worker status and the inadequacy and inaccuracy of the decision-maker guidance, all of which can steer decision-makers towards identifying atypical work as marginal and ancillary. The indirect discrimination faced by atypical workers, particularly when in already disadvantaged demographics, are highlighted in chapter six. This chapter examines the impact of the uniform approach to worker status, and the indirect discrimination faced by workers who encounter barriers to more standard employment, such as those arising from disability, care responsibilities (disproportionately borne by women) and domestic abuse. These problems extend beyond issues of compatibility and can reflect a combination of problems with the UK's approach and the EU concept of worker.

The final two substantive chapters of the book turns to EU citizenship as a source of rights for excluded atypical workers. The first step is to set out the expectations of EU citizenship. Chapter seven looks to theoretical models and political challenges of Union citizenship, addressing criticism in the literature that it has not outgrown its market origins. Through this investigation, EU citizenship is understood within its market constraints, and its capacity to protect the rights of

EU citizens who are both economically active and potentially dependent on welfare is questioned. Chapter eight then explores the rights of EU citizenship with a focus on the terms by which EU atypical workers who are excluded from workers status can claim access to a host Member State's national welfare system. This details the transition of these rights, from calls for a 'degree of financial solidarity' to the CJEU's recent restrictive interpretation of Directive 2004/38 as creating a ceiling to citizenship rights, considering the political sensitivity of these free movement rights as a driver of restrictive applications. Ultimately, this chapter argues that EU citizenship has little to offer atypical workers who must still demonstrate *enough* economic activity to guarantee the protection of free movement and equal treatment rights.

Chapter nine brings these findings together, strengthening the case for the explicit inclusion of atypical workers in the scope of economic activity. The study of atypical workers' experiences of drawing on free movement rights illustrates that economic activity does not guarantee equal treatment rights in host Member States. This undermines the narrative of EU citizenship even as a market citizenship, suggesting instead a model of individual membership, subject to subscription requirements, club etiquette and manager discretion.

2

'What a Way to Make a Living': The Risks of the Atypical Labour Market

2.1. Introduction

In 2016, Damien Green MP, then UK Work and Pensions Secretary, declared that the concept of 'a proper job' with 'a fixed monthly salary, with fixed hours, paid holidays, sick pay, a pension scheme and other contractual benefits' had all changed with the rise of gig economy.[1] Green's suggestion was that gig employment gave people more ownership, control and flexibility over their work, time and who they provide services to.[2] Yet, in reality, gig work was not the beginning of this change. The European labour market has changed quite significantly since the introduction of free movement for workers in EU Member States nearly 70 years ago. Across Europe there has been an increase in all kinds of atypical contracts, including part-time, temporary, casual and agency work.

This chapter addresses how economic recessions, developments in technology and pressures to integrate those previously excluded from the labour market (from both the perspective of increasing equality of opportunity, but also more instrumental objectives of 'activating' the 'inactive') have shifted the standard conception of work. While the most common type of employment contract is still full-time and permanent,[3] atypical work sectors have been growing, and new forms of flexible working have emerged.

While flexibility can mean higher employment rates, space for those who have limited capacity for full-time work and more freedom in work, the price of that flexibility is shifted onto those same workers. A high employment rate does not guarantee good employment. Far from the 'everyday entrepreneur' of Green's speech with greater autonomy and control over their working lives, atypical work

[1] D Green MP, 'Keynote Speech: A Welfare System that Works for All' (Reform Welfare Conference, 16 November 2016), www.reform.uk/research/welfare-system-works-all-rt-hon-damian-green-mp-secretary-state-work-and-pensions.

[2] ibid.

[3] Full-time permanent work still makes up 59% of employment in the EU. A Broughton, M Green, C Rickard and S Swift, 'Precarious employment in Europe part 1: patterns, trends and policy strategy' (European Parliament Committee on Employment and Social Affairs, July 2016) 32–33.

can lead to financial insecurity, irregularity of work opportunities, less control and little real flexibility.

To adjust to the increase of atypical contracts in the labour market,[4] in-work benefits have become more commonplace in welfare systems, reflecting Davies' assertion that the 'assumption that those in employment are self-sufficient is not reflected in many European societies'.[5] Yet, EU migrant workers face the extra hurdle of having to establish worker status to exercise free movement rights and access social assistance systems in Member States. EU migrants stuck in a labour market which is less likely to offer secure employment may struggle to insert themselves into the scope of 'worker status' and are left without access to essential 'in-work' benefits.

Before considering the suitability of the definition of an EU migrant 'worker' for atypical workers, it is important to reflect on the reality of work in the labour market it serves. Given that, as Nic Shuibhne states, EU legislation on workers has 'barely changed notwithstanding transformative change in the practice of work itself'.[6] This chapter builds a contextual understanding of the European labour market and identifies some of the challenges for the legal framework to accurately reflect the experience of cross-border workers. The increased dependence on social assistance to alleviate risks associated with precarious employment will also be considered.

Together, this begins to highlight some of the barriers to free movement for the increasing number of EU citizens in precarious work. It will also be built on to establish an expectation of what the EU definition of worker will need to include for atypical workers to access equal treatment rights in a host Member State. This expectation will then be taken forward in chapter three to analyse the suitability of the definition of work in EU law.

The full array of free movement rights for EU citizens are contingent on economic activity. Yet the changing labour market depicts a growing number of EU migrant workers who may be relying on the edge of the definition of worker while facing the risks of precarious employment making access to welfare more essential. Atypical workers therefore play a key role in the discussion of EU citizenship and free movement; they are simultaneously economic actors and likely recipients of social assistance. Should atypical workers face exclusion from equal treatment rights, the full array of EU citizenship rights are reserved, not just for those who engage in the market, but those who engage *enough* and in the right way.

Firstly, section 2.2 introduces the value of worker status. Section 2.3 then highlights common trends in labour statistics which show an increase in various

[4] C Belfield, J Cribb, A Hood and R Joyce, 'Two decades of income inequality in Britain: the role of wages, household earnings and redistribution' (Institute for Fiscal Studies, 2017).

[5] G Davies, 'Migrant Union Citizens and Social Assistance: Trying to Be Reasonable About Self-Sufficiency' (2016) College of Europe Research Papers in Law No 2/2016 5.

[6] N Nic Shuibhne, 'Reconnecting free movement of workers and equal treatment in an unequal Europe' (2018) 43 *European Law Review* 477, 479.

forms of non-traditional employment across both Europe and the UK. Section 2.4 looks to the rise of the gig economy, and how it encroaches on many traditional work arrangements. Section 2.5 focuses on the experience of atypical work, and the shift of financial risk onto the worker. This includes how increased flexibility, often touted as a benefit to those in atypical work, can lead to further precarity in workers lives. Access to welfare and social rights emerge as necessary remedies for workers to alleviate some of the risks associated with atypical employment. Finally, section 2.6 examines how atypical work particularly impacts women, Disabled, younger and migrant workers, including any specific risks these groups may face in the atypical labour market. This section, therefore, disputes the narrative that flexible work inevitably benefits individuals alienated from the traditional labour market. Instead, it can push risk disproportionately on those workers, while the benefits promised may not fully materialise.

2.2. Worker Status in EU Law

Under EU free movement law, a substantial divide exists between the rights available to those who acquire 'worker' status and those who do not. All EU citizens have the fundamental freedom to move to another Member State in Article 21 TFEU;[7] however, moving to another Member State as a worker guarantees some of the most robust EU rights for individuals. As Dougan and Spaventa write, work as

> a direct contribution to the economic life of the host community enables the foreign worker to overcome the exclusive nature of the group identity, and to benefit from the assimilation model as regards access to (even non-contributory, non-employment related) social benefits.[8]

As such, work is seen as breaking the barrier of territorial restrictions to national welfare systems and extends social solidarity through the recognition of the economic contribution made to the host Member State.

While it is possible to establish extended periods of residence rights through being a student or being self-sufficient,[9] these routes require that the EU citizen does not become a burden on the host Member State's social assistance system and has comprehensive sickness insurance. These requirements mean that, in practice, it can be almost impossible for EU citizens to access social assistance systems in some Member States. It is therefore work that remains the key to unlocking

[7] Consolidated Version of the Treaty on the Functioning of the European Union [2012] OJ C326/47 (TFEU), Art 21.

[8] M Dougan and E Spaventa, '"Wish You Weren't Here …" New Models of Social Solidarity in the European Union' in M Dougan and E Spaventa (eds), *Social Welfare and EU Law* (Hart Publishing, 2005) 190.

[9] Directive 2004/38/EC of the European Parliament and of the Council of 29 April 2004 on the right of citizens of the Union and their family members to move and reside freely within the territory of the Member States [2004] OJ L158/77 (Directive 2004/38), Art 7.

access to equal treatment and full enjoyment of the free movement rights that EU citizenship promises. It is this reality of free movement rights that prompts many to criticise EU citizenship as a market citizenship, on protecting the rights of economically active or wealthy citizens.[10]

EU citizen workers have additional and reinforced protection of their free movement rights in Article 45–48 TFEU and Regulation 492/2011.[11] These provisions existed, albeit in different legislation,[12] before the introduction of EU citizenship and demonstrate the enhanced status of economically active EU nationals under EU law.

Work also acts as a catalyst for access to other residence rights. Worker status can be retained in instances of illness, involuntary unemployment or at the late stages of pregnancy.[13] It can also provide a right of residence for family members of the worker,[14] or activate a derived right of residence for EU worker's children in compulsory education and their primary carers to stay in the host Member State.[15] Future residence rights can also be secured through work; for example, it can contribute towards establishing the five years of lawful residence required for a permanent right of residence.[16] Work in another EU Member State can also act as a gateway to secure residence rights for a third-country-national spouse when returning to a home EU state.[17] These rights will be explored in more detail in chapter three.

As a status that is vital for so many EU nationals looking to make use of free movement rights, it is important that the conditions reflect the reality of work opportunities in European labour markets. The free movement of workers has been around for nearly 70 years, but the types of work available and the characteristics of workers over this time have changed significantly. Before the adaptability of the definition of worker status can be examined against the experience of work for EU migrant workers, it is useful to understand the range of work and workers trying to fit into it. The European labour market is shifting away from traditional full-time and permanent jobs as the norm. Instead, atypical forms of work such as

[10] See M Everson, 'The Legacy of the Market Citizen' in J Shaw and G More (eds), *New Legal Dynamics of European Union* (Oxford University Press, 1995); N Nic Shuibhne, 'The Resilience of EU Market Citizenship' (2010) 47 *Common Market Law Review* 1597; C O'Brien, 'I Trade Therefore I am: Legal Personhood in the European Union' (2013) 50 *Common Market Law Review* 1643. See chs 7 and 8 for criticism of EU citizenship as a market citizenship.

[11] Regulation (EU) No 492/2011 of 5 April 2011 on freedom of movement for workers within the Union Text with EEA relevance [2011] OJ L141/1.

[12] Treaty establishing the European Economic Community [1957] Art 39, Regulation (EEC) No 1612/68 of the Council of 15 October 1968 on freedom of movement for workers within the Community [1968] OJ L257/2.

[13] ibid Art 7(3).

[14] ibid Art 7(2).

[15] Case C-480/08 *Teixeira* ECLI:EU:C:2010:83, [2010] ECR I-01107, Case C-310/08 *Ibrahim* ECLI:EU:C:2010:80, [2010] ECR I-01065.

[16] Directive 2004/38, Art 16.

[17] Case C-370/90 *The Queen v Immigration Appeal Tribunal and Surinder Singh, ex parte SSHD* ECLI:EU:C:1992:296, [1992] ECR I-04265.

part-time, temporary and casual contracts are increasing. As AG Geelhoed stated in *Baumbast*, it is not necessarily the case that these forms of work are new, but that 'the intensity with which and the scale on which they now occur have become so considerable' that the Union must take account of them.[18] A failure to incorporate this range of work would result in the exclusion of many economically active migrants from free movement rights in the EU.

2.3. Atypical Work in Numbers

The rise of atypical work can be hard to measure due to problems with overlapping and differing definitions, and a reliance on self-reporting. This section aims to consolidate some of the research into the changes in the labour market in Europe, and specifically the UK, to get a snapshot of how diverse the labour market is.

Atypical work can include various types of employment. It is broadly seen as any work that does not conform to the standard working relationship of full-time and permanent contracts, often worked on a Monday to Friday, nine-to-five basis. This research adopts a broad definition of atypical work to capture all employment in part-time, fixed-term, casual, seasonal and agency work alongside work conducted in the gig economy. This approach is necessary to examine the wide variety of working situations reflected in the experiences documented in the case studies collected for this research. It also provides a measure to examine the scope of worker status and, by proxy, the rights of EU market citizenship against the backdrop of a full variety of work experienced in the European labour market.

Overall trends across Europe and the UK show that atypical work is becoming more prevalent. Statistics show that many different forms of flexible work are increasing in the EU and UK, and the EU Commission has recognised that the trajectory suggests they will likely continue 'to be a feature of the EU labour market in years to come'.[19]

The Commission's impact assessment for the Directive on transparent and predictable working conditions reported that across the EU, more than half of all new jobs created between 2006 and 2016 were considered 'non-standard' contracts (not full-time permanent contracts).[20] Additionally, data from the European Labour Force Survey compiled in Broughton et al's 2016 report shows that 'standard' full-time, permanent contracts has decreased from 62 per cent of all employment contracts in 2003 to 59 per cent in 2016 in Europe, with the trend

[18] Case C-413/99 *Baumbast*, Opinion of AG Geelhoed ECLI:EU:C:2001:385, [2002] ECR I-7091 [26].

[19] Commission, 'Impact Assessment Accompanying the document Proposal for a Directive of the European Parliament and of the Council on transparent and predictable working conditions in the European Union' SWD(2017) 478 final, 13.

[20] Commission 'Proposal for a Directive of the European Parliament and of the Council on transparent and predictable working conditions in the European Union' COM(2017) 797 final, 1.

expected to continue.[21] Overall this pictures shows a slow breakdown of the traditional and more secure working arrangements to atypical work contracts. Before examining the risks of atypical working arrangements on workers and the disparate impact on different demographics of the working population, it is useful to understand how the growth of atypical employment is reflected across the variety of non-standard working arrangements.

This brief summary will focus on statistics up to 2019. While some figures from 2020 onwards will be referred to, it should be recognised that the levels of employment changed significantly due to the COVID-19 pandemic and that atypical employment was disproportionately impacted.[22]

2.3.1. Part-time Work

According to the European Labour Force Survey, part-time work made up about 19.2 per cent of EU Member States' total employment in 2019.[23] This varied considerably between Member States, with part-time work making up just 2.2 per cent of employment in Bulgaria, but 51.2 per cent in the Netherlands. Broughton et al found that part-time work of less than 20 hours was 'constantly growing'.[24] The Commission has also reported an increase in part-time work of eight hours or less from 3.4 million in 2005 to 3.8 million in 2016.[25]

The UK is recorded as having a higher than average rate of part-time work of under 20 hours, compared to other EU Member States.[26] In 2020, the Office for National Statistics (ONS) recorded approximately 8.6 million part-time workers in the UK.[27] In 2019, the Resolution Foundation recorded part-time work as making up around 26.5 per cent of total employment in the UK.[28] However, this percentage had only increased by 1.1 per cent over the last 10 years.[29]

Overall part-time work makes up a significant number of employment contracts across both the EU and the UK. While part-time work itself may not have increased in recent years, there is a concern that part-time work with lower contracted hours appears to be growing.

[21] Broughton et al (n 3) 32–33.

[22] T Weber, J Hurley and D Adăscăliței, 'COVID-19: Implications for employment and working life' (Eurofound, COVID-19 series, Publications Office of the European Union, 2021).

[23] 'Part-time Employment' (European Centre for the Development of Vocational Training (CEDEFOP)), www.cedefop.europa.eu/en/tools/skills-intelligence/part-time-employment?country=EU&year=2019#1.

[24] ibid 77.

[25] SWD(2017) 478 final (n 19) 13.

[26] Broughton et al (n 3) 46.

[27] B Chiripanhura, 'Labour market economic commentary' (ONS, April 2020), www.ons.gov.uk/employmentandlabourmarket/peopleinwork/employmentandemployeetypes/articles/labourmarketeconomiccommentary/april2020.

[28] S Clarke and N Cominetti, 'Setting the record straight: How record employment has changed the UK' (Resolution Foundation, January 2019).

[29] ibid.

2.3.2. Non-permanent, Fixed-term and Temporary Contracts

'Fixed-term contracts' were reported as around seven per cent of employment in Europe in 2014 by Broughton et al,[30] and 5.7 per cent of employment in the UK in 2019.[31] This figure does not account for the other categories such as 'marginal part-time' or 'temporary agency work', which can include both permanent and fixed-term contracts.[32]

When looking at a broader category of 'temporary employment', the EU LFS in 2019 recorded that 15.1 per cent of all people in employment across the EU were in temporary forms of work.[33] Once again, this figure varies significantly between Member States (1.4 per cent for Romania, while the maximum is 26.4 per cent for Spain). A Eurofound report provides data showing that temporary work (which includes fixed-term contracts, on-call work, probationary jobs, leave replacements and sometimes temporary agency work)[34] increased by 25 per cent between 2001 and 2012 in the EU-27.[35] This is a proportionately faster rise than that of permanent contracts, which increased by seven per cent in the same period.[36]

Additionally, most of these temporary contracts tend to be short term. Across Europe, only around 27.6 per cent of fixed-term contracts lasted for over 12 months.[37] Those working under fixed-term contracts lasting less than one month were recorded as increasing from '373,000 in 2002 to almost 1.3 million in 2016'.[38] This suggests that, similar to part-time work, it is the most insecure examples of temporary work that are increasing.

2.3.3. Zero-hours Contracts

Zero-hours and on-demand contracts are also on the rise. Zero-hours contract (ZHC) workers have no guaranteed income and hours can range from over full-time to zero each week. It provides employers with the opportunity to keep staff on the books for when they are needed, but not commit to budgeting for wages all year round. The EU Commission proposal for the directive on transparent and predictable working conditions estimates that 'between 4 and 6 million workers

[30] Broughton et al (n 3) 33.
[31] Clarke and Cominetti (n 28) 45.
[32] Broughton et al (n 3) 24.
[33] 'Temporary employment' (European Centre for the Development of Vocational Training (CEDEFOP)), www.cedefop.europa.eu/en/tools/skills-intelligence/temporary-employment?year=2019&country=EU#1.
[34] C Vacas-Soriano, 'Recent developments in temporary employment: Employment growth, wages and transitions' (Eurofound, 2015) 4.
[35] ibid 9.
[36] ibid.
[37] Broughton et al (n 3) 13.
[38] SWD(2017) 478 final (n 19) 13.

are on on-demand and intermittent contracts' with little indication of their work hours.[39] While exclusivity clauses are prohibited for ZHCs in the UK,[40] up to one million on-demand workers in Europe are prevented from finding other work due to being subject to exclusivity clauses.[41]

Again, Broughton et al identify the UK as having a higher-than-average level of ZHCs.[42] The ONS recorded a considerable increase of 373 per cent for those on ZHCs in the UK from 2011 to 2017 (190,000–900,000).[43] Overall, ZHCs are recorded as occupying around 2.5 per cent of employment in the UK, a significant increase from 0.5 per cent in 2008.[44] The ONS reports approximately 900,000 workers report as working in ZHCs in the UK.[45]

2.3.4. Agency Work

A range of studies analysed by the International Labour Organization indicate that agency work, where an employee is contracted by an agency and temporarily supplied to an employer by that agency, is a growing trend in most EU Member States.[46] Eurostat records show that in 2019, across the EU, temporary agency work made up around 2.2 per cent of employed men and 1.5 per cent of employed women.[47]

While the Eurostat statistics show the UK's share of agency work to be lower than the majority of other EU countries, at around only 0.5 per cent, a 2016 Resolution Foundation report considering a wider definition of agency work – including temporary, permanent, those with second jobs and where individuals are recorded as self-employed in an agency setting – found that it could amount to approximately three per cent of the UK workforce. This estimated percentage would equate to 865,000 workers, similar in size to the number of workers on ZHCs.[48] The presence of agency work in the UK has increased dramatically since the 1980s when there were only approximately 50,000 agency workers.[49] In the five years between 2011 and 2016 agency work was found to have increased

[39] COM(2017) 797 final (n 20) 1.

[40] Small Business, Enterprise and Employment Act 2015, s 153.

[41] COM(2017) 797 final (n 20) 1.

[42] Broughton et al (n 3) 46.

[43] Though this rise in reporting of ZHCs may be affected by an increased awareness of the term. Y Petkova, 'Contracts that do not guarantee a minimum number of hours: April 2018' (Office for National Statistics, 23 April 2018), www.ons.gov.uk/employmentandlabourmarket/peopleinwork/earningsandworkinghours/articles/contractsthatdonotguaranteeaminimumnumberofhours/april2018.

[44] Clarke and Cominetti (n 28) 45.

[45] Chiripanhura (n 27).

[46] N Countouris et al, 'Report on temporary employment agencies and temporary agency work' (ILO Governance and Tripartism working paper series, 2017) 23.

[47] 'Employment statistics' (Eurostat, May 2019), ec.europa.eu/eurostat/statistics-explained/index.php/Employment_statistics.

[48] L Judge and D Tomlinson, 'Secret Agents: agency workers in the new world of work' (The Resolution Foundation, 2016) 17.

[49] C Forde, G Slater and F Green, 'Agency Work in the UK: What do we know?' (Centre for Employment Relations Innovation and Change, 2008) 9.

by 30 per cent and was expected to continue to increase to up to one million workers by the end of the decade.[50]

Overall, studies indicate that nearly all forms of atypical work are increasing across Europe and more specifically in the UK. In the few instances where forms of atypical work are not necessarily increasing in the UK, they appear to have stagnated and not returned to the lower levels seen before the 2008 recession.[51] The number of workers in atypical contracts is not insignificant and is likely to either continue to grow or, at least, remain a significant part of the European labour market. Considering that the 2008 financial crisis is identified as one of the drivers of the increase in atypical work,[52] it is likely that further fragmentation of the labour market can be anticipated in the wake of further significant economic events, such as the COVID-19 pandemic.[53]

As the number of atypical workers in the European labour market increases, so too will the number of EU migrant workers in atypical contracts. The accuracy with which the definition of work under EU free movement law reflects the reality of the labour market will therefore be relevant to an increasing number of EU migrants. Failing to adapt to these changes could see a growing number of atypical workers unable to access equal treatment rights in another Member State. This shift also threatens the 'fundamental-but-market citizenship' claims of EU citizenship, by increasing not just the number of citizens who are excluded from free movement rights, but the number of economic actors who face the same exclusions.

Just as the definition of work fails to reflect this shift away from traditional working arrangements, it does not sit easily with relatively new and emerging areas of work such as the gig economy. The rise of gig and digital platform work and how it transcends some of the traditional ways we view work is worth closer inspection.

2.4. The Rise of the Gig Economy

The gig economy acquires its name from workers taking on 'gigs' or trading in on often 'low value, one-off exchanges' and tending to be paid for set tasks.[54]

[50] Judge and Tomlinson (n 48) 17.

[51] Clarke and Cominetti (n 28) 45.

[52] Broughton et al (n 3) 10.

[53] While the Resolution Foundation found that in the wake of the pandemic 'insecure work remain[ed] below pre-crisis levels', those in atypical work were more affected by job losses and furlough. Also 'zero-hours, temporary [and] agency contracts [are] beginning to rise' again. M Brewer, C McCurdy and H Slaughter, 'Begin Again? Assessing the permanent implications of Covid-19 for the UK's labour market' (The Economy 2030 enquiry, May 2021). See also R Sehmi and H Slaughter, 'Double trouble, Exploring the labour market and mental health impact of Covid-19 on young people' (Resolution Foundation, 13 May 2021); A Powell, B Francis-Devine and H Clark, 'Coronavirus: Impact on the labour market' (House of Commons Library Briefing CBP8898, 9 August 2022).

[54] Eurofound, 'Aspects of non-standard employment in Europe' (Publications Office of the European Union, 2017) 21.

Gig work can overlap with other types of atypical work, but is worth distinguishing.[55] Rather than working in a single type of employment and receiving an hourly rate such as the case with ZHCs, they are working in situations which are, as Webster describes it, 'as temporary as is possible for them to be'.[56]

Gig work takes on many different forms. Its most common uses are for 'the delivery of electronically transmittable' work or to assist in the organisation of 'physical labour-intensive services'.[57] Cherry states that the ubiquity of the internet and reliance on it developed 'new ways to buy and sell not only objects, but also time, effort, and labo[u]r'.[58] Work under a gig economy template can therefore cover skilled and low-skilled work, manual and intellectual labour, short- and longer-term projects, on-call style set-ups and flexible hours, in sectors as varied as transportation, housekeeping, delivery services, web development, translation and data inputting.

Degryse argues that this new form of work presents 'a severe disruption to the organisation of national labour markets' affecting 'their regulations, their social dialogue, their social rights financed by their social contributions and their taxes'.[59] In the free movement context, it is necessary to analyse the extent to which the gig economy is growing, the risks faced by gig workers to their working conditions and social rights[60] and whether gig workers exercising free movement can access the necessary rights in host Member States to mitigate some of these risks.

Huws et al describes the attempt to define and measure the gig economy as like 'nailing jelly'.[61] One issue in defining the gig economy lies in the many terms and labels used to describe it. This can include, but is not limited to, 'the "sharing economy", the "collaborative economy", "crowd-employment or crowd-working", "digital platform working" and the "on-demand economy"'.[62] There is also an array of terms for gig workers.[63] On top of this, contractual classifications as employed or self-employed, part or full time, temporary or permanent,

[55] U Huws, NH Spencer, DS Syrdal and K Holts, 'Work in the European Gig Economy: Research results from the UK, Sweden, Germany, Austria, The Netherlands, Switzerland and Italy' (Foundation for European Progressive Studies, November 2017) 50.

[56] J Webster, 'Micro-workers of the Gig Economy: Separate and Precarious' (2016) 25 *New Labor Forum* 56.

[57] C Codagnone, F Abadie and F Biagi, 'The Future of Work in the "Sharing Economy": Market Efficiency and Equitable Opportunities or Unfair Precarisation?' (European Commission, Joint Research Centre, 2016) 10.

[58] MA Cherry, 'Beyond Misclassification: The digital transformation of work' (2017) 37 *Comparative Labor Law and Policy Journal* 577.

[59] C Degryse, 'Digitalisation of the economy and its impact on labour markets' (European Trade Union Institute Working Paper, 2016) 50.

[60] J Prassl, *Humans as a Service: The promise and perils of work in the gig economy* (Oxford University Press, 2018).

[61] Huws et al (n 55).

[62] Codagnone et al (n 57) 10; Broughton et al (n 3) 115–16.

[63] Including, but not limited to '"micro-entrepreneurs", "gigs", "contractors", "on-demand workers, freelancers"' and platform workers in Codagnone et al (n 57) 10–11.

vary, with some misclassification ('bogus self-employment') thrown in.[64] This can create confusion for researchers seeking to understand the full scale of the gig economy.[65] Notwithstanding these difficulties in measurement,[66] there are several indications of scale and growth. A 2019 Joint Research Centre report found that around 11 per cent of workers 'across the 16 EU Member States surveyed had provided services via online platforms at least once'.[67] A 2021 Commission proposal to improve the working conditions of digital platform workers identified that 'over 28 million people in the EU work through digital labour platforms' and that by 2025 this number 'is expected to have reached 43 million'.[68] A 2017 Commission impact assessment for the Directive on transparent and predictable working conditions, analysed various studies to conclude the frequency of gig work has significantly increased over the last five years and, as technology advances, that trend is expected to continue.[69]

Estimates of the proportion of those in employment in the UK who engage with the gig economy range from four per cent,[70] to nine per cent,[71] or 12.8 per cent engaged in platform work[72] or 11 per cent (or five million workers) engaged in the crowd economy.[73] The percentage of total workers reporting that they rely on gig work for their main source of income also varies between 1.5 per cent to around three per cent[74] (or around 1,330,000 workers).[75] Between 2016 and 2019, participation in the UK's gig economy reportedly doubled in size.[76]

The presence of this type of work is statistically non-marginal,[77] and has grown over the last five years to such an extent that Codagnone et al found it to be 'an empirically consequential hypothesis that they could encroach on traditional and long-term forms of employment'.[78] Importantly, the growing presence of atypical and gig work impacts the stability of workers' lives, who must now navigate fluctuating income, hours and availability of work. As the world of work evolves, without

[64] Eurofound (n 54) 22.
[65] Huws et al (n 55) 14; Eurofound (n 54) 21.
[66] SWD(2017) 478 final (n 19) 13.
[67] Joint Research Centre (JRC) 'The Changing Nature of Work: and skills in the digital age' (Publications Office of the European Union, 2019) 58.
[68] European Commission, 'Proposal for a Directive of the European Parliament and of the Council on improving working conditions in platform work' SWD(2021) 395 final, 1.
[69] SWD(2017) 478 final (n 19) 13.
[70] The Chartered Institute of Personnel and Development (CIPD), 'To gig or not to gig? Stories from the modern economy' (March 2017) 4.
[71] Huws et al (n 55) 26.
[72] JRC (n 67) 60–61.
[73] U Huws and S Joyce, 'Crowd Working Survey: Size of the UK's gig economy revealed for the first time' (Foundation for European Progressive Studies, February 2016).
[74] 1.5% in JRC (n 67) 58; 3.2% or 29% of the full 11% of workers in the gig economy in Huws and Joyce (n 73).
[75] Huws et al (n 55) 26.
[76] Statistical Services and Consultancy Unit, 'Platform Work in the UK 2016–2019' (Foundation for European Progressive Studies, 26 June 2019); gig work is also likely to increase (CIPD (n 70)) 7.
[77] JRC (n 67) 58.
[78] Codagnone et al (n 57) 5–6.

an explicit revisiting of the EU free movement framework, a growing number of EU migrant workers engaged in atypical forms of work could find themselves relying on ineffective rights under EU citizenship which deprives them of the protection of vital free movement and equal treatment rights.

2.5. Flexibility, Risk and Precarity

The Confederation of British Industry has found that countries with flexible labour markets 'enjoy higher employment rates and lower unemployment than those with more rigid approaches'.[79] But higher aggregate employment, especially when in atypical contracts, is coupled with fewer individual protections.

Workers in the atypical labour market must plan their lives around short-term contracts, periods of unemployment and resulting unstable income. The EU Commission has recognised that with the increase in non-standard employment[80] there is a risk that a growing part of the working population in the EU will be left without essential social protection.[81] The report builds on the twelfth principle in the European Pillar of social rights, which calls for social protection for workers 'regardless of the type and duration of their employment relationship'.[82] Those in precarious employment do not have 'access to social protection on a par with workers in standard contracts',[83] jeopardising the welfare of workers and their families.[84] These risks can affect workers' ability to prepare for potential times of unemployment, health needs and ultimately pensions, all of which puts them at a disadvantage to other workers in permanent or full-time work.

In the UK, the Taylor Review, while largely positive about the benefits of atypical work, warns that workers face 'one way flexibility' where they are required to be available at all and for any number of hours, often at short notice and with no reciprocation of this flexibility or no guarantee that hours will be provided.[85] Often this one-way flexibility is accompanied with a fear that future hours will be withheld if any work is turned down, if a worker raises legitimate complaints about conditions, or makes reasonable requests. In these circumstances, responsibility

[79] Confederation of British Industry, 'Submission to the Taylor review: Work that Works For All: Building a fair and flexible labour market that benefits everyone' (2017) 1, www.cbi.org.uk/articles/cbis-response-to-the-governments-consultation-on-the-taylor-review.

[80] Commission, 'First phase consultation of Social Partners under Art 154 TFEU on a possible action addressing the challenges of access to social protection for people in all forms of employment in the framework of the European Pillar of Social Rights' SWD(2017) 205, 2.

[81] ibid 4.

[82] 'European Pillar of Social Rights' (2017), ec.europa.eu/commission/publications/european-pillar-social-rights-booklet_en.

[83] SWD(2017) 205 (n 80) 5.

[84] ibid 8.

[85] M Taylor et al, 'Good Work: The Taylor Review of Modern Working Practices' (July 2017) 2443.

and risk has shifted from the employers, platforms, intermediaries and corporations to workers while employers focus on the most effective extraction of profits.[86]

MacDonald and Giazitzoglu argue that increasing precarity goes hand in hand with the degradation of workers' rights and the UK benefits system, in the shift towards more client responsibility to take on work.[87] They argue that precarity and risk have long been increasing, with early signs becoming apparent with the increase of subcontracting and neoliberal policies in the 1970s. The increase in atypical work with limited job security, lower levels of income, lack of career progressions, long periods without employment and unpredictable and irregular income and hours promotes further individualism and ultimately leaves workers in an ever more precarious position.[88] This section will therefore examine some of the main risks faced by those in more flexible work, focusing on the impact of being underemployed, the pay penalty, loss of employment rights and the risks to health. Each of these issues speak to the necessity of access to welfare support for EU migrant atypical workers to mitigate some of these disadvantages and make free movement a viable option.

2.5.1. Underemployment

While part-time work can be, to use the CJEU's own words, an 'effective means of improving … living conditions',[89] this will only be the case if the hours worked and the regularity of those hours are enough to improve a workers' living conditions and if part-time work is a voluntary decision.

A report for the European Parliament found that the 2008 financial crisis was a driver of precariousness in Europe,[90] creating an environment in which businesses wanted more flexible employment arrangements to financially suit them in unstable times,[91] justified with the belief that those seeking work could choose to either accept or refuse these offers of employment. However, the choice here is something of an illusion. In the UK, for example, increasing conditionality punishes unemployment, and now underemployment;[92] failing to search for work or take up an offer of paid work can result in a high-level sanction.[93]

[86] Prassl (n 60) 85–86; see also J Hacker, *The Great Risk Shift: The New Economic Insecurity and the Decline of the American Dream*, 2nd edn (Oxford University Press, 2019).

[87] R MacDonald and A Giazitzoglu, 'Youth, enterprise, and precarity: or, what is, and what is wrong with, the 'gig economy'?' (2019) 55 *Journal of Sociology* 724.

[88] Broughton et al (n 3) 66.

[89] Case 53/81 *Levin* ECLI:EU:C:1982:105, [1982] ECR I-1035 [15].

[90] Broughton et al (n 3) 10.

[91] Prassl (n 60).

[92] HM Treasury, 'The Autumn Statement' (CP 751, 2022) para 3.7.

[93] P Dwyer and S Wright, 'Universal Credit, ubiquitous conditionality and its implications for social citizenship' (2014) 22 *Journal of Poverty and Social Justice* 27.

A significant number of workers are considered to be involuntarily working under atypical contracts. Statistics from the European Central Bank, utilised in the Commission impact assessment for the Directive on transparent and predictable working conditions, records that three per cent of the total working population, are 'working fewer hours than they would like'.[94] The Commission recognised that, while this number has declined between 2015 and 2017, this has been 'only very modestly' and 'despite robust employment growth'.[95] Around a quarter of part-time workers in Europe are recorded as involuntarily working part-time with income levels lower than they need.[96]

With regard to temporary contracts, Broughton et al also found that a large share (53 per cent) of individuals were involuntarily on fixed-term contracts.[97] Additionally, across Europe, only around 27.6 per cent of fixed-term contracts lasted for over 12 months, with a further 25 per cent lasting between seven and 12 months, meaning many fixed-term contracts only last for six months or less and were found not to represent 'stepping stones' to more permanent positions.[98] The chance of transitioning to permanent contracts has also decreased, meaning that many workers may find themselves stuck in rolling fixed-term contracts or being involuntary unemployed at the end of periods of fixed-term contracts.[99] The Resolution Foundation has also reported that those in the atypical labour market have been more likely to lose hours, be furloughed or lose their job during the COVID-19 crisis.[100]

In the UK, the Taylor Review found that since 2004 the number of 'under-employed', or workers who want more hours, has sharply risen.[101] Two-thirds of those on ZHCs would prefer to be in a job with guaranteed hours.[102]

While the gig economy might be presented as a means to flexibly top up wages from a more permanent job or plug a gap between employments,[103] 'as many as 60%' of gig workers in the UK were found to utilise multiple platforms at a time to build an income, rather than supplementing a main (more stable) job.[104]

[94] SWD(2017) 478 final (n 19) 20.

[95] ibid.

[96] Involuntary part-time work has also increased in Europe to 28% by 2016 in COM(2017) 797 final (n 20) 1; one in four are recorded as underemployed in Broughton et al (n 3) 70; Eurostat have also recorded that around nine million part-time workers in the EU-28 would prefer to work more: 'Underemployment and potential additional labour force statistics' (Eurostat, May 2018).

[97] Broughton et al (n 3) 103.

[98] ibid 13.

[99] ibid; the chance of transitioning to permanent contracts decreased from 27.3% in 2007 to 22.8% in 2013.

[100] L Gardiner and H Slaughter, 'The effects of the coronavirus crisis on workers: Flash findings from the Resolution Foundation's coronavirus survey' (The Resolution Foundation, May 2020) 3.

[101] The Taylor Review (n 85) 20.

[102] TUC, 'Great Jobs with Guaranteed Hours: What do workers really think about "flexible" zero-hours contracts?' (TUC, 4 December 2017).

[103] CIPD (n 70) 7.

[104] Codagnone et al (n 57) 6.

That some workers are involuntarily stuck in atypical work indicates that the profitability of contracting on a flexible basis is being prioritised over worker welfare and 'choice'. The statistics covered in this section suggests that a significant number of workers struggle to find suitable permanent, regular or full-time work that meet their needs let alone 'improve their living conditions'.

2.5.2. Pay Penalties

Work in the atypical labour market is likely to mean that workers take home less income and income that is unstable or fluctuating.

2.5.2.1. Lower Income

Fixed-term and agency work are also more likely to earn less per hour than those in full-time and permanent employment. The Resolution Foundation found that in 2018, on average, atypical workers earned less (£9.20 per hour) than those in full-time employment (£12.80 per hour).[105] After controlling for key variables relating to personal and job characteristics, it is reported that the average pay penalty in the UK between 2011 and 2018 equates to around 66p per hour for temporary workers (–6 per cent), 45p per hour for ZHC workers (–5 per cent), and 29p per hour for part-time workers (–3 per cent).[106]

There is also a trend in most EU countries that agency,[107] fixed-term, seasonal employment is more available in low-skilled, low-income work 'in mostly labour-intensive sectors, such as retail, industrial cleaning, the care sector and agriculture'.[108] In 2002, workers in Belgium who were under temporary contracts earned five per cent less than permanent contract workers with comparatively similar experience and education.[109] There is a double-penalty – firstly being concentrated in low-income sectors, and then receiving less pay than 'typical' workers in the same sector.

Gig work also comes with a pay penalty. Earnings in the digital labour market tend to 'range from very low to modest, with only a small minority of workers making above middle-level incomes'.[110] Huws et al found that, in the UK, gig workers' earnings are 'generally modest' with 42 per cent of gig workers earning

[105] Clarke and Cominetti (n 28) 51.
[106] ibid 52.
[107] Agency workers in the UK earned on average £2.57 less per hour than the non-agency workforce: Judge and Tomlinson (n 48) 34.
[108] Sweden and Denmark are specifically excluded from this as they legislate against it: A Broughton, I Biletta and M Kullander, 'Flexible forms of work: "very atypical" contractual arrangements' (Eurofound, 4 March 2010), www.eurofound.europa.eu/publications/report/2010/flexible-forms-of-work-very-atypical-contractual-arrangements.
[109] Broughton et al (n 108); Broughton et al (n 3) 109.
[110] Codagnone et al (n 57) 6.

a total income (before tax and other deductions) of less than £20,000 a year and 30 per cent earn between £20,000 and £35,000.[111] The issue of low-income gig work is made more significant by the fact that 81 per cent of crowd workers (a term adopted by Huws and Joyce to include a variety of gig work that is organised via online platforms) in the UK are recorded as the main 'breadwinners' in their households.[112] Unlike in more traditional forms of work where income may be expected to increase over time, gig economy jobs reach a pay ceiling, trapping many workers on a low-income.[113]

Atypical workers are therefore at greater risk of 'in-work' poverty and being unable to prepare a personal financial safety net for breaks in employment or periods of low hours. Despite an increasing employment rate,[114] the proportion of UK households deemed as being in 'in-work' poverty has risen from 37 per cent in 1994–95 to 58 per cent in 2017–18,[115] with this figure increasing by over one million between 2015 and 2018.[116] The Joseph Rowntree Foundation attributes this increase to the widespread conditionality prevalent in the UK welfare system and the rise in more insecure flexible employment, which traps workers in low-income jobs.[117]

'In-work' poverty across Europe has not gone unnoticed by the Commission, which adopted the promise of 'Adequate minimum wages' and the prevention of 'in-work' poverty as the sixth principle in the 2017 European Pillar of Social Rights.[118] Broughton et al also shows that the risk of 'in-work' poverty is more than doubled for temporary workers compared to permanent workers on average across the EU.[119] A report for the European Parliament highlights the clumsy and rigid 'interaction of … social security systems with low pay' as a driver of precarity.[120] The report goes on to recommend that, as atypical forms of employment are increasing, national welfare systems need to be amended to support individuals in these types of employment 'in order to avoid poverty traps due to inadequate social security coverage'.[121]

Financial insecurity also comes with a cost. Citizens Advice recorded that households with volatile incomes are 'five times more likely to turn to high-cost

[111] Huws and Joyce (n 73).
[112] ibid.
[113] M Benton and Patuzzi, 'Jobs in 2028: How will changing labour markets affect immigrant integration in Europe?' (Migration Policy Institute Europe, October 2018) 2.
[114] B Watson, 'Employment in the UK: August 2020' (Office for National Statistics, August 2020), www.ons.gov.uk/employmentandlabourmarket/peopleinwork/employmentandemployeetypes/bulletins/employmentintheuk/previousReleases.
[115] P Bourquin, J Cribb, T Waters and X Xu, 'Why has in-work poverty risen in Britain?' (Institute for Fiscal Studies Working Paper W19/12, 2019) 2.
[116] 'Budget 2018: tackling the rising tide of in-work poverty' (Joseph Rowntree Foundation, 2018).
[117] ibid; D Innes, 'What has driven the rise of in-work poverty?' (Joseph Rowntree Foundation, February 2020).
[118] 'European Pillar of Social Rights' (n 82) 15.
[119] ibid 66.
[120] Broughton et al (n 3) 10.
[121] ibid 14.

credit' including payday loans and rent to own schemes.[122] Reliance on such schemes will often only exacerbate financial problems and lead to a spiralling debt.

2.5.2.2. Insecure and Fluctuating Income

When gig workers are paid per task or job, rather than hourly, their income can be sporadic, hard to predict and low – often equivalent to less than the national minimum wage.[123] High-profile examples of gig work platforms, such as Uber, have attracted specific attention exploring the income levels of their registered workers. Research conducted by the Independent Union Workers of Great Britain into the income of Uber workers in the UK found that the average income equated to about £5 an hour, far below the national minimum wage in the UK[124] (which was £8.21 for workers aged 23 and over at the time of the Union's research) and the real living wage (£9.30). This amount is disputed by Uber, which points to research using its own data showing that the average hourly rate for its drivers in London is close to £11 an hour.[125] However, this research does not consider drivers based outside of the London area.

Similarly, Deliveroo records its average hourly rate as £10,[126] but as 87 per cent of 'riders' are paid per delivery, income can vary greatly from £0 to £17 per hour.[127] Additionally, a CIPD survey into gig work found that the median self-reported hourly rate for gig workers providing rides or deliveries was £6.[128] For gig workers performing short-term, often digital, tasks – typically expected to be the higher earners among gig workers – the median rate only increases to £7 or £7.70.[129]

For gig workers who are (mis)classified as self-employed, there is also often a need to cover expenses including commuting, equipment or insurance in these earnings.[130] Further risks of misclassification of gig workers will be covered below.

As a result of low pay, pay-per-gig models can also result in long hours being necessary to make up for the income shortfall. Uber reports that 30 per cent of its drivers are logged in to the app, waiting for rides, for over 40 hours a week, with six per cent logged in for over 60, 2.6 per cent for 70 and 0.8 per cent for

[122] G Hardy and J Lane, 'Walking on thin ice: The cost of financial insecurity' (Citizens Advice, February 2018) 23.

[123] Commission (n 68) 2.

[124] 'Uber drivers plan national shutdown on 8 May before Uber IPO' (Independent Union Workers of Great Britain, 3 May 2019), www.iwgb.org.uk/en/post/5ccbedcee58ac/uber-drivers-plan-national-shu.

[125] T Berger, CB Frey, G Levin and SR Danda, 'Uber Happy? Work and Wellbeing in the "Gig Economy"' (Working Paper for the 68th Panel Meeting of Economic Policy, October 2018).

[126] 'Your Earnings with Deliveroo' (Deliveroo), www.roocommunity.com/your-earnings.

[127] F Field and A Forsey, 'Delivering Justice: A report on the pay and working conditions of Deliveroo riders' (July 2018), www.frankfield.co.uk/latest-news/press-releases/news.aspx?p=1021645.

[128] CIPD (n 70).

[129] ibid.

[130] Cherry (n 58).

80 hours.[131] A *New Statesmen* article found that, since Deliveroo switched to a pay-per-delivery system, drivers 'making one delivery per hour would have to work nearly 74 hours to cover the average UK rent for a single room'.[132] Those in atypical and gig work are at risk of working longer hours than is recommended (for example, the Working Time Directive limits weekly working hours to 48 hours per week for the protection of the health and safety of workers).[133] Cherry highlights the 'temporal chaos' of working in the gig economy, where a gig worker may face the cancellation of tasks before completion, or jobs being double-booked,[134] which result in additional costs for the worker and extra, unpaid hours of work. While this is hard to measure, gig workers face extra tasks and pressures that are likely to increase the hours they do, and therefore potentially decrease their average hourly salary.

Beyond the risks of poverty and long hours, workers facing a low or volatile income will often be unable to prepare for the fluctuating hours and gaps in work which are ubiquitous with the atypical labour market. The impact of insecure work is likely to bite harder when income is low to begin with.

2.5.3. Loss of Employment Rights

The increase in flexible and atypical working arrangements can erode the employment rights of workers and are often not included in the legal frameworks established for the more traditional labour market.

2.5.3.1. Barriers to Employment Protections

Broughton et al raise the concern that many of the rights and protections available to workers in national and EU law, including 'working conditions, protection against discrimination and dismissal', have been built around the concepts of 'standard' full-time or permanent contacts.[135]

EU legislators have taken steps to ensure some recognition of atypical work in relation to employment rights. On the one hand, casual work was specifically excluded from the coverage of some protective legislation, such as Directive 1997/81, which concerns the employment rights of part-time workers.[136] On the other, fixed-term work was acknowledged by the EU as a type of employment in

[131] Letter from A Byrne (Uber Head of Public Policy) to R Reeves MP (Chair of Business, Energy and Industrial Strategy Committee) (8 November 2017).

[132] J Rampen, 'A Deliveroo driver would need to work 74 hours to cover the average UK rent for a single room' *New Statesman* (18 August 2016), www.tech.newstatesman.com/business/deliveroo-disaster.

[133] Commission 'Proposal for a Directive of the European Parliament and of the Council concerning certain aspects of the organisation of working time' COM(2002) 0336 final, 10.

[134] Cherry (n 58).

[135] Broughton et al (n 108) 10.

[136] Directive 1997/81/EC of 15 December 1997 concerning the Framework Agreement on part-time work concluded by UNICE, CEEP and the ETUC [1997] OJ L 14/9, clause 2(2).

need of protection from discrimination as early as 1999.[137] Additionally, rights to non-discrimination were recognised for temporary agency work in Directive 2008/104.[138] This Directive also gave Member States the option to include agency workers in social security schemes such as 'pensions, sick pay or financial participation schemes'.[139] Rights and entitlements can thus vary between Member States, with the UK fairly conspicuously not opting for greater protections.

The Organisation for Economic Co-operation and Development's (OECD) 2015 employment protection index rates the UK's regulations for temporary employment as the least strict in all recorded European countries.[140] A Trade Union Congress (TUC) reported that 82 per cent of workers on ZHCs did not have access to sick pay, 63 per cent did not have maternity or paternity rights, 70 per cent were not able to receive redundancy pay and 46 per cent did not get holiday pay.[141]

2.5.3.2. Misclassification

Atypical workers are also at risk of being misclassified as self-employed, and so excluded from a range of rights reserved for employees. As a cost-saving technique,[142] it appeals to employers who can avoid paying traditional employee benefits, compensation and insurance.[143] The Commission estimates that 'up to five and a half million people working through digital labour platforms could be at risk of employment status misclassification'.[144] A Work and Pensions Committee inquiry into the gig economy and self-employment in the UK found evidence that 'some companies are using self-employed workforces as cheap labour' as it frees them from 'both responsibilities towards their workers and from substantial National Insurance liabilities, pension auto-enrolment responsibilities and the Apprenticeship Levy'.[145] The inquiry concludes that 'Profit, not flexibility is the motive for using self-employed labour in these cases'.[146]

[137] Directive 1999/70/EC of 28 June 1999 concerning the framework agreement on fixed-term work concluded by ETUC, UNICE and CEEP [1999] OJ L 175/43.

[138] Directive 2008/104/EC of 19 November 2008 on temporary agency work [2008] OJ L 327/9.

[139] ibid Art 3(2).

[140] 'OECD Indicators of Employment Protection', www.oecd.org/employment/emp/oecdindicatorsofemploymentprotection.htm.

[141] TUC (n 102) 5.

[142] 'In the US, for example, this can lead to savings of up to 30% on labour costs in comparison with traditionally recruited workers': Hunt and Samman (n 143) 10.

[143] A Hunt and E Samman, 'Gender and the gig economy: Critical steps for evidence-based policy' (ODI Working Paper 546, 2019) 10.

[144] Commission (n 68) 2.

[145] House of Commons Work and Pensions Committee, *Self-employment and the gig economy* (HC 2016–17, HC 847) 3.

[146] ibid 13.

Several court cases have tackled the misclassification of gig workers as self-employed on high-profile platforms.[147] Globally, judges have sought to ensure that the classification of worker, employee and self-employed status, irrespective of what any written terms may dictate, reflects the reality of the working situation.[148] While digital platforms' 'tight control over many aspects of service delivery' will often result in a finding of employment status, Prassl notes that this line of cases is far from settled and must respond frequently to changes to platforms' policies, business models and litigation strategies 'mak[ing] it difficult to paint a consistent picture'.[149]

Some commentators suggest that gig economy jobs sit in a grey area of work, where the situation does not fit well in 'the existing employee–independent contractor dichotomy'.[150] The 2017 Taylor Review looking into the state of work in the UK recommended renaming the category of people who are eligible for worker rights who are not employees as 'dependent contractors'.[151] Others propose introducing a new in-between definition, 'dependent self-employed workers',[152] for those who do not have an employer but are in a position of dependence with limited autonomy. This definition has already been adopted as a category of work in Portugal, Slovenia and Spain, with similar formulations adopted in a number of other Member States.[153] However, drawing the boundaries between independent contractors and dependent contractors may cause unnecessary exclusions or fail to distinguish between those who choose to be a 'dependent self-employed workers' from those who are forced.[154] Instead, Codagone et al argue that already existing and regulated concepts of workers and self-employed persons should be interpreted broadly to be inclusive of dependent workers and be adaptable to potential changes in the future of work.[155] The EU has taken steps to improve the working conditions in platform work through a proposed new Directive which will come into force in late 2024 and aims to broaden the guidelines on when platform work should be deemed an employment relationship and place duties on platforms for more transparency in algorithmic management system.[156]

[147] See *Autoclenz Limited v Belcher and others* [2011] UKSC 41 [35]; *Uber BV and others v Aslam and others* [2021] UKSC 5; *Addison Lee Ltd v Lange & Ors* [2018] UKEAT/0037/18/BA; In 2018, Deliveroo settled an employment rights case brought by 50 couriers on their status as workers; see S Butler, 'Deliveroo couriers win six-figure payout in employment rights case' *The Guardian* (28 June 2018), www.theguardian.com/business/2018/jun/28/deliveroo-couriers-win-six-figure-payout-in-employment-rights-case.

[148] Prassl (n 60) 96.

[149] ibid 99–100.

[150] SD Harris and AB Kreuger, 'A Proposal for Modernizing Labor Laws for Twenty-First-Century Work: The "Independent Worker"' (The Hamilton Project, 2015) 8.

[151] The Taylor Review (n 85) 35.

[152] 'OECD Employment Outlook 2014' (OECD, 3 September 2014) 146.

[153] C O'Brien, E Spaventa and J De Coninck, 'Comparative Report 2015: The concept of worker under Art 45 TFEU and certain non-standard forms of employment' (FreSsco, European Commission, 2016) 53.

[154] W Eichhorst et al, 'Social protection rights of economically dependent self-employed workers' (European Parliament, 2013).

[155] Codagnone et al (n 57).

[156] Commission (n 68).

While identifying a solution is beyond the scope of this research, it is important to note that those sitting in these grey areas of economic activity, including EU migrant workers, will struggle to access important employment rights. They may be unaware of their registration and tax responsibilities and could be vulnerable to exploitation. Access to welfare could mitigate this risk.

2.5.4. Risks to Health

Precarity in atypical work does not only carry financial risks, but also creates risks to well-being and health. Job insecurity, financial instability and long hours can all increase the risk of mental health problems.[157] Workers face further stress where they are engaged in temporary contracts or gig work from regularly, or sometimes constantly, having to work. Additionally, Bambra et al found that those in 'tiring working positions' and 'temporary work' were 'the most strongly associated with worse self-rated health in Europe'.[158]

Cherry also highlights the additional pressures of work in the gig economy from constant ratings and surveillance, sometimes with public ranking where 'workers are expected to out-achieve each other'.[159] Workers face increased pressure from ratings which can determine whether you will be selected for future work or, in the case of Uber drivers with an average rating below 4.6 out of five, suspension from the platform.[160] Over half of skilled gig workers have reported that their work is often stressful.[161] Without access to sick pay, gig workers who must take time off for their health have little by way of a safety net. For example, Deliveroo riders who get injured in a cycling accident, whether during the course of their work or not, have no right to sick pay nor an entitlement to be rehired. In these circumstances, workers must rely on emergency payments from trade unions or the social security system.[162]

2.5.5. Precarity and Free Movement of Atypical Workers

There is a significant chance that workers relying on atypical employment may be vulnerable to destitution and 'in-work' poverty, unstable employment,

[157] R Dunstan and D Anderson, 'Vulnerable workers: preliminary findings from the Citizens Advice client research' (Department for Business, Enterprise and Regulatory Reform, 2008) 9.

[158] C Bambra, T Lunau, KA Van der Wel, TA Eikemo and N Dragano, 'Work, Health, and Welfare: The Association between Working Conditions, Welfare States, and Self-Reported General Health in Europe' (2014) 44 *International Journal of Health Services* 113, 130.

[159] Cherry (n 58) 601.

[160] J Cook, 'Uber's internal charts show how its driver-rating system actually works' *Business Insider* (11 February 2015), www.businessinsider.com/leaked-charts-show-how-ubers-driver-rating-system-works-2015-2?r=US&IR=T.

[161] JRC (n 67) 9.

[162] H Khaleeli, 'The truth about working for Deliveroo, Uber and the on-demand economy' *The Guardian* (15 June 2016), www.theguardian.com/money/2016/jun/15/he-truth-about-working-for-deliveroo-uber-and-the-on-demand-economy.

exploitation and excessive strain on health. As such, reliance on social services and welfare benefits to provide a safety net can be necessary to alleviate some of the temporary and permanent precarity in atypical workers' lives. EU migrant workers in these positions face additional risks to security, in barriers to accessing support in a host Member State.

This highlights the importance of migrant worker status for the purposes of free movement. Should the definition of work be too narrow, equal treatment rights will not be meted out to EU migrant atypical workers, who are then exposed to all the risks of precarity, without any of the protections. This could be a significant barrier to free movement and residence in a host Member State.

The precarity faced by atypical workers and potential loss of access to welfare support undermines the justification for full free movement and equal treatment rights being reserved for economically active EU citizens. For De Witte, it is essentially part of 'a quid pro quo', where economic and functional engagement of migrant workers with a host Member State society is exchanged for access to welfare benefits.[163] For Nic Shuibhne, the justification for this focus is lost 'when it cannot be taken for granted that work or self-employment produces financial self-subsistence'.[164] The CJEU has typically recognised work as an important form of integration in a host Member State, whether or not it provides enough income to be self-sufficient.[165] It must also recognise that atypical work illustrates participation in a host Member State's labour market.[166] This participation should justify the extension of social solidarity with EU migrant atypical workers.

Reliance on some social assistance is no longer a phenomenon just for non-workers. As such, the division in treatment between 'recipients of support and non-recipients of support is' as Davies suggests, 'no longer viable'.[167] If nationals of a Member State can utilise access to welfare to allow flexible working options to be viable, but such support is withheld from EU workers in the same position, their ability to sustain a life in the host Member State, including continuing in their employment, is compromised. Risks are shifted onto workers, and due to the make-up of the atypical work sectors, those risks are disproportionately borne by workers vulnerable to discrimination and exclusion on the grounds of sex, age, disability, care and nationality.

[163] F De Witte, 'Transnational Solidarity and Conflicts of Justice' (2012) 18 *European Law Journal* 705.

[164] Nic Shuibhne (n 6) 502.

[165] See ch 3; for example Case 53/81 *Levin* (n 89), Case 171/88 *Rinner-Kuhn* ECLI:EU:C:1989:328, [1989] ECR I-02743; Case C-444/93 *Megner and Scheffel* ECLI:EU:C:1995:442, [1995] ECR I-4741; Case 139/85 *Kempf* ECLI:EU:C:1986:223, [1986] ECR I-1714.

[166] Research conducted over 16 countries reported that flexible working would contribute more than $10 trillion to the economies analysed by 2030; this includes £148 billion to the UK economy; S Lucas, 'Flexible working solid facts: A summary review of the socio-economic benefits of flexible working in 16 countries' (Regus, July 2018).

[167] Davies (n 5) 5.

2.6. A Brief Equality Impact Assessment

This section will examine how some groups of workers are affected by the growth of the atypical labour market. Firstly, it will examine the over-representation of certain groups occupying atypical work and how that shifts the burden and precarity disproportionately. It will then analyse the specific discrimination faced by these groups in atypical work.

The burden of atypical work (including part-time work) can fall disproportionately on the same demographics who are at risk of exclusion from the labour market (mothers, single parents, women, Disabled people, those with lower qualifications, young people, ethnic minorities and immigrants.[168] Those same groups are therefore more likely to be exposed to the risks this type of work entails, as discussed above.

2.6.1. Women in Atypical Work

Women are far less likely to be in full-time, standard employment than men.[169] In 2018, the labour force survey found that across the EU 30.8 per cent of women worked on a part-time basis compared to and only eight per cent of men.[170] This finding is repeated in the UK statistics where, in 2017 to 2018, women were estimated to make up 73.5 per cent of the part-time work force.[171] Half of working women in the UK are in forms of atypical forms of work, which is significantly more likely than the total share of workers in atypical contracts (39 per cent).[172]

Women's over-representation in gig work is not as clear-cut. Women are reported as making up just over half of the European digital labour market population[173] and 54 per cent of UK crowd workers.[174] As women make up less than half of the labour force in the UK (46.8 per cent),[175] this suggests that women are more likely to be in gig employment than men. On the other hand,

[168] Clarke and Cominetti (n 28) 50.

[169] Broughton et al (n 3) 33.

[170] 'Employment Statistics' (Eurostat, May 2019), ec.europa.eu/eurostat/statistics-explained/index.php/Employment_statistics#Precarious_employment.

[171] R Clegg, 'UK Labour market April 2018: Estimates of employment, unemployment, economic inactivity and other employment-related statistics for the UK' (Office for National Statistics, 17 April 2018), www.ons.gov.uk/employmentandlabourmarket/peopleinwork/employmentandemployeetypes/bulletins/uklabourmarket/latest.

[172] Clarke and Cominetti (n 28) 50.

[173] Codagnone et al (n 57) 6.

[174] Huws and Joyce (n 73).

[175] 'Labor force, female (% of total labor force) – United Kingdom' (The World Bank, September 2019), www.data.worldbank.org/indicator/SL.TLF.TOTL.FE.ZS?locations=GB; fewer women (71.8%) than men (80.3%) are recorded as being in employment in the UK: D Leaker, 'Labour market overview, UK: November 2019' (Office for National Statistics, 12 November 2019), www.ons.gov.uk/employmentandlabourmarket/peopleinwork/employmentandemployeetypes/bulletins/uklabourmarket/november2019.

the Joint Research Centre found that, when covering a wider range of platform work, men occupy around two-thirds of gig employment.[176] But it is generally recognised (including in the JRC report)[177] that women's involvement in this area of the labour market is increasing, particularly if they have dependent children.

Women's growing participation in the atypical workforce could reflect the increase in jobs offering fewer than 20 hours a week, supposedly accommodating primary carer roles.[178] The Joint Research Centre found that 'platform workers are considerably more likely than offline workers to have dependent children'.[179] The rate of mothers engaging in freelancing work increased by 79 per cent between 2009 and 2017, drastically faster than other forms of growth in the gig economy and self-employment.[180] The likelihood of being in atypical employment increases for women (generally around 49 per cent) if they have any dependent children (58 per cent) and if they are a lone parent (56 per cent).[181]

This overrepresentation of women amongst part-time workers can leave them at a disadvantage. Women are expected to reconcile their career and family life, yet, this reconciliation more closely resembles an assimilation into an unequal male-centric world of work.[182] Commonly these jobs are contracted in 'female-dominated sectors' and limited to low-wage, low-skilled and precarious employment.[183] This means that 'women pay the price of reconciling work and family' as they must often downgrade their career,[184] perpetuating 'current patterns of income inequality'.[185] The compromise of pay and job security that supposedly ensures women have more flexibility for caring responsibilities is also exposed by Shultz, who finds that the sectors with a higher proportion of women in the workforce are 'not on the whole more family-friendly than male jobs'.[186]

[176] JRC (n 67) 62.

[177] ibid.

[178] Almost three in 10 mothers (28.5%) with a child aged 14 years and under had reduced their working hours because of childcare, compared with one in 20 fathers (4.8%): T Vizard, 'Families and the labour market, UK:2019' (ONS, 24 October 2019), www.ons.gov.uk/employmentandlabourmarket/peopleinwork/employmentandemployeetypes/articles/familiesandthelabourmarketengland/2019; 'Of the 2.9 million lone parent families in the UK in 2016, the majority (86%) were headed by a female lone parent': E Knipe 'Families and Households: 2016' (Office for National Statistics, 4 November 2016), www.ons.gov.uk/peoplepopulationandcommunity/birthsdeathsandmarriages/families/bulletins/familiesandhouseholds/2016; 72% of those receiving carers allowance in the UK are women: Carers UK, 'The Importance of Carers Allowance: Recognising and supporting family care' (July 2015) 9.

[179] JRC (n 67) 62.

[180] A Chamberlain, 'The Taylor review overlooks the big issue – clarifying what self-employment is' *The Guardian* (12 July 2017), www.theguardian.com/law/2017/jul/12/matthew-taylor-overlooks-the-big-issue-clarifying-self-employment-review-modern-working-practices.

[181] Clarke and Cominetti (n 28) 50.

[182] C O'Brien, *Unity and Adversity: EU Citizenship, Social Justice and the Cautionary Tale of the UK* (Hart Publishing, 2017) 94–95.

[183] Broughton et al (n 3) 69.

[184] M Gregory and S Connolly, 'The Price of Reconciliation: Part-Time Work, Families and Women's Satisfaction' (2008) 118 *The Economic Journal* F1, F7.

[185] N Fraser, *Justice Interruptus: Critical Reflections on the 'Postsocialist' Condition* (Routledge, 1997) 27–33 cited in V Shultz, 'Life's Work' (2000) 100 *Columbia Law Review* 1881, 1916–17.

[186] Shultz (n 185) 1895.

As the participation of women with caring responsibilities increases, the flexibility of the jobs they occupy should not justify paying women less. Nor should it be used to rationalise an expansion of casualisation and atypical contracts, to the degradation of permanent, fixed-hour contracts, in female-dominated areas of work, especially if the flexibility is 'one-way'. The discrimination already faced by women across all types of employment,[187] and extra barriers for those with family responsibilities or balancing the cost of wrap around childcare[188] will only be further exacerbated by their over-representation in atypical work – and again, if their ability to access welfare is compromised by an out-dated or restrictive definition of work.

2.6.2. Disabled Workers

Disabled workers are often over-represented in 'non-standard' work. In the UK, 34 per cent of Disabled workers are in part-time employment compared to 23 per cent of non-Disabled workers.[189] 48 per cent of Disabled workers in the UK are recorded as working atypical jobs, compared to 39 per cent of total workers in 2018.[190]

Just as the burden on reconciliation of work and caring responsibilities falls on women, Disabled workers are also expected to reconcile their disability with a world of work that previously 'designed out "nonstandard" people'.[191] This expectation does not challenge the ableist 'hegemonic constructions of productive value'[192] and therefore, Disabled workers are often expected to compromise by working in low-paid,[193] low-progression, insecure and often poorly adapted work.[194] Additionally, workplace adjustments that may have

[187] 'Median pay for all employees was 17.3% less for women than for men at April 2019': B Francis-Devine and D Pyper, 'The Gender Pay Gap' (House of Commons Library Briefing Paper 7068 2020); M Costa Dias, R Joyce and F Parodi, 'Wage progression and the gender wage gap: the causal impact of hours of work' (The Institute of Fiscal Studies Briefing note BN223, 2018); L Jones, 'Women's Progression in the Workplace' (Government Equalities Office, October 2019); Joseph Rowntree Foundation (n 116) 2.

[188] eg one in three parents in the UK find it difficult or very difficult to meet their childcare costs: Department for Education, 'Childcare and early years survey of parents 2022' (27 July 2023), www.explore-education-statistics.service.gov.uk/find-statistics/childcare-and-early-years-survey-of-parents/2022.

[189] A Powell, 'People with disabilities in employment' (House of Commons Library, Number 7540, 2020) 9.

[190] Clarke and Cominetti (n 28) 50.

[191] A Roulstone, 'Disability, work and welfare' in C Grover and L Pignott (eds), *Disabled people, work and welfare: Is employment really the answer?* (Policy Press, 2015) 257, 260.

[192] ibid.

[193] In 2019, the disability pay gap for all employees stood at 15.5%, equivalent to not being paid for two months of the year: 'Disability Pay Gap Day: disabled people work 2 months of the year for free, says TUC' (TUC, 4 November 2019; S Longhi, 'The disability pay gap' (Equality and Human Rights Commission: Research report 107, 2017).

[194] L Sayce, 'Switching Focus: Whose responsibility to improve disabled people's employment and pay' (London School of Economics, November 2018) 31.

been secured can be quickly lost when moving between temporary roles and organisations.[195]

Disabled gig workers are also at risk of facing discriminatory ratings systems which are subject to customer biases.[196] They are also at risk of disciplinary systems in gig work which penalise days off for illness, being late, not hitting demanding targets measured through algorithms, or taking too long for breaks.[197]

2.6.3. Young Workers

A report on precarious employment in Europe found that 50 per cent of European workers aged between 15–24 are employed in part-time or temporary contracts, compared to just 16 per cent in those aged 25–54 years old.[198] The higher proportion of younger workers could be, at least partly, explained by the likelihood that workers aged 15–24 are balancing employment and education.

In the UK various studies have found that young workers are more likely to be employed in part-time roles,[199] seasonal and casual roles,[200] agency work[201] and ZHCs.[202]

Young workers are also over-represented among gig workers. The Joint Research Centre has found that those working in digital labour markets across Europe tend to be younger and more educated.[203] Similarly, Huws et al demonstrate that crowd workers under 35 make up 51 per cent of the workforce.[204] While it could be claimed that these figures are distorted by the prevalence of students picking up jobs alongside their studies, only 10 per cent of digital platform workers are recorded students.[205]

Atypical work is often disproportionately occupied by younger workers, creating extra and distinct precarity. For example, younger workers are less likely to have built a sufficient personal safety net from previous employment and earnings.

[195] ibid 51.

[196] Prassl (n 60) 62.

[197] J Bloodworth, *Hired: Six Months Undercover in Low-Wage Britain* (Atlantic Books, 2018).

[198] Broughton et al (n 3).

[199] For workers aged 18–21, one-third of women and one-fifth of men were working part time. A Berrington et al, 'Measuring Economic Precarity among UK Youth during the Recession' (University of Southampton, ESRC Centre for Population Change Briefing Paper, 2014).

[200] 42% of seasonal and causal workers were aged between 16 and 19 years old, 24% between 20 and 24 years old: Forde et al (n 49).

[201] Around a third of agency workers aged between 16 and 24. ibid 12.

[202] 36% of workers aged 16–24 are on ZHCs compared to just 18.2% and 19.8% of 25–34-year-olds and 35–44-year-olds respectively. Petkova (n 43).

[203] Codagnone et al (n 57) 6; The average age of platform workers in this study was found to be just under 34, with those aged 16–25 accounting for a disproportionate percentage of over 26% of all secondary platform workers and 23% of main platform workers: JRC (n 67) 63.

[204] Huws and Joyce (n 73).

[205] Codagnone et al (n 57) 6.

Due to their age, younger workers are also more likely to be in the early stages of their career or an entrance job and may face lower wages because of this. They may also face a significant disadvantage if a country's minimum wage is tiered based on the age of the worker. In the UK, for example, a worker is only entitled to the full national living wage once they are aged over 21 (this was reduced from 23 in April 2024).[206] Young workers in apprenticeships also face lower wages; for example, in 2024 the UK minimum hourly rate is just £6.40. The additional hurdles for younger workers can result in more overwhelming precarity and will only be intensified by the insecurity of hours, income and availability of work.

2.6.4. Migrant Workers

Migrant workers are also more likely to be in atypical employment and so experience precarity. Eurostat record that on average EU migrant workers across the EU occupy a larger percentage share of part-time work and temporary work compared to nationals of the host Member States.[207] In the UK, the Migration Observatory's analysis shows that EU national workers are more likely than UK nationals to be in non-permanent, shift and ZHCs.[208] Migrant workers are also slightly more likely to be in all types of atypical work (41 per cent) than national workers (39 per cent).[209]

Across Europe, foreign-born workers make up over 50 per cent of workers who rely on platform or gig work as their main economic activity.[210] The gig economy can be less exclusionary than local labour markets. Some types of gig work have less stringent language requirements where platforms handle communication with the requester and can be operated in any language of choice.[211] Gig work is also more accessible to migrant workers as it reflects 'a breakdown of traditional word-of-mouth methods of finding work'.[212] Platforms are accessible anywhere with internet access and there is often only the need to register on a platform, rather than go through a hiring process and the hurdles of employer discrimination.[213]

[206] 'National Minimum Wage and National Living Wage rates', www.gov.uk/national-minimum-wage-rates.

[207] 'Migrant integration statistics – employment conditions' (Eurostat, May 2019), ec.europa.eu/eurostat/statistics-explained/index.php/Migrant_integration_statistics_-_employment_conditions#Youth_part-time_employment.

[208] M Fernández-Reino and C Rienzo, 'Migrants in the UK Labour Market: An Overview' (Migration Observatory, 15 July 2019) 13.

[209] Clarke and Cominetti (n 28) 50.

[210] JRC (n 67) 62.

[211] D Papademetriou and M Benton, 'Towards a Whole-of-Society Approach to Receiving and Settling Newcomers in Europe' (Migration Policy Institute Europe, November 2016) 16.

[212] Huws et al (n 55) 50.

[213] M Benton et al, 'Aiming Higher: Policies to Get Immigrants into Middle-Skilled Work in Europe' (Migration Policy Institute Europe, November 2014) 7.

An increased exposure to gig work and the insecurity it entails results, as warned by the Migration Policy Institute, in migrants ending up 'with a raw deal'.[214] They also face additional discrimination through the system of customer ratings and reviews, which are 'highly likely to be subject to either explicit or implicit bias'.[215] Alongside this, a review of qualitative studies of EU nationals in the UK speaks to a high prevalence of EU nationals being underpaid and overqualified.[216] EU nationals who have moved to a new Member State will be among those over-represented foreign-born gig workers; they face precarity and may require access to the necessary welfare safety nets.

While the flexibility of atypical work has increased accessibility for those who may be have traditionally been isolated from work, this has come with a cost. The disadvantages of the atypical labour market – increased instability of income, irregular hours and job insecurity – fall disproportionately on women, migrant, young and Disabled workers; groups that are often in a more vulnerable position to begin with. The interplay between this over-representation and the risk of exclusion from the rights provided by EU worker status means that women, Disabled and young EU citizens are likely to face further barriers to effectively exercising free movement.

2.7. Summary

This chapter has detailed how the world of work has changed with the growing presence of atypical work, increasing precarity in workers' lives and making access to welfare in a host Member State essential for many EU migrant atypical workers. As the number of atypical workers in the European labour market increases, so too will the number of EU migrant workers in atypical contracts, making it all the more important for the definition of genuine and effective work, as a gateway to free movement and equal treatment rights, to accurately reflect the changes in the make-up of the labour market.

Additionally, section 2.5 detailed the extra precarity and disadvantages endured by atypical workers, including lower incomes, underemployment, lack of employment rights and poorer health. In the face of increasing in-work poverty, reliance on social assistance is no longer reserved for non-workers. EU migrant atypical workers, in particular, may require access to welfare support to effectively exercise their free movement rights. This is especially so for EU migrants who face cumulative disadvantages and discrimination; the detrimental

[214] Benton and Patuzzi (n 113) 2.

[215] A Hunt and F Machingura, 'A good gig? The rise of on-demand domestic work' (Development Progress Working Paper 07, 2016) 27.

[216] P Teodorowski, R Woods and K Catriona, 'The Mental Health and Wellbeing of EU Citizens in the UK: A Systematic Review of the Qualitative Literature' (2020) 10 *Border Crossing* 43, 53.

impacts of atypical work also fall disproportionately on women, Disabled, carers, the young, and migrant workers.

By outlining both the growing prevalence of atypical work and the importance of social rights to alleviate temporary and permanent insecurity in the flexible labour market, this chapter sets the context for the variety of work that will need to be included in the EU legal concept of 'worker'. It also illustrates the risk of exposure to discrimination and precarity that EU migrant workers could face, especially if they are excluded from the definition of 'worker' and equal treatment rights. An insufficient definition of a 'worker' can mean that, for EU migrant workers, precarious employment is met with precarious residence status. As Thym puts it, 'Union citizens with scarce resources or with an instable employment position live in a grey zone with a precarious residence status and without much legal certainty'.[217] This can establish substantial barriers to exercising free movement, including the opportunity to access the flexible labour market at all. The next chapter will examine how the EU determines who is 'worker' and whether this takes an inclusive approach allowing for the wide variety of atypical work.

An insufficient definition for 'worker', which fails to capture the reality of work in Europe, could result in a growing number of economic actors being excluded from free movement rights. Chapter three, which examines the definition of worker, will also analyse the extent to which this problem has materialised in EU law and specifically in its application in the UK, revealing a considerable risk of exclusion for EU citizens *even* when they are engaged in atypical work across the internal market.

[217] D Thym, 'The Elusive Limits of Solidarity: Residence Rights of and Social Benefits for Economically Inactive Union Citizens' (2015) 52 *Common Market Law Review* 17, 41.

3

Schrodinger's Worker: When is a Worker Not a Worker?

3.1. Introduction

Work is often characterised as the golden ticket to free movement rights. The status provides a rite of passage for those who can demonstrate their economic activity credentials and be rewarded with the protections granted through EU law, most notably the right to equal treatment with nationals of the host Member State. However, simply working does not always mean that individuals are treated as a 'worker' under the free movement rules. 'Worker status' must be acquired, and importantly, recognised by decision-makers when seeking to assert these rights. With the variety of working arrangements and the increase in part-time, casual, temporary and gig work in the European labour market, as explored in the previous chapter, there is a risk that the rights provided to remove obstacles to free movement under Article 45 TFEU are reserved for those EU citizens who are deemed to be economically active *enough*.

This chapter seeks to establish what 'economically active enough' means. For EU migrants in atypical work, classification as economically active enough will fall to the determination of whether they meet the conditions to have status as a worker of self-employed person under EU law. If established, worker status provides free movement rights enshrined in Articles 45–48 TFEU and Regulation 492/2011,[1] and grants a right of residence.[2] EU migrant workers have the right to equal treatment with nationals of the host Member State,[3] without the requirement for them to be 'self-sufficient' or to have 'comprehensive sickness insurance'.[4] As such, EU migrants with worker status can access the majority of welfare rights available in the host Member State.

The previous chapter established that the labour market across Europe has become increasingly fragmented. The definition of worker is a gatekeeping

[1] Regulation (EU) No 492/2011 of 5 April 2011 on freedom of movement for workers within the Union Text with EEA relevance [2011] OJ L141/1 (Regulation 492/2011).

[2] Also relevant for Directive 2004/38/EC of the European Parliament and of the Council of 29 April 2004 on the right of citizens of the Union and their family members to move and reside freely within the territory of the Member States [2004] OJ L158/77 (Directive 2004/38), Art 7.

[3] Directive 2004/38, Art 24.

[4] Directive 2004/38, Art 7.

mechanism, which could limit the access of mobile citizens in atypical work to free movement and equal treatment rights. The Commission, in a proposal seeking to tackle the barriers to social protection for workers in non-standard employment, has recognised that 'The gaps in access to social protection, due to labour market status … may hinder the take-up of opportunities to move from one labour market status to another'.[5] Similarly, gaps in access to social protection, due to the inadequate coverage of the EU concept of work, could hinder EU nationals' take-up of opportunities for other work, including that in another Member State.

If they do not meet the conditions of worker status, EU citizens must rely on less secure rights which will either be dependent on the actions of another (family member) or reliant on demonstrating financial independence. These hurdles will be explored in more detail in chapters seven and eight.

It is also necessary to delineate the boundaries of this research. It examines the equal treatment rights of EU national workers who both reside and work in the same host Member State. It does not address issues relating to frontier workers,[6] or the definitions of work used in aspects of EU law not concerned with free movement.[7] Issues relating to how the social security coordination rules relate to atypical work is also not addressed for two main reasons. First, these issues did not come up in the case studies examined for this research, so it would be difficult to examine how atypical work is treated in this context. Secondly, the issues are substantially different to those for the definition of worker status, such as the risk of interruptions to work or changing family conditions that disproportionately impact women, as highlighted by Paskalia.[8]

This chapter explores the definition of worker status and its value to EU migrants, to assess whether its coverage of atypical employment is adequate to ensure that equal treatment rights are protected for atypical workers. By detailing and analysing the scope and limitations of the definition of worker, the chapter provides the framework for this book's test of the UK's implementation of the definition and analysis of whether it is compatible with EU law. It also highlights gaps in the definition and EU case law that could lead to the exclusion of atypical workers from free movement rights under Article 45 TFEU, leaving them to rely on the less secure rights of EU citizenship. To address the suitability of the definition of work this chapter first considers, in section 3.2, the value of worker status in relation to the social and residence rights it bestows on EU workers and other individuals. Section 3.3 then provides the starting point for analysing the definition

[5] Commission, 'Proposal for a Council Recommendation on access to social protection for workers and the self-employed' COM(2018) 0132 final.

[6] Case C-212/05 *Hartmann* ECLI:EU:C:2007:437, [2007] ECR I-6303; Case C-287/05 *Hendrix* ECLI:EU:C:2007:494, [2007] ECR I-06909.

[7] M Risak and T Dullinger, 'The concept of worker" in EU law: status quo and potential for change' (European Trade Union Institute Report 140, 2018) 17; H Verschueren, 'Being Economically Active: How it Still Matters' in H Verschueren (ed), *Residence, Employment and Social Rights of Mobile Persons: On how EU Law defines where they belong* (Intersentia, 2016) 187, 194.

[8] See more on the gendered issues in social security coordination and work in V Paskalia, *Free Movement, Social Security and Gender in the EU* (Hart Publishing, 2007).

of worker, located in EU case law. Section 3.4 provides a more in-depth analysis of where the CJEU has considered and included non-traditional forms of work in this definition. Finally, section 3.5 discusses the limitations of this definition, including where atypical workers may be left out and the problematic approach of adopting a vague definition to be interpreted by Member States.

3.2. The Value of Worker Status

Moving to another Member State as a worker guarantees some of the most robust EU rights for individuals. The value of a worker status under EU law and the subsequent rights attributed to those with the status is worth exploring to understand its importance.

3.2.1. Present Work

Before EU citizenship emerged in the Maastricht Treaty as a status granting free movement rights to all EU citizens,[9] the rights of workers to move and reside in another Member State were protected.[10] Free movement for workers and protection from discrimination based on nationality is now found in Article 45 TFEU.[11] This allows nationals of EU countries to freely accept offers of employment in other Member States and to move and reside there to work, and included a prohibition on discrimination based on nationality in matters of employment, remuneration and conditions of work. These rights are guaranteed subject to 'limitations justified on grounds of public policy, public security or public health'.[12]

Under Regulation 492/11,[13] EU migrant workers must have access to the same social and tax advantages as national workers (Article 7(2)), access to trade unions (Article 8) and education for their children (Article 10). '[S]ocial and tax advantages' are interpreted broadly,[14] including social assistance benefits.[15] Nic Shuibhne identified that CJEU case law has established a 'deep-rooted bond between work,

[9] Consolidated Version of the Treaty on European Union [1992] OJ C 325/5 Art 8 (Maastricht Treaty) and Consolidated Version of the Treaty on the Functioning of the European Union [2012] OJ C326/47 (TFEU), Art 21.

[10] Previously in Treaty Establishing the European Economic Community [1957], Art 39.

[11] TFEU, Art 45.

[12] ibid Art 45(3).

[13] Previously Regulation (EEC) No 1612/68 of 15 October 1968 on freedom of movement for workers within the Community [1968] OJ L 257/2 (Regulation 1612/68) which was codified into Regulation 492/11.

[14] Social advantages 'includes all advantages 'which, whether or not linked to a contract of employment, are generally granted to national workers': Case 207/78 *Even* ECLI:EU:C:1979:144, [1976] ECR I-2019 [22].

[15] Case 249/83 *Hoeckx* ECLI:EU:C:1985:139, [1985] ECR I-973.

equal treatment and access to social advantages',[16] including benefits guaranteeing a minimum means of subsistence as a social advantage.[17]

The introduction of EU citizenship developed the free movement of 'people', rather than solely workers, it is subject to significant 'limitations and conditions laid down in the Treaties and the measures adopted to give them effect'.[18] Despite mobile citizens theoretically being protected from discrimination on the grounds of nationality,[19] this has more recently been limited to citizens residing within the scope of Directive 2004/38,[20] effectively excluding those who are deemed economically inactive where they have not acquired permanent residence.[21]

An EU national with worker status fulfils the requirements of Article 7(1)(a) Directive 2004/38 for a right of residence in the host Member State for longer than three months.[22] Worker status is free from the condition to have sufficient resources not to become a burden on the social assistance system of the host Member State or to hold comprehensive sickness insurance.[23] A right of residence also provides EU citizens with the right to equal treatment to nationals of the host Member State including in relation to welfare benefits.[24]

Although there are alternative routes to establishing a right of residence, such as through being a student or self-sufficient person, these require EU citizens to meet extra conditions such as having sufficient resources not be an unreasonable burden on the social assistance system of the host Member State and to have comprehensive sickness insurance (CSI).[25] The requirement to have these resources creates a barrier for many EU nationals. The amount required for self-sufficiency cannot exceed 'the threshold below which nationals of the host Member State become eligible for social assistance'[26] and resources can come from a family member.[27] While a claim for social assistance should not automatically result in a finding that the claimant lacks sufficient resources for these rights

[16] N Nic Shuibhne, 'Reconnecting free movement of workers and equal treatment in an unequal Europe' (2018) 43 *European Law Review* 477, 485; Case 235/87 *Matteucci* ECLI:EU:C:1988:460, [1988] ECR I-5589 [16].

[17] Case C-249/83 *Hoeckx* (n 15) [22].

[18] TFEU, Art 21.

[19] ibid Art 18.

[20] N Nic Shuibhne, 'Limits Rising, Duties Ascending: The Changing Legal Shape of Union Citizenship' (2015) 52 *Common Market Law Review* 889, 937; Case C-333/13 *Dano* ECLI:EU:C:2014:2358, [2014] ECR I-2358.

[21] See section 3.2.3 of this chapter.

[22] The initial three months' right of residence is available to all EU citizens under Directive 2004/38, Art 6.

[23] As required for students and self-sufficient persons: Directive 2004/38, Art 7.

[24] ibid Art 24.

[25] ibid Art 7(1)(b). Although it should be noted that students are only required to make a declaration of self-sufficiency: Art 7(1)(c).

[26] Directive 2004/38, Art 8(4).

[27] Case C-218/14 *Singh* ECLI:EU:C:2015:476, [2016] CMLR 12 [76]; Case C-93/18 *Bajratari* ECLI:EU:C:2019:809, [2020] 1 CMLR 29 [31].

of residence, in the UK a claim for Universal Credit is often treated as all but definitive. In the UK, those relying on past self-sufficiency to establish a permanent right of residence are expected to prove they had sufficient resources at the 'outset' of their residence to see them through a five-year-period.[28]

Turning to CSI, the recent CJEU judgment in *VI* found that registering with a national healthcare service can fulfil this requirement. However, up until 2022, EU citizens in the UK were required to meet the extra and unusual hurdle of holding private health insurance in addition to their access to the National Health Service (NHS) to demonstrate holding CSI, excluding many from establishing this right of residence.[29] Many therefore struggle to fit into these categories to rely on equal treatment provisions in the Directive. Even where the requirements are met at first, those who require access to welfare benefits or housing may struggle to continuously meet the self-sufficiency condition.

The right to equal treatment, which secures access to social rights and welfare, has been reserved for those who are economically active or wealthy enough to not need to work. However, many will never have the resources necessary to meet the conditions of self-sufficiency without work. Work therefore continues to represent the most reliable route to secure the necessary protection from discrimination and vital access to public services in times of need.

3.2.2. Rights for Family Members of Workers

Alongside the rights conferred to workers, under Article 7(1)(d), family members can derive a right to reside in a host Member State from an EU migrant who meets the requirements of Article 7(1) Directive 2004/38. A finding of worker status can therefore provide an EU national the ability to secure rights for family members in the host Member State. This includes:

- spouse or registered partner;[30]
- non-married partner in a durable relationship;[31]
- children, grandchildren or great-grandchildren (etc) of the worker or his or her spouse or registered partner who are under 21 years old;[32]

[28] *VP v SSWP (JSA)* [2014] UKUT 32 (AAC) [84].

[29] *Ahmad v SSHD* [2014] EWCA Civ 988 [70]–[71]. While an European Health Insurance Card issued by another Member State can be used to satisfy the CSI requirement, these should only be used for temporary stays in a host Member State.

[30] Directive 2004/38, Art 2(a)–(b); Case 267/83 *Diatta* ECLI:EU:C:1985:67, [1985] ECR I-567 finds that marriage is subsisting until the completion of divorce.

[31] Directive 2004/38, Art 3.

[32] Directive 2004/38, Art 2(c); step-children are also included: Joined Cases C-401/15 to C-403/15 *Depesme and Kerrou* ECLI:EU:C:2016:955. The parent–child relationship is defined through economic terms rather than legal terms, ie whether the step-parent contributes to the child's maintenance.

- grandparents, great grandparents (etc) or children, grandchild or great-grandchildren (etc) over 21 (provided they are dependent).[33]

A family member receives equal treatment on the same basis as workers and can include family members with a non-EU nationality.[34]

Family rights derived from an EU worker are particularly valuable in the case of children as 'Children are not on the radar of the directive'.[35] EU children, even if born in the host Member State, cannot benefit from having a direct right to reside unless they fulfil the criteria in Article 7 of the Citizens' Rights Directive.[36] As rights under the Directive are often reliant on economic activity or wealth, this matter is often 'out of the child's hands'[37] and reliant on an EU adult's activity.[38] While there is a call for children's rights to be recognised in EU law,[39] as it stands children are reliant and therefore directly benefit from a parent's status of worker under EU law.

Notwithstanding the usefulness of family member rights, the justification and design of these rights are constructed with 'reference to market ideology'.[40] The CJEU has made clear that family members' rights are parasitic on and derive from the rights of the worker[41] and are established in recognition of the need to relieve workers of an obstacle to free movement.[42] This is despite many 'non-traditional' contributions made to the market by family members, through domestic work, and caring roles to the benefit of workers and their employers alike,[43] but which without payment do not, according to the CJEU, constitute work.[44] The traditional economic model of work leaves family members dependent on the status of their 'economically active' relative; this is a gendered dependence. The definition of work therefore, plays an important role for more than an individual worker.

[33] Directive 2004/38, Art 2(c)–(d); Dependency means to receive 'material' support including financial support, meals, accommodation or informal care if the relative is disabled or ill; see Case C-316/85 *Lebon* ECLI:EU:C:1987:302, [1987] ECR I-2811 [21]–[23]; Case 200/02 *Chen* ECLI:EU:C:2004:639, [2004] ECR I-9925 [43]; The UK Upper Tribunal found that translation, emotional and social support are not included in *SSWP v MF* (SPC) [2018] UKUT 179 (AAC).

[34] Directive 2004/38, Art 24(1).

[35] C O'Brien, 'The rights of EU nationals in the UK post-Brexit – five pessimistic predictions' (Free Movement Blog, 19 February 2018), www.freemovement.org.uk/rights-eu-nationals-uk-post-brexit-five-pessimistic-predictions/.

[36] For derivative rights see section 3.2.4 of this chapter.

[37] C O'Brien, *Unity in Adversity: EU Citizenship, Social Justice and the Cautionary Tale of the UK* (Hart Publishing, 2017) 74.

[38] Case C-115/15 *SSHD v NA* ECLI:EU:C:2016:487 [78].

[39] See O'Brien (n 37) 74–77.

[40] TK Hervey, 'Migrant workers and their families in the European Union: the pervasive market ideology of Community Law' in J Shaw and G More (eds), *New Legal Dynamics of European Union* (Oxford University Press, 1995) 91, 110.

[41] Case 157/84 *Frascogna* ECLI:EU:C:1985:243, [1985] ECR I-1739 [15].

[42] Regulation 1612/68 stated that 'the right of freedom of movement, in order that it may be exercised … requires that … obstacles to the mobility of workers shall be eliminated, in particular as regards the worker's right to be joined by his family'.

[43] Hervey (n 40) 105.

[44] Case C-77/95 *Züchner* ECLI:EU:C:1996:425, [1996] ECR I-5689 [14]–[15].

3.2.3. Long-term Resident Workers

Beyond current residence rights, the adequacy of the definition of worker can also affect the lives of EU national atypical workers many years after their work when seeking to establish a permanent right of residence.

The right to permanent residence can be acquired by EU citizens after five continuous years of 'lawful residence' in a Member State.[45] Lawful residence in this context is considered, predominantly, through the lens of Directive 2004/38, not simply through rights as a EU citizen exercising free movement rights.[46] As their right of residence is covered by Directive 2004/38, family members can also acquire permanent residence on the same basis as the EU national they derive their rights from. Fulfilment of residence under these categories must be for a continuous period of five years; if an EU citizen loses their right of residence for even a short period of time, the five-year-period will restart and all previous years of lawful residence are lost.[47] Absences from the Member State are permitted provided they do not exceed six months in any 12-month period.[48] However, a single absence of 12 months is permitted for an important reason.[49]

As a 'key element to social cohesion',[50] once permanent residence has been acquired, an EU national is entitled to equal treatment without having to show that they are exercising any other right to reside under the Directive,[51] meaning that they are treated as 'nationals in all but name'.[52] Once permanent residence is acquired, EU free movement rights are no longer conditional on economic activity or self-sufficiency. Permanent residence can only be lost after an absence from that Member State for 'a period exceeding two consecutive years',[53] or revoked on 'serious grounds of public policy or public security' as part on an expulsion measure.[54]

Article 17 of the Directive also provides for important exceptions to the five-year residence requirement for some workers and their family members. A worker can receive permanent residence after three years of residence if they have reached the age of entitlement for an old age pension or take an early retirement,

[45] Directive 2004/38, Art 16.

[46] Joined cases C-424/10 and C-425/10 *Ziolkowski* ECLI:EU:C:2011:866, [2011] ECR I-14035 [47].

[47] C O'Brien, 'The pillory, the precipice and the slippery slope: the profound effects of the UK's legal reform programme targeting EU migrants' (2015) 37 *Journal of Social Welfare and Family Law* 111, 118.

[48] Directive 2004/38, Art 16(3).

[49] ibid. 'Important reasons' include pregnancy, childbirth, serious illness, study, vocational training or a posting in another Member State or a third country. This list is not exhaustive.

[50] Case C-162/09 *Lassal* ECLI:EU:C:2010:592, [2010] ECR I-09217 [32]; referring to Directive 2004/38, preamble recital 17.

[51] Directive 2004/38, Art 24.

[52] C Barnard, *The Substantive Law of the EU*, 6th edn (Oxford University Press, 2019) 440.

[53] Directive 2004/38, Art 16(4).

[54] ibid Art 28(2).

and they have been working in the Member State for the preceding 12 months.[55] Only two years' residence is required where a worker has had to cease work as a result of permanent incapacity.[56] There is no 'period of residence' requirement at all if the worker is permanently incapacitated as the result of an accident at work or occupational disease.[57] Provision is also made for workers who, after three years' residence in the host Member State, take up work in another Member State, provided they maintain their place of residence and return at least once a week.[58] A permanent right of residence is also safeguarded for surviving family members of deceased EU workers, if the worker had either resided in the host Member State for at least two years, or died as a result of an accident at work.[59] These provisions reflect the EU's pursuit of removing risks to exercising free movement for economic activity and further highlights the salience of work in accessing rights.

3.2.4. Rights Acquired from Previous Work

The definition of work can also play a role in EU citizens' lives after they have stopped working, including the ability to retain worker status and access further derivative rights.

3.2.4.1. Retained Worker Status

An EU migrant worker can benefit from the provisions in place to ensure they retain the status of worker when they stop working due to a variety of circumstances usually beyond their control. These circumstances, of course, require the EU national to prove that they met the requirements for worker status, before it can be retained.

The circumstances where an EU national can retain their worker status are provided for in Article 7(3) of the Citizens Directive including where an EU national is temporarily unavailable for work due to illness or accident, involuntarily unemployed, or embarking on vocational training.[60] Importantly, for those in atypical work, involuntary unemployment does not require the worker to have been dismissed, but also covers situations where a worker reaches the end of a fixed-term or temporary contract.[61] The reason for retaining worker

[55] ibid Art 17(1)(a).
[56] ibid Art 17(1)(b).
[57] ibid.
[58] ibid Art 17(1)(c).
[59] ibid Art 17(4).
[60] Directive 2004/38, Art 7(3).
[61] Case C-413/01 *Ninni-Orasche* ECLI:EU:C:2003:600, [2003] ECR I-13187 [32].

status can also change over time; for example, an individual can retain their worker status first by being involuntarily unemployed and then from being unavailable due to illness.[62] The ability to retain worker status during gaps in employment is highlighted in a 2016 FreSsco report as vital 'For those who move in and out of work – possibly due to the rise in flexible and atypical contracts'.[63]

The CJEU have also found that this list is not exhaustive, and have included circumstances where workers must take time away or leave work due to the late stages of pregnancy in *Saint Prix*.[64] Workers are required to return to work or self-employment within a reasonable period after the birth of the child, taking account of 'the applicable national rules on the duration of maternity leave'.[65] However, where causes of interruptions to work are not explicitly covered, it is unlikely to be recognised by Member States as resulting in the retention of worker status, including the need to leave employment to provide informal care.[66]

The length of time for which an EU national can retain their worker status, in circumstances of illness, accident or involuntary unemployment where the EU national had been employed for over one year, is not specified. As such, some Member States have interpreted this as being up to the discretion of a national decision-maker. However, for EU nationals who have been employed for less than one year and are involuntarily unemployed,[67] the Directive 'sets a floor' requiring worker status to be retained for no less than six months.[68] This has allowed Member States to take a restrictive approach.[69] The UK, for example, treats this 'floor' as a 'ceiling',[70] by only allowing the retention of worker status in this situation for a *maximum* of six months.[71] This approach is also taken by Germany and was seemingly endorsed by the CJEU in *Alimanovic*.[72]

[62] *GE v SSWP* [2017] UKUT 145 (AAC) [41].

[63] C O'Brien, E Spaventa and J De Coninck 'Comparative Report 2015: The concept of worker under Art 45 TFEU and certain non-standard forms of employment' (FreSsco, 2016) 9.

[64] Case C-507/12 *Saint Prix* EU:C:2014:2007, [2015] 1 CMLR 5. This route to retaining worker status was extended to self-employed persons in Case C-442/16 *Gusa* ECLI:EU:C:2017:1004, [2018] WLR(D) 10.

[65] Case C-507/12 *Saint Prix* (n 64) [42]. In the UK, this 'reasonable period of time' has been interpreted as 52 weeks after the birth of the child and can include re-entering the employment market, making arrangements to return or to become a jobseeker: *SSWP v SFF* [2015] UKUT 0502 (AAC).

[66] C O'Brien, 'Social blind spots and monocular policy making: the ECJ's migrant worker model' [2009] 46 *Common Market Law Review* 1107.

[67] This includes completion of a fixed-term contract of less than a year: Case C-483/17 *Tarola* EU:C:2019:309, [2019] 3 CMLR 23.

[68] O'Brien, Spaventa and De Coninck (n 63) 9.

[69] Verschueren (n 7) 208.

[70] O'Brien (n 37) 145.

[71] The Immigration (European Economic Area) Regulations 2016, SI 2016/1052, Reg 6(3).

[72] Case C-67/14 *Alimanovic* ECLI:EU:C:2015:597, [2016] 1 CMLR 29.

3.2.4.2. Derivative Rights

The benefits of acquiring worker status in the past can also outlive the economic activity by activating a form of derivative right of residence. As EU citizens, children have a right to free movement.[73] The CJEU has recognised that for EU children to be able to fully enjoy their right to free movement, it is also necessary to impart a right of residence to their primary carers. However, these derivative rights are limited to specific circumstances.

The key derivative right concerning workers is established in the CJEU cases *Baumbast*[74] and *Teixeira*.[75] These cases concern EU migrant workers' right to bring their family to the host Member State and for their child to access education in that state (Article 10 of Regulation 492/2011). In *Baumbast*, the CJEU found that this must also include a right to remain in that education should the worker cease economic activity and that the primary carer of the child must also acquire a right to reside.[76] Education being withdrawn from an EU worker's child should their economic activity end represented an unjustifiable obstacle to free movement.[77] This right is therefore still embedded in the value of work. To ensure the continuation of education in the host Member State, the CJEU found in *Teixeira* that this derivative right of residence was 'not even implicitly' conditional on self-sufficiency.[78] Establishing a *Teixeira* right of residence therefore provides primary carers with access to welfare benefits.[79]

This route can be a useful alternative if worker status cannot be established at the time, providing that it has been found or can be proven at some point in the past. However, the CJEU has specifically excluded time spent with this derivative right to reside from contributing to the five years' continuous 'lawful residence' required for permanent residence.[80] This means residence as a *Teixeira* carer can result in a sudden loss of rights once the child has left education. Other forms of derivative rights (including as a *Chen*[81] or *Zambrano*[82] carer) do not currently offer clear access social benefits.

[73] TFEU Art 21.

[74] Case C-413/99 *Baumbast* ECLI:EU:C:2002:493, [2002] ECR I-07091.

[75] Case C-480/08 *Teixeira* ECLI:EU:C:2010:83, [2010] ECR I-01107.

[76] Case C-413/99 *Baumbast* (n 74).

[77] ibid [52].

[78] Case C-480/08 *Teixeira* (n 75) [67].

[79] Case C-480/08 *Teixeira* (n 75); Case C-310/08 *Ibrahim* ECLI:EU:C:2010:80, [2010] ECR I-01065 [57].

[80] Case C-529/11 *Alarape and Tijani* ECLI:EU:C:2013:290, [2013] 3 CMLR 38 [40].

[81] It is unlikely that a right to reside as a *Chen* parent would create entitlement given that it is premised on self-sufficiency, C-200/02 *Chen* (n 33); self-sufficiency cannot be established through work; Case C-86/12 *Alokpa and Others* ECLI:EU:C:2013:645.

[82] Zambrano residence rights are for TCN primary carers of children who would otherwise have to leave the territory of the EU, Case C-34/09 *Zambrano* ECLI:EU:C:2011:124, [2011] ECR I-1177 and Case C-256/11 *Dereci and others* ECLI:EU:C:2011:734, [2011] ECR I-11315 [66]. The UK Supreme Court found that Zambrano carers did not benefit from equal treatment and access to welfare benefits: *R (on the application of HC) v SSWP and others* [2017] UKSC 73. The CJEU has not had an opportunity to rule on this question; see C O'Brien, 'Acte cryptique? Zambrano, welfare rights, and underclass citizenship in the tale of the missing preliminary reference' (2019) 56 *Common Market Law Review* 1697.

3.2.5. Post-Brexit Residence Rights in the UK

Since Brexit, EU citizens in the UK and UK citizens in the EU must still rely on their worker status to grant equal treatment rights, and sometimes residence rights, under the Withdrawal Agreement.[83]

As the case studies informing this research are gathered from EU and EEA nationals living in the UK, sometimes after the end of the transition period, it is useful to consider the ongoing importance for worker status in the UK after Brexit. The UK opted to adopt a constitutive scheme to register EEA nationals and their family members living in the UK before the end of the transition period. EEA nationals must apply to the EU Settlement Scheme (EUSS) to establish new residence rights in the UK.[84] A successful application to the scheme will result in a grant of either 'settled status' to EEA nationals who can demonstrate residence for more than five years in the UK or 'pre-settled status' for those who can only demonstrate residence of less than five years.[85] The EUSS takes a 'more generous', or a necessary administratively simpler,[86] approach than the Withdrawal Agreement, by not making the status conditional on residence within the confines of Directive 2004/38. Instead, applicants must rely on evidence that they were *actually* resident.[87] However, the construction of a system that is treated as a separate domestic operation leaves EU nationals in the UK potentially vulnerable to any changes under domestic rules which may adjust the conditions on residency.[88] The relationship between the scope of Withdrawal Agreement rights and its relationship to the EUSS has been and is currently the subject of litigation.[89]

Despite the appearance of generosity, the UK has constructed a scheme that withholds equal treatment rights in the Withdrawal Agreement from those with pre-settled status unless they can demonstrate an additional right of residence

[83] Agreement on the withdrawal of the United Kingdom of Great Britain and Northern Ireland from the European Union and the European Atomic Energy Community [2019] OJ C 384/1 (Withdrawal Agreement), Arts 13 and 15.

[84] Home Office, *EU Settlement Scheme: Statement of Intent* (21 June 2018) para 1.3.

[85] Settled status is an indefinite leave to remain and pre-settled status is a limited leave to remain: Immigration Rules; Appendix EU, Rule EU14.

[86] C O'Brien, 'Between the devil and the deep blue sea: Vulnerable EU citizens cast adrift in the UK post-Brexit' (2021) 58 *Common Market Law Review* 431.

[87] This approach has caused significant issues for those with problems accessing evidence of their residence including, for example, the homeless and those fleeing domestic violence. F Costello and C Barnard, 'The EU Settlement Scheme – ongoing issues from the frontline' (UK in a Changing Europe, December 2022), ukandeu.ac.uk/the-eu-settlement-scheme-ongoing-issues-from-the-frontline. M Sumption, 'Not Settled Yet? Understanding the EU Settlement Scheme using the Available Data' (The Migration Observatory, April 2020).

[88] M Dougan, 'So Long, Farewell, Auf Wiedersehen, Goodbye: The UK's Withdrawal Package' (2020) 57 *Common Market Law Review* 631, 670.

[89] For example, see *SSWP v AT (AIRE Centre and IMA Intervening)* [2022] UKUT 330 (AAC). On current issues relating to scope of the Withdrawal Agreement, see *Juraj Hynek v London Borough of Islington* (County Court at Central London, 24 May 2024).

under the free movement rules.[90] This means that where an EEA national with pre-settled status requires access to welfare or public services, this generosity is an illusion.

The provisions excluding those with pre-settled status from equal treatment rights were challenged in the UK courts where it was found that the policy resulted in direct disclination.[91] However, when referred to the CJEU, it was instead found that those with confirmation of a domestic residence status were not entitled to protection from discrimination in Article 18 TFEU the EU treaties.[92] Instead, the Court found that those with pre-settled status could rely on protection from the risk of violating fundamental rights under the Charter of Fundamental Rights of the EU.[93] Assessment of whether the policy was discriminatory was therefore deemed unnecessary. As it stands, an EEA migrant atypical worker with pre-settled status could be denied access to benefits if they are found not to have worker status. Such a decision would mean that the only option to access welfare support is to return to the Member State of nationality and risk losing the right to return and live in the UK altogether.[94] The compliance of this policy with the Withdrawal Agreement has been questioned by O'Brien, but has yet to be tested in litigation.[95]

For many of the millions of applicants who have been granted pre-settled status,[96] worker status continues to play a vital role in ensuring access to means-tested welfare benefits and social housing. Many who could not demonstrate five years of residence for their initial EUSS application will continue to struggle when seeking to upgrade to settled status and be left with the less secure pre-settled status and needing to demonstrate the additional right of residence to access welfare benefits. Since the UK High Court found that pre-settled status could not expire, it is possible that the need to rely on worker status could be necessary for a significant number of years yet.[97] This is also the case for those with pending applications (100,000 applications were still pending by December 2023)[98] either

[90] Social Security (Income-related Benefits) (Updating and Amendment) (EU exit) Regulations 2019, SI 2019/872, Reg 8(3)(d) amending Universal Credit Regulations 2013 (UC Regulations), SI 2013/376, Reg 9(3)(c)(i).

[91] *R (Fratila and Tanase) v SSWP* [2020] EWHC 998 (Admin).

[92] Case C-709/20 *CG* ECLI:EU:C:2021:602, [2022] 1 CMLR 26; see also A Welsh, 'Permission to discriminate – EU nationals, pre-settled status and access to social assistance' (2022) 44 *Journal of Social Welfare and Family Law* 133.

[93] ibid [88]–[93].

[94] Those with pre-settled status would not be eligible for settled status if they are absent from the UK for more than six months in a 12-month period. Immigration Rules, Appendix EU, Annex 1, under 'continuous qualifying period'. Pre-settled status will lapse after an absence of two years.

[95] O'Brien (n 86).

[96] 2.8 million applications have resulted in a grant of pre-settled status by the end of December 2023. Some of these will be repeat applications to either correct a wrong decision or to upgrade to settled status. It is therefore difficult to determine how many with pre-settled status are resident in the UK. Home Office, 'EU Settlement Scheme quarterly statistics, December 2023' (March 2024), www.gov.uk/government/statistics/eu-settlement-scheme-quarterly-statistics-december-2023/eu-settlement-scheme-quarterly-statistics-december-2023.

[97] *R (Independent Monitoring Authority for the Citizens' Rights Agreements) v SSHD* [2022] EWHC 3274 (Admin).

[98] Home Office (n 96).

to acquire status, correct status or to upgrade to settled status.[99] The accuracy of how worker status is defined will continue to be relevant and gatekeep access to social rights for EEA nationals in the UK for many more years to come.

This section has aimed to illustrate the value of worker status. It grants the most effective and secure rights for EU nationals, allowing them equal treatment with nationals of a host Member State including access to many welfare benefits. The ability to establish worker status can therefore go a significant way to alleviating many of the risks that are created by the precarity of flexible employment, as identified in the previous chapter. Worker status can also open the door to both more permanent rights and rights that outlive the economic activity itself. Ultimately, the definition of worker determines who can access these rights and conversely excludes those who do not meet its requirements. Worker status continues to be relevant for millions of EEA nationals living in the UK after Brexit. The CJEU has recognised that systematic denial of benefits to workers is 'tantamount to an outright negation of the freedom of movement for [Union] workers'.[100] Workers who are excluded from the definition of work are stripped of equal access to benefits, damaging their ability to move between states to work. It is therefore vital that the definition of worker under EU law encompasses a wide variety of work and does not limit these rights to full-time or permanent workers.

3.3. When Work = Work under EU Rules

A substantial divide exists between the rights available to those who acquire 'worker' status and those who do not. Without a sufficiently broad and inclusive test for worker status that recognises the full varieties of economic activity, it is possible that many EU atypical workers may lose or never acquire worker status under Article 7 Directive 2004/38 and the rights accompanied with it. This has implications for free movement more generally. It has been argued that equal treatment rights are often practically limited to only those EU migrants who are deemed to be economically active or wealthy.[101] Therefore the definition of work must be carefully scrutinised; it plays an important role as the tool which determines which EU citizens have been *sufficiently economically active* to access free movement rights at all.

The CJEU has declared the goal of establishing a common and unified definition of a worker for free movement purposes under EU law as 'settled'.[102] However, the use of vague concepts, such as 'genuine and effective' work, has left more

[99] ibid.

[100] Nic Shuibhne (n 16) 494; Case C-208/05 *ITC Innovative Technology Center GmbH* ECLI:EU:C:2007:16, [2007] ECR I-181 [44].

[101] This is discussed in more detail in ch 8 at section 8.5.1.

[102] Joined Cases C-22/08 and C-23/08 *Vatsouras and Koupatantze* ECLI:EU:C:2009:344, [2009] ECR I-4585 [26].

unanswered questions about the precise boundaries of the definition and created space for restrictive applications. This section will detail the basic formulation of the EU definition of work, in order to then ask how inclusive it is of atypical work.

3.3.1. Worker Status

It is accepted that a 'worker' is a Union concept and therefore its scope is to be defined by the CJEU. While this is then left for Member States to interpret and apply, this should not be 'unilaterally fixed and modified by national law'.[103] The CJEU recognised the importance of creating an EU definition of work as differing approaches by Member States could risk the effectiveness of EU law and could 'jeopardize' the achievement of the objectives of the Treaties.[104] For Mancini, giving the concept of worker a Community meaning established the Court as having a 'hermeneutic monopoly' to counteract potential 'unilateral restrictions on the application of rules' relating to free movement of workers.[105] The Court has taken this responsibility on by offering a deliberately broad definition – but also a vague one. Leaving the implementation of the definition to Member States inevitably gives them the responsibility and power to refine the terms set by the CJEU. To avoid an abuse of this power, it is understood that the EU concept of worker cannot be undermined by national definitions.[106] This can be important for certain types of atypical work where, even if a type of employment is considered as *sui generis* under national law, it cannot have any consequence on the determination of worker status under EU law.[107] With this in mind, it is necessary to examine the CJEU case law to understand the scope of the definition of worker with which Member States should comply.

The definition of worker under EU law has been established broadly in *Lawrie-Blum* as: 'for a certain period of time a person performs services for and under the direction of another person in return for which he receives remuneration.'[108] This criteria is regarded alongside the test offered in *Levin*, where the CJEU determined that a worker must be in pursuit of 'genuine and effective' activities that are not 'on such a small scale as to be regarded as purely marginal and ancillary'.[109]

[103] Case 75/63 *Hoekstra* ECLI:EU:C:1964:19, [1964] ECR I-0177.

[104] Case 53/81 *Levin* ECLI:EU:C:1982:105, [1982] ECR I-1035 [15].

[105] F Mancini, 'The Free Movement of Workers in the Case Law of the European Court of Justice' in D Curtin and D O'Keeffe (eds), *Constitutional Adjudication in European community and national law: essays for the Hon. Mr. Justice T. F. O'Higgins* (Butterworth, 1992) 68 cited in AP van der Mei, *Free Movement of Persons within the European Community: Cross Border Access to Public Benefits* (Hart Publishing, 2003) 35.

[106] Case C-216/15 *Betriebsrat der Ruhrlandklinik gGmbH* ECLI:EU:C:2016:883, [2017] 2 CMLR 13 [43].

[107] Case C-116/06 *Kiiski* ECLI:EU:C:2007:536, [2007] ECR I-7643 [26].

[108] Case 66/85 *Lawrie-Blum* ECLI:EU:C:1986:284, [1986] ECR 2121 [17].

[109] Case 53/81 *Levin* (n 104) [17].

3.3.2. Self-employed Persons

While this book concerns the rights of atypical workers, some may be classified, perhaps incorrectly, as self-employed persons.[110] It is worth noting that the definition for self-employment follows a similar approach to the definition of a worker.

In *Jany*, the CJEU identified that a self-employed person must perform services for a certain period of time for which they receive remuneration but must not be performed under the direction of another person or in 'a relationship of subordination'.[111] This also entails the condition that any services provided must be 'genuine and effective'.[112] Those who are considered self-employed persons must also establish genuine and effective activity.

The requirement of 'genuine and effective' work takes a deliberately broad approach to guaranteeing worker status, arguably to ensure that many different types of work are caught in the definition. Yet, an imprecise definition, while seemingly useful to mould around different circumstances, also leaves more room for Member States to refine the definition while interpreting and applying a 'genuine and effective' test.[113] While, the CJEU has found that the concept of a 'worker' under EU law 'must not be interpreted restrictively',[114] or modified to 'eliminate at will the protection afforded by the Treaty to certain categories of person',[115] Member States are ultimately left to interpret and apply the rules that decide whether someone's work is *enough* to have achieved 'worker' status and the rights this entails. As a result, Member States have tested the parameters of the definition, while the CJEU has often responded with judgments which are inclusive of atypical work. Nevertheless, as Nic Shuibhne has argued, it is the vague terminology of 'genuine and effective' work that 'still shape[s] the functioning and reach' of the definition of work and subsequently of free movement.[116]

3.4. The Inclusion of Non-traditional Work

The case law dealing with part-time and non-traditional work reinforces the flexibility of the genuine and effective test. The CJEU has clearly stated that the test should be applied generously and inclusively, recognising that reserving rights 'solely to persons engaged in full-time employment' through a narrow definition would jeopardise 'the objectives of the Treaty'.[117] This section will detail how the

[110] See ch 2 at section 2.5.3.
[111] Case C-268/99 *Jany and Others* ECLI:EU:C:2001:616, [2001] ECR I-8615 [33]–[34].
[112] ibid.
[113] F Schauer, 'The Convergence of Rules and Standards' (2003) 3 *New Zealand Law Review* 303, 305.
[114] Case C-3/90 *Bernini* ECLI:EU:C:1992:89, [1992] ECR I-1071 [1].
[115] Case 75/63 *Hoekstra* (n 103).
[116] Nic Shuibhne (n 16) 497.
[117] Case 53/81 *Levin* (n 104) [15].

definition of worker is applied to non-traditional work in CJEU case law and what aspects are determined to be relevant to a finding of 'genuine and effective' work. This will ask whether the EU definition of worker is capable of including a large variety of atypical work.

The 'genuine and effective' criterion has consistently been interpreted broadly to encapsulate many varieties of work. This has included a consideration of the level of hours and pay along with other aspects of employment including consistency, longevity and formality of employment, various types of remuneration and distinctions for work designed to rehabilitate or (re)integrate individuals into the labour market.

3.4.1. Discrimination and Part-time Work

The CJEU has been clear that worker status cannot be denied solely because it is part time.[118] In *Levin*, the CJEU identified that part-time work is 'an effective means of improving the … living conditions' of Union citizens.[119]

However, a difference in treatment of part-time work has been permitted for frontier workers. The CJEU in *Geven* found that, even when work is recognised by the national court as 'genuine and effective',[120] insufficiently substantial part-time work can require a test for a 'genuine link' with the host Member State to establish a right to social advantages under what is now Regulation 492/2011.[121] This test was previously reserved for those deemed to be economically inactive.[122] While the impact of this case may be limited to the rights of frontier workers, it demonstrates a willingness from the Court to discriminate on the basis that part-time work can be evidence of *insufficient* economic activity to warrant social and welfare rights.

3.4.2. Remuneration and Hours

Importantly, the CJEU takes a flexible approach to levels of remuneration, stating that a limited amount of remuneration cannot have 'any consequence' on the finding of worker status.[123] Member States cannot apply a strict threshold of

[118] Case C-106/91 *Ramrath* ECLI:EU:C:1992:230, [1992] ECR I-3351 [25].
[119] Case 53/81 *Levin* (n 104) [15].
[120] Case C-213/05 *Geven* ECLI:EU:C:2007:438, [2007] ECR I-6347 [25]–[26].
[121] ibid.
[122] S O'Leary, 'Developing an Ever Closer Union between the Peoples of Europe? A Reappraisal of the Case Law of the Court of Justice on the Free Movement of Persons and EU Citizenship' (2008) 27 *Yearbook of European Law* 167, 188–89; H Verschueren, 'Free Movement of EU Citizens: Including for the Poor?' (2015) 22 *Maastricht Journal of European and Comparative Law* 10, 17.
[123] Case 53/81 *Levin* (n 104) [16]; Case 344/87 *Bettray* ECLI:EU:C:1989:226, [1989] ECR I-1621 [15]; Case C-456/02 *Trojani* ECLI:EU:C:2004:488, [2004] ECR I-7573 [16]; Case C-188/00 *Kurz*

earnings or hours to decide worker status, even though many do adopt a type of threshold as part of the decision process for worker status.[124] The UK, for example, has adopted a minimum earnings threshold (MET) as the first tier of the worker test, the consequences of which for the finding of worker status will be the main concern of chapters four and five.

In *Kempf*, the CJEU clarified that part-time work cannot be disregarded just because the remuneration derived from it is below the minimum means of subsistence and must be supplemented by public funds of the host state.[125] Member States cannot decide that an individual does not have 'worker' status on the basis that they rely on welfare support, so long as their work is genuine and effective. However, the qualification that work must be genuine and effective *before* supplementation from public funds becomes irrelevant could be confusing. It offers no further guidance to Member States on how to balance these two concepts; is there a point where remuneration would be so low that it *becomes relevant* to a finding that work is not genuine and effective? CJEU case law is unclear on this, but for now ensures that low earnings and access to public funds should not be the sole reason for refusing worker status.

Circumstances of long working hours with low pay have also been found to be potentially genuine and effective work, for example in *Birden*, where the worker was employed for 38.5 hours a week but received a relatively low income.[126] Progressive increases in remuneration have also been used by the CJEU as an 'indication that the work performed … was of growing economic value to his employer' and therefore a sign that the work is genuine and effective.[127]

The concept of remuneration is also interpreted broadly. Many CJEU judgments refer to 'remuneration' rather than 'pay' or 'wages'. This semantic choice is significant, as the CJEU has demonstrated that remuneration need not be monetary, as the supply of 'materials needs' such as accommodation, food and living expenses has been accepted as an 'indirect quid pro quo for' genuine and effective work.[128]

The CJEU has recognised the worker status of EU migrants where working hours are relatively low. This includes examples where employment consists of 10 hours work a week,[129] even when the work is done for a relatively low income and the work is completed on just two hours a day for five days a week.[130] The

ECLI:EU:C:2002:694, [2002] ECR I-10691 [32]; Case C-14/09 *Genc* ECLI:EU:C:2010:57, [2010] ECR I-0931 [20]; Case C-10/05 *Mattern and Cikotic* ECLI:EU:C:2006:220, [2006] ECR I-3145 [22]; Joined Cases C-22/08 and C-23/08 *Vatsouras* (n 102) [27].

[124] O'Brien, Spaventa, and De Coninck (n 63) 24–25; see ch 4 at section 4.2.3.

[125] Case 139/85 *Kempf* ECLI:EU:C:1986:223, [1986] ECR I-1714 [14].

[126] Case C-1/97 *Birden* ECLI:EU:C:1998:568, [1998] ECR I-7747 [27]–[28]. This case concerned a Turkish national, but the same 'genuine and effective' assessment applied.

[127] C-188/00 *Kurz* (n 123) [35].

[128] Case 196/87 *Steymann* ECLI:EU:C:1988:475, [1988] ECR I-6159 [11]–[14].

[129] Case 171/88 *Rinner-Kuhn v* ECLI:EU:C:1989:328, [1989] ECR I-02743.

[130] Case C-444/93 *Megner and Scheffel* ECLI:EU:C:1995:442, [1995] ECR I-4741.

CJEU, in *Genc*, also found that someone working for as a little as five hours a week should not be precluded from worker status and therefore could potentially meet the requirements of a genuine and effective test after an assessment of other relevant factors, which will be discussed below.[131]

Hours worked do not have to be regular or long term. In *Ninni-Orasche* the CJEU found that there is nothing inherent about temporary, short-term, seasonal, on-call, agency or zero-hour contracts that prevents a finding of worker status.[132] Work for just 16 days has been considered by the CJEU, finding that temporary or short-term work does not prevent an individual from having worker status.[133]

3.4.3. Further Aspects Characterising an Employment Relationship

Beyond hours and pay, the CJEU has instructed national courts to consider an array of factors which may indicate that the employment was genuine and effective even where remuneration and hours are low. Among 'the aspects characterising [an] employment relationship'[134] to consider are the length of time in work, an employment contract, contributions made and the nature of these contributions, and whether the individual has working entitlements. These were raised as aspects of an employment relationship to consider when making a genuine and effective test in circumstances of low hours and pay (in *Genc*, employment for 5.5 hours a week and pay of £7 an hour)[135] or to mitigate the short-term nature of the employment (in *O v Bio Philippe Auguste*, employment for four days).[136] Other normative measures to consider include whether the individual has completed enough time in employment to 'familiarize [themselves] with the work', but levels of productivity, in one case as a trainee,[137] must have no consequence in regard to the test of genuine and effective work.[138]

3.4.4. Employment for Rehabilitation or Integration into the Labour Market

The CJEU has taken a less inclusive approach for rehabilitative work. In *Bettray*, an EU national was in remunerated, rehabilitative work after receiving support for

[131] Case C-14/09 *Genc* (n 123).
[132] C-413/01 *Ninni-Orasche* (n 61) [25].
[133] Case C-357/89 *Raulin* ECLI:EU:C:1992:87, [1992] ECR I-1027 [14].
[134] Case C-46/12 *L. N.* ECLI:EU:C:2013:97, [2013] 2 CMLR 37 [44].
[135] Case C-14/09 *Genc* (n 123) [27].
[136] Case C-432/14 *O v Bio Philippe Auguste SARL* ECLI:EU:C:2015:643 [25].
[137] Case C-3/90 *Bernini* (n 114) [16].
[138] Case C-188/00 *Kurz* (n 123) [32].

drug addiction. The Court found that work which was specifically rehabilitative for reintegration into employment was not genuine and effective.[139] This finding threw into question the status of Disabled workers in rehabilitative or integrational employment,[140] not least as the Court suggested one of the features preventing the work from being genuine and effective was the adaptability of the work to cater to 'the physical and mental possibilities' of each person.[141]

However, later judgments in *Birden* and then *Fenoll* saw the CJEU state that the judgment of *Bettray* was not a general trend and instead should be limited to the particular facts of the case.[142] In *Fenoll* the Court made it clear that rehabilitative work or employment intended to assist with the integration or reintegration of the Disabled workers into the labour market was not necessarily marginal and ancillary.[143] The Court reasserted that levels of productivity should not be relevant to the determination of worker status.[144] For Bell, the *Fenoll* judgment was 'a substantive shift' in the CJEU's approach as it turned to an assessment of 'whether the activity in question possessed "economic value"'.[145] The determination of worker status was ultimately left to the national court. While seeking to confine the potential damage of *Bettray*, the judgments still leave problematic additional barriers for Disabled workers in integrational, rehabilitative or sheltered employment. As O'Brien identifies, alongside proving that their work meets the standard 'genuine and effective' criteria, they must also convince a decision-maker or court 'that they provide an economic benefit to others', where non-disabled workers do not.[146]

Given that the exclusion of part-time work would jeopardise the objectives of free movement, it is in the interest of the EU to ensure that Member States apply an inclusive approach to work and subsequent access to social rights. The CJEU's broad definition of work is, in theory, capable of including non-traditional forms of work. The case law examined takes an expansive and flexible approach to 'genuine and effective' work, remuneration (type and quantity), hours, and the consideration of other employment relationship factors to offset some characteristics that may be deemed marginal and ancillary.

However, these cases have developed rather imprecise boundaries for the definition of worker. Verschueren suggests that this makes it difficult 'to draw the line

[139] Case 344/87 *Bettray* (n 123) [17].

[140] M Bell, 'Disability, rehabilitation and the status of worker in EU Law: *Fenoll*' (2016) 53 *Common Market Law Review* 197.

[141] Case 344/87 *Bettray* (n 123) [17].

[142] Case C-1/97 *Birden* (n 126); Case C-316/13 *Fenoll* ECLI:EU:C:2015:200.

[143] Case C-316/13 *Fenoll* (n 142) [40].

[144] Case C-1/97 *Birden* (n 126) [30]–[31]; Case C-316/13 *Fenoll* (n 142) [38]; Case C-316/13 *Fenoll*, Opinion of AG Mengozzi ECLI:EU:C:2014:1753 [39]; C-456/02 *Trojani* (n 123) [19].

[145] Case C-316/13 *Fenoll* (n 142) [40]; Case C-316/13 *Fenoll*, Opinion of AG Mengozzi (n 144) [42]; Bell (n 140) 204.

[146] C O'Brien, 'Union Citizenship and Disability: Restricted Access to Equality Rights and the Attitudinal Model of Disability' in D Kochenov (ed), *EU Citizenship and Federalism: The role of rights* (Cambridge University Press, 2017) 527.

between "work" that falls under these definitions and "work" that does not'.[147] Leaving it to Member States to determine the exact limits of worker status could lead to different rules applying across the EU and 'seemingly arbitrary outcomes'.[148] Vague inclusivity does not provide legal certainty.

To utilise Schauer's work on the 'tyranny of choice', Member States may opt to 'supplement' imprecise and vague CJEU case law 'with more specific "guidelines" or "rules of thumb" that in practice have all of the characteristics of rules'.[149] This might aim to ease administrative burdens, encourage consistency among street-level bureaucrats or to cynically narrow the scope of worker status and the access to welfare it entails. The UK authorities, for example, have used the vagueness of the EU concept to justify introducing an earnings threshold to tackle what it presented as some EU nationals benefiting from worker status 'even if, in reality, they do very little work'.[150] While the validity of these claims can be disputed,[151] this policy illustrates how Member States may respond to the discretion bestowed on them. For Van der Mei, this transfer of power allows Member States to, perhaps intentionally, restrict access to benefits.[152] Irrespective of the motive, excessive discretion can leave the outer edges of the definition of work to be, more or less, defined and narrowed by Member States.

This discretion can damage the rights of those in atypical work, even when their work exhibits criteria that have been expressly included by the CJEU in the definition of work.[153] However, many aspects of atypical work have not yet been expressly included (or excluded) in the CJEU's case law on the definition of work.

3.5. The Case for Explicit Inclusion of Atypical Work

While the EU case law on the definition of a worker has interpreted the concept as relatively broad and inclusive of a large variety of working conditions, the EU has not had the opportunity to extend the same attention to more volatile forms of atypical work. This section will consider these gaps and identify where atypical workers may struggle to fit into the current EU definition of work.

The preamble of Directive 1999/70 concerning fixed-term workers reiterates the need for national social security systems to '[adapt] to new patterns of work and [provide] appropriate protection to those engaged in such work'.[154]

[147] Verschueren (n 122) 15.
[148] Verschueren (n 7) 197.
[149] Schauer (n 113) 316.
[150] 'Minimum Earnings Threshold for EEA migrants introduced' (DWP, 21 February 2014), www.gov.uk/government/news/minimum-earnings-threshold-for-eea-migrants-introduced.
[151] See ch 4 at section 4.3.
[152] van der Mei (n 105) 130.
[153] O'Brien (n 37) 156–60; See ch 4 at section 4.4.
[154] 'Dublin European Council 13 and 14 December 1996 Presidency Conclusions: Annexes' (European Parliament, December 1996) Annex II.

Additionally, the desire to update the Written Statement Directive raised the need to address the rising availability of casual and precarious work and recognised that, while they provide benefits to those looking for flexible employment, there is increased danger to working conditions.[155] The first consultation report for this update recommended using the opportunity to clarify a common EU definition of work,[156] which would recognise more casual and precarious employment. Risak and Dullinger argue that the differing contexts for these definitions of work make it unsuitable to transpose one to the other.[157] The free movement definition of work is supposedly broad to ensure the success of the single market and is arguably 'efficiency-oriented'[158] or aiming for the 'greatest possible freedom',[159] but matters of labour law tend to be concerned with safeguarding equity, voice and dependency.[160] Yet this call for an update in labour law could influence and inform positive and more expansive changes to the definition of migrant work.

Rather than establishing an updated and bespoke definition, the newly adopted Directive 2019/1152 on transparent and predictable working conditions relies on the definition set by the CJEU in *Lawrie-Blum*.[161] It also makes explicit reference to atypical work in the context of the Directive's specific purpose, stating that: 'Provided that they fulfil those criteria, domestic workers, on-demand workers, intermittent workers, voucher based-workers, platform workers, trainees and apprentices could fall within the scope of this Directive.'[162] The Directive also includes those who are in 'bogus self-employment', stating that 'determination of the existence of an employment relationship should be guided by the facts … not by the parties' description of the relationship.'[163] However, the adoption of the 'genuine and effective' definition here assumes that it is inclusive of these categories.

3.5.1. Requiring Regularity and Consistency from Precarious Work

The definition for work including its flexible yet vague concept of 'genuine and effective' work leaves a number of worrying gaps which can disadvantage those in

[155] Commission, 'First phase consultation of Social Partners under Art 154 TFEU on a possible revision of the Written Statement Directive (Directive 1991/533/EEC) in the framework of the European Pillar of Social Rights' SWD(2017) 205, 10–11.
[156] ibid 8.
[157] Risak and Dullinger (n 7) 17.
[158] ibid 18.
[159] Nic Shuibhne (n 16) 494.
[160] Risak and Dullinger (n 7) 18.
[161] Directive 2019/1152 of the European Parliament and of the Council of 20 June 2019 on transparent and predictable working conditions in the European Union OJ L186/105, preamble, recital 8.
[162] ibid.
[163] ibid.

forms of atypical work. Broadly speaking, it takes an inclusive approach, but the room for the discretion of each Member State means that it would be useful for EU legislation or case law to explicitly include guidance on common features in atypical working arrangements, such as irregular remuneration, erratic hours, the layering of short-term contracts, gaps in work or difficulty identifying relationships of subordination. Without specific guidance from the Court, Member States may opt to view these features as indicative of marginal and ancillary work.

The CJEU has established that work that is temporary, short-term, casual, seasonal or 'on-call' should not be automatically precluded from worker status.[164] There is also no requirement that work is completed for a specific period of time before worker status can be established.[165] However, certain features of atypical work, such as short duration of contracts or irregularity, have been expressly identified as potential indicators of marginal and ancillary employment. For example, in *Raulin*, which concerned a short-term, casual, 'on-call' employment (60 hours worked in 16 days), the CJEU advised national courts to take into account 'the irregular nature and limited duration' of the employment, stating that the 'very limited number of hours in a labour relationship may be an indication that the activities exercised are purely marginal and ancillary'.[166] Atypical work that is irregular or inconsistent may fall through the gaps. Or it may take longer for workers on casual contracts to demonstrate that they do not have a 'very limited number of hours'. It is also important to note that a requirement for some level of consistency can become problematic for atypical workers even after an initial finding of genuine and effective work; atypical workers may be more vulnerable to losing worker status on account of it being considered, even temporarily, to be marginal and ancillary.

The gaps in the definition of worker could lead to the exclusion of a growing number of economic actors from free movement rights. AG Szpunar's opinion in *Tarola*, concerning the right to retain worker status after an employment period of less than a year, warned that distinguishing between different types of employment would 'amount to unjustified difference in treatment' and 'would result in "reserving" … the right to move and reside freely … to workers who are in a more stable position' at the exclusion of workers in more flexible contracts and 'who are therefore in a clearly vulnerable position'.[167] The CJEU, in this case, found that where worker status is identified by the national court, including in the circumstances of the case where work lasted only two weeks, the rights under Article 7(3)(c) to retain worker status for at least six months must also apply to those in fixed term work.[168]

[164] Case C-413/01 *Ninni-Orasche* (n 61) [25]; C-357/89 *Raulin* (n 133) [11]; C-444/93 *Megner and Scheffel* (n 130) [18]; C-3/90 *Bernini* (n 114) [16].

[165] Case 39/86 *Lair* ECLI:EU:C:1988:322, [1988] ECR I-3161 [42]; Case 197/86 *Brown v The Secretary of State for Scotland* ECLI:EU:C:1988:323, [1988] ECR I-3205 [22].

[166] Case C-357/89 *Raulin* (n 133) [14].

[167] Case C-483/17 *Tarola*, Opinion of AG Szpunar.ECLI:EU:C:2018:919 [46].

[168] Case C-483/17 *Tarola* ECLI:EU:C:2019:309, [2019] 3 CMLR 23 [54].

On the other hand, the CJEU has decisively distinguished between the rights of those in work and self-employment when faced with the question of whether primary carers of the children of self-employed EU nationals in education could derive a qualifying right of residence in the same way as *Teixeira* primary carers[169] for the children of EU workers.[170] This judgment, in *Czop*, relied on the literal interpretation of Article 12 of Regulation 1612/68, which established rights for *Teixeira* carers. This Regulation, and Regulation 492/11 which replaced it, contains rights relating to the free movement of workers, and Article 12 refers directly to the children of EU nationals 'who is or has been employed'. In effect, this judgment allows Member States to withhold vital welfare benefits from children and their primary carers simply because the EU national parent is in the wrong kind of economic activity. This difference in treatment is particularly problematic in light of the growth in atypical work and the increasingly blurred division between work and self-employment in gig work and the prevalence of 'bogus' self-employment, as covered in chapter two.

The difference in treatment that could arise from an underinclusive definition of work could therefore be viewed as unjustified and reserving the rights of free movement to an exclusive group of more permanent or full-time workers. This different treatment can also be viewed as particularly unjust when considered alongside the data on who is most likely to occupy atypical work.[171]

3.5.2. An Equality Case for Inclusion

In the context of free movement and the extension of social welfare systems to EU migrants, the definition of work is a tool which assesses whether a migrant worker's level of economic contribution is sufficient to warrant equal treatment with nationals. This approach sets up EU nationals as competitors to demonstrate their worth to the host Member State, yet it fails to recognise the 'unequal starting points for the competitors'.[172]

This problem manifested itself in the single market's initial focus on men's mobility. Writing in the mid-1990s, both Hervey and Ackers highlighted the persistent emphasis on ensuring men's mobility as a worthwhile commodity while 'policies such as childcare facilities, protection of atypical employees and flexible careers, which could increase women's mobility as workers', were pushed to the sidelines as a negligible investment.[173] While some of these problems have

[169] Case C-480/08 *Teixeira* (n 75).

[170] Joined Cases C-147/11 and C-148/11 *Czop and Punakova* ECLI:EU:C:2012:538, [2012] WLR(D) 264.

[171] See ch 2 at section 2.6.

[172] Hervey (n 40) 108.

[173] Hervey (n 40) 107; L Ackers, 'Women, Citizenship and European Community Law: The Gender Implications of the Free Movement Provisions' (1994) 16 *Journal of Social Welfare and Family Law* 391, 393–94.

been identified and attempts have been made to address them, such as extending more employment rights to atypical workers, the definition of work has not been updated and still relies on traditional conceptions of employment as its starting point.

As an alternative, a definition of work that is inclusive of various forms of part-time and atypical work could be put forward on the basis of equality law.[174] Eurofound argue that EU law presents an extension of equality law from first protecting equal treatment 'regardless of characteristics such as sex, race, age and disability' to the 'new dimension' of equal treatment of workers 'regardless of working hours, duration of employment, place of work or the nature of the employment relationship'.[175] This seems to be a logical step as the two are intrinsically linked. It is well documented that gender, age, race and disability identities play a role in the likelihood of individuals being employed on an atypical basis – not necessarily as a matter of choice, but reflecting that these groups of workers tend to face significant barriers to the traditional labour market.[176] This also means that these workers are more likely to face the most precarity in their lives because of their employment conditions. A traditional scope of work 'perpetuates particularism and inequality' for marginalised groups already facing exclusion from the labour market because of these societal presumptions.[177] This disadvantages women, ethnic minorities,[178] Disabled workers[179] and those in 'low-skilled' and low-income work.[180] As such, where worker status acts as a significant gatekeeper to free movement rights, a limited definition of a worker has a discriminatory impact on these groups by making the exercise of free movement a greater risk.

Many workers in atypical employment will face precarious and erratic phases of work which could hinder their ability to pass the genuine and effective test. This section illustrates the gaps that exist in the current EU definition of worker and how characteristics of atypical work can synchronise with the understanding of what 'marginal and ancillary' work looks like. Therefore, while broad, the 'genuine and effective' test does not precisely cover common features of atypical employment. The EU's broad and vague approach to the definition of worker results in Member States being handed a significant amount of discretion, granting the power to tweak the finer details and ultimately restrict access to welfare and residence rights. How this power may be abused was discussed briefly above and will be considered in more detail in chapters four and five in relation the UK's MET.

[174] O'Brien (n 66).

[175] 'Atypical work' (Eurofound, 24 November 2017), www.eurofound.europa.eu/observatories/eurwork/industrial-relations-dictionary/atypical-work.

[176] See ch 2 at section 2.6.

[177] Hervey (n 40) 92.

[178] ibid 91.

[179] O'Brien (n 146) 524–28.

[180] C O'Brien, 'Civis Capitalist Sum: Class as the New Guiding Principle of EU Free Movement Law' (2016) 53 *Common Market Law Review* 937, 953.

3.6. Summary

Acquiring worker status activates substantial free movement and equal treatment rights in relation to both immigration and welfare benefits. These rights can be essential for many workers in atypical employment and can help balance periods of sporadic income, times of ill health and temporary unemployment or under-employment. They can also extend beyond the period of economic activity and beyond the individual worker by providing rights for family members. With the protections that it offers, worker status can make free movement a realistic option for many EU nationals, especially as being deemed economically inactive can significantly hinder access to these rights, as will be discussed in chapter eight.

The CJEU has established worker status as a flexible concept where 'genuine and effective' activity can be moulded to fit a range of employment circumstances. The EU concept of worker has the potential to be inclusive, but it relies on vague concepts and does not set clear guidelines for Member States to follow. While the CJEU has referred to some aspects of atypical work, such as part-time hours, levels of remuneration and formal characteristics of employment, other common characteristics have either not been addressed or, as in the case of casual or irregular work, been labelled as potential indicators of marginal and ancillary work. The concept of migrant work in free movement law has therefore not yet been formally expanded to specifically meet the changing aspects of the labour market, as covered in the previous chapter.

By adopting a vague and imprecise definition, many EU citizens who are working will have to rely on a generous application of the definition by the host Member States to be able to claim equal treatment with nationals. This leaves the potential for the exclusion of large groups of low-paid workers and creates a substantial barrier to them being able to enjoy the full array of free movement rights that are supposedly available to workers. Instead, it would result in, as O'Brien warns, 'alienating the working poor, and effectively awarding rights on the basis of socio-economic class'.[181] Given that the number of mobile EU workers in these forms of employment is significant and will continue to grow,[182] it would help if the EU legislature could make a clear determination on the scope of this status, to avoid the necessarily piecemeal and understandably imprecise approach of definition-by-case law. Any review of worker status and the overall free movement framework must also consider the potentially discriminatory impact of a standard one-size-fits-all approach to work to those who face barriers to the 'standard' labour market.

The impact of the limits to the EU concept of work and the consequences of granting significant discretion to Member States to fine-tune and interpret the specific limitations of the status are explored next. Chapters four, five and six will analyse how the UK applies its test alongside case studies of EU atypical workers

[181] ibid 939.
[182] See ch 2 at section 2.6.

navigating these rules. The analysis in this chapter of worker status at the EU level has established the standards which the UK definition should meet – it is now time to analyse the compatibility of the UK's approach with EU law. This will also illustrate how the discretion provided to Member States essentially allows the reclassification of worker status, demanding that EU citizens not only work, but do 'enough of the right type of work, with sufficient stability, and earning enough'.[183] It will also provide evidence of atypical workers excluded from the concept of work and how this presents significant hurdles to moving and working in another Member State.

[183] O'Brien (n 180) 939.

4

Taking Liberties: The UK's Minimum Earnings Threshold Narrows the EU Concept of Work

4.1. Introduction

The EU concept of worker, though theoretically uniform, is defined by reference to broad yet vague criteria and is susceptible to becoming 'lost in translation' as 'discretion is decentralised' and filtered down to benefit decision-makers.[1] Member States are left to flesh out the broad concept of 'genuine and effective' work to apply to specific individual employment circumstances. Some of this task is inevitably delegated to frontline decision-makers, leaving open-ended definitions vulnerable to being refined by a reliance on shortcuts, such as setting limits and thresholds. While this can make decision-making processes more efficient and standardised, it also can neglect the outer edges of the worker definition.[2] This sacrifices much of the breadth and flexibility instilled in the EU definition of work and risks the exclusion of many EU nationals who are factually working but not considered to be working *enough*.

In the UK, a two-tier test has been adopted. The first tier adopts a minimum earnings threshold (MET) to essentially fast-track decisions of worker status to those workers who earn above the threshold for the period of time required. The second tier allows for the further scrutiny of cases that fall below the threshold, which is meant to apply the 'genuine and effective' test set by the CJEU. The high level of the MET forces many atypical workers to bear the extra burden of having to demonstrate how their work is genuine and effective *despite* not meeting the threshold, and must rely on the correct and fair application of this test at this second tier. However, this process is accompanied with complex and often misleading advice for decision-makers (ADM),[3] which can fail to reflect, and sometimes conflicts with, EU law.

[1] J Sampson Thierry and D Sindbjerg Martinsen, 'Lost in translation: how street-level bureaucrats condition Union solidarity' (2018) 40 *Journal of European Integration* 819, 831.

[2] F Schauer, 'The Convergence of Rules and Standards' (2003) 3 *New Zealand Law Review* 303.

[3] This is referred to as decision-maker guidance (DMG) for legacy benefits guidance; Department for Work and Pensions (DWP), 'DMG Vol 2 Chapter 7 Part 3 Habitual Residence and Right to

The next three chapters address whether the application of the worker test to EU atypical workers in the UK is compatible with the EU definition of worker. In order to do this, the analysis adopts a mixed-methods approach, providing a doctrinal analysis of the compatibility of the UK's approach alongside an empirical critique of the MET by utilising qualitative data analysis from cases advised by the AIRE Centre and the EU Rights and Brexit Hub. Together this evidence will also contribute to the enquiry into what the UK's MET demonstrates about the availability of free movement and equal treatment rights in the changing labour market.

This chapter begins the analysis by examining the UK's approach to the worker status test. Section 4.2 considers the worker test in the UK, including the introduction of the MET in 2014 and how it compares to the practice in other Member States. This is followed by an examination of the intended purpose of the MET and the potential for restrictive signalling to decision-makers in section 4.3. The compatibility of the MET is then interrogated in section 4.4. Chapter five looks to the case studies collected for this research to examine how the MET and second-tier is applied to those in atypical work. Chapter six focuses on how the EU definition and certain aspects of the UK's approach to worker status excludes marginalised workers.

This chapter identifies how the MET was devised to exclude part-time and atypical workers from worker status and restrict their access to equal treatment rights in the UK. It explores how the new threshold was pitched to the public and the risk that this could signal a more restrictive approach on worker status more generally to decision-makers. Ultimately, the compatibility of the MET with EU law is scrutinised, finding that its potential to withhold worker status from many low-paid and atypical workers could unlawfully limit the ability to realistically exercise free movement to only those who earn *enough* and in the right way.

4.2. The EU Worker in UK Law

4.2.1. Habitual Residence Test and Worker Status

In order to receive any means-tested benefits in the UK, an EEA migrant must first pass the Habitual Residence Test.[4] This test has two parts. First, they must demonstrate that they have a right to reside. The Immigration (EEA) Regulations 2016

Reside – IS/JSA/SPC/ESA' (Vol 2 Amendment 39, February 2018) [073038]; the advice concerning worker status is the same in both. This chapter therefore only refers to the ADM.

[4] This chapter refers to EEA nationals as the group to which the UK rules applied before it left the EU. The term is also used in the text to mean those who have registered under the EU Settlement Scheme, unless stated otherwise. The European Economic Area (EEA), in the UK rules, includes all Member States of the EU with the addition of EEA countries (Iceland, Liechtenstein and Norway) and Switzerland. As this research is concerned with the fundamental status of EU citizenship, EU nationals are the primary focus.

(EEA Regulations) give effect to Directive 2004/38 and therefore transpose the requirement for EEA nationals to meet one of the qualified residence categories,[5] in these cases, as a 'worker' or sometimes a 'self-employed person'.[6] The second part requires applicants to be 'habitually resident', which looks at many different factors to determine how much of an applicant's life is in the UK, for example work, property, length of time in the country, having family here and whether a bank account has been opened in the UK.

While both parts of the test must be met, the 'right to reside' requirement is trickier to demonstrate. Establishing a right to reside is an eligibility condition to access a wide range of benefits including Universal Credit, Pension Credit, Council Tax Reduction and many of the 'legacy' benefits such as Income Support, Employment and Support Allowance (ESA), Housing Benefit and Child Tax Credit. Therefore, a decision on whether work meets the criteria for the right to reside as a 'worker' is vital to many EEA nationals' wellbeing.

As noted in chapter three, since the UK left the EU, millions of EEA nationals with pre-settled status continue to rely on establishing an additional right of residence in the EEA Regulations such as having worker status, to access benefits in the UK. While in theory those on pre-settled status can upgrade to settled status after five years of continuous residence, this is contingent on satisfying the Home Office with sufficient evidence. Some of the case studies examined from the EU Rights and Brexit Hub showed EEA nationals who had been resident in the UK for well over five years only being granted pre-settled status. As a recent High Court ruling found that pre-settled status cannot expire,[7] it may be many more years down the line before the definition for worker status is no longer required in the UK.

Additionally, EEA migrant workers across the EU, and in particular those in Member States who have adopted an earnings or hours threshold, may experience similar issues with restrictive implementation of the EU definition of work. Examining how the use of thresholds impacts workers' access to rights is necessary to examine whether EU citizens more likely to be in atypical work face more risks when exercising free movement rights to another Member State.

4.2.2. The MET

Before the introduction of the MET, the Court of Appeal approached worker status as a question of the genuine economic value of the work for the employer; for

[5] The Immigration (European Economic Area) Regulations 2016, SI 2016/1052 (EEA Regulations).

[6] Directive 2004/38/EC of the European Parliament and of the Council of 29 April 2004 on the right of citizens of the Union and their family members to move and reside freely within the territory of the Member States [2004] OJ L158/77 (Directive 2004/38), Art 7.

[7] *R (Independent Monitoring Authority for the Citizens' Rights Agreements) v SSHD* [2022] EWHC 3274 (Admin).

example, would another employee need to be found to do the work instead?[8] A few years later the Upper Tribunal, in *JA*, qualified its definition of worker to reflect closely the judgments of the CJEU, as services that have to be economic, genuine and effective and not marginal and ancillary.[9] Judgments regarding worker status identified 'genuine and effective' work in a broad range of employment scenarios such as where the individual earned £65 a week[10] and where someone had been employed for only two weeks,[11] although this was after already having worked in the UK. The Upper Tribunal had also identified genuine and effective self-employment where work was part-time for three to four hours a week, despite having only been set up for two months and not yet making any profit.[12] However, decision-making outside of courts did not necessarily reflect the same expansive approach. Sibley and Collins highlighted their experiences of the poor application of the genuine and effective test, reporting how decision-makers were frequently 'turning down EEA migrants even where they were working 11 or more hours per week'.[13]

In 2014, the UK introduced a new MET to adapt how worker status would be assessed. This involved a two-tier test which required decision-makers to establish if an EEA worker met either of the following criteria:

- First tier: Have an average gross earnings, currently set at no less than £242 a week, for the past three months,[14]
- Second tier: Employment must be genuine and effective.

These are discussed in turn below.

4.2.2.1. First Tier

To meet the first tier of the test an EEA national must earn above the set threshold. The earnings required is informed by the primary threshold used to trigger the payment of Class 1 National Insurance Contributions, and increases in conjunction with that amount on a yearly basis. The threshold for 2024/25 stands at £242 a week. This is equivalent to 22 hours a week at the national minimum wage (NMW) for over-25s.[15] A worker's average earnings must meet this threshold over a continuous period of three months immediately before the benefit application.[16] If this first tier is met, the EEA national will be automatically deemed to have

[8] *Barry v London Borough of Southwark* [2008] EWCA Civ 1440 [23].
[9] *JA v SSWP* [2012] UKUT 122 (AAC).
[10] *SS v Slough Borough Council* [2011] UKUT 128 (AAC).
[11] *Barry* (n 8).
[12] *TG v SSWP* [2009] UKUT 58 (AAC).
[13] E Sibley and R Collins, 'Benefits for EEA migrants' (2014) 22 *Journal of Poverty and Social Justice* 165, 169.
[14] DWP 'ADM International Issues Chapter C1: Universal Credit' (January 2023) [C1487].
[15] 'National Minimum Wage and National Living Wage rates', www.gov.uk/national-minimum-wage-rates.
[16] DWP (n 14) [C1487].

worker status. This threshold is applied strictly, meaning that even where earnings are close to requirements it will not pass and must instead be considered under the second tier.

Table 4.1 MET, NMW and hours required to meet MET between 2014 and 2023

Tax year	MET	National minimum/ living wage	Minimum hours required to earn enough to meet MET
2013/14	£149	£6.31	24
2014/15	£153	£6.50	24
2015/16	£155	£6.70	24
2016/17	£155	£7.20	22
2017/18	£157	£7.50	21
2018/19	£162	£7.83	21
2019/20	£166	£8.21	21
2020/21	£183	£8.72	21
2021/22	£184	£8.91	21
2022/23–July 2022	£190	£9.50	20
July 2022–April 2023	£242	£9.50	26
2023/24	£242	£10.42	24
2024/25	£242	£11.44	22

The use of a threshold is immediately a threat to the compatibility of the UK's approach to worker status. The CJEU has determined that a limited level of remuneration for work cannot have 'any consequence' for deciding worker status.[17] The MET ignores this and runs directly against it by examining the level of earnings as a key indicator of worker status, fast-tracking those who have a high level of earnings and submitting any worker with limited remuneration under the threshold to additional scrutiny. Noticeably, as shown in Table 4.1 above, the level of earnings required and the subsequent hours necessary to meet it when earning minimum wage are more than double the level that EU case law seemingly recognises as genuine and effective work. Analysis by the New Economics Foundation in 2019 showed that around nine per cent of the total workforce in the UK (roughly 2.4 million people) earnt below the threshold at the time.[18] While this might not

[17] See ch 3 at section 3.4.2; Case 139/85 *Kempf* ECLI:EU:C:1986:223, [1986] ECR I-1714 [14]. A Pieter van der Mei, *Free Movement of Persons within the European Community: Cross Border Access to Public Benefits* (Hart Publishing, 2003) 37: 'a general and uniform minimum level of remuneration applicable throughout the Community cannot be given'.

[18] 'The 2.4 million lowest paid employees would see no benefit from an increase in NICs threshold' (New Economics Foundation, 20 November 2019), www.neweconomics.org/2019/11/national-insurance-tax-cut-does-nothing-for-the-2-4-million-lowest-paid-employees.

directly transfer on the EEA migrant worker population in the UK, there will be a significant number of workers who do not meet the requirement of the first tier and therefore rely on the application of the second tier. Additionally, the requirement for EEA nationals to meet the threshold for a period of three months runs counter to CJEU judgments stating that the determination of worker status cannot be conditional on the completion of work for a specific period of time.[19]

The MET clearly strays from the rulings of the CJEU and in some cases runs counter to it. However, this is just the first stage of the test. The UK aims to comply with EU law by ensuring that all workers who cannot meet the requirements of the MET are examined by the second tier which should act as a catch-all and apply the CJEU case law consistently to ensure that genuine and effective work is granted worker status.

4.2.2.2. Second Tier

For the second part of the test, the guidance directs decision-makers to decide whether the work done was genuine and effective, and not on such a small scale as to be regarded as purely 'marginal and ancillary'.[20] This second tier requires decision-makers to 'examine each case as a whole, taking account of all circumstances'.[21] This stage of the test is ostensibly in line with CJEU case law. However, the ADM makes specific reference to five relevant 'secondary criteria' referred to in the guidance:

(1) whether the work was regular or intermittent,
(2) the period of employment,
(3) whether the work was intended to be short-term or long-term at the outset,
(4) the number of hours worked and
(5) the level of earnings.[22]

These considerations represent the various ways that discretion can be exercised to find work that is below the MET as meeting the genuine and effective criteria. The list of considerations are broadly in line with CJEU case law.[23] However, the inclusion of the level of earnings is problematic as it means that, once again, it does not reflect the CJEU's position that a limited level of remuneration for work cannot have 'any consequence' for the determination of worker status.[24]

[19] Case 39/86 *Lair* ECLI:EU:C:1988:322, [1988] ECR I-3161 [42]; Case 197/86 *Brown v The Secretary of State for Scotland* ECLI:EU:C:1988:323, [1988] ECR I-3205 [22].

[20] DWP (n 14) [C1498].

[21] ibid [C1489].

[22] ibid [C1499].

[23] For regularity and a short duration of employment, see Case C-357/89 *Raulin* ECLI:EU:C:1992:87, [1992] ECR I-1027 [14]; for number of hours, see Case 171/88 *Rinner-Kuhn* ECLI:EU:C:1989:328, [1989] ECR I-02743, Case C-444/93 *Megner and Scheffel* ECLI:EU:C:1995:442, [1995] ECR I-4741 and Case C-14/09 *Genc* ECLI:EU:C:2010:57, [2010] ECR I-0931.

[24] See n 17.

The guidance stipulates that decision-makers may balance the criteria against each other to determine worker status, stating that they 'will have to weigh, for example, low hours against long duration of work'.[25] While this guidance seeks to reflect what is necessary to be compatible with EU law, it steers decision-makers to give more weight to earnings and presume marginality for workers whose earnings fall below the threshold (see section 4.6 below). The guidance also refers to a number of principles found in CJEU case law concerning the definition of work. Some of the problematic or incorrect references here are discussed further in section 4.7. This chapter will conclude that the problems with the ADM's approach to the 'genuine and effective' test could lead to the exclusion of many atypical workers, unless they can demonstrate that their work is particularly exceptional.

4.2.3. Worker Status in Other Member States

The UK was not the only EU Member State to adopt an earnings threshold to determine when EU nationals have worker status. It is therefore useful to consider the MET with reference to the practices of other Member States to establish if it is an outlier or creating unique problems.

It is not uncommon for Member States to take a restrictive approach to applying free movement rights. In Martinsen et al's analysis of how domestic signals can impact frontline decision-makers, all three of the Member States examined (Denmark, Austria and France) adopted more limited approaches than the CJEU 'towards EU migrants and their cross-border access to welfare benefits', which were fed through to street-level bureaucrats.[26] More specifically on worker status, a comparative report requested by the EU commission revealed that many Member States imposed either formal or de facto thresholds, requiring that EU nationals meet either a minimum hours of work (Belgium, France, Lichtenstein, Cyprus and Malta), a minimum income (Italy, UK) or a mixture of both (Finland, Greece, the Netherlands and Poland).[27] Many of these thresholds impose higher limits in both hours worked and income (if working at the rate of NMW) than the CJEU case law, which has identified potential genuine and effective work in circumstances of 10–12 hours work per week or even 5.5 hours per week.[28] Additionally, many of the rules in Member States would not adequately accommodate those on

[25] DWP (n 14) [C1294].

[26] D Sindbjerg Martinsen, M Blauberger, A Heindlmaier and J Sampson Thierry, 'Implementing European case law at the bureaucratic frontline: How domestic signalling influences the outcomes of EU law' (2018) 97 *Public Administration* 814, 826.

[27] C O'Brien, E Spaventa and J De Coninck, 'Comparative Report 2015: The concept of worker under Article 45 TFEU and certain non-standard forms of employment' (FreSsco, 2016) 24–25.

[28] Case 53/81 *Levin* ECLI:EU:C:1982:105, [1982] ECR I-1035; Case C-444/93 *Megner and Scheffel* (n 23); Case C-14/09 *Genc* (n 232317).

zero-hours, on-call or fixed-term contracts as they often require a level of regular and consistent hours.[29] This is a particularly challenging criteria for atypical workers to meet where the very nature of the work is erratic or inconsistent. An atypical worker in a casual or zero-hours contract may work for the same overall hours and receive the same amount of earnings per year as an individual in more regular employment, but may not be found to have had worker status for that whole year if the bulk of economic activity is condensed into a few months. The issue of requiring consistency from atypical work is covered in more detail in chapter five.[30] Overall, it is noticeable that the UK's threshold currently stands as the most demanding, in terms of the earnings required or the hours needed to meet those earnings with NMW, among Member States – but the practice is far from unique.[31]

4.3. The Intention and Representation of the MET

Before examining the compatibility of the MET, it is important to briefly note that the policy was not an isolated reform. It was introduced by the coalition Government in 2013/14 as part of a series of measures to address alleged abuse of free movement by EEA nationals supposedly moving to the UK to access welfare benefits. These were also brought in alongside the broader context of austerity and increased welfare conditionality as part of what the then prime minister David Cameron described as his 'moral mission'.[32] This included, for example, an increase in the use of sanctions, stricter health assessments, the 'bedroom tax' and a cap on the total amount of benefits received.

For EEA migrants, the reforms prevented jobseekers from accessing Housing Benefit,[33] restricted access to Jobseekers Allowance (JSA), Child Benefit and Child Tax Credit for the first three months of residence[34] and introduced a new cut-off for accessing benefits for jobseekers after six months (reduced to 91 days in November 2014), unless they met the problematic evidence requirements of the 'genuine prospects of work test'.[35] New policies were also introduced which

[29] O'Brien, Spaventa and De Coninck (n 27) 25–26.
[30] See ch 5 at section 5.3.2.
[31] O'Brien, Spaventa and De Coninck (n 27) 25–26.
[32] D Cameron, 'Why the Archbishop of Westminster is wrong about welfare' *The Telegraph* (18 February 2014), www.telegraph.co.uk/news/politics/david-cameron/10646421/David-Cameron-Why-the-Archbishop-of-Westminster-is-wrong-about-welfare.html.
[33] Housing Benefit (Habitual Residence) Amendment Regulations 2014, SI 2014/539.
[34] The Jobseeker's Allowance Regulations 1996, SI 1996/207 as amended by the Jobseeker's Allowance (Habitual Residence) Amendment Regulations 2013, SI 2013/3196, Reg 85A(2); Child Benefit (General) Regulations 2006, SI 2006/223 and the Tax Credits (Residence) Regulations 2003, SI 2003/654 as amended by the Child Benefit (General) and the Tax Credits (Residence) (Amendment) Regulations 2014, SI 2014/1511, Reg 23(5).
[35] EEA Regulations, Reg 6(7), (8)(b).

directly impacted EEA nationals' ability to access welfare, such as withdrawing access to interpreters in jobcentres.[36]

Overall, this package of reforms sought to limit EEA migrants' and their families' access to welfare benefits and attracted criticism from commentators concerned about incompatibility with EU law, the impact of the measures on the lives of particularly vulnerable people and the motive of such reforms without evidential basis.[37] More of the intention of the MET can be drawn from government messaging at the time.

4.3.1. Domestic Signalling

By including the genuine and effective criteria in the second part of the test, the UK's approach appears, at least on paper, to be compliant with EU law. Yet if the introduction of the MET does not alter the actual test applied to EEA nationals, the purpose of the reform remains elusive, especially if the result is no different from the previous worker status decisions. The context and announcement of the threshold sheds some light on the reform's purpose to cut migration and welfare. The purpose of the policy matters as it steers the discretion of decision makers towards a restrictive application of the rules.

For example, in an article for the *Financial Times*, titled 'Free movement within Europe needs to be less free', David Cameron argues that the EU needs to introduce qualifications to free movement to prevent vast migrations. He uses the article to introduce the new policies adopted in the UK, including the MET: 'We are also toughening up the test which migrants who want to claim benefits must undergo. This will include a new [MET]. If they don't pass that test, we will cut off access to benefits.'[38] This indicates that the MET was expressly devised to prohibit certain migrants from claiming benefits. It is also clear that the new threshold will be determinative for deciding worker status, as those who 'don't pass the test' will have their access to benefits 'cut off'.

When the MET was introduced in February 2014, the Department for Work and Pensions (DWP) press release asserted the policy's necessity to reduce migration and benefit claimant numbers and prevent abuse, stating that:

> [I]n order to help ensure benefits only go to those who are genuinely working a [MET] will be introduced as part of the government's long-term plan to cap welfare and reduce

[36] DWP 'Further curbs to migrant access to benefits announced' (April 2014), www.gov.uk/government/news/further-curbs-to-migrant-access-to-benefits-announced.

[37] C O'Brien, 'The pillory, the precipice and the slippery slope: the profound effects of the UK's legal reform programme targeting EU migrants' (2015) 37 *Journal of Social Welfare and Family Law* 111; M Williams, 'Kapow to GPOW: The "Genuine Prospect of Work Test"' (Child Poverty Action Group, November 2015); M Evans, 'EU migrants, abuse and access to welfare' (2015) 29 *Journal of Immigration, Asylum and Nationality Law* 273.

[38] D Cameron, 'Free movement within Europe needs to be less free' *Financial Times* (26 November 2013) www.ft.com/content/add36222-56be-11e3-ab12-00144feabdc0.

> immigration so our economy delivers for people who actively contribute and want to work hard and play by the rules.
>
> Currently European Union case law means the definition of a 'worker' is very broad, meaning some people may benefit from this even if, in reality, they do very little work.[39]

Not only does this statement signal the main intentions of the MET as capping welfare and reducing immigration, but it also closely ties the need to earn above the threshold to whether an EEA migrant's work is 'genuine'. By situating the MET as a tool to catch people out who are not genuinely working or who 'do very little work', the DWP is implying that those who do not earn above the threshold are abusing the system. This implication is repeated more plainly in other press releases stating that 'abuse and clear exploitation of the UK's welfare system will not be tolerated' and how the new 'tough' rules were, in the DWP's words, aiming to 'stop people abusing Britain's benefit system' and to 'stop rogue EU benefit claims'.[40] O'Brien argues that the adoption of accusatory language 'conjures up the association of threat with EU nationals'.[41] Based on the press coverage and the Government's language during the introduction of the MET, it seems that the 'only possible, logical reason for introducing the threshold is to reduce the number of people who are defined as workers', and as a result deny them access to welfare benefits.[42] It is understandable that decision-makers may presume, from this signalling, that the introduction of a threshold should operate as the entirety of the worker status test.

In a different DWP press release, the future implementation of the MET was said to ensure that EEA migrants 'who claim to be in work or self-employed in order to gain access to a range of benefits … face a more robust test, which includes satisfying a [MET]'.[43] This statement could be easily construed as introducing a new test where, among other requirements, EEA nationals must satisfy the MET. O'Brien warns that the presentation of the MET in this way mispresents the threshold as 'definitive of *genuine* work'.[44]

Clearly stating that the intention of the MET is to cut welfare in conjunction with the misrepresentation of the threshold as an overall assessment of genuine and effective work acts as strong domestic and political signals that can limit or steer the discretion of decision-makers.[45] Just as Martinsen et al identified significant signalling for decision-makers through negative politicisation of free movement and 'welfare tourism' in Denmark, Austria and France,[46] the Government's assertion of the MET as a tool to stop welfare abuse is likely to trickle down to

[39] DWP, 'Minimum Earnings Threshold for EEA migrants introduced' (February 2014), www.gov.uk/government/news/minimum-earnings-threshold-for-eea-migrants-introduced.

[40] DWP (n 36).

[41] C O'Brien, *Unity and Adversity: EU Citizenship, Social Justice and the Cautionary Tale of the UK* (Hart Publishing, 2017) 119.

[42] O'Brien (n 41) 155.

[43] DWP (n 36).

[44] O'Brien (n 41) 155.

[45] Martinsen et al (n 26) 816.

[46] ibid 826.

decision-makers. This is even more pertinent in the application of EU rules, where complexity and ambiguity can push decision-makers to domestic guidance and signals more.[47]

Additionally, the overall package of restrictions on EEA nationals' access to welfare, alongside David Cameron's 'moral mission' of cutting welfare more generally,[48] will no doubt cultivate an increase in awareness of the changes and intensify these signals to decision-makers.[49]

4.3.2. Justifications for Reform

The evidence concerning the impact of EU migration to the UK runs counter to the concerns raised by the coalition Government and press announcements for the MET. A 2013 report compiled for the EU Commission shows that EU nationals in the UK are more likely to be employed and less likely to access welfare benefits than nationals.[50] The higher employment rate for EU nationals in the UK is also corroborated by evidence from the Migration Observatory.[51] Overall, EU nationals are found to contribute far more to the UK in payment of taxes than what is received in benefits or public services,[52] while any negative impact on wages is reported as either minimal or non-existent.[53] Even at the time the policy changes were made, while there was some belief that limiting access to in-work benefits may discourage some migration, the Migration Observatory doubted 'how significant the effects of such a policy would be on the number of people choosing to migrate'.[54] Research completed for the EU Commission also found little evidence that 'the main motivation of EU citizens to migrate and reside in a different Member State

[47] ibid.

[48] Cameron (n 32).

[49] Martinsen et al (n 26) 816.

[50] ICF GHK Milieu, 'A fact finding analysis on the impact on the Member States' social security systems of the entitlements of non-active intra-EU migrants to special non-contributory cash benefits and healthcare granted on the basis of residence' (2013).

[51] 'Among the working-age EU population, 81% were in employment. This compares to 75% among the UK born' in C Vargas-Silva and M Fernández-Reino, 'Briefing: EU Migration to and from the UK' (The Migration Observatory, September 2019) 7.

[52] European migrants pay 'substantially more' in taxes than they receive in benefits or public services, with total contribution in 2016–17 at £4.7 billion; see Migration Advisory Committee, 'EEA migration in the UK: Final report' (September 2018) 73; Oxford Economics, 'The Fiscal Impact of Immigration on the UK: A report for the Migration Advisory Committee' (June 2018) 21; J Wadsworth, S Dhingra, G Ottaviano and J Van Reenen, 'Brexit and the Impact of Immigration on the UK' (Centre for Economic Performance, London School of Economics, 2016) 13.

[53] Migration Advisory Committee (n 52) 2: 'lower-skilled workers face a negative impact while higher-skilled workers benefit, however the magnitude of the impacts are generally small'; alternatively low wages have been found to be the result of the 2008 recession rather than EU migration in Wadsworth et al (n 52).

[54] M Sumption and W Allen 'Election 2015 Briefing – Migration and Welfare Benefits' (Migration Observatory, May 2015): 'the number of people whose initial migration decision might be affected by the immediate availability of tax credits is only a small share of the total'.

is benefit-related as opposed to work opportunities or family connections'.[55] The new policies aiming to cap EU migration to the UK and access to welfare claims lacked justification. The decision to introduce policies without reason echoes the lack of evidence to support the four-year brake on in-work benefits featured as part of the (now defunct) 2016 settlement between the UK and EU.[56]

The free movement of workers should allow EU nationals to engage in other Member States' labour markets and integrate into their solidarity systems. However, in unduly seeking to reduce the number of EU nationals who claim welfare benefits, the UK opted to limit the scope of the definition of worker with the risk of falling foul of EU requirements.

4.4. (In)compatibility of the MET with EU Law

The MET's compatibility with EU law is questionable.[57] A decision on worker status based on earnings alone would not be consistent with EU law. The UK Government insists, as the MET includes a general assessment of whether work is 'genuine and effective' in its second tier, it 'is compatible'.[58] However, the CJEU has found that the concept of 'worker' in this context relates to the definition under EU law and not national law and that it would be inappropriate to allow a Member State 'to modify the meaning of the concept of 'migrant worker' and to eliminate at will the protection afforded by the Treaty to certain categories of person'.[59]

The introduction of the policy sparked concern from the Commission, a spokesperson was quoted as intending to scrutinise the new policy closely, stating that 'a definition of a worker' which ignored case law and was assessed 'according to the amount [a worker] earns is not compatible with EU law'.[60] Additionally, in May 2020, the Commission launched infringement proceedings against the UK (Infringement number: INFR(2020)2202), believing it to be in breach of Directive 2004/38, Article 21 TFEU, Article 45 TFEU and Article 49 TFEU. This includes concern that national legislation 'limits the scope of beneficiaries of EU free movement law in the United Kingdom'.[61] While the specific details of the infringement have not been made available and the case is still active (as of July 2024), the UK's

[55] ICF GHK Milieu (n 50) 14.

[56] Decision of the Heads of State or Government, meeting within the European Council, concerning a new settlement for the United Kingdom within the European Union OJ C691/1 Annex VI; see ch 8 at section 8.4.1.

[57] O'Brien (n 37).

[58] B Waterfield, 'Earnings threshold for European migrants to get benefits 'illegal' under EU law' *Telegraph* (19 February 2014), www.telegraph.co.uk/news/uknews/immigration/10648866/Earnings-threshold-for-European-migrants-to-get-benefits-illegal-under-EU-law.html.

[59] Case 75/63 *Hoekstra* ECLI:EU:C:1964:19, [1964] ECR I-0177.

[60] ibid.

[61] 'May infringements package: key decisions' (European Commission, 14 May 2020), ec.europa.eu/commission/presscorner/detail/en/inf_20_859.

MET may be one of the Commission's concerns as a limitation of the scope of working EU nationals who can benefit from equal treatment in the UK.

If applied as conclusive of the worker status test, the UK's earnings threshold would undoubtedly be incompatible with EU law and would result in the exclusion of many low-paid atypical EU workers from the protections of the free movement regime. Equally, by setting such a high threshold that requires at least over 22 hours a week at minimum wage, many workers who would be expected to have worker status under EU law will be relying on the application of the second tier genuine and effective test. Therefore, the METs compatibility with EU law can be separated into two key considerations. Firstly, that the threshold must not applied determinatively. Secondly, that the second tier must correctly reflect the breadth and flexibility of the worker definition under EU law.

4.5. Summary

This chapter has shown that the adjustment to defining an EU worker introduced by the MET could lead decision-makers to take a more restrictive approach than is compatible with EU law. Such an approach is arguably, on the surface, technically compatible with the requirements of EU law, yet was openly devised as a tool to restrict access to worker status.

The key to whether the UK's MET is compatible with EU law, and other Member States who adopt a similar strategy, will be contingent on whether it is utilised as a streamlining tool rather than entirely determinative of the worker status test. A threshold that is overly restrictive or further encourages decision-makers to take a restrictive approach would also be in conflict with the approach at the EU level. Chapter five will therefore examine how the MET has been applied and its reduction of the genuine and effective work test to a calculation of earnings. It will also examine how atypical workers are further caught out through the way the MET is calculated and the limited tolerance for inconsistent, flexible or multi-job work arrangements.

The concerns raised here also reflect a larger issue with the EU definition of work and the free movement rights of all EU citizens. Where Member States create shortcuts to ease the administrative burden of implementing a vague EU definition of work, such as an earnings threshold, EU nationals in atypical work are at risk. Without further guidance and clarity around the outer edges of the definition, Member States are able and may be tempted to scale back the rights of atypical workers. As will be explored later in this book, without worker status, many EU nationals will rely on the inadequate protection of rights for EU citizens. The exclusion of large groups of low paid workers therefore creates a substantial barrier to them being able to enjoy their free movement rights at all. Instead, treating the higher earning workers as more 'deserving' of these freedoms.

5

Show Me the Money: The UK's Reductive Approach to Worker Status in Action

5.1. Introduction

The UK's introduction of the minimum earnings threshold (MET) into the decision-making process could limit the discretion of decision-makers and risks arbitrary outcomes that do not properly reflect the complexities and intricacies of work and individual circumstances.[1] The formulation of the earnings threshold alongside the press tour touting the new policy as a tool to restrict access to benefits signals to decision-makers that too many people are found to have worker status, and the new MET should result in fewer EU nationals passing the test. This approach is particularly problematic as the CJEU has ruled that worker status must not be 'interpreted restrictively'[2] by Member States or modified to the point of 'eliminat[ing] at will the protection afforded by the Treaty to certain categories of person'.[3] Where a restrictive approach is adopted, those on the 'fringes' of the definition of work, atypical workers and those facing barriers to standard employment, are most likely to face exclusion from free movement and equal treatment rights.

This chapter utilises case studies from the AIRE Centre and the EU Rights and Brexit Hub to demonstrate how the definition of worker is applied in the UK and identify where parts of the test falls foul of the broad approach required by EU law. This chapter therefore contributes to the existing analysis and concerns about the worker test in the EU and the UK.[4] The empirical data presented offers a fresh

[1] A Molander, *Discretion in the Welfare State: Social Rights and Professional Judgment* (Routledge, 2016) 12.

[2] Case C-3/90 *Bernini* ECLI:EU:C:1992:89, [1992] ECR I-1071 [1].

[3] Case 75/63 *Hoekstra* ECLI:EU:C:1964:19, [1964] ECR I-0177.

[4] C O'Brien, *Unity and Adversity: EU Citizenship, Social Justice and the Cautionary Tale of the UK* (Bloomsbury, 2017); N Nic Shuibhne, 'Reconnecting free movement of workers and equal treatment in an unequal Europe' (2018) 43 *European Law Review* 477; H Verschueren, 'Being Economically Active: How it Still Matters' in H Verschueren (ed), *Residence, Employment and Social Rights of Mobile Persons: On how EU Law defines where they belong* (Intersentia, 2016) 187; C O'Brien, 'Social blind spots and monocular policy making: The ECJ's migrant worker model' (2009) 46 *Common Market Law Review* 1107; S Giubboni 'Being a worker in EU law' (2018) 9 *European Labour Law Journal* 223.

perspective on the specific elements of the UK's worker test and how it directly penalises irregular and precarious employment. First, section 5.2 examines how the MET can be treated as entirely determinative of the worker status test, ignoring the need to assess work yielding an income less than the threshold under the 'genuine and effective' criteria. Next, the chapter critiques the way that the MET is calculated to exclude those with lower earnings or fluctuating incomes (section 5.3) and those who have multiple jobs or overlap work with self-employment (section 5.4). The second tier of the test is then examined, including how guidance reasserts the centrality of earnings and limits the CJEU's expansive approach to 'remuneration' (section 5.5). Section 5.6 highlights how decision-makers may selectively apply the genuine and effective criteria to exclude those in atypical employment.

Overall, the chapter focuses on aspects of the UK's approach to worker status that excludes atypical workers and risks incompatibility with EU law. By excluding those in atypical working arrangements from 'worker status', the UK makes equal treatment rights with regard to accessing social rights and a secure residence status conditional on an EU citizen 'earning access'.

5.2. What Second Tier? The Determinative Threshold

It is vital for compatibility with EU law that the threshold is not treated as entirely determinative of worker status. The CJEU has been clear that a low level of earnings cannot be the sole basis used to withhold worker status.[5]

Street-level bureaucrats, or decision-makers, may seek to simplify the process of decision-making to overcome the gap between demands on them and the lack of resources, workforce, time and information.[6] Schauer identifies that, for decision-makers, 'more choice is not always better than less'.[7] To increase efficiency for more open-ended decisions, he argues that it may be 'highly appealing' to gravitate towards tools that narrow the factors to be considered.[8] An earnings threshold may provide this opportunity and, alongside the domestic signalling detailed in chapter four, a conclusive earnings threshold could become received wisdom among decision-makers.

It is therefore not entirely surprising that the case studies examined included multiple examples of the MET being applied as the only tier involved in the consideration of genuine and effective work. In these cases, the second tier was

[5] Case 53/81 *Levin* ECLI:EU:C:1982:105, [1982] ECR I-1035; Case 139/85 *Kempf* ECLI:EU:C:1986:223, [1986] ECR I-1714 [14].

[6] A Heindlmaier, '"Social Citizenship" at the Street Level? EU Member State Administrations Setting a Firewall' (2020) 58 *Journal of Common Market Studies* 1252; M Lipsky, 'Toward a Theory of Street-Level Bureaucracy' (IRP Discussion Paper No. 48–69, Institute for Research on Poverty, 1969).

[7] F Schauer, 'The Convergence of Rules and Standards' (2003) 3 *New Zealand Law Review* 303, 316.

[8] ibid.

ignored entirely, with decision-makers declaring individuals' work to be not genuine and effective on the basis that they did not meet the earnings threshold.

Tomas

Tomas began working in a food production company in June 2014. He was contracted to work part-time for 10 hours a week, but often worked between 20–24 hours a week. He earned minimum wage which, at the time, was £5.50 an hour.

In November 2014 he applied for Housing Benefit from the local council, which was denied as he had not provided enough evidence to show consecutive earnings over three months. He applied again and brought in payslips showing his income for the previous three months. While this income fluctuated, it averaged out at £135 a week. His highest income during this period was recorded at £175 and his lowest income during this period was £56. The MET at the time was £153 per week.

The council refused his application again. The reasoning of the decision-maker is outlined in a short letter from the council which states:

> Unfortunately, your income, although it is now consecutive and over three months, does not meet the [MET] Criteria – you are not entitled to Housing Benefit and Local Council Tax Reduction Scheme.

The letter does not mention the second tier or any other aspects of Tomas's work being considered under a genuine and effective test.

This strict application of the MET meant that, as Tomas's average earnings fell below the MET, he was not a worker. It did not matter that some of his weekly earnings were over the MET. Nor did any of the other aspects of his work merit consideration. This approach to worker status is highly problematic as it takes an arbitrary and strict reading to an otherwise relatively nuanced and broad EU definition.

While Tomas's earnings were fluctuating, the hours required to meet these earnings (based on his hourly rate of £5.50) often fell above hours considered by the CJEU as potentially genuine and effective.[9] Even his lowest earning week represented the equivalent of nine hours' work. The same approach to the MET can be seen in other local authority decisions, including assessing whether self-employment is genuine and effective.

[9] See ch 3 at section 3.4; 10 hours in Case 171/88 *Rinner-Kuhn* ECLI:EU:C:1989:328, [1989] ECR I-02743; Case C-444/93 *Megner and Scheffel* ECLI:EU:C:1995:442, [1995] ECR I-4741; five hours in Case C-14/09 *Genc* ECLI:EU:C:2010:57, [2010] ECR I-0931.

Naomie

Naomie applied for Housing Assistance in October 2016. She was a full-time carer for her mother and had worked as a self-employed housekeeper for three years. This job involved working around 3.5 hours a day, five days a week, and was paid £6.50 an hour.

Naomie also tried to make ends meet by taking on extra employment. However, she could only find informal and flexible work distributing leaflets due to her care responsibilities and self-employment. She had no 'official' evidence of this income.

> Naomie's application to her local council requesting Housing Assistance was refused. The decision letter takes account of Naomie's earnings from self-employment, showing between £104 and £125 a week and therefore not meeting the MET:
>
> > The income you claim to get from your self-employment is below the stipulated [MET] of £155 a week for self-employed persons. *I am therefore of the view* that your employment is not genuine and effective.' (emphasis added)

The decision letter also retrieved evidence from HMRC of Naomie's earnings from her work distributing leaflets. It identified income varying from £429 to £4427 per annum, but stated that:

> The income you earn falls below the MET of £153 for National Insurance Contribution.

No further consideration is given to whether Naomie had a right to reside as a worker.

Yet again, Naomie's case illustrates a failure to consider or mention the second tier of the test for both worker and self-employed status. Naomie's combined income from employment and self-employment may even have met the threshold, but it is considered separately. The problem of assessing co-existing periods of work separately is discussed in section 5.4.

While there is no consideration of the second tier, the decision-maker mentions the need for employment to be 'genuine and effective', instead determining that earning below the threshold is conclusive of this concept. Failing to examine the second-tier criteria meant that relevant aspects of Naomie's self-employment are ignored, such as regularity of working days, three years of employment and 17.5 hours of work a week.

Laura

Laura is a lone parent caring for her 13-year-old daughter who struggles with periods of ill health and was taken out of school. Laura took on a variety of employed and self-employed work, but struggled balancing this with her caring responsibilities for her daughter.

Laura's applications for Housing Benefit and Council Tax Reduction in May 2018 were refused by the local council on account of her not having a right to reside. A mandatory reconsideration was requested by Laura and the decisions upheld. The reconsideration decision letter from the council considered Laura's work, finding that:

> As an employed/self employed EEA national, *you are required to be earning above the [MET]*. You have informed us that you returned to work on 27/10/17, however your average earnings are below the [MET] and there were periods where you did no work at all … **As a result**, you are treated as a Person from Abroad and therefore you have no entitlement to Housing Benefit/Council Tax support at this time. (emphasis added)

Shortly after receiving this refusal, Laura faced the threat of a possession order for her house.

This decision is illustrative of local authorities relying on the MET. The decision-maker states that, to be a worker, an individual is 'required to be earning above the MET', reducing the test to only its first tier. It is notable that this strict application of the MET comes from the first stage of the appeal process (mandatory reconsideration) where it might be expected that errors are corrected.

These three cases are a snapshot of some of the examples found in this research. Eight of the cases examined included a direct reference to the MET and a failure of decision-makers to consider or mention the second tier of the test. Many of these instances involved local authority decision-makers. O'Brien's research on EU migrants rights in the UK also highlighted advisers' experience of worker status tests made at local authorities where the second tier is ignored altogether.[10]

Further to the case studies, evidence from a 2017 freedom of information request demonstrates Sandwell Metropolitan Borough Council's ability to identify the number and proportion of Housing Benefit applications that had been rejected based on a failure to meet the MET. The response, provided as a table, includes a clearly stated proportion of applications refused 'due to' them failing to meet the

[10] Advice workers reported that worker status was often refused without even 'cursory consideration of whether their work was genuine and effective' and that 'anyone earning less than the threshold is automatically refused' in O'Brien (n 4) 158.

threshold. While this data does not clearly show that decisions ignored the second tier entirely, there appears to be an issue with local councils opting to view the threshold as a reason why an application would be refused. It is perhaps an indication that the problem could be more systematic than the individual case studies examined.

Table 5.1 Data from Freedom of Information request to Sandwell Metropolitan Borough Council[11]

	Total claims by EEA nationals	**Refused due to [MET]**	**Percentage**
18 February 2015–31 March 2016	1855	92	4.95%
1 April 2016–31 March 2017	1342	25	1.86%
1 April 2017–[May 2017]	178	3	1.68%

That this reliance on the MET as a reason to refuse worker status was present almost exclusively in local government decisions could reflect the particular constraints on local authorities. Firstly, they may lack the necessary expertise for complex right to reside decision-making, especially as the DWP had, until recently, utilised a specialist EU decision-making team.[12] Secondly, local councils in the UK face budgetary and resource pressure stemming from the 'fetishizations' of localism alongside the programme of austerity, pushing more responsibilities than resources to local government.[13] Local authorities may therefore be more likely to turn to shortcuts which produce quick, binary results.

Should this problem be isolated to local authorities, arbitrary decisions on the MET will result in the withholding of necessary benefits such as Housing Benefit, Housing Assistance and Council Tax Reduction. While the introduction of Universal Credit (UC) should take some of these decisions away from local councils,[14] even after the completion of the rollout, Housing Benefit decisions are still made for those in supported, sheltered or temporary housing and those over state pension age. Decisions regarding Council Tax Reduction and Housing Assistance also remain the remit of local authorities.

[11] Letter from C Comely, Benefits and Awards Team Manager at Sandwell Metropolitan Borough Council to R Bains (26 May 2017), www.whatdotheyknow.com/request/housing_benefit_minimum_earnings#incoming-984473.

[12] O'Brien (n 4) 215.

[13] C Schwab, G Bouckaert and S Kuhlmann, 'Conclusion: Lessons and Advice for Future Local Government in Europe' in C Schwab, G Bouckaert and S Kuhlmann (eds), *The Future of Local Government in Europe Lessons from Research and Practice in 31 Countries* (Nomos, 2017) 101, 103; V Lowndes and L Pratchett, 'Local Governance under the Coalition Government: Austerity, Localism and the 'Big Society'' (2012) 38 *Local Government Studies* 21; D Featherstone, A Ince, D Mackinnon, K Strauss and A Cumbers, 'Progressive localism and the construction of political alternatives' (2012) 37 *Transactions of the Institute of British Geographers* 177.

[14] *Hansard* HC Deb Vol 671, Col 175 (4 February 2020).

In *RF*, the Upper Tribunal ruled that the MET couldn't be applied determinatively.[15] It concerned a refused Housing Benefit application for an EEA worker on the basis that their work was marginal and ancillary *solely because* it did not meet the MET. Judge Jacobs identified that the MET was 'read as a rule of law' and the second tier was ignored entirely.[16] The Upper Tribunal therefore set aside the decision for the First-tier Tribunal to rehear. However, the requirement of the Upper Tribunal to make this judgment demonstrates that this misapplication was replicated through both the administrative and First-tier Tribunal appeals.[17] Ignoring the second tier of the test is clearly not *just* a local authority problem. An Upper Tribunal judgment in *DD* addressed the inaccuracy of the HMRC guidance, unavailable to the public, used to determine right to reside.[18] While the case concerns a decision on the genuine prospect of work test, Judge Wright addressed the general inaccuracies of the HMRC guidance, including 'one particular flaw … earnings below the MET are not decisive'.[19] The guidance is not available to the public so the exact information provided to decision-makers cannot be analysed and the Upper Tribunal was notified that this guidance was being amended in 2019.[20] However this case shows that HMRC decision-makers had, until at least 2019, been directed to apply the threshold as decisive.

These case studies provide examples of local authority decision-makers abandoning EU case law, instead choosing to give preference to perceived domestic rules. This approach is clearly incompatible with EU law. By failing to recognise the existence of the second tier, work is reduced to a sum of earnings, neglecting the many aspects of work identified in EU law that are relevant to the genuine and effective test. Workers who expect to rely on the second tier instead find that their work is automatically classified as marginal and ancillary. Rather than workers, they are treated as economically inactive and subsequently become disentitled to welfare benefits. The case studies also show that requesting a mandatory reconsideration or tribunal appeal does not necessarily offer a reprieve from these errors.

5.3. Earnings Thresholds in a Diverse Labour Market

Where an MET is adopted and applied, even correctly as part of a two-step process to determining genuine and effective work, the level at which it is set and the way

[15] *RF v London Borough of Lambeth* [2019] UKUT 52 (AAC).
[16] ibid [4].
[17] ibid [5].
[18] *DD v HMRC and SSWP (CB)* [2020] UKUT 66 (AAC).
[19] ibid [26].
[20] ibid [24].

it is calculated must be closely inspected to determine potentially exclusionary impacts. This section will investigate how an expectation for consistent and well-paid work is baked into the calculation of the MET.

5.3.1. Setting a Steep and Restrictive Threshold

As identified in chapter four, the compatibility of the MET with EU law hinges on its conception as a streamlining tool to improve efficiency in decision-making and not, as the UK's own press releases allude to, an exclusionary and definitive device.[21] Where a threshold is adopted with efficiency in mind, the level of earnings required should closely reflect the EU's flexible and broad approach. More generally, the Commission has highlighted its concerns with 'income and time thresholds' in national welfare systems, as they may result in 'an unduly high obstacle to access social protection for some groups of non-standard workers and for the self-employed'.[22] Setting any kind of earnings threshold will disproportionately impact atypical workers who are more likely to have lower earnings than those in more typical employment.[23]

By adopting a threshold that is too high, the UK pushes many atypical workers into the second tier where, as will be discussed in section 5.5, they face higher levels of scrutiny and an increased burden to offset a presumption of marginality.

The current threshold requires those earning minimum wage to work at least 22 hours a week consistently for over three months. This sets the benchmark of hours for low earners above the average for part-time workers in the UK (16.1 hours).[24] It is also far beyond the CJEU's suggested hours; where part-time work of around 10 hours per week,[25] and even 5.5 hours,[26] were not prevented from constituting 'genuine and effective' employment. Requiring those earning the minimum wage to work over double the amount suggested in CJEU case law is a glaring indication that the threshold is set at an unreasonable level. The 22-hour calculation above can also be considered a 'best-case scenario' as gig and self-employed workers' earnings do not correlate to hours worked.

[21] DWP, 'Minimum Earnings Threshold for EEA migrants introduced' (February 2014), www.gov.uk/government/news/minimum-earnings-threshold-for-eea-migrants-introduced.

[22] Commission, 'Proposal for a Council Recommendation on access to social protection for workers and the self-employed' COM(2018) 0132 final.

[23] See ch 2 at section 2.5.2; S Clarke and N Cominetti, 'Setting the record straight: How record employment has changed the UK' (Resolution Foundation, January 2019) 52.

[24] D Leaker, 'Average actual weekly hours of work for part-time workers (seasonally adjusted)' (Office for National Statistics, 17 March 2020), www.ons.gov.uk/employmentandlabourmarket/peopleinwork/earningsandworkinghours/timeseries/ybvb.

[25] See ch 3 at section 3.4; Case 53/81 *Levin* (n 5).

[26] Should other aspects of the employment suggest it is genuine and effective; see Case C-14/09 *Genc* (n 5).

Marie

Marie has lived in the UK since 2008. After leaving her job in 2014 due to ill health, she tried to find new flexible employment to ease back into work. She began working as a leaflet distributer and was paid £40 for every 1,000 leaflets distributed. She reported working around five hours a day, six days a week, and had evidence of earnings for the previous three months that fell below the MET.

In June 2015, Marie was once again signed off from work due to ill health. She applied for ESA and this was refused as she was deemed to not meet the MET. In turn this triggered the cancelling of the Housing Benefit and Working Tax Credits she had been receiving.

Someone working as many hours at the NMW as Marie would meet the MET automatically. However, workers who require more flexible arrangements and take on work where pay is not calculated at an hourly rate will find meeting the earnings threshold particularly difficult. Already disadvantaged demographics are overrepresented among those in work that is not paid per hour,[27] including migrant workers.[28] Setting an earnings threshold indirectly discriminates against those who may have to work far more than the 22 hours to reach the threshold.

The same is true for undeclared or cash-in-hand work. The Upper Tribunal case of *JA* ruled that worker status under EU law is an economic status, not a legal one.[29] The fact that the worker in question was receiving payment in cash and did not pay taxes or National Insurance contributions as a result did not preclude them from obtaining worker status.[30] While worker status should not be withheld from those who are in undeclared work, they may not be earning the national minimum hourly rate and therefore may have to work considerably more hours to meet the threshold. They may also struggle to meet some of the evidentiary requirements to calculate their average earnings over three months. Workers in this situation may include victims of exploitation and trafficking, and so the measurement of 'genuine and effective' work through earnings could result

[27] See ch 2 at section 2.4.

[28] Foreign-born workers make up over 50% of workers who rely on platform work as their main economic activity: Joint Research Centre, 'The Changing Nature of Work: and skills in the digital age' (Publications Office of the European Union, 2019) 62.

[29] The economic relationship, and not its legality, controls whether someone is a worker under EU law: *JA v SSWP* [2012] UKUT 122 (AAC).

[30] ibid.

in the withholding of welfare benefits or permanent residence on the grounds that they have been exploited.[31]

The UK's NMW also enables employers to pay younger workers less. As can be seen in Table 5.2, this can result in younger EEA nationals having to work even more hours than the already problematic requirement of the threshold.

Table 5.2 MET, NMW and how age impacts hours of work required, 2020–2025

Tax year	MET	Age	NMW	Hours required to meet MET
2020/21	£183	25 and over	£8.72	21
		21–24	£8.20	23
		18–20	£6.45	29
		Under 18	£4.55	40
		Apprentice	£4.15	45
2021/22	£184	23 and over	£8.91	21
		21–22	£8.36	23
		18–20	£6.56	29
		Under 18	£4.62	40
		Apprentice	£4.30	43
2022/23 *from July 2022	£242	23 and over	£9.50	26
		21–22	£9.18	27
		18–20	£6.83	36
		Under 18	£4.81	51
		Apprentice	£4.81	51
2023/24	£242	23 and over	£10.42	24
		21–22	£10.18	24
		18–20	£7.49	33
		Under 18	£5.28	46
		Apprentice	£5.28	46
2024/25	£242	21 and over	£11.44	22
		18–20	£8.60	29
		Under 18	£6.40	38
		Apprentice	£6.40	38

[31] See ch 6 at section 6.3.4.

Younger workers are overrepresented in several forms of atypical work.[32] Additionally, around 40 per cent of EEA nationals recorded as living in the UK in 2015 were below 30.[33] Any EEA migrant worker below 23, or since April 2024 below 21,[34] and earning NMW will therefore be required to work more hours to be able to meet the threshold set by the UK. The combination of a high earnings threshold and the UK's tiered approach to minimum wage places further hurdles in front of young EEA workers to access their rights. As a result, younger EEA workers may not have the same access to equal treatment rights as workers over 23 or 21.

5.3.2. Calculating Consistency in Inconsistent Work

The MET is also calculated based on average earnings on a monthly basis extracted from the immediate previous three months.[35] This can disproportionately affect workers in casual or zero-hour contracts, gig work or temporary contracts whose earnings may fluctuate over time. The MET is applied strictly, meaning that atypical workers cannot rely on averages over a longer period of time to meet the threshold, nor can earnings over the threshold in one month be carried over to make up for quieter months. Even if one month shows earnings well beyond the threshold, subsequent monthly earnings which fall below will result in a failure to meet the threshold.

There are two potential issues here: firstly, that earnings can differ from week-to-week for many casual workers; and secondly, the requirement to show income for three months.

5.3.2.1. Fluctuating Income

The UK courts have recognised that self-employment often results in periods of 'feast and famine'.[36] Taking this into account, an income test relying on a stable income seems unsuitable. Just as self-employed workers face ebbs and flows in business, so do the workers employed in zero-hours, gig, temporary and seasonal contracts. As features of atypical employment and self-employment become more closely aligned, recognition of periods of 'feast and famine' should be incorporated in the worker status test. However, the calculation of the MET requires consistency

[32] See ch 2 at section 2.6.3; for Europe, see A Broughton, M Green, C Rickard and S Swift, 'Precarious employment in Europe part 1: patterns, trends and policy strategy' (European Parliament Committee on Employment and Social Affairs, July 2016) 35; for the UK, see A Berrington, P Tammes, S Roberts, T McGowan and G West, 'Measuring Economic Precarity among UK Youth during the Recession' (ESRC Centre for Population Change Briefing Paper, 2014).

[33] About 24% of all EEA citizens living in the UK were below the age of 30: Migration Observatory, 'Young People and Migration in the UK: An Overview' (December 2016) 9.

[34] Before April 2021 NMW was only paid to those over 25.

[35] DWP, 'ADM International Issues Chapter C1: Universal Credit' (January 2023) [C1487].

[36] *SSWP v JS* [2010] UKUT 240 AAC [5].

and does not cater for fluctuating income. A closer inspection of Tomas's case, discussed above, exemplifies how the requirement of consistency can impact flexible work.

Tomas (continued)

Tomas was found to be ineligible for Housing Benefit as he failed to meet the MET. The second tier was not applied. Tomas worked in a flexible contract for a food production company. He provided wage slips for the most recent three months, which showed an average wage of £135 (the MET for the relevant financial year was £153).

The wage slips show that Tomas earned over the MET for seven of the 13 weeks. Two weeks of these earnings stand out as significantly lower (£56 and £70). They cover the period over Christmas and New Year where Tomas was not able to work his usual hours due to scheduled closures. There is no information on whether Tomas was entitled to any holiday pay. These two weeks represent anomalies and are the only payslips when Tomas's weekly earnings fell below £100.

A worker test that places significance on average earnings fails to account for any short periods of sickness, lulls in business or other circumstances that could reduce the ability of the worker to take on paid hours. A worker with a full-time contract would likely have access to holiday and sick pay, and other cover, whereas a worker in a casual contract is more likely to face a fluctuation of income and to require access to benefits to fill gaps in work, especially when access to holiday and sick pay are not guaranteed and may have to be accrued. Yet it is precisely when a worker may need this access that they may find that their work fluctuates too much to be considered as 'genuine and effective'. Or workers who have lived in a host Member State for over five years might only discover that their work was too flexible at the point of making an application for permanent residence.

5.3.2.2. *Three-month Requirement*

The second issue relates to the requirement to provide average earnings over the three months immediately prior to an application for benefits if relying on current worker status.[37] Unless establishing permanent residence or retaining worker status, an EEA worker cannot select their own period of three months where work has been consistent and instead must rely on the immediate three months prior

[37] DWP (n 35) [C1487].

to application. Any new work, short-term contracts of less than three months or gaps in the availability of hours in the previous three months can result in failure to meet the MET. This seems to diverge from CJEU case law, where an EU national working just 16 days was not precluded from being a 'worker'.[38] Additionally, some social risks (such as illness and disability) can result in earning capacity beginning to diminish in the preceding weeks and months before the point of claiming a welfare benefit, meaning that earnings are likely to be lower during the three-month period assessed by the MET.

As work becomes more fragmented, it is increasingly difficult to justify a worker status test that relies on consistency and excludes based on the characteristics commonly present in atypical work. Despite the CJEU ruling that being employed under an on-call or zero-hours contract cannot preclude an individual from being a worker,[39] the MET is calculated in a way which weaponises a worker's irregular earnings or short-term contracts as a reason to exclude them. This calculation of 'genuine and effective' work ignores a growing area of the labour market and pushes many atypical workers to the second tier of the test, which may be ignored altogether, and which can steer decision-makers towards findings of marginality, as discussed below.

Cases from the EU Rights and Brexit Hub show that decision-makers can treat the three-month rule for the MET strictly and potentially as an overarching rule for anyone seeking to establish worker status.

Isabella

Isabella's benefits adviser had contacted the EU Rights and Brexit Hub about the client's difficulty in accessing Universal Credit. She had been in self-employment for just under a year, but then stopped work for the next few years to care for her young son.

Isabella had recently taken up a couple of flexible work contracts earning £770 a month. She spoke to the DWP about making a new Universal Credit application and was told that she should *only* submit a new claim once she had completed three months' work. A note on the client's online Universal Credit journal states:

> It has been determined that you have not demonstrated an EEA right to reside. You have provided us with a contract of work. *After working for three-months you may* be considered as an EEA worker.

It is not clear from the decision if the 'three months' is a reference to the MET itself, or conflating the three-month calculation of the MET with the entirety of

[38] Case C-357/89 *Raulin* ECLI:EU:C:1992:87, [1992] ECR I-1027 [14].
[39] ibid.

the genuine and effective work test. Either way, the decision-maker states that it is only possible to have worker status after three months of work. EU law is clear that EEA nationals must not be required to show three months of earnings for worker status; the short duration of employment cannot, in itself, exclude it from being genuine and effective.[40]

The current threshold discredits the value of low-income work and fails to recognise the disparity between the value of work and the income attached to it. It is an approach that privileges an outdated and potentially discriminatory standard.[41] It fails to accommodate many aspects present in atypical work, such as fluctuating income and the prevalence of irregular hours and short-term contracts.

Using an earnings threshold that demands stable and regular income is an entirely inappropriate tool to the assess whether work is 'genuine and effective'. Yet, if an MET is to remain as a form of administrative streamlining, it is necessary to ensure that it more accurately reflects CJEU case law and the reality of the diverse labour market. Setting the income to NMW earnings of approximately 10–12 hours a week would be a more inclusive and accurate interpretation of worker status under EU rules. An alternative option, which would not unfairly disadvantage low-income workers, is an hours *or* income threshold. The threshold could also permit EEA workers to provide evidence of income/hours from any months in the last six months. Moulding a test for worker status that more precisely reflects the diversity of work arrangements would reduce the risk of automatic exclusion for atypical workers. As the prevalence of atypical work grows, the UK's approach to worker status should adapt to fit this reality, including the recognition of workers building income from a variety of atypical work arrangements.

5.4. Separate Consideration for Each Source of Income

Data collected for this research saw decision-makers assess both a change in employment contracts and concurrent employment and self-employment as separate periods of worker status.

The ADM requires decision-makers to assess the 'average gross earnings from employment or self-employment'; it does not restrict this to one single occupation.[42] Nevertheless, this research encountered negative worker status decisions emerging from the individual examination of different sources of income. This problem was prevalent in both calculations for the MET and applications of the second-tier 'genuine and effective' test. In both instances this approach

[40] Case C-413/01 *Ninni-Orasche* ECLI:EU:C:2003:600, [2003] ECR I-13187 [25].

[41] See ch 2 at section 2.6 and ch 6.

[42] DWP (n 35) [C1487].

disadvantages atypical workers on the basis that they work multiple jobs or mix employment with self-employment to build an income. The case studies illustrate the problem with a lack of clarity in both EU law and the UK guidance for decision-makers on how to approach an assessment of worker status for those who work in the atypical labour market.

5.4.1. Changing and Overlapping Employment

Fredrik

Fredrik had lived in the UK for over 20 years when he applied for Universal Credit. The application was refused. He was supported by a benefits adviser to request a mandatory reconsideration, arguing that he had acquired a right of permanent residence from an extensive work history spanning over six years. The reconsideration decision did not agree and pointed to Fredrik's multiple employments as evidence:

> [Y]ou have provided evidence from HMRC that you were employed in the years from 2007/8 to 2012/13. However, the information you have given shows *you did not have a consistent employer for that time, you changed employment at least four times* from 2008 to 2012.

The EU Rights and Brexit Hub helped to appeal this and DWP decided to revise the decision and award Universal Credit before the tribunal hearing.

Here, the decision-maker has highlighted how not having a consistent employer had led to their decision to discount four years of work. There is no requirement that a worker has a consistent employer, let alone one that lasts for such a significant time. It is a clear and incorrect application of both the EU and UK rules and was eventually overturned, but demonstrates the way that changes in employment can be detrimental to an EEA national's status in the UK and sometimes fatal to future reliance on establishing a permanent right of residence.

Krzysztof

Krzysztof arrived in the UK in 2015 and was a victim of trafficking. He managed to escape this situation and from late November 2017 worked a full-time job for four months (ending February 2018). He left this job due to difficult personal circumstances and tried to find new work. From March 2018, he started a full-time but temporary contract with an agency, the job ending when he was no longer required. He received a full-time salary from this position for three weeks.

Krzysztof made an application for Jobseeker's Allowance, relying on his retained worker status on the basis that he was involuntarily unemployed.[43] The decision-maker found that Krzysztof's first job between November 2017 to February 2018 was genuine and effective:

> by taking the following factors into account – the length of employment, number of hours, if the work was regular or erratic and the level of earnings

However, when considering his second job, the decision-maker found that:

> Due to the short-term nature of your last job, it has been determined that this employment was not genuine and effective to give you 'worker' status.
>
> The 'worker' status you had previously gained from [employment A] would be lost as you have not continued in genuine and effective employment.

The decision-maker concluded that Krzysztof had not retained his worker status at the date of the claim for JSA. The AIRE Centre provided advice and helped argue that the consecutive months of income should contribute to a single period of worker status, and not be considered separately. While this argument was not accepted in the mandatory reconsideration, the First-tier Tribunal overturned the decision and found that Krzysztof did have a right to reside to access Jobseeker's Allowance.

Additionally, Krzysztof's case demonstrates how a decision-maker examined employment in two jobs as two separate periods of worker status, rather than a continuous period of work. This is not in line with UK case law, where the Upper Tribunal found that short gaps in between different agency contracted work does not prevent an EEA national from having worker status throughout that time.[44] This suggests that consecutive contracts of employment should be assessed cumulatively. The two employment contracts in Krzysztof's case were full-time positions and yielded income in consecutive months without a gap. It can therefore be assumed that if they were jointly assessed, Krzysztof would have secured worker status for this period. The decision-maker's treatment of each employment separately meant that, despite an accumulation of nearly five months of full-time work,

[43] The Immigration (European Economic Area) Regulations 2016, SI 2016/1052, Reg 6(2)(b).
[44] *NE v SSWP* [2009] UKUT 38 [9]–[10].

Krzysztof's earlier work counted for nothing simply because he had a change of contract. While this decision was overturned at the First-tier Tribunal, an EU Rights and Brexit Hub case also saw separate employers examined separately in the First-tier Tribunal.

Nikolai

Nikolai had arrived in the UK as a child. After 15 years of residence, during which he had worked in several different jobs and self-employment, his health deteriorated. Nikolai became street homeless and was later supported by a mental health unit, which helped him to apply for Universal Credit.

The DWP decided that Nikolai did not have a qualifying right of residence to access Universal Credit as he had not established five years of continuous lawful residence for the purpose of acquiring a permanent right of residence. Both the request for a mandatory reconsideration and appeal to the First-tier Tribunal resulted in the decision being upheld.

The First-tier Tribunal judge and the DWP decision-maker listed Nikolai's extensive history in atypical work and often dismissed it as marginal and ancillary due to the level of earnings or short duration of work. For example, Nikolai had worked for seven different overlapping employers in a space of six months between August 2017 and January 2018. Each of these employments were examined separately and were seen as offering 'no indication of genuine and effective work and no status'.

Here, separate employers in concurrent employments are examined individually, resulting in Nikolai being found to be a run of 'marginal and ancillary' work, rather than an overall period of work activity. Taken together, Nikolai should have been found to be in economic activity for a period of six months, which may have suggested he was in genuine and effective work.

Treating different work contracts or employers individually excludes those who build an income through overlapping jobs, have short gaps between contracts or who rely on short-term work.

The CJEU is clear that when considering worker status, 'account should be taken of all the occupational activities which the person concerned has pursued with the territory of the host Member State'.[45] The ADM requires decision-makers to follow this approach, but this specific guidance is buried in a section of leftover 'principles derived from EU law'.[46] Instead, the need to examine the entirety of an EEA national's recent economic activity should be front and centre of the guidance

[45] C-357/89 *Raulin* (n 38) [2].
[46] DWP (n 35) [C1492].

on both the MET and the second tier of the test. Different workers should not be treated differently simply because their over-threshold income, or genuine and effective employment, may come from one employer or several.

5.4.2. Concurrent Employment and Self-employment

This problem also extends to where EEA migrant workers overlap concurrent employment and self-employment to build-up their income. The 'right to reside' test, like Article 7 Directive 2004/38, separates the categories of 'workers' and 'self-employed person[s]'.[47] The ADM deals with each category separately, but both direct decision-makers to the same two-tier process in assessing whether work is 'genuine and effective', including the MET.[48] Importantly, the ADM is silent on how to assess applicants combining work and self-employment. This can lead to decision-makers insisting that at least one of these activities stands up to the 'genuine and effective' test based entirely on its own merits, and any aspects of the other activity are considered irrelevant. This approach becomes particularly problematic where decision-makers may also apply the MET definitively.

Naomie (continued)

In an application for Housing Assistance, Naomie's self-employment as a housekeeper was deemed to not yield enough income to pass the MET. The second tier was not applied.

The decision-maker also considered employment that was completed alongside Naomie's self-employment. Due to her caring responsibilities, Naomie had limited time to fit extra work in. She found and took on informal work as a leaflet distributer. The hours were flexible, and she was paid per box of leaflets. She had no official record of this income. The decision-maker relied on data from HMRC records that recorded Naomie's income from this work as ranging from around £400 to £4,500 per annum. In assessing whether this was genuine and effective, the decision maker wrote:

> The income you earn falls below the MET of £153 for National Insurance Contributions.

Here, income generated from employment and self-employment is assessed separately to determine if either meets the MET. As a result, both fail, yet if

[47] Universal Credit Regulations 2013 (UC Regulations), SI 2013/376, Reg 9(4)(a).
[48] DWP (n 35); worker at [C1484]; self-employment at [C1505].

considered together they may have met the threshold. Of course, this example is already problematic given the decision-maker's treatment of the earnings threshold as conclusive of genuine and effective work, yet the separate examination of concurrent employment and self-employment, even where the second tier of the test is applied correctly, is still likely to disadvantage atypical workers. While not impossible, atypical workers in this situation face the prospect of trying to meet a required standard with one economic activity, while any time spent for other economic activity is detrimental to their ability to commit to activities that are more likely to be genuine and effective.

It is not clear if this method of assessing concurrent employment and self-employment is endorsed by EU law. On the one hand, free movement rights are mutually exclusive.[49] By taking this approach, a consideration of 'genuine and effective' work is applied, not to an EEA national's overall activity, but to the relevant activity, ie their employment *or* self-employment. An EEA national might not meet the requirements of the scope of one freedom by nearly fulfilling the requirements of two freedoms. Even the CJEU principle of examining 'all occupational activities which the person concerned has pursued with the territory of the host Member State' is limited to the assessment of worker status.[50]

Yet, with the fragmenting of the labour market and likely increase in those mixing employment and self-employment to build their right of residence, it would hardly seem in the spirit of the free movement regime and Directive 2004/38 to expose those who combine work and self-employment to the risks associated with being deemed 'economically inactive'. If key objectives of the Directive are to facilitate free movement and to ensure EU citizens do not become an 'unreasonable burden' on the host Member State,[51] it seems counterintuitive to treat workers differently depending on whether their work is employment, self-employment or a combination of the two.

The principles guiding the free movement of workers and self-employed persons are often closely aligned.[52] In particular, the rules concerning access to welfare benefits for the self-employed often emulate or are encompassed in the rules applicable to workers.[53] Further to this, the CJEU has shown reluctance to differentiate between the entitlements of workers in different employment situations in *Tarola*[54] and between those in employment and those

[49] Case C-275/92 *Schindler* ECLI:EU:C:1994:119, [1994] ECR I-1039.

[50] Case C-357/89 *Raulin* (n 38) [2].

[51] Directive 2004/38/EC of the European Parliament and of the Council of 29 April 2004 on the right of citizens of the Union and their family members to move and reside freely within the territory of the Member States [2004] OJ L158/77 (Directive 2004/38), Preamble.

[52] '[T]hey are based on the same principles both in so far as they concern the entry into and residence in the territory of Member States of persons covered by community law and the prohibition of all discrimination between them on grounds of nationality.' Case 48/75 *Royer* ECLI:EU:C:1976:57, [1976] ECR 0497 [12] and Case 118/75 *Watson and Belmann* ECLI:EU:C:1976:106, [1976] ECR 1185 [9].

[53] AP van der Mei, *Free Movement of Persons within the European Community: Cross Border Access to Public Benefits* (Hart Publishing, 2003) 41–42.

[54] Case C-483/17 *Tarola* EU:C:2019:309, [2019] 3 CMLR 23.

in self-employment in *Gusa* and *Dakneviciute*.[55] While *Tarola* concerned the ability to retain worker status under Article 7(3)(c) Directive 2004/38 when in fixed-term employment, AG Szpunar found 'no objective justification' for a difference in treatment between those who pursue an occupational activity as a worker or self-employed person as both would have 'contributed to the social and tax systems' of the host Member State.[56] *Gusa* and *Dakneviciute* both concerned the extension of rights, which had been provided to those in employment, to those in self-employment (respectively the ability to retain worker status after involuntary unemployment[57] and the rights to retain worker status when temporarily out of work due to the late stages of pregnancy as found in *Saint Prix*).[58] The CJEU identified that 'employees and the self-employed are in a comparable vulnerable position if obliged to stop working, and therefore cannot be treated differently as regards retention of their right of residence in the host Member State'.[59] Contrastingly, the CJEU did not extend the ability to derive a right of residence under the *Teixeira* rules[60] to those in self-employment,[61] as a primary carer of a EEA workers child in education. It is worth noting that these judgments concern the substance of rights to retain a residence status as a worker or self-employed person in Directive 2004/38, rather than the scope of Article 7(1). Nevertheless, the difference in treatment or inclusion in Article 7(1) for those who combine work and self-employment compared to their solely employed or self-employed counterparts would have the same effect: a loss of a right of residence, even though these workers pursue occupational activity and contribute to the social and tax systems of the host Member State.

As it stands, the separate consideration of status as a worker *or* as a self-employed person fails to reflect the reality of a labour market which has seen a proliferation in overlapping and temporary contracts and occupations which sit in a grey area between the definitions. Such fixed distinctions creates a significant barrier for atypical workers, who, like Naomie, Nikolai, Fredrik and Krzysztof, could be penalised because the nature of their work is atypical.

The assessment of individual employment or self-employment disadvantages those in atypical work arrangements. As these types of work arrangements become more common, both EU rules and UK guidance could be clearer on how decision-makers should approach those who build an income from multiple sources. The current worker status test and lack of guidance on this issue risks the exclusion of those who are clearly economically active in a 'genuine and effective' way. Taken together, the MET and the inclination to assess multiple employments

[55] Case C-442/16 *Gusa* ECLI:EU:C:2017:1004, [2018] WLR(D) 10; Case C-544/18 *Dakneviciute* ECLI:EU:C:2019:76, [2020] 1 CMLR 22.

[56] Case C-483/17 *Tarola*, Opinion of AG Szpunar ECLI:EU:C:2018:919 [50].

[57] Directive 2004/38, Art 7(3)(b).

[58] Case C-507/12 *Saint Prix* EU:C:2014:2007, [2015] 1 CMLR 5.

[59] Case C-544/18 *Dakneviciute* (n 55) [33]; referring to Case C-442/16 *Gusa* (n 55) [42]–[43].

[60] Case C-480/08 *Teixeira* ECLI:EU:C:2010:83, [2010] ECR I-01107.

[61] Joined Cases C-147/11 and C-148/11 *Czop and Punakova* ECLI:EU:C:2012:538, [2012] WLR(D) 264.

and self-employment separately risks the exclusion of many atypical workers and leaves their ability to access welfare or establish permanent residence as entirely contingent on the second tier of the test, a tier that is often ignored altogether. This places a considerable burden on EEA workers who must evidence that their work is genuine and effective *despite* the fact that they have not earned enough to meet the MET.

5.5. The Pervasiveness and Mistreatment of Earnings in the Second Tier

The second tier of the UK's worker test must be applied broadly to act as a 'catch-all' for the many workers who will not meet the strict requirements of the earnings threshold but are in 'genuine and effective' work. The EU concept of worker, while neither precise nor adequately inclusive of some characteristics common in atypical employment, is theoretically available to all types of work (provided it is genuine and effective).[62] Additionally, there is nothing to prevent a Member State from adopting more inclusive rules. At the very least, the UK guidance must ensure worker status decisions reflect the broad approach adopted by EU law.

Martinsen et al's research on applying EU rules in Member States found that when decision-makers must consider 'rather opaque and ambiguous rules, they turn to their domestic superiors for instructions'.[63] Additionally, a FreSsco report comparing Member State approaches to non-standard work found that, while national rules did not often overtly ignore EU law, in practice it was the national restrictions that were decisive.[64] Therefore national guidance for decision-makers plays a crucial role in directing the process of applying the worker test, and decision-makers are unlikely to turn to other resources on the EU legal framework to fill any gaps or correct mistakes.

5.5.1. Genuine and 'Exceptional' Part-time Work

Crucially, adopting an earnings threshold as the first step of worker status tests could steer decision-makers. O'Brien argues that setting an income threshold, especially one that is introduced in a package to prevent abuse of the welfare system, can inevitably create 'a presumption of marginality for those who fall

[62] See ch 3 at section 3.3.

[63] D Sindbjerg Martinsen, M Blauberger, A Heindlmaier and J Sampson Thierry, 'Implementing European case law at the bureaucratic frontline: How domestic signalling influences the outcomes of EU law' (2018) 97 *Public Administration* 814, 826.

[64] C O'Brien, E Spaventa and J De Coninck 'Comparative Report 2015: The concept of worker under Article 45 TFEU and certain non-standard forms of employment' (FreSsco, 2016) 8.

below the threshold'.[65] This establishes a higher standard of proof for EEA workers who must now evidence that aspects of their work are compelling enough to offset the fact that they have not earned enough to meet the MET.[66] This is a different test to that required by EU law, which simply requests that EEA workers show that their work is 'not on such a small scale as to be considered marginal and ancillary', not to compensate for failing to meet the higher earnings threshold.

For example, the guidance steers decision-makers towards a presumption of marginality in its treatment of part-time or low-paid work. Decision-makers are told that 'work below the [MET] that is part time or low paid is not necessarily always marginal and ancillary'.[67] The suggestion that part-time or low paid work '*is not necessarily always* marginal and ancillary' could easily be replaced with is '*usually* marginal and ancillary', '*frequently* marginal and ancillary' or '*almost always* marginal and ancillary'. O'Brien reminds us that 'Any language pertaining to probability is important in guiding decision makers',[68] as it 'operates from an assumption that the reader would be inclined to treat part time work as "necessarily always" marginal'.[69] This provides a strong steer for decision-makers to start from a position of marginality, leaving genuine and effective part-time or low-paid work to be the exception.

The suggestion that part-time or low paid work must be the exception to be genuine and effective ignores the judgments of the CJEU, which has sought to ensure that part-time work is included in the concept of a 'worker' in recognition of its role as 'an effective means of improving the … living conditions' of Union citizens.[70] Again, the CJEU has handed down rulings that find lower earnings to not have 'any consequence' in regard to worker status,[71] even when 'their remuneration is largely provided by subsidies from public funds'.[72] Additionally, part-time and limited hours do not prevent work from being 'genuine and effective'.[73] By emphasising that part-time and low paid work is likely to be marginal and ancillary, the UK guidance directly conflicts with these judgments.

5.5.2. Re-examination of Earnings

The pertinence of income is reiterated in the ADM by requiring a re-examination of earnings in the second tier. Repeating aspects already considered under the first tier of the test, or features that are a proxy for earnings such as hours, reasserts

[65] O'Brien (n 4) 156.
[66] ibid.
[67] DWP (n 35) [C1295].
[68] C O'Brien, 'The pillory, the precipice and the slippery slope: the profound effects of the UK's legal reform programme targeting EU migrants' (2015) 37 *Journal of Social Welfare and Family Law* 111, 119.
[69] O'Brien (n 4) 156.
[70] Case 53/81 *Levin* (n 5) [15].
[71] Case C-188/00 *Kurz* ECLI:EU:C:2002:694, [2002] ECR I-10691 [32]–[33].
[72] Case 344/87 *Bettray* ECLI:EU:C:1989:226, [1989] ECR I-1621 [15].
[73] Case C-3/90 *Bernini* (n 2) [16].

its importance. Considering the level of earnings a second time, immediately after an EEA worker has been found to fail the MET, could negatively steer decision-maker discretion, especially when the guidance fails to indicate the level of earnings relevant to the second tier, which, if provided, could benefit those who only just miss the threshold. At worst, this reassessment could be conflated to mean that anything below the MET is, in fact, an indication that work is marginal and ancillary. And at best, it may encourage decision-makers to give further significance to their initial finding under the MET, particularly when balanced against other factors that indicate genuine and effective work.

Silvia

Silvia has lived in the UK for 10 years. Her application for Universal Credit was refused and Silvia requested a mandatory reconsideration, arguing that she had automatically acquired a permanent right of residence.

The mandatory reconsideration decision from the DWP examined over five years of self-employment history. Each year where Silvia had 52 weeks of National Insurance contributions were deemed to demonstrate genuine and effective self-employment. However, any years where Silvia's profits fell below the small profits threshold and therefore did not result in National Insurance contributions were regarded as demonstrating 'insufficient information to show if this was genuine and effective – no status'.

Silvia was not asked for more information on these periods of work and there is no evidence that the decision-maker considered the length of her self-employment (2015 to 2020) or regularity of earnings. As a result, years of Silvia's self-employment were entirely discounted.

Anton

Anton had lived in the UK for over 15 years. Due to health issues he had stopped working and was living in a shelter after a period of street homelessness. He was supported to apply for Universal Credit and Housing Benefit, as the shelter could not support him without funding. His application was refused on the basis that he had not acquired a right of permanent residence and had no other right of residence. Anton's support worker helped him appeal this decision to the First-tier Tribunal.

The DWP's appeal submissions examined Anton's previous work in the UK, discounting over four years of full-time employment due to his lack of registration under the worker registration scheme (WRS). The remaining employment records from April 2009, after the WRS was no longer in place, were examined during each tax year with each employment examined separately:

> 2 × periods of employment with [employer A] – Total Earnings Factor £282 – not established as genuine and effective – NO STATUS
>
> Work for [employer B] from around 01/2/2019 to 06/4/2019, total earnings £1261.68 – not established as genuine and effective – NO STATUS

While not directly referring to the MET, the decision listed Anton's employers, cited only earnings and then declared that the work was not genuine and effective. There does not appear to be an attempt to engage with other aspects of the genuine and effective test, including seeking evidence of Anton's hours of work, regularity of shifts or whether the job was intended to be long-term.

These cases show DWP decision-makers briefly considering years of work history and only noting the level of earnings when deciding to dismiss it as marginal and ancillary. While the MET was not mentioned by name, earnings take centre stage to the overall test for genuine and effective work, with no other relevant aspects of work examined such as hours or regularity of work. In Silvia's case in particular, low level of earnings for some tax years are detrimental to establishing a permanent right of residence despite having five consistent years of records for her self-employment. Earnings frequently played a pivotal role in the communication of decisions in the case studies examined and suggested that, even when looking beyond the MET, decision-makers often identify income as the primary measure of genuine and effective work.

Alongside earnings, hours are to be assessed in the second tier of the test. Those who have failed to meet the threshold, unless earning less than NMW, will usually be working less than 20–25 hours a week.[74] There is a risk that hours may be treated as a direct proxy for earnings. The assessment of hours could steer decision-makers into assuming that working less than the hours necessary for the threshold at a minimum wage is consequently a sign of marginal and ancillary work.

[74] See ch 4, Table 4.1.

Stephan

In August 2015 Stephan made an application for State Pension Credit after he became homeless. The application was refused on the grounds that he did not have a right to reside as a self-employed person. Stephan was a 72-year-old German national who had lived in the UK with his wife since at least February 2014. At this time he began self-employment as a micro-entrepreneur. He reported working an average of 20–25 hours a week and earning around £23 a week.

In assessing whether Stephan's self-employment was genuine and effective, the decision-maker only referred to Stephan's earnings as reason that he had no right to reside as a self-employed person:

> [Y]our work as a [micro-entrepreneur] was on such a small scale, and your earnings were on average £23.12 per week for 25 hours work, that your earnings were considered as marginal and ancillary and therefore were not considered to be genuine and effective employment.

With the help of the AIRE Centre, Stephan requested a mandatory reconsideration, arguing that full consideration of his work should be taken account of. The reconsideration decision letter upheld the original decision. Again, his earnings were the only cited reason for the finding that his work was marginal and ancillary:

> Your work is not considered to be genuine and effective because your employment yields an income on such a small scale as to be regarded as purely marginal and ancillary … Your employment yields an income lower than the minimum required for subsistence. In the present context this would not be considered as 'effective' employment.

This decision was appealed and the First-tier Tribunal upheld the finding that Stephan's self-employment was not genuine and effective.

The decision-makers, for both the initial decision and reconsideration, explicitly reference Stephan's earnings as marginal and ancillary, rather than his work as a whole. The hours, regularity and length of time in self-employment are all elements that could have shown genuine and effective work. Instead, the other criteria were almost ignored entirely, with hours mentioned merely as exemplary of how low his earnings were. Stephan's earnings may have been so low that even a correct application of EU law could result in a finding that his work was marginal and ancillary. Nevertheless, failing to consider and balance aspects beyond income reduces the second tier of the test to a duplication of the MET.

The decision-maker in Stephan's case also incorrectly applies EU concepts. The decision-maker highlights that Stephan's earnings are 'lower than the minimum required for subsistence', despite the judgments in *Levin and Kempf*, which directly recognised that this did not preclude work from being genuine and effective.[75] Additionally, the decision-maker in this case relied on the everyday understandings of the relevant terms rather than their legal meaning. An example of this is when Stephan's self-employment is found to be 'genuine' but his income means that the employment is not 'effective'. This incorrect interpretation of the EU test relies on a general definition and understanding of what work is 'effective'; in this case, whether it yields enough income. It also highlights how unhelpful broad terms can be in a worker definition without clear guidance. The mandatory reconsideration decision-maker misquotes EU law, switching the terms so that 'income', rather than 'activity', cannot be 'on such a small scale as to be regarded as purely marginal and ancillary', perhaps revealing some of the invasiveness of the MET into the EU worker test.[76] These issues closely reflect findings in O'Brien's research on EU rights in the UK, where confusion and steers from the guidance have generated decisions where work was declared 'genuine but not effective' and decision-makers resorted to dictionary definitions to apply EU concepts like 'marginal and ancillary'.[77]

5.5.3. Earnings to Meet Subsistence

EU case law is clear that neither earnings below a minimum level of subsistence[78] nor seeking to supplement earnings with public funds such as welfare benefits[79] preclude an individual from having worker status. While the ADM mentions both principles, they are not always clear or followed by decision-makers.

Regarding the irrelevance of whether earnings meet a minimum level of subsistence, the ADM states that:

> [A]s long as the work is 'genuine and effective' it is irrelevant whether it yields an income lower than the amount considered the minimum required for subsistence in the host Member State.[80]

This statement could be viewed as technically correct, as particularly low earnings could form part of a justification for work being considered marginal and ancillary. It even follows similar language in the judgment. However, the assertion that the level of earnings is only irrelevant 'as long as the work is genuine and effective' is unclear for decision-makers, who may read this as the existence of a

[75] Case 53/81 *Levin* (n 5) [15]–[18]; 139/85 *Kempf* (n 5) [14].

[76] This also ignores the CJEU ruling that remuneration does not need to be monetary; see Case 196/87 *Steymann* ECLI:EU:C:1988:475, [1988] ECR I-6159 [11]–[14].

[77] O'Brien (n 4) 156–60.

[78] Joined Cases C-22/08 and C-23/08 *Vatsouras and Koupatantze* ECLI:EU:C:2009:344, [2009] ECR I-4585 [28]; Case 53/81 *Levin* (n 5) [15]–[16].

[79] Case 139/85 *Kempf* (n 5) [14].

[80] DWP (n 35) [C1492].

point at which low remuneration is relevant to a worker status determination. On the other hand, guidance on supplementing remuneration from work with public funds is much clearer with the ADM opting to closely reflect the language in the *Kempf* judgment.[81] Yet, even this much more evident matter has been misapplied by decision-makers. For example, O'Brien's research reported decision-makers 'suggesting that work can only be genuine and effective where a worker poses no "burden on the state"'.[82] Additionally, a case from this research saw a decision-maker use this as a relevant factor for consideration when assessing whether self-employment was genuine and effective.

Stephan (continued)

The mandatory reconsideration decision letter refers to worker and self-employed status as requiring enough income to support himself and his family:

> When looking at a person's self-employment, the Decision Maker has to determine if the work is genuine and effective ... i.e. that the work is active enough to support you/your wife and not low paid, with slight earnings.

The decision letter also cites a repealed residence directive (replaced by Directive 2004/38) suggesting that it requires work to earn enough to not be a burden on a Member State, when this requirement would have only come into effect if Stephan was relying on his rights as a self-sufficient person:

> Although you are registered as self-employed and may be genuine, Directive 90/364/EEC states that Member States can require of nationals of other states who wish to reside within their territory that they have sufficient resources to avoid becoming a burden on their social assistance system ... Your employment yields an income lower than the minimum required for subsistence
>
> When this case was appealed to the first tier tribunal, the judge corrected the mistake by the DWP decision letter: [Stephan] did not have to show that his self-employment was sufficient to meet all of his needs but he does have to show that it is effective.

In Stephan's case, the requirement for him to earn enough to support himself and his family and to not be a burden on the state are incorrect applications of EU law. While the tribunal decision corrected these mistakes, albeit still finding the work to be marginal and ancillary, it took until the point of appeal for this correction to be made. This will not be an option for many EEA nationals,

[81] ibid; Case 139/85 *Kempf* (n 5) [14].
[82] O'Brien (n 4) 158.

especially where they lack language skills, legal literacy and do not have the financial means or access to free advice or support to make an appeal. The more socially excluded an EU national is, the further excluded they may be from their rights, particularly if they require a tribunal to enforce them.

5.5.4. Strict Interpretation of Remuneration

Another potential issue in the ADM is its unclear treatment of remuneration. The guidance states that 'a worker must receive remuneration', and this is determined as economic in nature therefore a decision-maker should not consider worker status when looking at an EEA nationals delivering 'unpaid voluntary work'.[83] This contradicts the decisions of the CJEU that, as discussed in chapter three, found that remuneration could include material needs even if they received no pay.[84] This matter is given some clarity in the examples given in the ADM. One example describes an EEA national receiving low pay and free board who was found to be a worker and another who had done unpaid charity work who was found to not meet the requirements for worker status.[85] While this goes some way to clarifying the difference, it would be beneficial for the guidance to include the specific recognition of remuneration of any value. The current guidance risks decision-makers treating all work that does not receive monetary income as marginal and ancillary.

Worker status cannot be withheld based on low earnings alone. However, the guidance encourages decision-makers to view part-time work, low earnings and potentially any sign that earnings fall under MET as proof of marginality. With this steer, extra hurdles are put in place for part-time and low-earning workers who must seek to offset this finding and demonstrate that *despite* their earnings their work is still genuine and effective. This is further exacerbated by the reassessment of earnings, especially when no further guidance is provided on how this is to be distinguished from the MET. This approach to part-time and low-paid work is incompatible with EU law and risks decisions, like those for Silvia, Anton and Stephan, where income alone is prioritised. For many part-time and low-earning workers, this second tier is reduced to a performative step, with the true test ending at the earnings threshold.

Taken together, 14 case studies in this research involved worker status decisions which only examined level of earnings, including whether work was deemed to fail the MET or not be genuine and effective due to low levels of earnings. Decisions based entirely on the MET, or on earnings alone, were not an

[83] DWP (n 35) [C1492].
[84] Case 196/87 *Steymann* (n 76) [11]–[13]; see ch 3 at section 3.4.2.
[85] DWP (n 35) [C1501].

anomaly, nor were these decisions limited to one particular region[86] or government department.[87] A focus on earnings was the most common issue identified in the research and is directly incompatible with the CJEU ruling that a low level of earnings cannot be the sole reason to exclude work from being considered as genuine and effective.[88] Atypical workers who must first contend with an unreasonably high earnings threshold, are unlikely to find solace in the second tier.

5.6. Selective Consideration at the Second Tier

Decision-makers are guided to consider 'each case as a whole, taking account of all circumstances' when assessing work under the second tier.[89] On paper, this approach would allow significant discretion and could be beneficial for atypical workers. However, some of the listed considerations that decision-makers must take into account could lead to the exclusion of atypical work. The five considerations are:

(1) whether the work was regular or intermittent,
(2) the period of employment,
(3) whether the work was intended to be short-term or long-term at the outset,
(4) the number of hours worked and
(5) the level of earnings.[90]

While they tend to represent some of the directions given in CJEU judgments,[91] this is by no means an exhaustive list of relevant considerations. Although the guidance covers some further relevant factors from CJEU judgments under a leftover section covering principles that 'can be derived from EU case law',[92] they are not part of this core 'genuine and effective work' list after the MET has been applied. Additionally, the guidance is not clear on how each consideration should be weighed up, stating that:

> In some cases the [decision-maker] will have to weigh, for example, low hours against long duration of work as part of their overall assessment of whether work is genuine and effective. However, case law does not identify one consistent approach to applying these and other factors: each case must be decided on its own merits.[93]

[86] Not all cases showed which local authority made the decision. Of the cases recorded, local councils applying the test as determinative spanned from inside the London area, the East Midlands, South Yorkshire, Berkshire and the West Midlands.
[87] Decisions relying on earnings came from the DWP, HMRC and local authorities.
[88] Case 139/85 *Kempf* (n 5) [14].
[89] DWP (n 35) [C1489].
[90] ibid [073050].
[91] See ch 3 at section 3.4.
[92] DWP (n 35) [C1492].
[93] ibid [073050].

This leaves plenty of room for discretion and, while this can be useful to reflect the breadth of the EU definition, it can result in overly restrictive approaches. Decision-makers could be tempted to focus on the aspects of work that fail to meet the criteria and conclude that employment is marginal and ancillary.

Krzysztof's case (discussed earlier in section 5.4.1) also shows a decision-maker selectively applying aspects of the second tier to the detriment of atypical workers. While Krzysztof's first job lasted four months on a full-time basis and would have subsequently yielded an income over the MET, the decision-maker still addressed the criteria in the second tier to show precisely how it was genuine and effective. This was not necessary and instead sets the decision-maker up to compare the second period of employment against the first. Despite working full time, Krzysztof's second employment had not yet lasted three months so could not meet the MET; instead, the second tier was used to distinguish how the former employment was clearly genuine and effective and not the latter. This is not the correct test and adopts a unique interpretation, where the decision-maker models the remits of the second tier around work that already meets the steep requirements of the MET. Additionally, in dismissing the second period of work as marginal and ancillary, the decision relies solely on 'the short-term nature' of the work without considering the other criteria, which would have likely assisted Krzysztof's case, such as the hours worked and income received. Selectively applying criteria will likely result in arbitrary decisions which may become overly exclusive, or in some cases inclusive,[94] to worker status.

The selective approach places more importance on the length of employment than is intended by the ADM. The CJEU, in *Ninni-Orasche*, stated that a short-duration of employment cannot, in itself, exclude that employment from the scope of worker status.[95] In the UK, the Court of Appeal, in *Barry*, found that employment which was, and always known to be, of two weeks' duration could be sufficient for worker status.[96] Additionally the Upper Tribunal in *NE* found that where work ends prematurely (rather than a fixed-term contract that was always intended to be temporary), it may be more likely to be considered genuine and effective.[97] By basing a decision of marginality on the short duration of Krzysztof's second employment, the decision-maker appears to take the exact approach that both the CJEU and UK courts have prohibited.

A selective approach to applying relevant criteria is likely to lead to the exclusion of many atypical workers who must challenge decision-makers to consider other aspects of their work. Overall, the second tier of the UK's test falls short of replicating the broad approach of the EU and is far from the catch-all necessary

[94] 'Accidental generosity' at the point of a benefit application might come back to haunt EEA nationals who are misled about the lawfulness of their residence. When making a future application that relies on the same period, for example a permanent residence application, the time period is reassessed.

[95] Case C-413/01 *Ninni-Orasche* (n 40) [25].

[96] *Barry v London Borough of Southwark* [2008] EWCA 1440 [44].

[97] *NE* (n 44) [9].

to include all the workers who are marginalised by the steep demands of the MET. Those relying on a fair application of the second tier of the test may find that the very nature of their work as atypical will lead to its exclusion, rather than a full consideration of the merits of their work.

As the EU concept of worker is filtered down to decision-makers, the broad outer edges of the test more closely resemble a rigid boundary where the scope for discretion can be limited by thresholds, steers in the guidance or a lack of clear instruction on the array of employment situations present in the labour market. The projection of these issues in the case studies of atypical workers illustrates the exclusionary impact of this approach on a significant and growing number of EEA workers in the labour market. The impact of this narrowing of worker status is felt most by workers who are alienated from more 'standard' employment and have no choice but to take on part-time or atypical employment due to their personal circumstances.

5.7. Summary

This chapter has concluded that the adjustment to defining an EU worker, through the introduction of the MET, could and has shifted decision-makers to take a more restrictive approach than is compatible with EU law. The first issue identified is the tendency for decision-makers, mostly at local authorities, to apply the MET as entirely determinative of worker status. This is the clearest example of incompatibility with EU law and means that workers who earn under the threshold, sometimes marginally so, are at risk of being automatically denied access to benefits, without any consideration of the genuine and effective criteria.

This chapter has also sought to examine the UK's interpretation and application of the EU concept of 'worker' in light of the changes seen in the European labour market. This analysis has demonstrated how the discretionary outer edges of the worker definition are reduced to rigid boundaries, leaving 'non-standard' work to fall through the gaps. The earnings threshold has been set at an unreasonably high level and rewards consistency and permanence to the exclusion of many EEA nationals engaged in atypical work. Alongside this, the insufficient or absent guidance from the EU level and the ADM on issues arising in new forms of work, such as overlapping contracts, the combination of temporary work and inconsistency of earnings, means that many workers who are, by all accounts, in 'genuine and effective' economic activity can be unfairly excluded from worker status.

Without the thorough and accurate application of the second tier, the UK's approach to worker status could also be deemed incompatible with EU law. The guidance on assessing genuine and effective work under the second tier is misleading and sometimes deliberately contrary to EU law. This chapter has found that the overemphasis of earnings in the ADM steers decision-makers into starting from a position of marginality when assessing work below the threshold. Misleading or unclear guidance also results in the misapplication of established EU law on how to treat low earnings or alternative types of remuneration. Rather than a 'catch-all', the restrictive approach to the 'genuine and effective' test, as seen in the case studies, can result in EEA national's work being excluded on the grounds that it is atypical. These issues effectively create extra burdens on atypical workers who must prove that their work is genuine and effective *despite* their low earnings. Adopting an earnings threshold especially when it is particularly high, while problematic itself, cannot necessarily be redeemed by a secondary restrictively interpreted and poorly executed 'genuine and effective' test.

While many of these problems may be resolved through better application of the broad EU definition, the case studies have revealed some of the weak spots in the EU definition of worker status. Imprecision in the definition has allowed Member States to scale back rights for atypical workers by reducing the nuance of working arrangements to matter of income and little else. Many of the problems encountered in these case studies could be overcome with a slight tweaking of the EU definition, or even a statement clarifying the position of atypical workers. For example, a more precise definition outlining how different atypical work arrangements interact with the 'genuine and effective' test or a specific statement on the inclusion of atypical work such as gig work, agency work or other temporary employment.

A worker definition which, in practice, excludes many atypical workers will likely have a discriminatory impact on a growing section of the labour market that is disproportionately occupied by lone parents, carers, Disabled workers and young workers. Chapter six will therefore look to additional case studies to examine whether atypical aspects of work and personal circumstances are accommodated in the UK's worker status test.

6

Inequality Squared: How the MET Compounds Discrimination

6.1. Introduction

The European labour market is becoming more diverse, in terms of both work and workers.[1] Whether the definition of 'genuine and effective' work includes a variety of working situations is more relevant to a growing number of EU citizens, and more specifically to those who have previously faced barriers to employment such as lone parents, Disabled people and those with caring responsibilities. To ensure that free movement rights are not withheld from the atypical workforce, the definition of work must reflect these diversities. While the EU definition of work is relatively broad, implementation at a Member State level must not dilute the breadth of protection. As shown in the previous chapter, adopting earnings thresholds can greatly restrict the scope of the definition of work, which in turn could risk the disproportionate exclusion of these groups of workers from Article 45 TFEU free movement rights.

This chapter contributes to commentary on the adequacy of the EU concept of worker and its national implementation, focusing on the specific issues of the UK's approach in light of the changing labour market and the diverse workforce. While chapter five focused on the operation of the test, specifically on how an earnings threshold can exclude types of atypical work, this chapter looks at some of the more hidden discriminatory impacts and how the test excludes workers who face barriers to the more 'standard' labour market. The analysis in this chapter demonstrates how the UK's MET limits the availability and utility of free movement and equal treatment rights in the changing labour market. In particular, the rigidity with which the test has been applied to a range of already disadvantaged demographics is scrutinised against the status of free movement of workers as a fundamental right to be available to all EU citizens.

This chapter looks at the diversity of workers in the labour market and how the construction of the worker test leaves insufficient room for a consideration of personal circumstances. Section 6.2 considers the impact of pushing a homogeneous expectation of 'genuine and effective' work on all workers, ignoring the

[1] See ch 2.

diversity of the workforce. Section 6.3 examines the discriminatory impact on specific groups of workers who are more likely to be in atypical employment. Then, section 6.4 focuses on the contradictory circumstances of the provision of unpaid care not being treated as economic activity, especially even when receiving a carer's benefit.

6.2. Worker Status and the Diverse Workforce

Human lives are not simple and homogenous. Recognising inequality and barriers faced by some individuals due to impairments, health conditions or the limited capacity of those with care responsibilities requires a level of flexibility and discretion in the assessment of worker status. Any assessment of whether an individual is a worker, which relies on evaluating if they are working *enough*, should be applied relative to the individual and their circumstances rather than rigidly applying the same expectations to everyone.

As chapter three covered, the CJEU's imprecise broad approach to worker status may be anticipated to include those facing barriers to 'standard' work, but an explicitly required consideration of personal circumstances is lacking. While the CJEU has addressed the inclusion of work outside of the 'normal' labour market where it may assist workers with disabilities to integrate into standard work,[2] employment in the 'normal' labour market remains the EU's primary concern.[3] Explicit inclusion of personal circumstances could see a nuanced approach to the concept of 'genuine and effective' work and a more active role for proportionality in its assessment.

The UK's definition of work in its current form includes relatively little space for the consideration of personal situations. With regard to the first tier of the test, those who face barriers to more secure work are expected to meet the same requirements as those with no such barriers. The second tier, which applies the 'genuine and effective' criteria, could theoretically involve the holistic assessment of these circumstances, but the guidance does not require decision-makers to specifically or thoroughly acknowledge these aspects. Without consideration of these circumstances, there is no recognition of the difficulties faced by Disabled workers, those with caring responsibilities, or lone parents when trying to find suitable work. Nor are there concessions to recognise the hardship faced by those who have been victims of exploitation, trafficking or situations of domestic abuse.

The personal circumstances of workers have, to a limited extent, been recognised in the UK courts when considering self-employment. In the Upper Tribunal,

[2] See ch 3 at 3.4; Case C-316/13 *Fenoll* ECLI:EU:C:2015:200.

[3] C O'Brien, *Unity in Adversity: EU Citizenship, Social Justice and the Cautionary Tale of the UK* (Hart Publishing, 2017) 97–100.

when assessing whether the claimant should continue to have a right to reside during a gap in income from her self-employment, Judge Ward suggested that evidence on 'circumstances at the time' could provide 'important background that might be relevant to whether she was in a position to continue self-employment'.[4] However, there is still no formal recognition of the consideration of individual circumstances in an assessment of whether work or self-employment is 'genuine and effective'.

This section looks at how the UK's approach to worker status fails to accommodate the personal circumstances of workers. It first considers the flaws in approaching equality formally and treating all the workers the same. It then addresses the contradiction between the expectations placed on EEA workers to establish eligibility for benefits and how individual circumstances are treated once eligibility for benefits is established through the use of easements to conditionality. Finally, it examines how the guidance encourages decision-makers to use inappropriate guesswork when considering a worker's motivation for taking up employment and their physical capacity to undertake work.

6.2.1. The Inequality of the 'Same' Treatment

While the ADM asks decision-makers to approach 'each case as a whole, taking account of all circumstances',[5] a more explicit appreciation of barriers through the use of exceptions or concessions is absent from the guidance. Failure to do so risks the 'genuine and effective' and test being applied homogenously. It ignores the structural barriers limiting some workers' access to the labour market and full-time employment and is likely to disadvantage these groups further by excluding them from the benefits that come with worker status. This is particularly noticeable given that these barriers are recognised for national workers in the UK in the form of a sliding scale of conditionality.[6] Without such recognition in a free movement context, the rigid definition of work can be a significant barrier for many individuals who are left without equal treatment in access to welfare benefits.

The failure to build in mechanisms to account for personal circumstances and the barriers they face represents a larger shift towards neoliberal approaches to welfare. Humpage attributes this approach as treating inequality and social risk as 'emerging from individual inadequacies'.[7] Consequently, individuals are held 'personally responsible for, and expected to overcome, their vulnerable circumstances'.[8] As policies tend towards a focus on individual responsibility,

[4] *SSWP v JS* [2010] UKUT 240 AAC [8].

[5] DWP, 'ADM International Issues Chapter C1: Universal Credit' (January 2023) [C1489].

[6] See 6.2.2.

[7] L Humpage, *Policy change, public attitudes and social citizenship: Does neoliberalism matter?* (Policy Press, 2014) 29.

[8] H Stinson, 'Supporting people? Universal Credit, conditionality and the recalibration of vulnerability' in P Dwyer (ed), *Dealing with welfare conditionality* (Policy Press, 2019) 15; Humpage (n 7) 29.

there is a concern that 'social, economic and political causes of unemployment, poverty and disability will cease to be recognised',[9] rather than understanding that, for those with particular personal characteristics, atypical work and subsequent precarity is not a choice. Taking Amartya Sen's 'capability approach', Deakin argues that the lack of choice can stem from institutional and societal levels which fail to take the necessary 'state action to remove the conditions which inhibit effective market participation'.[10] Instead a formal equality approach is taken, focused on treating everyone the same, without consideration of these wider societal factors and barriers. This is only likely to further entrench inequalities. Holding disadvantaged groups to the same productivity standards treats them 'the same' but actually 'results in discrimination in favour of those in positions of established privilege'.[11] The problem with this expectation is brought into sharp focus when considered alongside the measures limiting the conditionality of some recipients receiving welfare benefits in the UK.

6.2.2. Contradictory Conditionality between Universal Credit and Worker Status

The UK has seen recent reforms to its welfare system, focused on activation and benefit claimant responsibility to improve their living standards through work. While this has taken place over many years and several administrations,[12] its most recent shift has come through the transition to Universal Credit. This welfare benefit introduced heightened mandatory job search requirements paired with sanctions regimes if the claimant fails to reach targets, which have since been shown to be ineffective and damaging.[13] This conditionality also extends beyond the unemployed, to part-time and low-paid workers[14] and to those who may have previously held relatively unconditional access to benefits, such as Disabled people[15] or lone parents of preschool-aged children.[16]

Some elements of this conditionality can be tailored to the personal circumstances of the individual. Universal Credit requires claimants to sign up to a 'claimant commitment' to work or seek work for an agreed amount of hours. Work

[9] P Dwyer, 'Rewriting the contract? Conditionality, welfare reform and the rights and responsibilities of disabled people' in D Horsfall and J Hudson (eds), *Social Policy in an Era of Competition: from global to Local Perspectives* (The Policy Press, 2017) 145.

[10] S Deakin, 'The "Capability" Concept and the Evolution of European Social Policy' in E Spaventa and M Dougan (eds), *Social Welfare and EU law* (Hart Publishing, 2005) 4–5.

[11] O'Brien (n 3) 100.

[12] Dwyer (n 9) 136.

[13] P Dwyer, 'Final findings report: Welfare Conditionality Project 2013–2018' (June 2018) 23.

[14] B Watts and S Fitzpatrick, *Welfare Conditionality* (Routledge, 2018) 6.

[15] Dwyer (n 9) 136.

[16] L Dewar and D Ben-Galim, 'An impossible bind: Requirements to work under Universal Credit' (Gingerbread, November 2017) 7.

coaches have the ability, although often applied inconsistently,[17] to modify the expectations of jobseeking where the claimant has a disability, is a lone parent or has caring responsibilities.[18] The claimant commitments can also be adapted to more temporary circumstances such as sickness, where a claimant has experienced domestic abuse or other extenuating circumstances that make them 'unfit for work'.[19]

While this recognition of limited capacity in the claimant commitment was originally withheld from EEA nationals, the relevant provision in the Universal Credit Regulations has been repealed[20] and they are now, in theory, available. However, for EEA migrants to even get to the point where they benefit from the relevant concessions, they must first be granted access to Universal Credit through the process of the Habitual Residence Test and right to reside requirements. Therefore, EEA workers must first meet the requirements of the restrictive two-tier test before they have any recognition of personal circumstances that could limit their capacity for full-time work. As UK nationals automatically pass the right to reside portion of this test, they do not have to meet the same expectations. This creates a situation where a UK national lone parent of a four-year-old child is only expected to work or seek work for 16 hours a week,[21] but an EEA national with the same caring responsibilities could have to work 22 hours a week continuously for at least three months to guarantee eligibility for Universal Credit. The effect of this is an important illustration of the contradiction in the UK welfare system for EEA nationals where, at the point of application, their personal circumstances are irrelevant, but once Universal Credit is awarded, these circumstances can have a significant impact on the level of conditionality faced.

Hanna

Hanna is an Italian national who has recently separated from her partner. She is a full-time carer for her son, who has autism.

Hanna has taken on work as a fitness instructor, earning just £80 a week. She says she would like to work more but is unable to take on more hours alongside her caring commitments.

Due to her low income, Hanna is currently relying on loans from her mother, but not sure how long she can do this. She made an application for

[17] Dwyer (n 13) 24.

[18] Universal Credit Regulations 2013 (UC Regulations), SI 2013/376, Reg 88.

[19] DWP, 'Chapter J3: Work-related requirements' (March 2013) [J3180–J3233].

[20] UC Regulations, Reg 92 (repealed).

[21] 'Universal Credit: further information for families' (30 November 2017), www.gov.uk/government/publications/universal-credit-and-your-family-quick-guide/universal-credit-further-information-for-families.

Universal Credit which was refused on the basis of Hanna's employment not being genuine and effective. She is still in receipt of child benefit, but is worried that this will also be stopped.

Without any support from Universal Credit Hanna is looking into whether she will have to move back to Italy, but is reluctant to take her son out of the UK since he has only ever lived there, does not speak Italian and she fears he will struggle with the adjustment.

This case highlights the lack of logical coherence between the UK's worker status test for EU nationals and how UK nationals in the same circumstances are treated when accessing welfare benefits. When accounting for Hanna's personal circumstances as a lone parent and full-time carer, it cannot be fair to expect her to take on more work.[22] In this example, if Hanna had been granted access to Universal Credit, her claimant commitment would have been tailored to reflect these responsibilities; it is likely that she would have been placed in the 'no work requirements' category and received Universal Credit with relatively little conditionality.[23] Yet it is the same circumstances that would ease conditionality in the Universal Credit system that are ignored in the 'genuine and effective' test to exclude her from welfare benefits in the first place.

The difference in treatment is also confusing for decision-makers and EEA nationals. Should an EEA national see that claimant commitments should be tailored to personal circumstances, they may reduce their hours in line with the requirements for Universal Credit. As a result, they risk losing entitlement to the welfare benefit on the grounds of not meeting the genuine and effective work test.

Beatrice

Beatrice had worked in the UK for several months. She stopped work and lived off savings for a few months before she gave birth to her child. When the child was two years old she separated from her partner and successfully applied for Universal Credit on a single basis.

She did not pursue any work after receiving advice from her work coach at the job centre that she was not required to, because she had a child under the age of three. Beatrice had also seen online that, as she had a young child, she would not be required to look for work.

[22] See 6.4.

[23] Work and Pensions Committee, *Valuing and Supporting Carers* (HC 2007-08, 485-I) para 187; UC Regulations, Reg 89(1)(b).

> A year later, Beatrice received a letter stating that she had been wrongly awarded Universal Credit as she had no right of residence, and she therefore had been overpaid £10,000, which she was required to repay.

The Department for Work and Pensions (DWP) in this case may have been technically correct in identifying that Beatrice did not have a right of residence, but misinformation from the work coach and online resources resulted in Beatrice believing that she had no requirement to look for work or to start working to maintain her access to benefits. Instead, it was only after a year of receiving Universal Credit that Beatrice was told that her lack of employment would not only result in her losing access to benefits but also to receiving a devastatingly high overpayment. When Universal Credit was introduced, the Government introduced stricter rules on overpayments, meaning that the DWP could recover the overpayment regardless of the cause, even when it is the department's own error.[24] The difference in treatment between UK nationals and EEA nationals in these circumstances can act as a tripwire, not only resulting in a loss of continuous lawful residence, but also access to benefits and potentially a significant debt to the DWP.

6.2.3. Presumptions and Speculations in the Guidance

The guidance on the second-tier of the worker status test also increases the likelihood of further discrimination for diverse workers in atypical employment. It requires decision-makers to make subjective findings on aspects of EEA nationals' motivation for seeking employment and of their physical capacity to fulfil the requirements of an employment. Without training and further guidance on personal circumstances, these considerations are likely to impact lone parents, carers, older and Disabled workers. Neither of these considerations are grounded in EU law and both require an element of inappropriate guess work.

6.2.3.1. Motivation for Work

The CJEU has been clear that the motives of an EU national seeking work 'are of no account and must not be taken into consideration'.[25] Instead, the issue is simply whether they perform work that is genuine and effective.

[24] Welfare Reform Act 2012, s 105.

[25] Case 53/81 *Levin* ECLI:EU:C:1982:105, [1982] ECR I-1035 [22]; Case C-46/12 *L. N.* ECLI:EU:C:2013:97, [2013] 2 CMLR 37 [47]; motive for migration is also considered immaterial, see Case C-109/01 *Akrich* ECLI:EU:C:2003:491, [2003] ECR I-9607 [55]; Case C-542/09 *Commission v Netherlands* EU:C:2012:346 [68]; Case C-237/94 *O'Flynn* ECLI:EU:C:1996:206, [1996] ECR I-2617 [21].

However, a number of national courts in Member States, including the UK, have shown a willingness to consider a perceived intention of taking employment with fewer hours as a way to access welfare benefits.[26] The UK Court of Appeal has interpreted EU law on motivation of seeking employment as *relevant*, but only when determining whether an EEA national is genuinely pursing activity as an employed person.[27] But once this has been established, motivation for seeking employment 'is of no relevance' to the genuine and effective test.[28] The 2015 FreSsco report warns that discrediting the genuineness of work in instances where there is a perceived ulterior motive for work 'does not have a sound basis in EU law'.[29] Adopting motivation as a relevant factor to any part of the test risks worker status being refused due to what is *assumed* to be the EU nationals' motives to work in a Member State, even when they are factually performing work.

Stephan (continued from chapter five)

In the arguments presented by the DWP in Stephan's appeal, they claimed that during a telephone conversation to the Department, Stephan had asserted that a judge told him that through selling products as a micro-entrepreneur he would be entitled to Pension Credit. The DWP's representative argued that:

> Such an assertion would confirm that [Stephan] took up his self-employment solely for the purpose of accessing social assistance benefits in the UK and therefore, his work is not genuine.

Stephan received advice and support from the AIRE Centre for this appeal, which argued that this was factually inaccurate. Pointing to the mandatory reconsideration decision letter, which described how Stephan was advised by a judge (from an appeal in a previous benefits application) to keep records of his self-employment as evidence of his right to access benefits in the future, and not to take up self-employment. This issue was not discussed in the tribunal judgment.

Stephan's case illustrates some of the risks of permitting an assessment that relies on speculation, assumptions and perceived intention. This could be especially

[26] C O'Brien, E Spaventa and J De Coninck, 'Comparative Report 2015: The concept of worker under Article 45 TFEU and certain non-standard forms of employment' (FreSsco, 2016) 9.

[27] *MDB (Italy) v SSHD* [2012] EWCA Civ 1015 [61]–[65].

[28] ibid.

[29] O'Brien, Spaventa and De Coninck (n 26) 66.

problematic where signals from national government indicate that action needs to be taken to stop 'rogue EU benefit claims'.[30]

There is an additional risk that the ADM's approach to the motivation for seeking work fails to clearly make the distinction of when motivation is irrelevant. The ADM instructs decision-makers that: 'The motives which have prompted the worker to work in another Member State are irrelevant, provided the work is genuine and effective.'[31] This could confuse decision-makers trying to assess worker status. Stating that motivation is only irrelevant 'provided the work is genuine and effective' could be construed as meaning it is relevant to the genuine and effective test. Secondly, the guidance later instructs decision-makers to 'look at all the circumstances including the person's primary motivation in taking up employment' when considering 'whether the claimant is genuinely exercising their EU rights as a "worker"'.[32] While the guidance applies the interpretation of the UK Court of Appeal,[33] this has the potential to mislead decision-makers who are instructed to consider motives when deciding if an EEA national is *genuinely* exercising their rights as a worker, but not consider them in relation to their determination on whether the work is *genuine* and effective.

Decision-makers will be tasked with trying to speculate on whether a migrant has taken up work to pass the Habitual residence test. A worker's motivation is unlikely to be questioned where they are higher earners or in full-time employment. When decision-makers treat everyone equally regardless of their personal circumstances, a decision to take on work with lower hours becomes suspicious. There will be many workers with perfectly understandable reasons for taking up work with fewer hours, for example where they have caring responsibilities or limited work capability due to health issues or old age. These workers will therefore likely face much more scrutiny than those who can access full-time employment, including inappropriate questions about their motivation for work.

6.2.3.2. *Physical Capacity*

The consideration of physical capacity is also offered as a relevant factor. An example provided in the ADM, in which a worker's contract is terminated after two weeks because health problems prevented her from being able to continue in the post, states that: 'A claimant's physical incapacity to do the work she had undertaken and the fact that she had been dismissed from it after a short period were relevant to the issue of whether the work was genuine and effective.'[34]

[30] DWP, 'Further curbs to migrant access to benefits announced' (April 2014), www.gov.uk/government/news/further-curbs-to-migrant-access-to-benefits-announced.

[31] DWP (n 5) [C1492].

[32] ibid [C1496]; DWP 'JSA(IB) –Right to Reside – establishing whether an EEA National is/was a "worker" or a "self-employed person"' (2014, Memo DMG 1/14) [11]–[12].

[33] *MDB (Italy)* (n 27) [61]–[65].

[34] DWP (n 5) [C1492].

This assertion is based on just 'one judgment of a Social Security commissioner in 2007', not a CJEU judgment and, as O'Brien argues, 'invites speculative retrospective guesswork about physical capacity and job performance' while not requiring the review of expert evidence or occupational health and reasonable adjustment duties.[35] This runs counter to the goals pursued by the EU Charter of Fundamental Rights (The Charter) which recognises the rights of persons with disabilities to be supported in integrating with social, occupational and community life.[36] O'Brien also describes this as a 'too disabled' criterion,[37] which can be expected to have an adverse impact on Disabled EEA workers where their work may be considered marginal and ancillary due to a presumed physical incapacity. This potentially denies Disabled workers formal equality, as their disability is deliberately targeted as a reason to refuse worker status.

A formal approach to equality clearly results in an established disadvantage to workers who face barriers to the 'standard' labour market. Easements to work requirements are withheld from EEA migrants, and UK guidance encourages decision-makers to be suspicious of workers who take on fewer hours or have limited physical capacity without any direction on how personal circumstances should be considered. This issue exists at both the UK level, where guidance appears to be incompatible with EU law, and at the EU level, where Member States lack precise instructions on the role of personal circumstances or Charter Rights when examining worker status.

The one-size-fits-all approach to worker status could be adapted to address these issues. Firstly, it is worth noting that replicating the broad and flexible approach of the CJEU would be helpful to many whose personal circumstances affect their ability to work. Part of the problem for claimants here is that the test in the UK is too steep and rigid. However, it may also be necessary to introduce a tiered approach to the earnings threshold or to expectations of work that fall below the MET. This would allow decision-makers to assess the genuineness and effectiveness of work based on an expectation that is tailored to fit individual circumstances, similar to the easements seen in Universal Credit. Additionally, space in the guidance that allows for discretion to be exercised in these circumstances is essential when dealing with the diversity inherent in individuals' lives. This issue could also be addressed by EU legislators through establishing clearly that worker status must be interpreted to include those with limited capacity to work and, as a minimum, should require easements made available to nationals of a Member State in work capacity tests, to be available as part of the worker status test. As this would relate to the way that Article 7 of Directive 2004/38 is interpreted and applied, The Charter may already provide the necessary tools for this through non-discrimination rights in Article 21, protection of equality between

[35] C O'Brien, 'The pillory, the precipice and the slippery slope: the profound effects of the UK's legal reform programme targeting EU migrants' (2015) 37 *Journal of Social Welfare and Family Law* 111, 120.

[36] Charter of Fundamental Rights of the European Union [2012] OJ C 326/02 (The Charter), Art 26.

[37] O'Brien (n 35) 119.

women and men in all areas, including employment, work and pay and Article 23 on the integration of persons with disabilities in Article 26.

EEA nationals who face barriers to full-time, permanent work can have no or very little control over these situations and the barriers that impact their ability to work. Yet their personal circumstances can force them to take on atypical work and subsequently struggle to meet the requirements of the worker status test, as applied in the UK.

6.3. The Unequal Impact of Worker Status

Nearly all types of atypical work are occupied by workers who are alienated from more permanent and high-paid roles. This includes Disabled workers, carers,[38] migrant workers, lone parents (who are predominantly women) and women more generally.[39] The over-representation of workers with limited capacity in atypical forms of work will also push the impact of a restrictive worker definition disproportionately on these groups. As migrant workers are over-represented among atypical workers,[40] EEA nationals and their family members could, even generally, be more likely than nationals to be in the type of work that sits at the outer edges of the worker definition.

The statistics suggest that there is likely to be a significant cross-section of atypical workers who face the outdated and restrictive interpretation of work and workers who, due to individual circumstances, should not be expected to work more. As worker status acts as a gateway to many important free movement rights, this combination can indirectly discriminate by essentially excluding these groups. In addition, as the next chapters will explore in relation to the barriers to alternative free movement rights, exclusion from worker status can essentially exclude atypical workers from establishing lawful residence under the free movement rules.

6.3.1. Disabled Workers and Ill Health

Disabled workers face considerable obstructive barriers to the labour market. They are often expected to reconcile their health conditions and impairments with a world of work that previously 'designed out "nonstandard" people'.[41] This expectation does not challenge the ableist 'hegemonic constructions of

[38] 'Just over 2.1 million people have reduced their working hours in order to care': Carers UK, 'Juggling work and unpaid care A growing issue' (February 2019) 9.

[39] See ch 2 at 2.6.1.

[40] See ch 2 at 2.6.4.

[41] A Roulstone, 'Disability, work and welfare' in C Grover and L Pignott (eds), *Disabled people, work and welfare: Is employment really the answer?* (Policy Press, 2015) 257, 260.

productive value'[42] and therefore Disabled workers are often expected to compromise by working in low-paid, low-progression, insecure work. Despite the belief that more flexible working conditions support Disabled workers, Sayce points out that this trade-off instead leaves many in employment that is rarely suitable for their disability.[43]

For EEA Disabled workers this compromise can also inhibit their ability to access rights through worker status. Marie's case, in chapter five, shows that leaving standard employment and joining the flexible labour market due to health conditions led to her losing her status as a worker and therefore access to welfare benefits.[44] In her case, no account was taken of her health conditions and how they could impact the barriers to her engagement in more 'standard' and secure work. Informal carers are also affected by the restrictive approach to worker status. Their particular situation and the relationship between unpaid care and worker status is covered in more detail in section 6.4 below.

Disabled EEA nationals must also face the extra hurdle of the inclusion of physical capacity as a factor to consider for worker status, where their health conditions may be directly cited as a reason why they cannot be in genuine and effective work.

At an EU level, a definition of worker that ignores the barriers faced by Disabled workers sidesteps the general principle of EU law to guard against discrimination and the powers to combat that discrimination in Article 19 TFEU.[45] In particular, it ignores the broad prohibition of discrimination by EU institutions in Article 21 of the Charter and overlooks Article 26, which promises to respect the right of Disabled people to 'benefit from measures designed to ensure their independence, social and occupational integration and participation in the life of the community'. Instead, a Member State's use of thresholds and treatment of non-standard work as marginal and ancillary risks a disproportionate number of Disabled workers being pushed into dependence, social and occupational exclusion, and obstruction from participation in the life of the community, in particular obstruction to participation in free movement. While Article 26 was deemed to be a guiding principle for EU institutions when they legislate, rather than an enforceable right,[46] Lock argues that 'the binding character of a principle only removes the legislature's discretion as far as the question is concerned

[42] ibid.

[43] L Sayce, 'Switching Focus: Whose responsibility to improve disabled people's employment and pay' (London School of Economics, November 2018) 31.

[44] See ch 5 at 5.3.1.

[45] Consolidated Version of the Treaty on the Functioning of the European Union [2012] OJ C326/47 (TFEU), Art 19.

[46] Case C-356/12 *Glatzel* [2014] EU:C:2014:350, [2014] 3 CMLR 52 [74]–[79]. See D Ferri, 'The Unorthodox Relationship between the EU Charter of Fundamental Rights, the UN Convention on the Rights of Persons with Disabilities and Secondary Rights in the Court of Justice Case Law on Disability Discrimination' (2020) 16 *European Constitutional Law Review* 275 and C O'Brien, 'Driving Down Disability Equality' (2014) 21 *Maastricht Journal of European and Comparative Law* 723.

whether it needs to comply. It leaves intact the legislature's discretion as to *how* it should comply' (emphasis in original).[47] As shown through the case studies, a broad definition of work does not guarantee a broad and adaptable approach to worker status. Neglecting to create inclusive measures, such as specific instructions on the inclusion of Disabled workers or the relevance of proportionality to these decisions, could indicate a failure to comply with the principle set in Article 26.

6.3.2. Lone Parents

Lone parents are also more likely to be excluded from free movement rights due to the restrictive application of the worker test. The vast majority of lone parents are women.[48] Like Disabled workers, women with families often pay the price of the reconciliation that is expected of them by downgrading their employment, often with the unmet expectation of further flexibility.[49] In 2014, 32.4 per cent of lone mothers were in part-time work – more than those in full time work.[50] Lone parents who are subjected to work conditionality more generally find that it impacts their career progression and does not take account of 'individual preferences about whether to work or look after children, the impact on child wellbeing, the availability of work, the potential for flexible working and the quality of childcare'.[51] Case studies examined in this book have also demonstrated the difficulties in meeting the standard for worker status for lone parents, particularly when combined with other circumstances such as disability/health conditions (Marta), care (see Naomie, Beatrice and Laura) and fleeing domestic violence (Juliana and Sophie).

A definition of worker set at Union level, which is open to a discriminatory interpretation by Member States and results in such discrimination for women, could once again indicate a breach of Article 21 of the Charter. Additionally, Article 23 of the Charter concerning equality between women and men alongside Directive 2006/54 on equal opportunities and equal treatment of men and women in matters of employment could conflict with the exclusion some women

[47] T Lock, 'Rights and principles in the EU Charter of Fundamental Rights' (2019) 56 *Common Market Law Review* 1201.

[48] 'Of the 2.9 million lone parent families in the UK in 2016, the majority (86%) were headed by a female lone parent'; E Knipe 'Families and Households: 2016' (Office for National Statistics, 4 November 2016) www.ons.gov.uk/peoplepopulationandcommunity/birthsdeathsandmarriages/families/bulletins/familiesandhouseholds/2016.

[49] M Gregory and S Connolly, 'The Price of Reconciliation: Part-Time Work, Families and Women's Satisfaction' (2008) 118 *The Economic Journal* F1, F7.

[50] M Tinsley, 'Parenting Alone: Work and welfare in single parent households' (Policy Exchange, 2014).

[51] Dewar and Ben-Galim (n 16) 7.

face from worker status when exercising free movement.[52] It is not difficult to imagine how an exclusionary worker definition, which results in the withholding of social assistance or the ability to secure residence rights from lone parents, would result in women losing opportunities to move and work in another Member State. While the EU clearly has competence to tackle these gaps in the definition of worker, Union institutions have so far failed to adequately guard against the discriminatory impact on women. Nic Schuibhne argues that an abandonment of primary Union law – including the Charter and other non-discrimination rights – in favour of the limitations and conditions for free movement rights has been an ongoing trend.[53] Similarly, while it is legitimate to assess whether work is genuine and effective, this must not be conducted in a vacuum, free from the duties of fundamental rights and other non-discrimination provisions.

6.3.3. Victims of Domestic Abuse

Disruptions to life caused by domestic abuse also have a disproportionate impact on women and their exclusion from worker status.[54] Two of the cases examined in this research concerned lone parents who had fled situations of domestic abuse. Such circumstances can lead to trauma and create a lot of upheaval in an individual's life. The level of and effect of this upheaval is recognised by the requirement for work coaches to ease the requirements of the claimant commitment for claimants of Universal Credit.[55] But once again, this easement is not extended to the genuine and effective test for worker status. O'Brien found some recognition of these 'exceptional circumstances' for domestic abuse victims in the First-tier Tribunal.[56] However, as this does not set a precedent, the 'exceptional' circumstances are not formally recognised and leave a significant domestic abuse gap.[57]

One additional problem for EEA nationals facing domestic abuse is that their lawful residence can often stem from evidencing their EEA national partners' work once they have fled. Acquiring this evidence can be understandably difficult

[52] Directive 2006/54/EC of the European Parliament and of the Council of 5 July 2006 on the implementation of the principle of equal opportunities and equal treatment of men and women in matters of employment and occupation (recast) [2006] OJ L 204/23.

[53] N Nic Shuibhne, 'Limits Rising, Duties Ascending: The Changing Legal Shape of Union Citizenship' (2015) 52 *Common Market Law Review* 889, 935. Also see ch 8.

[54] UK statistics show that women are more likely to experience domestic abuse, and are also considerably more likely to experience repeated and severe forms of violence and sexual abuse: 'Domestic Abuse Statistics UK' (National Centre for Domestic Violence), www.ncdv.org.uk/domestic-abuse-statistics-uk. Domestic violence was identified as 'the single most quoted reason for becoming homeless' in H Cramer and M Carter, 'Homelessness: what's gender got to do with it?' (Shelter, 2002).

[55] DWP (n 19) [J3180].

[56] O'Brien (n 3) 168. These Tribunal decisions were made on the basis that the CJEU, in *Saint Prix*, identified that Directive 2004/38, Art 7(3) which lists the ways in which worker status can be retained, is not exhaustive; Case C-507/12 *Saint Prix* EU:C:2014:2007, [2015] 1 CMLR 5.

[57] O'Brien (n 3) 167–70.

or dangerous. While DWP has the power to look at the employment records of partners in difficult circumstances such as domestic abuse and estrangement,[58] case data from the EU Rights and Brexit Hub showed that this was rarely done, especially without being specifically requested by an adviser. Where EEA nationals cannot derive a right to reside from their partner, they must establish it themselves. Many in this position find that their ability to work is negatively affected[59] and they may have to leave their employment in the upheaval and disruption of fleeing domestic abuse. The restrictive worker test in the UK can mean that they are refused access to welfare benefits at this particularly vulnerable time. Juliana and Sophie in the case studies below were held to the same expectation as any worker, despite their responsibilities to care for their children as lone parents and the circumstances they faced while fleeing domestic abuse.

Juliana

Juliana is a Spanish national who arrived in the UK in August 2015. She is currently living in a refuge with her five-year-old child after fleeing domestic abuse.

Her ex-partner is currently serving time in prison and, while believed to be an EEA national, there is no evidence of his nationality or status in the UK, including evidence of work.

From December 2015 to June 2016, Juliana worked part-time for 10 hours a week, earning minimum wage (£6.70 per hour), with an income of around £67.50 a week. Juliana applied for Housing Benefit in February 2016, but her application was refused. Juliana's caseworker reported that the decision maker explained that Juliana is 'not earning the minimum required for her to have workers status'.

Sophie

In 2015, Sophie fled an abusive relationship. She had a young child and tried to get a place in a refuge, which was refused after she could not access Housing Benefit.

Sophie moved to the UK to study in 2013. Sophie was in the middle of studying for a bachelors degree, but took leave from this due to her circumstances. She started working part time at a fast-food restaurant and earned

[58] *Kerr v Department for Social Development* [2004] UKHL 23 [62].

[59] Women's Aid found that 56.1% of their sample 'who had left a relationship with an abuser felt that the abuse had impacted their ability to work': 'The nature and impact of domestic abuse', www.womensaid.org.uk/information-support/what-is-domestic-abuse/the-nature-and-impact-of-domestic-abuse.

approximately £135 per week, working approximately 20 hours a week. When she applied for Housing Benefit as a worker, it was refused due to her not being able to meet the MET (£155 in 2015).

6.3.4. Victims of Trafficking and Exploitation

While the Upper Tribunal has found that worker status is inclusive of undeclared work,[60] having no space to consider the wider difficulties associated with trafficking or its aftermath means that EEA nationals face the full force of the 'genuine and effective' expectations.

The ADM makes reference to the Upper Tribunal's ruling, stating that work can still be genuine and effective 'if the person is employed under a contract that is performed illegally'.[61] Nevertheless, the use of the MET and the homogenous approach to genuine and effective work means that victims of trafficking or modern-day slavery may struggle to assert their rights as an EEA worker. This, combined with the inadequacies of Home Office support for victims of trafficking, can leave EEA nationals in particularly vulnerable positions.

Krzysztof (continued from chapter five)

Before Krzysztof's run of employment, he had been a victim of trafficking. He received a positive decision identifying him as a victim of trafficking (known as a 'conclusive grounds' decision) from the Nationals Referral Mechanism (NRM), the UK system that identifies and supports victims of modern slavery. However, he was not granted discretionary leave which meant that after the 45-day 'recovery and reflection period' provided to those in the NRM, Krzysztof had to support himself or rely on his EU rights to access support.[62]

During this time, Krzysztof began working again, but left a full-time job due to difficult personal circumstances stemming from the trauma he had faced as a victim of trafficking. He then took on full-time temporary work that lasted just three weeks. His application for Jobseeker's Allowance was refused as he was deemed not to have had worker status for this second period of employment.[63]

[60] *JA v. SSWP* [2012] UKUT 122 (AAC).

[61] DWP (n 5) [C1492].

[62] Those with discretionary leave are exempt from the habitual residence test for at least 30 months; 'the most recent Home Office statistics show just 12% of confirmed [victims of trafficking] are granted this type of leave' in ATLEU 'Legal aid and immigration advice for victims of modern slavery' (April 2018), www.atleu.org.uk/news/legalaidimmigrationadvice.

[63] As discussed in ch 5 at 5.4.

Krzysztof had gone through the process of being officially identified as a victim of trafficking, receiving the support that comes with this and had gone on to find full-time employment. The support offered by the Home Office (including accommodation in a safe house) and the limited 45 day period of 'reflection and recovery' is criticised by charities as inadequate, abandoning victims of trafficking and modern-day slavery almost as soon as they are recognised as vulnerable.[64] The shortfalls in support are significant and can create temporary or ongoing barriers to rebuilding lives and specifically rejoining the labour market due to unstable accommodation, impacting physical and mental health and risking re-traumatisation.[65] Krzysztof's application for Jobseeker's Allowance was refused with no consideration of his personal circumstances as a victim of trafficking, or how this impacted on his ability to stay in his initial full-time employment.

Such decisions and refusals of support for EEA workers in these situations could risk further vulnerability, re-traumatisation or forcing individuals back into situations of exploitation and abuse.

6.3.5. Ongoing Impact

The inability to consider personal circumstances comes into even sharper focus when looking at the added value that should be gained from having worker status. The initial finding of worker status opens up the ability to retain worker status or establish other residence rights through permanent residence or derivative rights, such as where EEA national's children are in education.[66] By binding these rights to an inadequate assessment of worker status as a point of access, periods of time where an EEA national does not have worker status could deactivate routes to these rights of residence. For example, Marta's case shows some of the knock on-effect of a negative worker decision.

Marta

Marta lived in the UK with her 16-year-old daughter Francisca since 2011. After a period of work from June 2014 to March 2017, Marta was advised to stop working due to ill health. She applied for ESA, which was refused after finding that she did not have a right to reside (no details were recorded about this claim). Subsequently, Marta struggled to make ends meet and got into

[64] S Ferrell-Schweppenstedde, 'Day 46: Is there life after the Safe House for Survivors of Modern Slavery?' (Human Trafficking Foundation, October 2016).

[65] ibid 5, British Red Cross, 'Hope for the future: Support for survivors of trafficking after the National Referral Mechanism' (July 2019).

[66] See ch 3 at 3.2.

rent arrears. By the time she requested advice from the AIRE Centre in June 2018, Marta had received a court order to vacate the property. She went to an interview for housing assistance at her local council, where they assessed her right to reside and found that her work was not genuine and effective because she earned less than the MET:

> You previously worked from [June 2014–March 2017] as a cleaner. You had a contract to work 16 hours per week and your income was £99.20 per week. This is below the [MET] which is currently £162 per week.

The council then considered if she had a potential derivative right to reside as a primary carer of a worker's child in education.[67] These regulations emulate the rights found in the *Baumbast*, *Ibrahim* and *Teixeira* case law:[68]

> [I]t is acknowledged that you have a dependent child who is in full time education. I have therefore considered whether you could be said to have a derivative right of residence .... However, this right does not apply in your case because you are not currently working and your previous employment cannot be regarded as genuine and effective.

The finding that Marta's work was not 'genuine and effective' meant that she could neither retain the status nor acquire a derivative right to reside. While the initial finding on worker status can be challenged, as the MET was treated as determinative, a recognition of Marta's individual circumstances as a lone parent and as someone with health conditions could have eased the expectations on her. This decision can have devasting impacts, such as in Marta's case where access to means-tested welfare benefits is lost and she is left facing eviction and potential homelessness. This impact also extends to the rights of her daughter who, if worker status had been found, would have her free movement rights including her access to education.[69]

Flexible working arrangements and atypical work can play an important role in opening access to the labour market for those who are excluded from or not able to take on full-time work. Yet, if those relying on atypical work are excluded from the benefits associated with worker status or triggered after work, this structural discrimination is only exacerbated. Without recognising where Member States' interpretations of worker status limit its applicability to a diverse range of

[67] The Immigration (European Economic Area) Regulations 2016, SI 2016/1052, Reg 15A(3).

[68] Case C-413/99 *Baumbast* ECLI:EU:C:2002:493, [2002] ECR I-07091; Case C-480/08 *Teixeira* ECLI:EU:C:2010:83, [2010] ECR I-01107; Case C-310/08 *Ibrahim* ECLI:EU:C:2010:80, [2010] ECR I-01065.

[69] Case C-413/99 *Baumbast* (n 68) [71].

workers, the EU risks worker status being reserved only for those who do not face structural discrimination or exceptional circumstances. Disregarding personal circumstances and withholding worker status can become even more unreasonable when considering the labour of informal carers.

6.4. Discrediting the Value of Informal Care

Informal care, particularly when accompanied with Carer's Allowance, teeters on the definitional edge of work. While the 'unpaid' care provided by family and friends has been described by the former Minister of State for Disabled People as 'an invaluable service',[70] a DWP briefing paper states clearly that Carer's Allowance 'is not a payment for care provided or a "carer's wage"'.[71] The intention of the benefit has been recognised as the provision of 'a measure of income maintenance' for those who 'had forgone the opportunity of full-time employment in order to care for a severely disabled relative'.[72]

Nevertheless, carers in the UK are generally exempt from expectations to take on work. A 2007 Work and Pensions Committee report recognised that receiving a 'income replacement benefit' did not mean that carers should be treated as 'unemployed' and recommended placing no conditionality or compulsion on these carers to seek employment.[73] To reflect this, those with caring responsibilities for 35 hours a week, regardless of whether they receive Carer's Allowance, are exempt from the requirement to look for work when claiming Universal Credit.[74] Like other 'income replacement benefits' and earnings from employment, the receipt of Carer's Allowance triggers credits of Class 1 National Insurance contributions, is taxable and is counted as income for means-tested benefits.[75] Yet, an EEA national's time spent caring, even where it is supported through Carer's Allowance, will not be counted towards genuine and effective economic activity. This means they must meet the same rigid and restrictive worker definition through additional employment alongside their informal care work.

The tendency to overlook unpaid care as work is evident at the EU level, not just in the case of the UK. Excluding informal care from worker status can deprive EU nationals who are providing a service with an economic value of important

[70] 'Making it easier for carers to get government help' (1 December 2014), www.gov.uk/government/news/making-it-easier-for-carers-to-get-government-help.

[71] S Kennedy and M Gheera, 'Carer's Allowance' (House of Commons Briefing Paper, Number 00846, 9 January 2020) 17.

[72] ibid 4; DWP, 'Attendance Allowance, Disability Living Allowance and Carer's Allowance: Retrospective equality impact Assessment' (September 2019) [2.8].

[73] Work and Pensions Committee (n 23) para 187.

[74] UC Regulations, Reg 89(1)(b).

[75] Kennedy and Gheera (n 71) 4.

free movement rights. Hervey points to the treatment of unpaid domestic or caring work as an example of non-traditional work being considered 'outside "true" market activity' and therefore not valuable to the single market and subsequently not included within the scope of EU rights.[76] Family and caring roles are still gendered,[77] meaning that the brunt of precarity disproportionately impacts women.[78] In the UK specifically, women are recorded as constituting 73 per cent of recipients of Carer's Allowance.[79] The failure to accommodate the circumstances of those with unpaid caring responsibilities ignores the extent of restrictions on their ability to work, the value of this care to society and its discriminatory effect on women.

This section first examines the case for unpaid care to be considered work, critiquing the reasonings of the CJEU and UK case law on this issue. It then goes on to examine the paradox created by the earnings threshold of the MET and the earnings restrictions on those who receive Carer's Allowance. Finally, it addresses examples from the case studies to examine how worker status interacts with time spent caring for relatives and friends.

6.4.1. Care as Work

At the EU level, time spent providing informal care to family members has not been included in the definition of work. CJEU case law appears to differentiate between a family member providing care, which is not considered work,[80] and non-familial care work that is remunerated by a care benefit, which AG Tizzano described as 'undoubtedly "effective and genuine activities"'.[81] In the latter case, the CJEU avoided the opportunity to 'take a position' on whether this kind of care is work, instead opting to locate equal treatment rights with national

[76] TK Hervey, 'Migrant workers and their families in the European Union: the pervasive market ideology of Community Law' in J Shaw and G More, *New Legal Dynamics of European Union* (Oxford University Press, 1995) 91, 104.

[77] '[W]omen spend two to ten times more time on unpaid care work than men': G Ferrant, LM Pesando and K Nowacka, 'Unpaid Care Work: The missing link in the analysis of gender gaps in labour outcomes' (OECD Development Centre, December 2014) 2. In the UK, 20% of women said they had unpaid caring responsibilities, and 13% of men: Carers UK (n 38) 10.

[78] '[O]ver 20 million Europeans (two-thirds of whom are women) care for adult dependent persons, which prevents them from having a full-time job' and austerity has been found to have forced 'many people, mainly women, to cut their working hours' to care for dependants, elderly people, ill people or children': European Parliament, 'Motion for a Parliament Resolution on Women Domestic Workers and Carers in the EU' 2015/2094(INI) OJ C-66/30; K Scheiwe, 'EC Law's Unequal Treatment of the Family: The Case Law of the European Court of Justice on Rulings Prohibiting Discrimination on Grounds of Sex and Nationality' (1994) 3 *Social and Legal Studies* 243, 249.

[79] Kennedy and Gheera (n 71) 4.

[80] Case C-77/95 *Züchner* ECLI:EU:C:1996:425, [1996] ECR I-5689.

[81] Joined Cases C-502/01 and C-31/02 *Gaumain-Cerri and Barth*, Opinion of AG Tizzano ECLI:EU:C:2003:649, [2004] ECR I-6483 [130].

carers through the status of EU citizenship.[82] In *Züchner* (which did not relate to migrant work but whether the individual could utilise the protection from sex discrimination in Directive 79/7/EEC requiring her to be in the 'working population'),[83] a family member providing care on an informal basis was identified as requiring 'a degree of competence' which would have to be 'provided by an outsider in return for remuneration' should the family member be unable to take on the responsibility.[84] However the CJEU determined that it did not fall into the scope of 'work', citing a concern of the potential 'infinite extension' of the Directive or, as O'Brien puts it, an exercise of 'damage limitation'.[85]

The UK's approach has also added to the problems faced by carers. The UK courts have taken the approach that receipt of Carer's Allowance is not a reflection of economic activity under EU law, whether the recipient is a family member or not. When considering the inclusion of Carer's Allowance in the calculation of the benefit cap, a High Court judgment found that describing 'a household where care was being provided for at least 35 hours a week as workless was somewhat offensive' and that 'reasonable people would recognise that to care for a seriously disabled person is difficult and burdensome and could properly be regarded as work'.[86] However, when looking at the free movement rules, the Upper Tribunal has found that the definition of work does not include the time an EEA national spends providing care, even when in receipt of Carer's Allowance.[87] In an unreported case the Upper Tribunal recognised that the importance of the care provided should not be underestimated,[88] but ultimately decided that the receipt of Carer's Allowance did not reflect the employment relationship requirements found in *Lawrie-Blum*. To come to this conclusion, the Upper Tribunal echoed the distinctions drawn by the CJEU in *Züchner* between an employee receiving remuneration and an informal carer receiving a benefit from the state.[89] The Upper Tribunal judgment also regarded carers as not working under the direction or supervision of the state providing the benefit.[90] However, the conditions attached to the receipt of Carer's Allowance could arguably be viewed as quite clear directions. The requirements to provide care 'regularly and substantially' for a person in receipt of a qualifying disability benefit',[91] for specified minimum hours and to restrict their level of earnings from elsewhere, all closely reflect a level of control

[82] Joined Cases C-502/01 and C-31/02 *Gaumain-Cerri and Barth* ECLI:EU:C:2004:413, [2004] ECR I-6483 [130].

[83] Directive 79/7/EEC on the progressive implementation of the principle of equal treatment for men and women in matters of social security [1979] OJ L6/24.

[84] Case C-77/95 *Züchner* (n 80) [14]–[15].

[85] C O'Brien, 'Social blind spots and monocular policy making: The ECJ's migrant worker model' (2009) 46 *Common Market Law Review* 1107, 1119.

[86] *Hurley and Ors v. SSWP* [2015] EWHC 3382 [28].

[87] *JS v SSWP (IS)* [2019] UKUT 135 (AAC) [5]; *M and S v SSHD* [2018] UKAITUR EA045132017 [15].

[88] *M and S v SSHD* (n 87) [13].

[89] ibid [14].

[90] ibid.

[91] Kennedy and Gheera (n 71) 4.

and direction. Additionally, the 'remuneration' received is conditional on meeting these requirements.[92] Alternatively, should the benefit had been paid to the recipient of services to 'remunerate' the care, rather than directly to the carer themselves, it may be more likely to be recognised as akin to employment.

The conclusion that care is not of 'genuine economic value', as O'Brien highlights, is contrary to the fact that 'national economies are subsidised to a very significant degree by the unpaid labour of parents and carers'.[93] For example, the economic value and contribution of carers in the UK was calculated at around £132bn a year in 2015.[94] Care work is crucial as it provides an essential service that would otherwise require a paid worker or 'state-funded social care staff at a considerably higher cost to society'.[95] The informal care of family and friends can also support others to be able to work. By treating unpaid care work as a non-economic activity, many EU nationals providing this essential service will not have free movement rights as a worker and, as is explored in the next chapters, will be unlikely to meet the conditions of other free movement rights, particularly as many of them require access to public funds. As a result, these carers may not be able to risk exercising free movement at all.

Noor

Noor is a French national who has lived in the UK for over 12 years. Recently, her long-term British national partner passed away. They were not married.

Noor has not worked during her time in the UK. For the last 12 years, Noor has been a full-time carer for her 12-year-old Disabled son and has been receiving Carer's Allowance and other welfare benefits. Shortly after her partner's death, Noor applied for Universal Credit and this was refused on the basis of her not having a right to reside.

Noor's case reflects some of the long-lasting impact of full-time caring responsibilities being discounted for worker status. Noor has spent the last 12 years providing full-time care for her son and receiving Carer's Allowance for this. This decision meant that Noor cannot claim other means-tested benefits based on having a lawful right to reside. Noor's long period of residence is also treated as lost time. Despite living in the UK for over 12 years, Noor was not able to rely

[92] The Social Security (Invalid Care Allowance) Regulations 1976, SI 1976/409 (Carer's Allowance Regulations), Reg 4(1).

[93] O'Brien (n 3) 94.

[94] L Buckner and S Yeandle, 'Valuing Carers 2015: The Rising Value of Carers' Support' (Carers UK, November 2015) 4, www.carersuk.org/for-professionals/policy/policy-library/valuing-carers-2015.

[95] 'Carers deserve a liveable income' Letter, *The Guardian* (31 March 2015) in Kennedy and Gheera (n 71) 28.

on her time as a carer to be entitled to permanent residence as it would not be counted towards worker status. Neither did Noor's British partner offer a route to establish rights and access to welfare.[96] For many EEA full-time carers, it is only after many years of residence or when facing upheaval in their life and requiring further welfare support, that they discover that they have not worked *enough* to access their EU rights.

6.4.2. The Paradox of the MET and Carer's Allowance

As time spent providing care is not considered work, in order to access free movement rights carers will often rely on establishing a right to reside from additional work.

The UK's approach to the definition of work, in particular the MET, creates a paradox for those receiving Carer's Allowance in the UK where it becomes impossible to meet the requirements for both. Firstly, EEA national carers do not need to establish a right to reside to access Carer's Allowance, they must be habitually resident in fact. However, an EEA national in receipt of Carer's Allowance will still need to establish a right to reside to access other means tested benefits or to secure their future residence status. As discussed above, in order to receive Carer's Allowance, the claimant must be caring for over 35 hours a week[97] and must not earn more than £151 a week.[98] This limit has been reported by several charities as making it 'almost impossible for carers to combine paid work with their caring responsibilities'.[99] Many must face giving up work or reducing hours to provide care.[100] Nevertheless, for EEA nationals needing to combine work and care to establish a right to reside as a worker, these rules make it impossible for their work to be recognised under the MET without falling foul of the Carer's Allowance requirements.

EEA carers looking to establish a right to reside as a worker face the task of earning over the weekly threshold of £242, higher than the earnings limit permitted to continue receiving payment under the Carer's Allowance rules. EEA carers face a dilemma over whether to sacrifice state support for their care work in order to increase their earnings to more easily meet the MET or to find work that earns under the Carer's Allowance limit and rely on the problematic and earnings-focused genuine and effective test. This creates a potential welfare no-man's-land where a carer could earn over £151 but below £242 and risk being ineligible for either Carer's Allowance or other benefits that require a right to reside.

[96] Directive 2004/38, Art 3(1).

[97] Carer's Allowance Regulations, Reg 4(1).

[98] Carer's Allowance Regulations, Reg 8(1); DWP, 'Chapter 60 – Carer's Allowance Vol 10 Amendment 40 June 2015' [60025].

[99] Work and Pensions Committee (n 23) para 164.

[100] 5% of UK adults have given up work to provide care for an ill, Disabled or older relative or friend. A further 4% had reduced their hours. This equates to 2.6 million people: Carers UK (n 38) 9.

Additionally, if an EEA national is required to provide care for at least 35 hours, it becomes even more unreasonable to expect them to fit in 22 hours of additional work, if earning minimum wage. The unreasonableness of this expectation is reflected in the rules, discussed above, which exempt other carers in the UK from work requirements in their Universal Credit claim.[101] Many carers report caring for over the 35 hours required for Carer's Allowance.[102] It is therefore likely that EEA national carers, even if sacrificing their eligibility for Carer's Allowance through earning over £151, would have to provide care and work for a combined total of around 57–72 hours a week to meet the MET. This is much higher than the maximum recommended working time of 48 hours a week.[103] While it is not unusual for carers to have this kind of demand on their time, requiring it of EEA carers to establish a lawful right to reside and to access means-tested benefits is discriminatory and far from the promise of equal treatment.

6.4.3. Care and the Second Tier of the Test

Many EEA carers will struggle to meet the demands of the MET. Instead, they will be relying on the second tier of the test. As the ADM leaves little room for consideration of the personal circumstances of workers and any barriers that may prevent them working to the same capacity as others, any EEA worker with care responsibilities will be held to the same standards as other EEA workers free from these commitments.

Laura (continued from chapter five)

Laura lives in the UK with her 13-year-old daughter, Emma. They have both lived in the UK since 2016 and Laura has worked on and off in both employment and self-employment.

Due to ill health, Emma is no longer in full-time education and Laura took on work as a self-employed carer on a casual basis to allow for more flexibility to provide informal care for her daughter.

Laura made an application for Housing Benefit and Council Tax Reduction, which was refused; it was also found that she had no right to reside after a strict application of the MET. A mandatory reconsideration was

[101] Work and Pensions Committee (n 23) para 187; UC Regulations, Reg 89(1)(b).

[102] A third of carers in the UK were recorded as providing care for 50 or more hours in Buckner and Yeandle (n 94) 6.

[103] Directive 2003/88/EC of the European Parliament and of the Council of 4 November 2003 concerning certain aspects of the organisation of working time [2003] OJ L299/9, Art 6(b).

requested by Laura and the decision was upheld. The mandatory reconsideration letter from Slough Council considered Laura's work, finding that:

> As an employed/self-employed EEA national, you are required to be earning above the [MET]. You have informed us that you returned to work on 27/10/17, however your average earnings are below the [MET] and there were periods where you did no work at all.

By ignoring Laura's personal circumstances, the elements of her work history which accommodate care for her daughter are removed of all their context. Instead, Laura's break from and return to work, casual hours and the reduction of income are all referenced as indications of marginal and ancillary work.

The exclusion of carers can go further. Where the ADM lacks clarity and decision-makers turn to their own understanding of the definitions of 'genuine and effective' and 'marginal and ancillary', carers could be excluded from having a right to reside as a worker because of the strenuous nature of their caring responsibilities or where work is seen as a secondary activity.

Naomie (continued from chapter five)

Naomie works as a self-employed housekeeper and is employed casually to distribute leaflets. She is also a full-time carer for her mother and is a lone parent of a four-year-old son. She has been receiving Carer's Allowance since 2014.

She applied for housing assistance from her local council in October 2016. This was refused as she did not meet the MET. Alongside the issues in decision-making discussed previously, the decision-maker discussed the amount of time spent caring for her mother and the earnings limits that would be necessary for Naomie to be receiving Carer's Allowance, concluding that:

> The Carer's Allowance you receive is a welfare benefit and not remuneration for work carried out. To be able to qualify for Carer's Allowance you must not earn more than £110 per week [the limit in 2016]. You must also spend at least 35 hours a week caring for the person and I am satisfied that you care for your mother who is blind for a minimum of 35 hours in her home at [redacted] and receive a Carer's Allowance of £62.10. I am therefore of the view that the housekeeping services you render could only be marginal and ancillary to the support you give to your mother as a carer.

Here, the decision-maker has misunderstood the EU definition of 'genuine and effective' work, instead taking a more literal meaning of 'ancillary' to assume that work must be an EEA national's primary activity. The decision-maker uses the very fact that care work requires high levels of commitment and that Carer's Allowance places restrictions on a person's time and earnings to illustrate that any work alongside this *must* be ancillary to caring. There is no requirement or precedent for 'genuine and effective' work to be interpreted as the primary activity in an individual's life or the activity that takes the most time. This is a problematic approach which would make it almost entirely impossible for an EEA national in receipt of Carer's Allowance to fulfil the requirements for worker status, essentially barring EEA carers from accessing other benefits.

Carers must balance work with care and be mindful of how this may conflict with the earnings limit which, if surpassed, could strip them of Carer's Allowance. Alongside this, the combination of the earnings cap for recipients of Carer's Allowance and the steep level of earnings required to meet the MET can result in a near-automatic disqualification for many EEA carers from worker status. When relying on the second tier of the test, the atypical nature of their work or even the recognition of the pressures of care are used as the very reason to discount them from worker status. Instead, and considering that Carer's Allowance is calculated as income to offset the amount of means-tested benefit received, the UK should count the amount received from Carer's Allowance towards the MET. This would allow EEA carers to meet the threshold without falling foul of the eligibility requirements for Carer's Allowance and act as an indication to decision-makers that time spent caring is neither irrelevant, a burden on the social assistance system nor a counterargument for the genuine and effective test in the second tier. Instead, time spent providing care should be a strong indication of economic integration into the host Member State, through the provision of a service that would otherwise have to be provided and paid for by the state.

Leaving carers out of the protections offered in the free movement of workers framework is particularly illogical when considered alongside the context of an ageing population[104] and looming care crisis across Europe.[105] Going forward, the value of unpaid care should not be neglected and formal inclusion in the EU free movement regime would be welcome. The failure to recognise and adapt to the diversity of workers means that the expectation of work required from EEA

[104] '[T]he over 80 age group is projected to increase its share by 2.5 times between 2008 and 2050': R Fujisawa and F Colombo, 'The long-term care workforce: Overview and strategies to adapt supply to a growing demand' (OECD Health Working Papers no 44, 2009); the number of those over the age of 79 is expected to triple across EU by 2060: A Verashchagina and F Bettio, 'Long term care for the elderly: Provisions and providers in 33 countries' (European Commission, 2012) 62.

[105] There is 'a threat to the supply of long term carers from the decline in the number of people of working age' and from families being less likely to be able to provide informal care in Social Protection Committee and European Commission, 'Adequate social protection for long-term care needs in an ageing society' (Publications Office of the European Union, 2014) 33.33; R Horton, 'Caring for adults in the EU: Work–life balance and challenges for EU law' (2015) 37 *Journal of Social Welfare and Family law* 356; by 2032, there is projected to be a shortfall of 160,000 care-givers in England: L Pickard, 'A growing care gap? The supply of unpaid care for older people by their adult children in England to 2032' (2015) 35 *Ageing and Society* 96.

migrant carers is unreasonable. Informal carers face exclusion from the strongest rights and protections in Article 45 TFEU as they are not deemed to be exercising their free movement as workers. Instead, they must rely on the rights of EU citizenship which, as explored in the next chapters, are constrained by a market ideology limiting their utility for those who do not have the correct economic credentials. By failing to establish caring responsibilities as economic activity or to make more nuanced concessions for care in the scope of Article 45 TFEU, the UK and the EU more broadly discredit the work that is combined with care, the contribution of informal carers and risks leaving them out of the free movement framework altogether.

6.5. Summary

The UK has restricted the definition of work to such an extent that it barely resembles the broad and inclusive approach taken by the CJEU. The efforts to 'reduce welfare and cut immigration' through the use of the MET[106] have manifested themselves in the exclusion of many atypical workers from equal treatment rights.

These exclusions can be arbitrary, but they can also result in discrimination by ignoring the structural barriers which force the 'choice' to engage in atypical work. The one-size-fits-all approach to work ignores the diversity of workers who contribute to a large proportion of the atypical workforce alongside the barriers and structural discrimination they face when accessing work. A homogenous approach to expectations is brought into particularly sharp focus when compared to the changes in expectations and easements that would be offered to UK national workers in the same circumstances when receiving Universal Credit. Misleading and incorrect guidance also encourages decision-makers to weigh up irrelevant and inappropriate considerations, sometimes encouraging speculation, to the detriment of low-earning atypical workers.

Case studies from this research also illustrate examples of how specific circumstances of EEA workers present particular barriers to meeting the requirements of worker status such as disability, illness, the responsibilities of lone parents and carers, and the consequences of domestic violence and trafficking. These cases illustrate the problems with a homogenous application of the definition of work, in particular where it can result in creating additional barriers through exclusion from accessing welfare benefits, housing and other public services. Despite protections from discrimination and specific rights and principles in the Charter promoting equality and measures to improve integration, EU institutions have yet

[106] DWP, 'Minimum Earnings Threshold for EEA migrants introduced' (February 2014), www.gov.uk/government/news/minimum-earnings-threshold-for-eea-migrants-introduced.

to act to ensure that access to Article 45 TFEU rights is not limited to only those who face no barriers to the traditional labour market.

Lastly, the example of unpaid carers shows how failing to recognise personal circumstances can make it almost impossible for workers to meet the requirements of the UK's worker test and Carer's Allowance. If care is not capable of constituting economic activity for the purposes of Article 45 TFEU, there should be specific concessions available to carers; for example, the inclusion of income from care benefits or a reduced expectation on what makes genuine and effective activity while caring.

This chapter has also sought to suggest some ways the worker test in the UK could be adapted to be more inclusive of the changing labour market. However, these proposals are UK-specific, whereas the restrictive interpretation of worker status is apparent in a number of Member States.[107] Addressing the shortfalls of worker status could be achieved through legislating an updated and reframed EU concept of work. This could adopt a more precise approach to what 'genuine and effective' work looks like for different workers and explicitly and formally include new and emerging forms of work in the labour market. However, free movement and access to welfare is a politically sensitive topic, attracting reactionary restrictions at the EU level, as will be discussed in the next chapters.[108] Worker status is often perceived as a tool by which Member States exercise control over access to their social security systems,[109] and attempts to widen its scope might be met with resistance and should be dealt with sensitively. A more conducive response could utilise the tools already available. This could include more proactive EU intervention in Member States' attempts to narrow the definition of work. Non-discrimination rights in Article 18 TFEU or in the Charter could also be relied on to ensure that, where Member States have measures to reduce work-related conditionality to access social assistance, due to disability or caring responsibilities, these reductions are replicated for EEA nationals during a worker status assessment. Additionally, the importance of proportionality could be reasserted by EU institutions to direct Member States to consider personal circumstances when assessing worker status – capturing the barriers to the labour market for Disabled workers and those with care responsibilities.

Overall, the lack of explicit inclusion in the EU concept of work alongside the restrictive interpretation of the worker test at the UK level limits the ability of some economically active EU nationals to access rights as a worker under Article 45 TFEU. Adopting an anachronistic conception of work, which can result

[107] O'Brien, Spaventa and De Coninck (n 26) 24–25.
[108] See ch 8 at 8.4.
[109] AP van der Mei, *Free Movement of Persons within the European Community: Cross Border Access to Public Benefits* (Hart Publishing, 2003) 130.

in the exclusion of atypical workers and entrench inequality, cannot be justified on purely economic grounds and instead exposes the entrenched political value judgments taken in the inadequate construction of 'genuine and effective' work. Instead, EEA nationals in atypical work must turn to their status as EU citizens when exercising free movement. As the next chapters will explore, such rights have developed through a rationale of market citizenship and therefore offer little for those who cannot demonstrate the necessary economic credentials.

7

'Citizens of Nowhere'?: The Limitations and Challenges of Supranational Citizenship

7.1. Introduction

The EU's internal market and free movement are integral to the goals of an economically and politically united Europe. It is, then, perhaps not surprising that EU citizenship has been criticised as inappropriately tied to the internal market.[1]

The introduction of EU citizenship saw the consolidation of already existing free movement rights and the extension of free movement to all nationals of the Member States by attempting to decouple it from employment status.[2] It was perceived that the rights entailed in Union citizenship were 'open-ended and w[ould] grow with a passage from union towards federal statehood'.[3] However the creation of this citizenship was quite unique; it is neither a national citizenship nor a replacement for national citizenship. Instead, it sits additional to it, as a supranational citizenship.[4] As Thym identifies, the establishment of a new supranational fundamental status of citizenship would be 'no self-fulfilling prophec[y]' and would need to be more than a ceremonial treaty change.[5]

EU citizenship's potential to expand EU rights to all holders of the status has garnered a lot of interest and critique concerning the nature and aims of the citizenship. Ultimately, this has led many to consider EU citizenship to reflect only the nature and rights expected of a 'market' citizenship.[6] This chapter seeks to

[1] N Nic Shuibhne, 'The Resilience of EU Market Citizenship' (2010) 47 *Common Market Law Review* 1597.

[2] W Maas, *Creating European Citizens* (Rowman and Littlefield Publishers, 2007) 50.

[3] R Bauböck, 'Why European Citizenship? Normative Approaches to Supranational Union' (2007) 8 *Theoretical Inquiries in Law* 453, 460.

[4] Consolidated Version of the Treaty on the Functioning of the European Union [2012] OJ C326/47 (TFEU), Art 20(1).

[5] D Thym, 'The Judicial Deconstruction of Union Citizenship' in D Thym (ed), *Questioning EU Citizenship: Judges and the limits of free movement and solidarity in the EU* (Bloomsbury, 2017) 7.

[6] M Everson, 'The Legacy of the Market Citizen' in J Shaw and G More (eds), *New Legal Dynamics of European Union* (Oxford University Press, 1995); C O'Brien, 'I Trade Therefore I am: Legal Personhood in the European Union' (2013) 50 *Common Market Law Review* 1643; Nic Shuibhne (n 1).

examine how the introduction and evolution of EU citizenship has shaped the extent to which it has decoupled from its economic routes. If it has been successful in expanding social solidarity for not just the economically active, then atypical workers may find solace in their status as an EU citizen and may not have to rely on fitting into the scope of Article 45 TFEU. This chapter therefore examines what the characteristics of EU citizenship and its approach to equal treatment reveal about the limitations of a market 'citizenship' for atypical workers.

This chapter engages with the theoretical expectations of citizenship in general and the literature highlighting the shortfalls of EU citizenship to these expectations, including whether it follows a more social or market-based approach. The chapter sets the current standard of expectations for EU citizenship by taking account of the constraints of the market on available 'rights' and the challenges of establishing solidarity at a supranational level, the result of which is a status that can more accurately be described as a type of market membership where individuals must 'buy-in' to access their full free movement rights, to the exclusion of those whose personal circumstances do not meet the model market member. The chapter builds on previous findings of the book on the exclusion of atypical workers by highlighting the need to test EU market 'citizenships' remit against its ability to protect atypical workers. As such, this research contributes to the debate on free movement for EU citizens by investigating the extent to which an EU market 'citizenship' can protect citizens who are both market actors and potentially reliant on social protections.

It is first helpful to consider the circumstances under which EU citizenship evolved. This is discussed in section 7.2 and highlights whether the realisation of EU citizenship's full potential as a fundamental status is limited by the context of its development. Next, section 7.3 addresses theoretical approaches to social citizenship and contrasts this to 'market' citizenship. The section also conceptualises common expectations of citizenship and establishes two key components that guide the following sections of the chapter: rights and entitlements; and solidarity and participation. When applying this to EU citizenship, section 7.4 examines the rights and entitlements given to all EU citizens. This will address the extent to which rights and access to these rights have expanded or continue to be limited by requiring market engagement. Section 7.5 then focuses on the expectation of solidarity among citizens, as well as the challenges of the EU's solidarity deficit, and critiques the potential to foster solidarity through identity, integration and political participation.

Through these components, EU citizenship emerges as a hopeful concept, which attempts to transcend some of the territorial aspects of national citizenship, but one that cannot be said to have been fully realised. Two main challenges are presented in meeting the expectations of a social citizenship. First, EU citizenship is tied to a market ideology which limits the scope of rights available. Second, the establishment of solidarity among supranational communities has proven to be something of a challenge. Failing to reflect the expectations set out in this chapter reduces the likelihood that atypical workers can rely on this citizenship status to access redistributive arrangements in host Member States.

7.2. Market Origins and Union Citizenship

Before tackling the expectations and components of citizenship, it is first useful to remember the origins of EU citizenship to better understand its unique beginnings and foundations. EU citizenship's construction, from a supranational institution and an internal market, informs how some of the potential shortcomings have come to be.

Critique of EU citizenship regularly focuses on its origin in, and continuing strong association with, the internal market. It is often argued that market ideology has infiltrated the institution of EU citizenship and impacted negatively on many of the expectations of supranational citizenship, the value of identity and integration, the rights available and the conditions by which these rights are accessible. In 1995, Everson critiqued Union citizenship as a compromise between national and supranational interests resulting in a glorification of a market citizen status that simply continues to provide the opportunity to be part of a European single market, if one would choose to, with little in the way of entitlements and rights.[7] EU citizenship would, at this time, have struggled to claim that it has forged new rights based on a social citizenship model, rather it continued to represent a status intrinsically linked to the market. While there have been developments in EU citizenship, including some encompassing of social rights, Everson's critique remains a fitting descriptor and is therefore worth re-examining. The following section will look at the foundations of EU citizenship and critique its entanglement with the internal market.

7.2.1. Market Origins and Enduring Presence

The EU presents its beginnings as a 'purely economic union' with its origins in the European Coal and Steel Community (1951) and then the European Economic Community (1958).[8] It is then said to have expanded to a political union and adopted the name 'European Union' after the Maastricht Treaty (1993). This move reflected the expansion of policy areas now covered by the EU including climate, migration, employment and social affairs. However, to refer to this as a move from the purely economic to political is simplistic and misleading given that the economic is political. Decisions on the objectives of the market, how the market is defined and prioritising economic over social issues are political. Additionally, the notion that the origins of the EU were entirely centred around economic issues is not accurate. Maas documents some of the historical ideas that built the EU we see today, including initial calls for the creation of an economic *and political* union in Europe including a 'continental citizenship' as early as the 1940s.[9] This included

[7] Everson (n 6) 73.

[8] 'The EU in brief: From economic to political union' (Europa), europa.eu/european-union/about-eu/eu-in-brief_en.

[9] Maas (n 2) 12.

the desire for a free and united federal Europe in the Ventotene Manifesto 1941, as a response to the frequent wars in Europe.[10] The presence of more social and political desires in the origins of the EU must be noted, despite its initial beginnings as an economically prioritised unity.

Economic unity in the EU can also be viewed as intrinsically linked to the achievement of more ambitious political goals. While Nic Shuibhne identifies the EU's purpose as to 'encourage, secure, engineer and develop intensive forms of transnational cooperation', she argues that 'The market is a vitally important means through which those ideas are realized'.[11] The centrality of economic integration to the EU is something that 'almost goes without saying'.[12] Many of the rights given to EU citizens appear to be underpinned by, and potentially developed from, the objectives of the single market.

At the emergence of Union citizenship and its formal establishment in the Maastricht Treaty,[13] the EU, by opting to use this terminology, made a link to 'State-citizenship's primeval narrative of … meanings, ideologies and expectations'.[14] Many of these expectations looked for EU citizenship to 'help the Union out of an internal market *impasse*' and begin to realise stable legal rights for all individuals holding the status.[15] Academics, such as Everson, saw Union citizenship as a medium through which problems caused by the legacy of market citizenship could receive 'urgent attention'.[16] Establishing an EU citizenship was therefore, 'part of a desire to enhance the legitimacy of the European project and to bring the European Community closer to the nationals of the Member States'.[17]

However, as highlighted by Nic Shuibhne, Union citizenship appears to have, perhaps inevitably, continued to orientate itself around the internal market given the EU's disproportionate weighting to its economic function compared to that of states. She argues that the EU's main component that makes it 'citizenship-able' is its role as a 'polity' rather than an 'organisation'.[18] This determination is rooted in the acceptance that usually a 'polity is … a formalized and recognized unit having

[10] L Passerini, 'From the Ironies of Identity to the Identity of Irony' in A Pagden (ed), *The Idea of Europe: From Antiquity to the European Union* (Cambridge University Press, 2002) 191, 192.

[11] Nic Shuibhne (n 1) 1608.

[12] S Reynolds, 'Explaining the constitutional drivers behind the perceived judicial preference for free movement over fundamental rights' (2016) 53 *Common Market Law Review* 643, 646.

[13] Consolidated Version of the Treaty on European Union [1992] OJ C 325/5 Art 8 (Maastricht Treaty).

[14] Nic Shuibhne (n 1) 1600.

[15] D Kochenov, 'On Tiles and Pillars: EU Citizenship as a Federal Denominator' in D Kochenov (ed), *EU Citizenship and Federalism: The Role of Rights* (Cambridge University Press, 2017) 3–4.

[16] Everson (n 6) 74.

[17] S Currie, 'The Transformation of Union Citizenship' in M Dougan and S Currie (eds), *50 years of the European treaties: looking back and thinking forward* (Hart Publishing, 2009) 365, 366.

[18] Under O'Leary's definition of citizenship as 'a juridical condition which describes membership of and participation in a defined community or State [carrying] with it a number of rights and duties which are, in themselves, an expression of the political and legal link between the State and the individual'. S O'Leary, *The Evolving Concept of Community Citizenship: From the Free Movement of Persons to Union Citizenship* (Kluwer Law International, 1996).

political, constitutional and economic elements' rather than the EU's reverse order of importance bestowed on economic, constitutional and then political elements.[19] The result of this prioritisation can be witnessed in the balancing of economic aims over fundamental rights or matters of equal treatment.[20] The structural difference provides for a market bias, seen as ingrained into EU citizenship from the outset,[21] or as 'strongly suggest[ing] a market character' for EU citizenship.[22]

7.2.2. Market Orientation's Potential Impact on EU Citizenship

Although the European single market was originally guided by moral aims of 'dealing with the heritage' of World War II and uniting the Member States, Weiler argues that over time this purpose was lost to history, and from the 1990s, the internal market became entirely removed from this moral purpose.[23] Alternatively, Davies suggests that that the EU's market focus could stem from more practical considerations, such as the separate briefs of those concerned with the internal market compared to those engaged with constitutional matters. The consequence of this means that those adjudicating the internal market will 'often see it in economic and technocratic terms'.[24] Whether lost through history or the separation of briefs, such an approach to citizenship is likely to put the needs of the market before those of moral or social concerns.

With all this in mind, Kochenov has warned that an EU citizenship based purely on market considerations would 'provide too thin a foundation for the development of what could aspire to becoming a "real" citizenship'.[25] He argues that an ideological focus on economic integration and the internal market creates 'profoundly insufficient' citizenship rights that lack a 'moral essence'.[26] He further argues that this approach is not 'ethically sustainable' as a citizenship rooted in the success of the market is 'bound to ignore problems and voices not fitting well within its pre-set understanding'.[27] It is certainly the case that a market approach to citizenship holds a risk for those who are not deemed useful to its economic goals,

[19] Nic Shuibhne (n 1) 1601.
[20] Reynolds (n 12); see ch 8 at 8.3.
[21] D Kochenov, 'The Essence of EU Citizenship Emerging From the Last Ten Years of Academic Debate: Beyond the Cherry Blossoms and the Moon' (2013) 62 *International and Comparative Law Quarterly* 97, 110.
[22] Nic Shuibhn (n 1) 1601; Kochenov (n 21) 110.
[23] JHH Weiler, 'Bread and Circus: The State of European Union' (1998) 4 *The Columbia Journal of European Law* 223, 228.
[24] G Davies, 'Services, Citizenship, and the Country of Origin Principle' (Mitchell Working Paper (Edinburgh) No 2/2007) 20.
[25] Kochenov (n 21) 108; I Harden, 'The constitution of the European Union' (1994) *Public Law* 609, 620.
[26] Kochenov (n 21) 111 and 132.
[27] Kochenov (n 15) 15.

including many already marginalised groups. However, these are high standards to set for a supranational citizenship and, in some cases, it exceeds the reality of national citizenships. For Weiler, the establishment of EU citizenship was designed as 'a cynical exercise in public relations'.[28] Rather than shifting the goal posts to an aspirational version of EU citizenship, its potentially limited vision must be accounted for. Locating the value of EU citizenship, even if it must be within the constraints of its market origins, is necessary to avoid negating its achievements and setting it up to fail.

While a basis in the market is flawed, it must be recognised that it does not prevent a citizenship from extending beyond this remit or seeing the marketable value in a 'moral' approach. Nic Shuibhne contends that, while the current market focused citizenship may prove to be a phase of transition,[29] we underestimate the potential of the market as a foundational principle for enhancing rights in Union citizenship.[30] She demonstrates this through highlighting the 'tools-in-waiting' in the current incarnation of market citizenship to achieve further rights, for example where the treaties suggest that purely internal situations could be considered.[31] Not only does Nic Shuibhne recognise potential ways that market citizenship can improve the rights currently available, but also stresses that, in its current form, market citizenship has 'come an incredibly long way'.[32] However, conceiving an increase in citizenship rights within the boundaries of what is beneficial to the market can exacerbate inequalities.[33] A market approach may also create a fracture between the expectations that the concept of 'citizenship' gives to its citizens and the potential reality of EU citizenship.

The EU and its citizenship's origin and focus on the internal market could result in a skewed take on citizenship, where priorities are placed with the market and not on equality and social rights. The concerns discussed in this section suggest that the importance in market activity will continue to play a central role in access to citizenship rights for atypical workers. If this remains the case, the outer edges of the definition for economic activity will also continue to gatekeep these rights. Where ties to the internal market are too strong, rights of citizenship will likely be withheld from those deemed not to contribute *enough* to the market. In the context of this research, atypical workers' citizenship rights may be subject to their supposed value to the market. To examine these concerns, the next section analyses theoretical frameworks

[28] JHH Weiler, 'European Citizenship and Human Rights' in AE Kellermann, B de Witte, DM Curtin and JA Winter (eds), *Reforming the Treaty on European Union: The Legal Debate* (Kluwer Law International, 1996) 68.

[29] Nic Shuibhne (n 1) 1628.

[30] ibid 1615–16.

[31] TFEU, Art 21(1) 'refers to movement and residence "within" – not "across" – the territory of the States'; and Art 26(2) 'simply outlines an area "without internal frontiers", a sufficiently ambiguous reservoir of interpretative potential': Nic Shuibhne (n 1) 1615.

[32] Nic Shuibhne (n 1) 1628.

[33] C O'Brien, *Unity and Adversity: EU Citizenship, Social Justice and the Cautionary Tale of the UK* (Bloomsbury, 2017) 92–95.

of citizenship to compile some common and key expectations for the status. It will also consider where market citizenship, in contrast to social citizenship, sits within these frameworks. These expectations will then be used to inspect whether EU citizenship meets many of the expectations and has broken from its market origins.

7.3. Expectations for Supranational Citizenship

In critically analysing EU citizenship, it is helpful to identify a comparative framework in which supranational citizenship can be analysed. This involves looking at a variety of citizenship models to establish the core expectations of a citizenship and unpicking where this differs for supranational citizenships. Exploring different citizenship frameworks will also provide an opportunity to assess how differing priorities in social and market citizenship can play out. As discussed briefly above, the conception of EU citizenship has often been criticised for its dependency on the market,[34] and has been considered, at best, a market citizenship which has not yet progressed to the status of a social citizenship.[35] Instead of embodying much of the theoretical components and expectations of a citizenship, a market focus creates a clash of opposite ideals resulting in a rather hollow status that disempowers and commodifies the citizen. As such, a market approach to EU citizenship threatens its legitimacy and may be no more than a disguised elite membership where access to 'rights' and freedoms are bought.

National citizenships are not necessarily static models. There are many different formulations of national citizenship and they are all subject to overhauls and tweaks which impact the rights of holders of its status. We should also be cautious when attempting to streamline citizenship into definitive models as 'Citizenship means many different things to different people'.[36] There is no single definition for citizenship, as different aspects will be prioritised, emphasised or constructed depending on 'different social and historical contexts, or to fit different ideological or philosophical perspectives'.[37] It is also necessary to recognise, as Maas has, that different levels of citizenship exist at sub-state, state, suprastate and non-state political communities, resulting in different formulations of a citizenship status.[38] However, it is equally important that we avoid the notion that EU citizenship is so unique 'that no analysis is possible or worthwhile'.[39] Instead, rather than approaching EU citizenship with an 'unsatisfying shrug',[40]

[34] Bauböck (n 3).
[35] Everson (n 6) 73; Nic Shuibhne (n 1) 1597.
[36] Everson (n 6) 81–82.
[37] Nic Shuibhne (n 1) 1600.
[38] W Maas, 'Varieties of Multilevel Citizenship' in W Maas (ed), *Multilevel Citizenship* (Pennsylvania Press, 2013).
[39] ibid.
[40] R Schutze, 'On "Federal Ground": The European Union as an (Inter)National Phenomenon' (2009) 46 *Common Market Law Review* 1069, 1091.

we must hold it to external standards and measure its progress,[41] and not treat it as 'incomparable with other varieties of multilevel citizenship'.[42] Analysing EU citizenship in this way is an important exercise in recognising its value to citizens, the power it gives and the vulnerability it can create if the interests of marginalised groups are ignored. Rather than ignoring EU citizenships failings or areas of improvement, it should be held against different models and expectations. Importantly, this must ensure that the holders of EU citizenship are not misled and unknowingly risk their welfare and security based on a false anticipation of their status as an EU citizen.

This section starts by considering various theoretical conceptions of citizenship and how they fit with the ideas of social and market citizenship. It then explores the discord between the ideas of social and market citizenship in more detail, questioning whether a citizenship embedded in market credentials can be a citizenship at all. Expectations and baselines of citizenship are established, which are then discussed in section 7.4 in relation to EU citizenship.

7.3.1. Identifying Key Components of Citizenship

To begin with, it is useful to briefly outline the core differences between social and market citizenship as the two main concepts framing the debate around EU citizenship.

7.3.1.1. Social Citizenship

Firstly, social citizenship models view the concept of citizenship as inherently social. It requires a community to share a status that dictates how they relate to each other and are treated by governing bodies of the community. In a social citizenship, citizens' rights are not abstract; instead they are 'intricately connected to a social context'.[43] Marshall identified social citizenship as the equal provision of social rights to all citizens such as access to the necessary economic resources and as the essential next step after civil and political rights.[44] Social citizenship is also recognised by Gorham as aiming to benefit a society in the following four ways:

> (1) creating the economic conditions necessary for individuals to pursue their life choices and thus become freer; (2) increasing the general equality in society which

[41] ibid.

[42] Maas (n 38) 6.

[43] D Thym, 'The Evolution of Citizens' Rights in Light of the European Union's Constitutional Development' in D Thym (ed), *Questioning EU Citizenship: Judges and the limits of free movement and solidarity in the EU* (Bloomsbury, 2017) 112.

[44] TH Marshall, *Citizenship and Social Class* ([1949] Pluto Press, 1992) 8.

> helps lessen class tensions; consequently, (3) enhancing political stability; and (4) ensuring the perpetuity of a civilization, of a community to which all can become full, and proud, members.[45]

Under this model, a collective effort towards equality and rights is achieved through the protections given by the state, such as welfare and public services. It captures the idea that 'citizenship is … a refuge from the market' as rights are presented as entitlements, not as rewards or provisions for economic contribution, 'but because they are human and members of a community that transcends the boundaries of the market'.[46]

7.3.1.2. Market Citizenship

In contrast, market citizenship prioritises individual responsibility and has introduced a newfound 'obligation to become more self-reliant'.[47] Under market citizenship, government responsibility for social and welfare rights is replaced with 'a new political and social order in which governments are only responsible for helping citizens to help themselves'.[48] Individuals are also perceived differently. They are valued not as individual and equal citizens, but as production factors based on the labour they provide.[49] Everson's work on 'market citizenship', in relation to the EU, highlights the difference between rights, as seen in social citizenship above, and provisions as 'options such as the qualified choice to enter the labour market or to trade'.[50] Here, Everson locates the bulk of market citizenship offerings as 'provisions'.[51] Ultimately the market citizenship attempts to extract the 'social' aspects out of citizenship, instead making it a status focused on individualism and freedom of the market.

With these two brands of citizenship in mind, the key components and expectations of citizenship can be examined more thoroughly by considering how they relate to or are ignored by social or market citizenship. Examining this helps to identify the themes, aims and priorities of citizenship in more detail, including where different models of citizenship strike the balance between rights and obligations. This also begins to disentangle the reality of a citizenship status tied up in market dependency and citizens' value as a production factor.

[45] E Gorham, 'Social Citizenship and its Fetters' (1995) 28 *Polity* 25, 26.
[46] ibid 35.
[47] J Brodie. 'Restructuring and the New Citizenship' in I Bakker (ed), *Rethinking Restructuring: Gender and Change in Canada* (University of Toronto Press, 1996) 126, 131 cited in J Fudge, 'After Industrial Citizenship: Market Citizenship Or Citizenship at Work?' (2005) 60 *Industrial Relations* 631, 645.
[48] Fudge (n 47) 645.
[49] AP van der Mei, *Free Movement of Persons within the European Community. Cross Border Access to Public Benefits* (Hart Publishing, 2003) 23.
[50] Everson (n 6) 83.
[51] ibid 87.

7.3.1.3. Components of Citizenship

Despite centuries of academic debate, citizenship remains a 'contested and normative concept' of which 'there are no authoritative definitions'.[52] Nevertheless, patterns of identified key concepts and theories have emerged. For example, Delanty has identified four key features of modern citizenships: rights; duties; participation; and identity.[53] This is almost mirrored in Bellamy's work which finds that contemporary citizenships feature the key components of rights, participation and solidarity.[54] In this example, 'participation' can be interpreted as a duty to be actively involved in the community, and 'solidarity' can be said to reflect Delanty's notion of 'identity' in the sense that it reflects membership to a community. Additionally, Bartle identifies three traditional notions of 'citizenship-as-rights', 'citizenship-as-belonging' and 'citizenship-as-participation'.[55] O'Leary also offers a model of citizenship as:

> A juridical condition which describes membership of and participation in a defined community or State [carrying] with it a number of rights and duties which are, in themselves, an expression of the political and legal link between the State and the individual[56]

With these in mind, a brief look at academic work on citizenship will reveal repetitions of three popular ideas which I have categorised as: rights and duties; and solidarity and participation.

As an alternative, Kochenov offers a different set of key components in his work specifically looking at EU citizenship; identifying elements of justice, political participation and equality as providing 'a sound foundation for a supranational citizenship'.[57] Some of these requirements echo the ideas noted above; justice and equality reflect much of the content in rights and solidarity and the need for inclusion is similar to political participation. However, Kochenov goes a step further by requiring citizenship to display a moral purpose in the drive of each three components. This approach idealises the concept of citizenship beyond its exclusionary nature; citizenship is not necessarily an inherently moral construct. Where citizenship exists, individuals may have more rights or opportunities depending on the citizenship they hold. Carens highlights that this can be interpreted as 'the modern equivalent of feudal privilege – an inherited status that greatly enhances one's life chances'.[58] The status of citizenship provides the state with an excuse to

[52] T Faist, 'Social Citizenship in the European Union: Nested Membership' (2001) 39 *Journal of Common Market Studies* 37, 40.

[53] G Delanty, *Citizenship in a Global Age: Society, Culture, Politics* (Open University Press, 2010) 9.

[54] R Bellamy, 'Introduction: the Making of Modern Citizenship' in R Bellamy, D Castiglione and E Santoro (eds), *Lineages of European Citizenship* (Palgrave Macmillan, 2004) 6.

[55] I Bartle, 'Political Participation and Market Citizenship in a Global Economy: The European Union in Comparative Perspective' (2006) 29 *International Journal of Public Administration* 415, 417.

[56] O'Leary (n 18).

[57] Kochenov (n 21) 109.

[58] JH Carens, 'Aliens and Citizens: The Case for Open Borders' (1987) 49 *The Review of Politics* 251, 252.

withdraw or fail to provide to resident non-citizens, while citizens themselves can be perceived to benefit from the exclusion of non-citizens through acquiring privileges. It may seem unrealistic to expect a citizenship to hold a moral purpose, when its very nature is exclusionary.

Kochenov's model is an aspirational one, which expects more from supranational citizenship than most national citizenships have yet to achieve. For example, Kochenov argues that 'where equality is not safeguarded, there is no citizenship'.[59] However, inequalities are present and often permitted in many forms of national citizenship. The anticipation of equality, as a measurement of a successful citizenship, may be too steep a demand. Instead, it may be more realistic to expect citizenship to aim for formal equality or to establish provisions where those with certain characteristics experience disadvantages. While it is understandable to set high standards for citizenships, it is not always a helpful way to examine it. Especially when looking at the EU; a supranational institution that requires the support of Member States who would themselves struggle to meet this standard. Nic Shuibhne reminds us that unfair expectations may lead to 'unhelpful disappointment and a fated feeling of failure'.[60] Kochenov's requirements, while important, risks setting the EU up for failure.

Instead, this research will carefully establish expectations to measure EU citizenship and its achievements and flaws whilst also recognising the practical limits of the supranational context. It is important to recognise that much of the academic debate covered here originates from and considers only the evolution of citizenship in so-called 'western' or 'advanced' industrial democracies. In contrast, Chung highlights how citizenships in 'non-western' countries reveal how the concept is contingent.[61] In this respect, the focus on literature concerning so-called 'western' democracies is made relevant as Member States of the EU tend to subscribe to the 'western' formulations and theories of citizenship.

Taking the components identified above – rights and duties; and solidarity and participation – this section next details how each is perceived and what it entails. As these key concepts appear, albeit in differing terms and priorities, in various theoretical studies of citizenship, it is necessary to dive a little deeper into their substance. This will focus on how these concepts are interpreted through liberal, communitarian and republican lenses while beginning to unpick how they interact with social and market citizenship.

[59] D Kochenov, 'Citizenship without Respect: The EU's Troubled Equality Ideal' (2010) Jean Monnet Working Paper (NYU Law School 08/10) 5.

[60] Nic Shuibhne (n 1) 1628.

[61] Chung finds that 'non-western' citizenships are 'characterised by the prioritization of collective regulation over individual rights, contingent membership over universal membership, and subnational and supranational hierarchies over national democratic principles': EA Chung, 'Citizenship in Non-Western Contexts' in A Shachar, R Bauböck, I Bloemraad and M Vink (eds), *The Oxford Handbook of Citizenship* (Open University Press, 2017).

7.3.2. Rights and Duties

In his pivotal work on citizenship in the UK, Marshall argues that citizenship is formed in stages, firstly through civil rights including 'freedom of speech, thought and faith … to own property and … to justice', then political rights with the right to political participation as a representative or as an elector, and lastly, social rights which covers 'the right to a modicum of economic welfare and security … and to live the life of a civilised being according to the standards prevailing in the society'.[62] This theory has not been free from criticism, especially as it reflects the stages that citizenship rights were earned in relation to white males in the UK, forgetting that women, Disabled people and ethnic minorities did not earn these rights at the same time or necessarily in the same order,[63] with some people yet to earn this full assortment of rights depending on their identities, circumstances or country of residence.[64] Marshall also seeks equality for the purpose of eroding class inequality and protecting citizens from market forces, but this fails to recognise or aim to combat 'other key axes of inequality and other mechanisms and arenas of domination'.[65] With this criticism in mind, it is still useful to consider three elements of rights linked to citizenship – civil, political and social – but noting that the order of attainment is not fixed, and provision of each is not necessarily guaranteed to the same extent.

Some liberal approaches to citizenship can echo the requirements of social citizenship as a necessary means of ensuring the realisation of individual freedoms. Marshall recognises that social citizenship and the rights that it entails has a positive relationship with the autonomy necessary to enjoy civil and political rights. For Magnussen and Nilssen, it is also social rights, granted through the welfare state, 'rather than arbitrary benevolence', that provide the requisite social justice and inclusion to ensure that individuals can enjoy the status of citizenship.[66] This approach favours a 'positive' over 'negative' conception of liberty,[67] which recognises the importance of state intervention in ensuring that all citizens have the 'basic level of material well-being' necessary to pursue and enjoy their individual civil and political rights.[68]

However, stricter conceptions of liberal theories prioritise the individual rights of citizens and their freedom to pursue their individual interests in the private sphere. The only derogation from this is the expectation 'to respect in others the rights he or she enjoys'.[69] The purpose of this is to protect individuals from the

[62] Marshall (n 44) 8.

[63] S Walby, 'Is Citizenship Gendered' (1994) 28 *Sociology* 379.

[64] Chung (n 61) 434–35.

[65] N Fraser and L Gordon, 'Contract vs. Charity: Why is there no Social Citizenship in the United States' (1992) 22 *Socialist Review* 45, 49–50 cited in K Sadiq, 'Postcolonial Citizenship' in Shachar, Bauböck, Bloemraad and Vink (n 61) 181.

[66] Magnussen and Nilssen (n 97) 232.

[67] On positive and negative liberty see JJ Rousseau, *Social Contract* (Wordsworth Editions, 1998); I Berlin, 'Two Concepts of Liberty' in H Hardy (ed), *Liberty* (Oxford University Press, 2002) 166.

[68] Lister and Pia (n 80) 12–13.

[69] J Locke, *Two Treatises of Government* ([1683] Everyman, 1993) cited in Lister and Pia (n 80) 10.

imposition of obligations from the community or state 'that constrain or contradict his or her self-interest'.[70] Obligations to others are to be kept to an absolute minimum. This is where market citizenship can link in with liberal theories, reflecting the notions of individual responsibility to look after yourself and demanding reduced state interference. By valuing the freedom of individuals unhindered over any kind of collective responsibility, this approach ignores the impact on those who may be less able to access and enjoy these freedoms. This strict liberal approach is where critique is often concentrated as only certain individuals are valued over the needs of disadvantaged individuals or the collective.

Alternative focus is offered with communitarian and republican theories. These both approach the challenge of ensuring citizens have equal access to rights through the focus of achieving the common good, rather than what will enable individuals to live freely. In seeking the public good, communitarian theorists, such as Etzioni, recognise that an overwhelming pursuit of individual liberty can result in the concerns of a community or a common good being ignored, and rights for all jeopardised.[71] While individual rights are not deemed unimportant, they can sometimes take a back seat to what is seen as good for the community. Critics of this approach are concerned with where control lies in determining what the 'public good' will be, whether the rights of those who disagree with these decisions are protected, and finally the extent to which individual rights may be sacrificed for a perceived 'public good' such as public security.[72]

The clearest conflict between theories here lies between negative conceptions of rights which prioritise individual freedoms and positive rights which takes account of the accessibility of freedoms to all citizens.[73] Where rights in citizenship are expressed as a negative liberty, little effort is made to ensure that the right has any value for all or even most citizens. Some citizens may struggle to pursue a freedom, such as freedom of movement, due to limited choices and availability, and some may struggle to see the full realisation of that freedom without measures in place to support access, such as social protections in a host Member State. In the case of atypical workers and free movement, the option may exist to move to another Member State, but without more positive conceptions of this right, the support necessary for many to sustain this option is unavailable.

7.3.3. Solidarity and Participation

The other key concepts of citizenship – solidarity and participation – can be seen as the mechanism by which the 'common good' in communitarian and

[70] K Faulks, *Citizenship* (Routledge, 2000) 57 cited in Lister and Pia (n 80) 10.

[71] A Etzioni, *The Spirit of Community: rights, responsibilities and the communitarian agenda* (Fontana Press, 1995).

[72] Lister and Pia (n 80) 20.

[73] On positive rights as necessary to be free see Rousseau (n 67); on negative rights as the liberty and positive rights as a means for advancing totalitarian ideals see Berlin (n 67).

republican thinking, and the social policy to support individual rights in liberalism, can be achieved.

Communitarian theory sees the goal of ensuring common good within communities as requiring and fostering a shared identity and solidarity – solidarity is often required to ensure that social rights are secured and supported. As mentioned above, social citizenship is best achieved through the provision of social rights, most frequently institutionalised in a welfare state. The success of a welfare state relies on diffuse solidarity between members of a political community[74] in order to ensure that there is a mutual commitment to the moral good of redistributive social policy. It should also be noted that this is considered a cyclical process; the support provided by a welfare state corresponds to the 'moral orientations and expectations of citizens',[75] which leads to promoted feelings of solidarity and mutual obligation,[76] resulting in 'considerable public support' in the legitimacy of the welfare state and social citizenship.[77]

Without some solidarity between all citizens and the beneficiaries of the welfare state, this construction of social citizenship cannot be realised. This is clearly reflected in the territorial nature of welfare states, where, like national states, ease of access to social assistance discriminates between insiders and outsiders, or in this case nationals and non-nationals.[78] Communitarianism faces a similar criticism for regarding the duty to achieve the common good to be reliant on a type of solidarity that is formed around identity. However, a focus on identity limits the scope of this solidarity to only those who are in the community, at the exclusion of those who are not.[79] The lines drawn to determine who benefits from this common good can exclude individuals who may not conform to the duties expected of them in the community[80] or can lead to exclusion based on ethno-nationalism.[81]

Republicanism,[82] while recognising the need to achieve public good and individual rights, sees participation in the public sphere as the vital component to achieving this, rather than solidarity. Participation is seen as a tool to prevent relations of dominance, something which the prioritisation on individual rights

[74] Faist (n 52) 40; Solidarity is also described as the '*sine qua non*' of the welfare state in W Lamping, 'Mission Impossible? Limits and perils of Institutionalizing Post-National Social Policy' in M Ross and Y Borgmann-Prebil (eds), *Promoting Solidarity in the European Union* (Oxford University Press, 2010) 49.

[75] Lamping (n 74) 48.

[76] RM Titmuss, *Commitment to Welfare* (Unwin University Books, 1968) cited in Lamping (n 74) 48.

[77] B Rothstein, *Just Institutions Matter: The Moral and Political Logic of the Universal Welfare State* (Cambridge University Press, 1998) cited in Lamping (n 74) 48.

[78] A de Swaan, 'Perspectives for Transnational Social Policy' (1992) 27 *Government and Opposition* 33.

[79] Delanty (n 53) 27.

[80] M Lister and E Pia, *Citizenship in Contemporary Europe* (Edinburgh University Press, 2008) 8, 20.

[81] See section 7.5.1.

[82] Which is often conflated with communitarianism, while both focus on community and the public good, republicanism view legitimacy for social policy coming from political participation rather than solidarity see Maas (n 38) 5.

in liberalism ignores.[83] As a component of participation, different social groups should be active in pressing for their concerns – preventing one group from dominating the other.[84] It is in this way that republicanism envisages the achievement of equality, as otherwise there is a risk that one group will be dominant and have more rights than others. Participation also has a role in the realisation of social rights in citizenships. Social rights, especially those that require high levels of redistribution and solidarity, require a legitimate and justified institution to implement them.[85] Active political participation among citizens can fill a democratic deficit and help legitimise the political institutions in social citizenship.

In contrast, liberal approaches to these ideals are compounded in the same rights and duties discussed above. It is perceived, as Marshall puts it, that citizenship is an instrument to foster membership through the granting of equal individual rights to all.[86] Equally, participation is deemed as an important political right granted to citizens. In Marshall's conception of the stages of rights in citizenship, discussed above, political rights emulate much of the requirements of participation, such as the right to act as a representative or as an elector.[87] Liberalism therefore treats the very rights and duties provided by citizenship as establishing a cause for participation.

However, strict liberal approaches to this requires only the availability of the option to engage in participation and community solidarity.

This approach reflects closely with the absence of solidarity in market citizenship. Instead, the importance of social solidarity to achieve equality among citizens is substituted for self-realisation and self-interest of individual citizens.[88] In this sense there is no need for a market citizenship to be concerned with the overall good of the community as individuals are supposed to have the freedom to pursue what is good for them. In this environment, there is little opportunity for the creation of solidarity or 'allegiance' amongst market citizens who are guided by self-interest.[89] Solidarity to facilitate effective social policy is therefore unnecessary. Market citizenship also struggles to sit comfortably with the demand for political participation, as rather than envisioning citizens as 'collaborative partners' they are instead seen as 'consumers', 'clients' or as a production factor.[90] This risks increasing the legitimacy deficit with market citizenship.

Viewing these traditional ideas of citizenship through the lens of both social and market citizenship begins to unpick the shortcomings of the latter. Market

[83] P Pettit, *Republicanism: a theory of freedom and government* (Clarendon Press 1997).

[84] Q Skinner, 'Machiavelli on the Maintenance of Liberty' (1983) 18 *Politics* 3 cited in Lister and Pia (n 80) 24.

[85] Lamping (n 74) 47.

[86] Marshall (n 44).

[87] ibid 8.

[88] J Hayward, 'From Citizen Solidarity to Self-Serving Inequality: Social Solidarity, Market Economy and Welfare Statecraft' in J Connelly and J Hayward (eds), *The Withering of the Welfare State* (Palgrave Macmillan, 2012) 1.

[89] Everson (n 6) 89.

[90] Bartle (n 55) 418.

'citizenship' fails on many counts to interact with, effectively or at all, the key components of citizenship. Failing to integrate elements of rights for all, building solidarity for fellow citizens and encouraging political participation leads to a hollow status where differing priorities disempowers its citizens.

7.3.4. Equality and Empowerment in Citizenships

Notably, the pursuit of equality appears to be one key theme that intertwines the three strands of liberal, communitarian and republican contemporary citizenship theory. While the pursuit of equality is present in each, the three theories 'advance alternative perspectives' on the best way to realise freedom and equality among all citizens.[91] Liberalism seeks equality through universal rights for individuals to pursue freedom and interests, and is therefore seen to have 'an egalitarian impulse at its heart'.[92] Communitarianism pursues equality through 'acting in accordance with the shared understandings of its members'[93] to achieve good for all through notions of solidarity and community. Republicanism attempts to establish equality through recognition of the community's diverse citizens, where 'solidarity may be realized less through cultural commonality than intersubjective recognition and interaction',[94] stressing the importance of participation for all social groups.

It is widely held that the mark of a successful society can be measured by how it treats its most vulnerable members.[95] Social and economic rights for all therefore plays an important role as a litmus test of a civilised country and the citizenship which that country offers. Citizenship should therefore be a vehicle through which social justice is achieved. In other words, social rights to meet basic needs for income, shelter and living necessities should be perceived as a 'right of citizenship'.[96] From this, a key consideration for citizenships is posed; are individual rights maintained for people who are not able to 'claim' or 'earn' them through market credentials?[97] As discussed above, the anticipation of equality is not reflective of the reality often experienced by citizens. Instead, this core aspect of citizenship must be identified as a minimum of baseline provisions to address the inequalities for those with certain characteristics or – more specifically within market citizenship – those who face barriers to engage with the market. Failing to account for these structural barriers will lead to citizens being actively excluded from these rights.

[91] P Honohan, 'Liberal and Republican Conceptions of Citizenship' in Contexts' in Shachar, Bauböck, Bloemraad and Vink (n 61) 101.

[92] Lister and Pia (n 80) 9.

[93] M Walzer, *Spheres of Justice* (Basic Books, 1983) cited in Lister and Pia (n 80) 20–22.

[94] Honohan (n 91) 97.

[95] This quote is often attributed to Mahatma Ghandi and is widely repeated.

[96] Commission on Social Justice, *Social Justice: Strategies for National Renewal* (Vintage, 1994) 18.

[97] AM Magnussen and E Nilssen, 'Juridification and the Construction of Social Citizenship' (2013) 40 *Journal of Law and Society* 228, 232.

Market citizenship, however, falls short of this expectation, particularly when adopting a strict liberal approach, concentrating on the freedom of individuals to pursue their own goals with little responsibility to care for others. Rather than providing support for the most vulnerable in society and respecting the equal worth of all citizens, market citizenship instead awards citizens on the, often arbitrary, criteria of market engagement or wealth. An approach so absorbed in promoting individualism and self-interest results in the social rights and policies that should be 'implied by citizenship',[98] being ignored or neglected.

Empowerment of citizens is a further baseline expectation of the status of citizenship. This can be understood as the power to be free from reliance on the market, and therefore a goal of citizenship should be to decommodify its citizens. Esping-Anderson defines decommodification of citizens as when a 'person can maintain a livelihood without reliance on the market' and instead the services of citizenship are 'rendered as a matter of rights'.[99] In social citizenship, citizens can be effectively decommodified through the mobilisation of societies, solidarity and ultimately the provision of a welfare state that provides a basic standard of living,[100] which means that inability or lack of opportunity to engage with the market does not result in destitution.[101] In this instance, those who are not able to work, either at all or not to the same extent as others, or those who cannot find work, are protected.

In contrast, market citizenship does not offer this protection; rights or freedoms are rewarded on the basis of performance in the market rather than through citizenship,[102] resulting in almost all citizens being dependent 'on both the[ir] personal characteristics … and prevailing labour demands'.[103] Alongside this, in keeping state interference minimal and individualism promoted, social rights are 'severely curtailed', the result of which is the expansion of 'the obligation to be employed'.[104] Market citizenship therefore appears to disempower and commodify the citizen.

Citizenship comes with a number of expectations and baselines around the idea that 'the foundation of a free society is the equal worth of all citizens'.[105] Not only does market citizenship fail to rearticulate the expectations found in theoretical debates of citizenship, but it also fails to address the inequality in access to the

[98] Faist (n 52) 51.
[99] G Esping-Anderson, *The Three Worlds of Welfare Capitalism* (Polity Press 1990) 41–43.
[100] M Ferrera, 'Towards an "Open" Social Citizenship? The New Boundaries of Welfare in the European Union' in G de Búrca (ed), *EU Law and the Welfare State: In Search of Solidarity* (Oxford University Press, 2005) 23.
[101] S Shaw, 'Comparative Welfare' in P Dwyer and S Shaw (eds), *An Introduction to Social Policy* (Sage, 2013) 177.
[102] Rather than where 'social rights are … granted on the basis of citizenship rather than performance, they will entail a de-commodification of the status of individuals vis-à-vis the market' in Esping-Anderson (n 99) 40.
[103] Everson (n 6) 84.
[104] Fudge (n 48) 645.
[105] Commission on Social Justice (n 96) 17–18.

market, protecting the most vulnerable and to empower and decommodify its citizens. Market citizenship struggles to resemble anything close to what is expected from the status of citizenship. Instead, it appears to be a misnomer, for a set of rights which are pitched as available to all but in reality are exclusively available to those who are 'sufficiently' integrated into the market. Atypical workers in this model should be commended for their integration in the market, but in reality may find that they are deemed to not work *enough* to have earnt market citizenship rights.

7.3.5. Expectations of Citizenship

The aim of this section has been to analyse theories of citizenship to determine criteria against which EU citizenship can be assessed. However, it is important to recognise that 'there is, to greater and lesser degrees, blurring of the boundaries between'[106] different citizenship theories and that various academics have breached the gaps between them.[107] Taking this into account, and the assertions above that citizenship can vary greatly across multiple levels of governance and contexts, instead of modelling an exact single formula for citizenship, it is more prudent to pick out some of the expectations we can anticipate EU citizenship to fulfil. Using this approach, this section measures the extent to which EU citizenship interacts with the expectations and delivers on them.

Two key expectations of citizenship have emerged from the analysis above, and these form the basis of assessment of EU citizenship:

(i) The establishment of *rights and entitlements* covering the grounds of civil, political and social rights versus provisions.
(ii) The notion of membership of a community denoting a sense of *solidarity* which encourages and is enhanced by citizens enacting duties or *participating* in public and political life.

A third expectation concerning the active pursuit of equality for citizens extends across both the establishment of rights and solidarity. The analysis of how EU citizenship engages with the two components listed above will therefore consider the impact this may have on *equality*. Additionally, equality considerations will play an important role when analysing how atypical workers may be able to rely on their EU citizenship rights in chapter eight.

The following sections address expectations (i) and (ii) identified above and transpose them on to EU citizenship, starting with rights in section 7.4 and then

[106] Lister and Pia (n 80) 30.
[107] Lister and Pia (n 80) 30–31; for liberal communitarianism see Delanty (n 53); for liberal republicanism see R Dagger, 'Republican Citizenship' in EF Isin and BS Turner (eds), *Handbook of Citizenship Studies* (Sage Publishing, 2002); for overlaps between republicanism and communitarianism see W Kymlicka, *Contemporary Political Philosophy*, 2nd edn (Oxford University Press, 2000); Maas (n 38) 5.

looking closer at solidarity and participation in section 7.5. These discussions will also utilise these expectations to examine whether EU citizenship has expanded from its market roots to a social citizenship, or whether, by remaining a form of a market 'citizenship' or membership, it is unlikely to provide a route through which atypical workers can enjoy free movement rights, without having to meet a standard of market credentials.

7.4. The Rights and Entitlements of Union Citizenship

While the EU's ability to provide universal rights has traditionally been restrained by both its market focus and the limitations of its competence due to its institutional status as a supranational body, EU citizenship introduced the prospect and anticipation for notable advances in the rights and entitlements available. This section will therefore consider some of the ways that Union citizenship has either enhanced, protected or provided rights to its citizens. First, it will look at how EU citizenship has sought to enhance the scope of free movement, ensuring that rights in EU law are available to all mobile Union citizens. Secondly, it will cover the ability of Union citizens to choose their Member State of residence and enjoy free movement rights. Finally, the section will examine how EU citizenship protects access to EU rights by engaging with and restricting Member States from gatekeeping these rights through decisions on nationality law.

7.4.1. Enhancing the Scope of EU Law

For Spaventa, Union citizenship has had 'far-reaching effects' and has 'overwhelmingly enlarged' the scope of EU law in its personal and material application.[108] It has achieved this in two main ways: firstly, through enhancing the scope of the *rationae persone* test and subsequently the scope of the economic freedoms; and secondly, through forcing a reassessment of the CJEU's approach to what was previously considered purely internal matters.

Since the introduction of EU citizenship, arguably any Union citizen can now fall 'within the personal scope of the Treaty, regardless of'[109] the economic link that was previously required.[110] The consequence was that the scope of who could use EU law was extended from only workers and their family members to supposedly

[108] E Spaventa, 'Seeing the Wood Despite the Trees? On the Scope of Union Citizenship and its Constitutional Effects' (2008) 45 *Common Market Law Review* 13, 44; Kochenov (n 21) 119.

[109] Spaventa (n 108) 44.

[110] 'Under this test, three criteria ("limbs") have to be satisfied: a) the exercise of inter-state movement; b) the taking up of an economic activity; and c) the impediment to inter-state movement': A Tryfonidou, 'In Search of the Aim of the EC Free Movement of Persons Provisions: Has the Court of Justice Missed the Point?' (2009) 46 *Common Market Law Review* 1591, 1592–95.

all Union citizens who exercised free movement. This enlarged the potential scope 'from less than 2.3 per cent of Member States nationals to 100 per cent'.[111] Union citizens could now theoretically challenge Member State rules where they limit 'residence or discriminate on grounds of nationality'.[112]

However, the number of Union citizens who exercise free movement is relatively small.[113] For those that can, the CJEU has found that the scope of EU law extends to Union citizens so long as they establish their 'cross-border credentials'.[114] There are some limited exceptions to the cross-border requirement, such as that seen in *Zambrano* (here derivative residence rights are provided to the primary carers of Member State national children, where a finding that the primary carer does not have a right of residence would limit the child's 'genuine enjoyment of the substance' of EU citizenship rights).[115] And where EU law was found to extend to some non-mobile EU citizens in their home Member State.[116] However, these exceptions are very narrow in practice, both in scope and in substance, for example where Zambrano carers have been found to have no access to the UK's social assistance system.[117]

The CJEU has extended the scope of what is sufficiently 'cross-border' to cover some instances that were previously considered to be purely internal. This has included some 'hypothetical cross-border situations',[118] including, but not limited to, potential movements in the future.[119] However, as Nic Shuibhne points out, this approach still 'insists on the need to find some cross-border dimension, even a potential one'.[120] Still, a case relying on a purely hypothetical prospect of future movement or obstructions to that movement will likely fail to establish enough of a connection to warrant the intervention of EU rights.[121]

This debate warrants a more detailed discussion and analysis than there is space for here, especially as this research focuses on those who have exercised free movement and therefore fulfil the cross-border criteria. Nevertheless, for the purposes of assessing the rights of EU citizenship generally, it is worth noting the divide this criterion can create between mobile and non-mobile

[111] Kochenov (n 21) 112.
[112] Spaventa (n 108) 44.
[113] Eurostat found that only 4% of EU citizens of working age live in another EU Member State: 'EU citizens living in another Member State – statistical overview' (April 2018), ec.europa.eu/eurostat/statistics-explained/index.php?title=EU_citizens_living_in_another_Member_State_-_statistical_overview.
[114] E Spaventa, 'Earned Citizenship – Understanding Union Citizenship through Its Scope' in D Kochenov (ed), *EU Citizenship and Federalism: The Role of Rights* (Cambridge University Press, 2017).
[115] Case C-34/09 *Zambrano* ECLI:EU:C:2011:124, [2011] ECR I-1177.
[116] L Azoulai, '"Euro-bonds": The Ruiz Zambrano judgment or the real invention of EU citizenship' (2011) 3 *Perspectives on Federalism* E-31.
[117] C O'Brien, 'Acte cryptique? Zambrano, welfare rights, and underclass citizenship in the tale of the missing preliminary reference' (2019) 56 *Common Market Law Review* 1697.
[118] Kochenov (n 21) 120.
[119] Case C-200/02 *Chen* ECLI:EU:C:2004:639, [2004] ECR I-9925; C-34/09 *Zambrano* (n 115); Tryfonidou (n 110) 1592–95.
[120] Nic Shuibhne (n 1) 1615.
[121] Case C-40/11 *Iida* ECLI:EU:C:2012:691, [2013] 1 CMLR 47 [77].

EU citizens – one which Reynolds points out as exacerbating potential inequalities for those who are not able 'to move or find novel ways to satisfy the cross-border condition'.[122] If the scope of EU law is to be implemented with citizens in mind it shouldn't legitimately differentiate 'based on the sole ground that a border has been crossed'.[123] Nor should it construct situations of reverse discrimination, where EU citizens in their home Member State are treated less favourably than their EU migrant counterparts when a situation is deemed to be 'purely internal'. A clear example of this is where EU migrants can utilise EU law to bring certain categories of third-country national (TCN) family members to the host Member State,[124] yet nationals of that Member State who have not exercised free movement cannot rely on these rules and must instead follow the, usually stricter, requirements of national laws.

In still requiring a cross-border dimension, the CJEU has created a relatively trivial divide between citizens that results in the universality of rights and equality 'undergo[ing] something of an ideological battering'.[125] This expansion of scope can also be viewed sceptically as only reinforcing market ties. As 'the potency of cross-border movement' is emphasised in the case law, the guise of facilitating the exercise of movement and residence rights for all citizens mainly facilitates access to the labour market.[126] Through this lens, the enhanced scope can be credited as a success of the internal market and not just of citizenship.

7.4.2. EU Citizens and Free Movement

Union citizenship offers individuals the choice of which Member State to live in. With the introduction of EU citizenship, the ability to move freely within the territory of the Member States was extended to all who held the status 'subject to the limitations and conditions laid down in this Treaty and by the measures adopted to give it effect'.[127] This was previously only available to workers.[128] Directive 2004/38 (Citizens' Rights Directive) now sets out many of these limitations by providing all EU citizens a right of residence in another

[122] S Reynolds, 'Exploring the "intrinsic connection" between free movement and the genuine enjoyment test: reflections on EU citizenship after *Iida*' (2013) *38 European Law Review* 376.

[123] Spaventa (n 108) 44.

[124] Directive 2004/38/EC of 29 April 2004 on the right of citizens of the Union and their family members to move and reside freely within the territory of the Member States [2004] OJ L 158/77, Arts 2, 3, 6 and 7 (Directive 2004/38).

[125] N Nic Shuibhne, 'The European Union and Fundamental Rights: Well in Spirit but Considerably Rumpled in Body?' in P Beaumont, C Lyons and N Walker, *Convergence and Divergence in European Public Law* (Hart Publishing, 2002) 188.

[126] Nic Shuibhne (n 1) 1613.

[127] Now summarised in TFEU, Art 20(2)(a): 'Every citizen of the Union shall have the right to move and reside freely within the territory of the Member States, subject to the limitations and conditions laid down in this Treaty and by the measures adopted to give it effect.' See ch 8 at 8.2.

[128] Previously protected by EC Treaty (Treaty of Rome), Art 39 and Council Regulation (EEC) No 1612/68 of 15 October 1968 on freedom of movement for workers within the Community [1968] OJ L 257/2.

Member State for an initial three-month period without conditions.[129] Residence beyond this period of time is permitted under one of the qualified residence categories.[130] However, Member States' ability to expel EU citizens without a right of residence is limited.[131] While nearly all EU citizens may technically have the freedom to move and reside in any Member State (exceptions to this include where transitional measures are implemented, as discussed below), the right to equal treatment can be withheld from those who do not reside in compliance with Article 7 of the Citizens' Rights Directive. This essentially excludes EU citizens who are considered economically inactive from EU provisions which protect from discrimination based on nationality and creates a significant barrier to enjoying free movement rights. As demonstrated in previous chapters, the requirement for economic activity and the worker status test can also lead to the exclusion of workers in atypical employment, ie the economically active. While the substance of EU citizenship rights in relation to free movement and the limitations to this are covered in more detail in chapter eight, this section looks at the right to free movement stemming from a shared citizenship and the availability of this freedom to *all* citizens.

7.4.2.1. Free Movement for All *Citizens*

Importantly, free movement in the EU has consistently been identified as the most common answer from EU citizens when asked what the EU means to them.[132] Freedom of movement 'amounts to choosing friends, foes, and the law' and, beyond this, the choice of residence can be made based on what certain Member States offer in terms of healthcare, work, education and lifestyle choices.[133]

Kochenov argues that this reflects a federalist approach 'connecting the choice of jurisdiction and liberty'.[134] But it must also be recognised that many federal states have their limits when it comes to internal migration. For example, there are restrictions on professional qualifications and denial of health coverage for several months when moving provinces in Canada, different privileges are given to those with inherited membership to the province in Quebec which are not available to all Canadian citizens, and different tuition fees apply for in-state and outside-of-state

[129] Directive 2004/38, Art 6. However, Member States can restrict the rights of EU citizens relying on Art 6, such as restricting access to welfare support.

[130] Directive 2004/38, Art 7.

[131] For example, Directive 2004/38, Art 14(2) provides that verification on rights of residence cannot be carried out systematically; Under Art 14(3) expulsion cannot be the automatic consequence of recourse to the social assistance system; expulsion measures cannot be taken against workers, self-employed persons or jobseekers (Art 14(4)) and extra protection against expulsion is provided for long-term residents in Art 28 (see 7.5.2).

[132] Standard Eurobarometer, 'Public Opinion in the European Union' (No 89, March 2018) 71; W Maas, 'Equality and the Free Movement of People: Citizenship and Internal Migration' in W Maas (ed), *Democratic Citizenship and the Free Movement of People* (Martinus Nijhoff Publishers, 2013) 16.

[133] Kochenov (n 21) 130.

[134] ibid.

students in the US.[135] This shows that, while a broader and more open approach to internal migration in the EU can reflect a federalist system this should not be conflated with an expectation of completely barrier-free movement. Instead, Maas argues that federal systems entail 'constant negotiation between governments at different levels, but relative security for individual citizens'.[136]

Nevertheless, if freedom of movement is conceived as available to all EU citizens, then the ability to choose where to reside must be one that is thoroughly protected. Barriers to this choice of residence should be sought to be removed, especially when they limit the effective enjoyment of free movement. Yet, under EU citizenship many obstacles to free movement remain present and active, including perhaps the largest barrier to free movement: the economic focus to the rights of residence.[137] The available routes to establish a right of residence tend to reflect an over-reliance on economic activity as a path to rights. As Ackers and Dwyer put it, entitlement to equal treatment rights is 'by no means universal nor derived simply from Community nationality but turns on notions of contribution and family status'.[138] An overreliance on economic credentials alongside the restrictive interpretation of economic activity further limits the availability of equal treatment rights, reducing it to only those citizens who can demonstrate that they have worked *enough*.

Additionally, other barriers to free movement mirror those seen in the federalist systems above. While the Directive on the recognition of professional qualifications and a policy of mutual recognition exists to smooth the process of transferring qualifications across borders in the EU,[139] professionals from certain Member States whose qualifications were not deemed equivalent can be disadvantaged. Van Riemsdijk highlights this with the undervaluation of Poland's nursing qualifications at the time of accession, resulting in the Commission introducing obstacles to their transfer to other Member States – a decision which was seen as deliberate and influenced by the request to assist with Poland's shortage of nursing staff and Member State concerns of labour market saturation.[140]

Another potential barrier to free movement could be the restriction of political participation and the rights to vote in national elections, held by Nic Shuibhne as 'a defining feature of any citizenship'.[141] The CJEU has not recognised the lack

[135] W Maas, 'Boundries of Political Community in Europe, the US, and Canada' (2017) 39 *Journal of European Integration* 575.
[136] ibid 586.
[137] C O'Brien, 'Civis Capitalist Sum: Class as the New Guiding Principle of EU Free Movement Law' (2016) 53 *Common Market Law Review* 937.
[138] L Ackers and P Dwyer, *Senior Citizenship?: Retirement, migration and welfare in the European Union* (Bristol University Press, 2002) 3.
[139] Directive 2005/36/EC of the European Parliament and of the Council of 7 September 2005 on the recognition of professional qualifications (2005) OJ L 255.
[140] M van Riemsdijk, 'Politics of Free Movement in the European Union: Recognition and Transfer of Professional Qualifications' in W Maas (ed), *Democratic Citizenship and the Free Movement of People* (Martinus Nijhoff Publishers, 2013) 115–43.
[141] Nic Shuibhne (n 1) 1619.

of national voting rights as a barrier to free movement, understandably given the limitations of Union competence. However, the CJEU has been criticised as treating political rights as conditional.[142] Losing a key right associated with nationality, such as voting in their place of residence, could discourage EU citizens from exercising their free movement.[143]

Alongside the various potential barriers facing EU citizens should they wish to consider moving to another Member State, transitional measures adopted after the ascension of new Member States in 2004 and 2007 permitted the limitation of free movement for some citizens depending on when their Member State joined the EU.

7.4.2.2. Transitional Restrictions: The Creation of Second-tier Citizenship

The addition of new Member States to the EU has resulted in a growing acceptance of levels of citizenship, with new arrivals being temporarily given a second rate of Union citizenship. This is most prominent in the exercise of transitional restrictions for the A8 and A2 countries in 2004 and 2007 respectively. The Treaties established to oversee the accession of the A8 states allowed the older Member States to derogate from what was then Article 39 EC (on the free movement of workers), and Articles 1–6 of Regulation 1612/68,[144] effectively allowing them to withhold access to labour markets from A8 nationals for a period up to seven years.[145] This meant that the new EU citizens were not guaranteed key rights to free movement, even if they were seeking to engage in economic activity in a new Member State.

While some Member States decided to implement the full restrictions allowed in the accession treaty, the variation in time periods for restrictions and the exact limitations placed on A8 nationals were significant. For example, Spain, Belgium, Luxemburg, Greece and Portugal limited access for two years; France had limits for five years but only in particular sectors of work and in particular regions; and Denmark only allowed full-time workers access to their labour markets and restricted access to welfare for all workers, though there were no restrictions for self-employed persons. Sweden, Ireland and the UK did not choose to limit access to their labour markets at all.

[142] See 7.5.3.

[143] D Kochenov, 'Free movement and participation in the parliamentary elections in the Member State of nationality: An ignored link?' (2009) 16 *Maastricht Journal of European and Comparative Law* 197, 219.

[144] Council Regulation (EEC) No 1612/68 of 15 October 1968 on freedom of movement for workers within the Community [1968] OJ L 257/2.

[145] Treaty of Accession of the Czech Republic, Estonia, Cyprus, Latvia, Lithuania, Hungary, Malta, Poland, Slovenia and Slovakia (2003) OJ L236/875 (The Accession Treaty).

The UK's approach appeared, on the face of it, to be quite generous. However, the UK introduced a range of transition measures that restricted access to welfare and required work to be authorised under the Worker Registration Scheme (WRS).[146] Under the Scheme, A8 nationals must register their employment within one month of their start date.[147] Registration certificates were unique to specific employments, meaning that notification to the Home Office and a new certificate were required for any change of employment or where working multiple jobs. This would continue until 12 months of continuous lawful residence was covered by the registration scheme. Work that had not been properly registered could not be used to establish a right to reside and access welfare benefits or permanent residence status after five years.[148] This WRS required A8 nationals to have an awareness of the scheme, be willing to take the time to apply and incur an initial fee of £90. While opening access to labour markets may be less restrictive to the movement of new EU citizens than the available derogations in the Accession Treaty 2003, it introduced more ways in which equal treatment may be restricted based on nationality. Currie described the UK's transition measures as 'one of the more exploitative post-accession free movement regimes to have emerged' with the promise of an open labour market in this situation as a 'wolf in sheep's clothing'.[149] Given that no prosecutions were made against those who failed to register their employment, it suggests that the WRS was aimed at reducing access to welfare benefits, rather than monitoring labour market activity.

Additionally, Maas questioned whether EU authorities would have the legitimacy to prevent further restrictions from Member States, should they wish to extend the time period or type of restrictions.[150] This concern came to light, as the UK extended the use of the WRS for A8 nationals for two years after its expiry in 2009. The UK Supreme Court found that this extension was unlawful.[151] Yet Maas's concern remains: it is not clear whether the EU authorities would have the power to prevent further restrictions if national courts did not step in.

Ultimately, Currie argues that the practical impact of this was that accession state nationals were 'assigned the role of a flexible reserve army of labour' where the work they are called upon to do is 'characterised by poor working conditions, often resulting in a degree of de-skilling'.[152] This introduction of limits to the rights of new EU citizens, openly departing from the principle of equal treatment,[153]

[146] A Fihel, A Janicka, P Kaczmarczyk and J Nestorowicz, 'Free movement of workers and transitional arrangements: lessons from the 2004 and 2007 enlargements' (Centre of Migration Research, University of Warsaw, 2015) 11.

[147] The Accession (Immigration and Worker Registration) Regulations 2004, SI 2004/1219.

[148] DWP 'DMG Vol 2 Chapter 7 Part 3 Habitual Residence and Right to Reside – IS/JSA/SPC/ESA' (Vol 2 Amendment 39, February 2018) [073508].

[149] S Currie, *Migration, Work and Citizenship in the Enlarged European Union* (Ashgate, 2008) 22–23.

[150] W Maas, 'Unrespected, Unequal, Hollow? Contingent Citizenship and Reversible Rights in the European Union' (2009) 15 *The Columbia Journal of European Law* 265, 272.

[151] *SSWP v Gubeladze* [2019] UKSC 31.

[152] Currie (n 149) 201.

[153] O'Brien (n 33) 161.

established a form of 'second-class citizenship',[154] to which holders of EU citizenship are treated differently depending on their nationality. This is a direct affront to the concept of a shared citizenship, shared rights and entitlements and demeans the principle of equality.

Overall, due to the barriers discussed in this section, EU citizenship has been criticised for its short-lived and nominal recognition of personhood beyond economic contribution.[155] This approach commodifies its citizens and restricts rights based on market credentials, and as such it continues to reflect a market 'citizenship' approach. It also restricts access to free movement, even temporarily, based on how new a Member State is to the Union. Barriers to free movement create significant hurdles for atypical workers, and chapter eight explores this further with an analysis of the substance of EU citizenship free movement rights.

7.4.3. EU Citizenship's Influence on Nationality Law

While the scope of EU law may have increased under EU citizenship, it can be seen as problematic that acquiring the status of Union citizenship is entirely dependent on the regulating of Member State nationalities. This may bring into question the formidability of the rights of EU citizenship, as a citizen can lose access based on a revocation of nationality decided solely by a Member State with no EU involvement. The legitimacy of EU citizenship has also been questioned in relation to the status of long-term 'third country national' residents in the EU, as Union citizenship cannot be granted without a Member State nationality.[156] These issues have influenced the CJEU to require the consideration of EU law principles in cases of nationality law.

Although a derivative status dependent initially on the fact of national citizenship, Union citizenship has since acquired the potential to limit the ability of Member States to deprive an EU citizen of their existing nationality. In *Rottmann*, the CJEU stated that EU law and the principle of proportionality must be considered when looking at decisions that could result in the loss of Union citizenship.[157] From this, individuals who are faced with the prospect of losing their Member State nationality, and consequently their status as an EU citizen, can rely on EU law

[154] Maas (n 150) 277.

[155] Spaventa (n 114) 225.

[156] See TK Hervey, 'Migrant workers and their families in the European Union: the pervasive market ideology of Community Law' in J Shaw and G More, *New Legal Dynamics of European Union* (Oxford University Press, 1995) 91; Maas (n 150); Maas (n 2) 50; European Economic and Social Committee, 'Resolution addressed to the European Convention' (CES 1069/2002) point 2.11 'The Committee calls on the Convention to examine the possibility of granting Union citizenship to third country nationals with long-term resident status.'; Kochenov (n 21) 106–07.

[157] Case C-135/08 *Rottmann* ECLI:EU:C:2010:104, [2010] ECR I-1449 [59].

including a particularly thorough application of the principle of proportionality.[158] Davies argues that since this case, where nationality law and EU law clash, the CJEU can now be considered 'the final authority'.[159] While Shaw and Kochenov have questioned whether *Rottmann* paved the way for further restrictions on the sovereignty of Member States' nationality law, including refusals of an acquisition of nationality rather than just loss of citizenship.[160] On the other hand, Dougan points out that such an extension would be 'stretching even the Court's generous approach … beyond its logical limits'.[161] The boundaries of this can also be seen in the context of Brexit, which shows that EU citizenship cannot be guaranteed as a permanent status and remains reliant on Member State nationality and continued membership of the EU.[162] Despite its contextual limitations, *Rottmann* does highlight the potential of Union citizenship as a rights-providing status.

This is particularly notable given some Member States' reaction to a previous judgment on nationality law[163] discussed at the Edinburgh Summit 1992. During the summit, Denmark negotiated opt-outs of the Maastricht treaty including one that European citizenship would not replace national citizenship,[164] explicitly stating that the decision of whether an individual possesses national citizenship will be left solely to the Member State concerned.[165] Golynker regards this summit as demonstrating that Member States never intended 'delegation of competence on issues of nationality to the EU'.[166] A further example of this tension can be found in the 2004 Irish referendum resulting in the 27th amendment to the Irish Constitution removing birthright citizenship, irrespective of the parents' status. While the provision for citizenship by birthright was originally intended to ensure that those in Northern Ireland would not be deprived of their Irish citizenship, popular opinion began to favour the change after allegations that foreign nationals were engaging in 'birth tourism'. At the time of the referendum, the CJEU was

[158] M Dougan, 'Some comments on Rottmann and the "personal circumstances" assessment in the Union citizenship case law' in J Shaw (ed), 'Has the European Court of Justice Challenged Member State Sovereignty in Nationality Law?' (Working Papers, EUI RSCAS, 2011/62, EUDO Citizenship Observatory 2011) 17.

[159] G Davies, 'The Entirely Conventional Supremacy of Union Citizenship and Rights' in J Shaw (ed), 'Has the European Court of Justice Challenged Member State Sovereignty in Nationality Law?' (Working Papers, EUI RSCAS, 2011/62, EUDO Citizenship Observatory 2011) 6–7.

[160] J Shaw, 'Setting the Scene: the Rottmann case introduced' in J Shaw (ed), 'Has the European Court of Justice Challenged Member State Sovereignty in Nationality Law?' (Working Papers, EUI RSCAS, 2011/62, EUDO Citizenship Observatory 2011) 4 and Kochenov (n 21) 115.

[161] Dougan (n 158) 17.

[162] Case C-499/21 *P v Council of the European Union* ECLI:EU:C:2023:479.

[163] Case C-369/90 *Micheletti* ECLI:EU:C:1992:295, [1992] ECR I-4239.

[164] This was not originally included in the Maastricht Treaty, but was later incorporated through amendments in the Amsterdam Treaty stating that EU citizenship was 'complementary to' national citizenship. The Lisbon Treaty then amended this to 'additional'.

[165] 'Conclusions of the Presidency' Edinburgh Summit 1992, 57.

[166] O Golynker, 'The correlation between the status of Union Citizenship, the rights attached to it and nationality in Rottmann' in J Shaw (ed), *Has the European Court of Justice Challenged the Member State Sovereignty in Nationality Law?* (EUI Robert Schuman Centre for Advanced Studies Paper No 62, 2011) 20.

hearing the case of *Chen*,[167] concerning a Chinese mother residing and facing deportation from the UK. She was pregnant and, knowing that a second child would violate the 'one child policy' in China, gave birth in Northern Ireland. Her child acquired Irish and EU citizenship and through this she was found to have a right to reside in the UK as a primary carer of a self-sufficient EU citizen. This case was prominent during the referendum and was later pronounced by the Irish Government as 'vindication' of its decision to hold the referendum.[168] This ultimately resulted in the restriction of the ability to acquire EU citizenship.

While, through EU citizenship, EU law can have some influence over matters previously regarded as purely internal, it is clear that this power is far from unlimited. Incursions into these matters, such as with nationality law, are likely to face a backlash from the Member States. EU citizenship has not developed to the point where it is independent of nationality, as more recently asserted in the CJEU's decision that voting rights from EU citizenship cannot be preserved after a decision by a former Member State to withdraw from the Union.[169] Nor is it clear that independence of EU citizenship would be the next step, should a Member State revoke nationality despite disagreement from EU law. Nevertheless, it highlights an effort to protect citizens from losing access to rights under their status as Union citizens.

This brief overview has considered some of the rights and entitlements available to EU citizens that have been accredited to the introduction of EU citizenship. Union citizenship expanded access to EU law rights and protected citizens from being stripped of their status under EU law in some limited circumstances. However, many of the 'rights' associated with free movement, such as the protection from discrimination based on nationality and equal treatment, are withheld based on personal attributes, market credentials and other barriers. This questions the universality and credibility of the rights offered through EU citizenship, instead appearing more like the optional provisions highlighted by Everson. In this respect, the full array of rights available to EU citizens are only awarded on the basis of market engagement, rather than being universal, and therefore continue to reflect a market citizenship approach.

7.5. Solidarity and EU Citizenship

The second core expectation of citizenship is the anticipation of solidarity and participation amongst the membership of its citizens. It is important to remember that 'Rights are always contested' and for them to be sustained they require formal

[167] Case C-200/02 *Chen* (n 119).

[168] S Mullally, 'Children citizenship and constitutional change' in B Fanning (ed), *Immigration and Social Change in the Republic of Ireland* (Manchester University Press, 2007) 38.

[169] Case C-673/20 *EP v Préfet du Gers* ECLI:EU:C:2022:449 [62].

safeguarding and political support.[170] Rights and freedoms can only survive by 'developing a certain measure of loyalty … that cannot be legally enforced'.[171] As Dougan and Spaventa argue, if EU citizenship is to incorporate some level of 'morally demanding/compelling' social solidarity where all Union citizens have access to non-contribution benefits and/or public services paid for through tax contributions it will have to acquire the necessary support.[172] As a central feature to citizenship and a potential way to enhance its capabilities it is necessary to consider the different aspects of solidarity, how it can be fostered in a transnational community, and any prospective difficulties in realising this. After all, despite EU citizenship rights falling short of an acceptable standard for a status beyond market citizenship, as found above, 'all rights are reversible, no matter how fundamental they may appear'.[173] Therefore, citizenship rights cannot be taken for granted; they need to achieve and maintain some political and popular support.

This section is split into three subsections. The first looks at the possibility of enhancing solidarity through a common European identity; the second analyses approaches to solidarity through integration; and the third critiques how the low levels of political engagement among EU citizens can deprive the Union of the requisite legitimacy to encourage solidarity.

7.5.1. Creating a European Identity

Achieving solidarity and support for rights depends on, according to Maas, achieving 'a shared European identity' and belonging.[174] Everson argues that the best way to ensure allegiance and solidarity is through a 'certain measure of loyalty' to a state built from having a shared identity.[175] National identities are also identified by Bauböck as a 'very strong source of solidarity'.[176] Maas therefore suggests that 'the extent to which the Europe idea becomes part of national identities will ultimately determine how successful integration can be'.[177] EU citizenship was perceived to be a vital step in increasing a sense of European identity amongst

[170] Maas (n 2) 97–98.

[171] J Habermas, 'Struggles for Recognition in the Democratic Constitutional State' in C Cronin and P De Greiff (eds), *The Inclusion of the Other: Studies in Political Theory* (Cambridge, 1998) 227; Marshall also recognised that 'citizenship requires … a direct sense of community membership based on loyalty to a civilisation which is a common possession' in Marshall (n 44) 92.

[172] M Dougan and E Spaventa, '"Wish you weren't here …" New Models of Social Solidarity in the European Union' in M Dougan and E Spaventa (eds), *Social Welfare and EU Law* (Hart Publishing, 2005) 217.

[173] Maas (n 150) 267.

[174] Maas (n 2) 97–98.

[175] Everson (n 6) 73.

[176] R Bauböck, 'Citizenship and Collective Identities as Political Sources of Solidarity in the European Union' in K Banting and W Kymlicka (eds), *The Strains of Commitment: The Political Sources of Solidarity in Diverse Societies* (Oxford University Press, 2017) 80.

[177] Maas (n 2) 113.

those holding the status. For Kochenov, Union citizenship has gone some way in achieving this, stating that by 'releasing [EU citizens] from the "suffocating bonds"' of nationality, free movement allows them to embrace Europe as their identity.[178] On the other hand, free movement is only enjoyed by a relatively small number of EU citizens. This section will therefore explore the likelihood of social solidarity forming among EU citizens based on a shared identity.

Elsmore and Starup suggest the EU 'lacks the cultural … angle'[179] and has '"brand identity" problems',[180] which hinder the success of a 'euro-identity'. The blame for these problems is placed, at least partly, on the economically motivated development of the EU rather than 'selling the idea that national citizens will acquire a Euro-social identity … and join the spirit and consciousness of a new European society'.[181] However, it is important to remember, as Faist does, that the idea of sharing a common culture regularly places too much importance on a retelling of histories, traditions, religion or race that are often based on false narratives.[182] For example, a 'pure, pristine and true cultural tradition of Europe' does not exist.[183] Going further, Anderson recognises that, rather than just an invention based on fabricated commonalities, which could imply the existence of 'true' nations, all communities larger than those where individuals have 'face-to-face contact (and perhaps even these) are 'imagined'.[184] The EU must therefore be cautious when attempting to achieve commonality through a European identity to avoid this ethno-national approach due to its potential to divide and its false perception of Europe. The decision to remove a reference to 'Christian values' in the draft of the planned (but ultimately rejected) European Constitution illustrates awareness of this issue. The argument for inclusion, made by Weiler, identified Christian values as the closest shared 'European historical memory and common culture' which could be used to benefit European integration.[185] Cvijic and Zucca question this claim and argue that it fails 'to capture a phenomenon as complex as European culture'.[186] It therefore places too much importance on the potential false narratives that Faist warns against.[187] Instead, the decision to remove reference to 'Christian values' is illustrative of a desire to avoid an 'aggressive self-assertion' of a presumed European identity.[188] There is also a risk of creating a clear distinction

[178] Kochenov (n 21) 135.
[179] MJ Elsmore and P Starup, 'Union Citizenship – Background, Jurisprudence, and Perspective: The Past, Present, and Future of Law and Policy' (2007) 26 *Yearbook of European Law* 57.
[180] ibid 109.
[181] ibid 106.
[182] Faist (n 52) 53.
[183] ibid.
[184] B Anderson, *Imagined Communities: Reflections on the Origin and Spread of Nationalism* (Verso Books, 1983).
[185] JHH Weiler, *Un'Europa cristiana: un saggio esplorativo* (Rizzoli, 2003); S Cvijic and L Zucca, 'Does the European Constitution Need Christian Values? A review of Un'Europa cristiana: un saggio esplorativo by J. H. H. Weiler' (2004) 24 *Oxford Journal of Legal Studies* 739, 742.
[186] Cvijic and Zucca (n 185) 742.
[187] Faist (n 52) 53.
[188] Cvijic and Zucca (n 185) 746.

between perceived 'European and non-European'. Emphasising 'the *otherness*' of not only third-country nationals, but also EU citizens in ethnic, racial or religious minorities.[189] Such a distinction upholds the narrow perception of 'Europe' as a 'White Man's Club' ignoring its multicultural heritage, and the inhumane colonial histories of some Member States.[190]

While the creation of something akin to national identity could prove useful to fostering solidarity, it does not guarantee it. Even in national contexts, where minority communities exist, Bauböck argues that attempts to strengthen national identity 'have contributed to further disintegration'.[191] It is also important to note that the strength of the link between national identity and social solidarity is disputed.[192] A collective European identity may therefore not create the unity or solidarity with fellow EU citizens to translate into support for redistributive social policy.

Instead, Dougan and Spaventa suggest that a common European identity could be derived from 'shared social and cultural experiences and institutional and political bonds'.[193] Habermas theorises that a shared political culture crystallising around constitutional principles such as human rights and popular sovereignty can form into a type of 'constitutional patriotism' which 'can take the place originally occupied by nationalism'.[194] With a lack of 'true' traditional or historical commonalities to draw on and the dangers of relying on these, a focus on political culture and constitutional values could act as the common ground where solidarity can be forged. However, Müller notes the concerns that such ties are not strong enough to 'generate the kind of social solidarity that motivates large-scale egalitarian socio-economic policies'.[195] This concern may be particularly true in the post-national context of the European Union.

The potential for a shared political culture among EU citizens may also be stifled by the dominance of Member State allegiance and identity. Bellamy questions EU citizenships' substantive contribution to supranational solidarity.[196] He argues that while it gives holders of the status easier access to other Member States,

[189] Hervey (n 156) 98–99.

[190] ibid.

[191] Relying on examples such as sustaining solidarity between Belgium's linguistic communities or the calls for independence of Scotland from the UK and Quebec from Canada in Bauböck (n 176) 80.

[192] Hall's review of empirical studies concludes that 'stronger attachment to the nation does not promote support for redistribution': PA Hall, 'The Political Sources of Social Solidarity' in K Banting and W Kymlicka, *The Strains of Commitment: The Political Sources of Solidarity in Diverse Societies* (Oxford University Press, 2017) 202–03; R Johnston, K Banting, W Kymlicka, and S Soroka. 'National Identity and Support for the Welfare State' (2010) 43 *Canadian Journal of Political Science* 349; M Shayo, 'A Model of Social Identity with an Application to Political Economy, Nation, Class and Redistribution' (2009) 103 *American Political Science Review* 147.

[193] Dougan and Spaventa (n 172) 185.

[194] J Habermas, *The inclusion of the other: studies in political theory* (Polity Press 1998) 118.

[195] JW Müller, 'A general theory of constitutional patriotism' (2008) 6 *International Journal of Constitutional Law* 72.

[196] R Bellamy, 'Evaluating Union citizenship: belonging, rights and participation within the EU' (2008) 12 *Citizenship Studies* 597.

potentially leading to citizenship of those Member States, it does little to 'create a distinctive attachment to the EU itself'.[197] Instead he locates solidarity as remaining between the individual and Member States, with 'no transfer of allegiance to the EU'.[198] This approach treats allegiance as a zero-sum game and does not consider the ability for individuals to grapple with multiple identities and allegiances. The Summer 2022 Standard Eurobarometer shows that 74 per cent of EU nationals felt that they were European citizens;[199] however, this feeling has been mostly expressed as being secondary to that of national citizenship.[200] Perhaps a transfer of allegiance from Member State to the EU is not necessary, rather a fostering of solidarity towards to EU irrespective of allegiance to a Member State. Nevertheless, it is not insignificant that EU citizens have more affiliation with individual Member States than the EU itself, as it may restrict the potential for social solidarity for citizens beyond national borders.

Solidarity and identity are thus intertwined concepts that can assist each other to form. It seems that a sense of European identity is unlikely, potentially inappropriate and not necessarily effective, especially when focused on a false impression of shared culture and given its divisive and exclusionary nature. Alternatively, establishing a common identity based on a shared political culture and values that are reflected in constitutional provisions could be more helpful. While EU citizenship has taken some steps in establishing a shared supranational legal culture, this is perhaps too abstract a notion to foster a shared identity and solidarity. This begs the question of how far a common identity through EU citizenship can go, particularly if it is to 'justify the assimilation of economically inactive migrants into the traditional welfare societies of the Member States'.[201] Instead, it is necessary to consider other potential drivers of solidarity in the EU: integration and participation.

7.5.2. Integration and the Persistence of the Market

Solidarity and a sense of community in the EU could potentially be enhanced through greater recognition of integration as a key factor to belonging. By recognising the value of belonging-by-choice, the EU can play to its strengths, rather than fixating over its lack of 'national identity'. Free movement gives EU citizens the option to move, work, study and build a new life in any of the Member States.

[197] ibid 598.
[198] ibid 609.
[199] Standard Eurobarometer, 'European Citizenship' (No 97, June 2022) 24.
[200] The Eurobarometer identified that 88% of respondents either identified solely by their Member State nationality or first by their nationality and then as a European citizen. Of these 55% of respondents defined themselves first by their own nationality and then as a European citizen. Only 8% stated that they felt European first and 2% identifying solely as European, Standard Eurobarometer, 'European Citizenship' (No 91, June 2019) 46.
[201] Dougan and Spaventa (n 172) 217.

For example, in AG Wathelet's opinion in *NA*, the salience of integration was highlighted by determining that a German national who had no connection with that Member State and had been born and educated in the UK had 'constructed their citizenship'.[202] If EU citizenship can fashion a community based on the recognition of integration, rather than a common identity or involvement with the market, it may be able to establish further support and solidarity.

7.5.2.1. Integration as an Escape from the Market

In some ways, EU law pays homage to the value of integration. Spaventa argues that Union citizenship, a status that promoted a 'more fluid concept' of belonging determined by 'the actual links established by the (individual) citizen with the polity of reference',[203] enhances the importance of integration. This can be demonstrated in three main scenarios; firstly, through the enhanced protection granted to EU nationals in relation to deportation providing they have acquired the right of permanent residence[204] or have resided in the host Member State for 10 years;[205] secondly, through permanent residence itself, which provides more rights to individuals who have spent at least five years in a host Member State,[206] recognising that time can create a genuine link with a Member State;[207] and thirdly through the CJEU's approach to welfare benefits which is argued by Thym to display some recognition of integration into host societies.[208] All three of these scenarios appear to award the time spent in a host Member State, recognising the importance of integration and encouraging Union citizens to reach a certain level of integration to acquire further rights. However, problems arise in each of these when examining how levels of integration are assessed.

Spaventa recognises that these systems are often not awarded on time and social integration alone; the acquisition of permanent residence and access to many means-tested benefits includes a qualitative element: 'the citizen has to be migrant; economically active or economically independent; and she must have been "good"'.[209] Adding a qualitative hurdle that relies on economic situations

[202] Case C-115/15 *SSHD v NA*, Opinion of AG Wathelet ECLI:EU:C:2016:259 [115].
[203] Spaventa (n 114) 208–09.
[204] Directive 2004/38, Art 28(2).
[205] ibid Art 28(3).
[206] ibid Art 16; Art 17 contains specific circumstances where permanent residence can be acquired in a period of time shorter than five years. See ch 3 at 3.2.3.
[207] Spaventa (n 114) 217.
[208] D Thym, 'Towards "Real" Citizenship? The Judicial Construction of Union Citizenship and its Limits' in M Adams, H de Waele, J Meeusen and G Straetmans (eds), *Judging Europe's Judges: The Legitimacy of the Case Law of the European Court of Justice Examined* (Hart Publishing, 2013) 155, 162.
[209] Spaventa (n 114) 218. For example, the right of permanent residence requires individuals to have 'resided legally' for a continuous period of five years: Directive 2004/38, Art 16. 'Legal residence' in this context means residence which 'complies with the conditions laid down in the directive, in particular those set out in Article 7(1)' in Joined Cases C-424/10 and C-425/10 *Ziolkowski and Szeja* ECLI:EU:C:2011:866 [2011] ECR I-14035 [46]. See ch 3 at 3.2.3.

diminishes the importance of integration into the community, time and laying down roots in a Member State. This also creates a situation where two individuals who have lived in a Member State for the same amount of time have very different rights because one satisfies the economic hurdles and the other doesn't, with no room for the consideration of other forms of integration.

However, this approach to integration is likely to be most problematic when faced with accessing welfare benefits, as the easiest way to establish integration is through sufficient economic activity or independence, two scenarios where welfare benefits may not be required. Additionally, when it comes to welfare benefit systems, they are often built on a notion of membership with 'duties to contribute to the financing' of the system alongside the right to claim benefits.[210] Communities based on membership have a 'built-in bias towards "otherness"' and often 'shift from addressing structures of inequality and discrimination to individuals' responsibilities'.[211] An EU community based on market-focused integration and individual responsibility such as economic activity and contribution, seems unlikely to foster any kind of solidarity that will protect the rights of citizens who have integrated in other ways.

In these examples, the focus on the internal market taints the significance of integration. It is only the extra protection for those faced with deportation that does not rely on an economic-style integration, and this is only activated after 10 years of residence. Solidarity and loyalty may never be established if the rights available through EU citizenship continue to rely on economic considerations as benchmarks for deserving citizens. The continuing importance of the market to integration may continue to alienate Union citizens as when certain forms of welfare needs are ignored it 'effectively excludes many individuals from membership of the … community'.[212] It is also recognised that EU citizenship, being so encompassed by the market, creates a relationship between the citizen and the EU that hinders the development of allegiance.[213] An EU citizen's role in the market is integral to their rights as a citizen. In contrast, a social citizenship protects its citizens who are unable to engage in the market as their rights and entitlements are affirmed by the institution of citizenship rather than economic performance.[214] Instead, if the choice is made to engage in the internal market, there is no guarantee of success *or* entitlements to fall back on. Everson warns that without the benefits of status and entitlements granted from the traditional forms of citizenship, a Union citizen's only reason to engage with the single market is for 'self-interest'.[215] When the recognition of rights is dependent on the commodification of individuals it 'is most unlikely to win firm support among those it commodifies',[216] and

[210] van der Mei (n 49) 5.
[211] D Kostakopoulou, 'The Anatomy of Civic Integration' (2001) 73 *Modern Law Review* 933, 957.
[212] Dougan and Spaventa (n 172) 186.
[213] Everson (n 6) 73.
[214] ibid 87–88.
[215] Everson (n 6) 73.
[216] Kochenov (n 15) 8.

may therefore never encourage solidarity among other EU citizens or allegiance towards the EU.

7.5.2.2. Integration versus Assimilation

Where integration is replaced with expectations of assimilation, the notion can quickly introduce new forms of othering or alienation. While assessing integration beyond economic circumstances is a welcome approach, the methods adopted to test this can sometimes rely on an expectation for individuals to assimilate, rather than integrate. Spaventa recognises the risk that further qualifications to assess integration could be introduced, for example through language skills,[217] or cultural knowledge tests to establish access to EU citizenship rights. These language and cultural tests, which are often adopted for those who wish to naturalise as national citizens, can be a misleading, unnecessary and an inappropriate test of integration.[218] Kostakopoulou convincingly argues that integration tests based on national values, ways of life and sometimes political views can actually produce the opposite of the desired effect and result in individuals feeling 'more estranged, apprehensive, fixated and resistant'.[219] As Nic Shuibhne argues, 'The European anthem cannot be shoved down the throats of EU citizens. They will respond to it or they won't'.[220] There is equally a danger that if states do not offer classes on language and cultural knowledge, integration tests can create discriminatory boundaries for those with less access to education and where private tuition is not an option.[221] Integration, focusing on forced assimilation also often mirrors the issues of false narratives and ethno-nationalism discussed in section 7.5.1. It is therefore at risk of encouraging further alienation and, in the interest of fostering support for citizenship rights, should be avoided.

7.5.2.3. Supranational Integration

It is important to recognise the aspects of integration that can form a positive community which is less likely to alienate based on market credentials and 'otherness'. Kostakopoulou supports the pluralist approach, where 'developing partnerships, cultivating mutual respect, fostering interactions and dynamic learning in action' are prioritised.[222] To achieve this, it is imperative to prioritise 'equality

[217] Spaventa (n 114) 218.

[218] See TM Milani, 'Language Testing and Citizenship: A Language Ideological Debate in Sweden' (2008) 37 *Language in Society* 27, 49; SW Goodman, 'Integration Requirements for Integration's Sake? Identifying, Categorising and Comparing Civic Integration Policies' (2010) 36 *Journal of Ethnic and Migration Studies* 753.

[219] Kostakopoulou (n 211) 957.

[220] Nic Shuibhne (n 1) 1624-5.

[221] A Etzioni, 'Citizenship Tests: A Comparative, Communitarian Perspective' (2007) 78 *The Political Quarterly* 353, 361.

[222] Kostakopoulou (n 211) 957.

and non-discrimination', especially towards migrant communities to 'safeguard … the dignity of human beings … giv[ing] them the opportunity to thrive'.[223] This entails an equality which includes, in some ways, those who do not fit the mainstream demands of a capitalist market as 'fairness and sensitivity are crucial'.[224] Although this aspiration is both admirable and sensible, it is equally quite optimistic and a little too intangible. Against the backdrop of the 2008 economic crisis and the 'current of national protectionism in associated public debate', Nic Shuibhne predicts that the success of creating a transnational solidarity based on integration and community 'will be challenging, at best'.[225]

Indeed, even the CJEU has shown a willingness to reject notions of supranational integration as legitimate reasons for access to citizenship rights. While the CJEU has historically used proportionality tests to consider the individual circumstances of EU nationals, including levels of integration, more recently the Court has been reluctant to adopt these positions and in some cases have ignored it altogether.[226]

The case of *Alokpa* is an example of this.[227] The Court denied access to a residence and work permit, in Luxemburg, to a third-country national who was the primary carer of French national children on account of her not having the resources to be self-sufficient.[228] However, Ms Alokpa had been offered a job, which she was unable to take without the residence permit, but paradoxically, without the job she 'could not demonstrate that her children had sufficient resources' to qualify for the necessary residence right for the permit. In this case, the CJEU decided that no proportionality test was necessary if the residency requirements were not met, and that the children's French nationality meant that it was the responsibility of France to allow the family to reside there, despite the fact that Ms Alokpa's children had never lived in France and had no family life with their French father.[229] Spaventa draws attention to the fact that, in doing this, 'the Court is privileging an abstract notion of belonging' which is allocated at birth, almost always irrespective of the country of birth,[230] 'at the expense of the supranational notion of belonging-by-choice'.[231]

This is repeated in *Alarape*,[232] where the CJEU disregarded the level of integration and belonging that could form by residing in a Member State for five years under a lawful derivative right of residence. This case considered residence as a

[223] ibid.

[224] V Bader, 'The Cultural conditions of Transnational Citizenship: On the Interpenetration of Political and Ethnic Cultures' (1997) 25 *Political Theory* 771, 796 cited in Kostakopoulou (n 211) 958.

[225] Nic Shuibhne (n 1) 1625.

[226] See ch 8 at 8.3.2.

[227] Case C-86/12 *Alokpa* ECLI:EU:C:2013:645.

[228] Case C-86/12 *Alokpa* (n 227);Case C-200/02 *Chen* (n 119) [28]–[30] on how sufficient resources can come from the income of a parent.

[229] Case C-86/12 *Alokpa* (n 227) [12]–[19].

[230] *SSWP v Sequeira-Batalha* [2016] UKUT 511 (AAC).

[231] Spaventa (n 114) 215.

[232] Case C-529/11 *Alarape and Tijani v SSHD* ECLI:EU:C:2013:290, [2013] 3 CMLR 38.

Teixeira carer (a derivative right of residence provided to the child, and primary carer of the child, of an EEA national worker or former worker where that child is in education and where requiring the primary carer to leave the host Member State would prevent the child from continuing their education there).[233] Despite residence as a *Teixeira* carer qualifying as exercising a right to reside in other situations, including access to welfare benefits, the Court in *Alarape* specifically excluded it for the purposes of acquiring permanent residence under Article 16(2) of the Citizens Directive.[234] With the CJEU rejecting many notions of supranational integration through long periods of residence and belonging-by-choice, it seems even more unlikely that transnational solidarity will be formed in the way Kostakopoulou envisions.

With this analysis in mind, the concepts of identity and integration must be carefully navigated if they are to avoid further estrangement rather than solidarity. It is equally necessary to bear in mind the symbiotic nature of solidarity and rights. With more rights to equality and non-discrimination comes more of a sense of community and solidarity and equally, further solidarity provides the necessary support to justify the expansion of rights. As Faist notes, 'the causal arrows usually run both ways'.[235] Therefore, while nurturing a transnational solidarity seems in many ways unlikely and, at best, challenging, it will be necessary if EU citizenship is to expand from its market confines. Additionally, it will not be sufficient for the EU to wait to enhance citizenship rights until the support for rights has reached a substantial level, as the protection of human dignity through equality and non-discrimination is seemingly vital to the progression of solidarity. Equally, it is important to recognise, as Kochenov does, that sticking to an EU citizenship 'where the commodification of the human being is the core rationale behind the construction of personhood' may well receive a lot of support in law but is 'unlikely to win firm support among those it commodifies'.[236]

7.5.3. Participation and Solidarity

A final consideration that could enhance solidarity among EU citizens and support for the EU, is the value of political participation. As discussed above, political participation can be a tool for a citizenship to help ensure that the good of the community is pursued and that the institution is seen as a legitimate enough to warrant allegiance to. The EU's focus on economic integration and market interests can 'lead to pressures for more political participation'.[237] Yet this can be

[233] As the primary carer of an EU national worker's child who is in full-time education. See Case C-480/08 *Teixeira* ECLI:EU:C:2010:83, [2010] ECR 2010 I-1107; For more detail see ch 3 at 3.2.4.
[234] Directive 2004/38, Art 16(2).
[235] Faist (n 52) 52.
[236] Kochenov (n 15) 8.
[237] Bartle (n 55) 417.

difficult on the supranational or international arenas where engagement may be low compared to local or national levels. As Davies points out, while referring to Hirschman's work on 'Exit, Voice and Loyalty',[238] if the engaged and politically active 'customer' or citizen is denied a voice in encouraging improvements in a 'service' they may be likely to exit that 'service'.[239] When the 'service' is more social or political, a lack of voice also likely begets a lack of loyalty. As such, this section will briefly consider problems with participation in EU citizenship.

Currently, the political rights available to mobile Union citizens include the right to vote and stand in local (municipal) and European Parliament elections and access to consular protection of any Member State when in a third country. While limited, the CJEU has not even treated the voting rights that *are* available to mobile EU citizens as inherent or fundamental rights, but rather identifying them as conditional,[240] and granting states a 'wide margin of appreciation in imposing conditions'.[241] In Besselink's words, the CJEU has treated EU citizenship voting rights as 'a nice thing to have, but a privilege which does not of necessity have to be granted by law'.[242] Instead, Union citizens are dependent on thorough and consistent implementation of their voting rights at all levels of governance,[243] leaving only the security of active participation in politics at the European level.[244] Yet, even at the European Parliament level, EU citizens are vulnerable to unlawful restrictions on their voting rights in Member States.[245]

Union citizens residing in a Member State, even for long periods, continue to have no right to vote in national elections despite Union citizens showing support for the extension,[246] with just more than two-thirds (67 per cent) of respondents believing that EU nationals should be allowed to vote in the national elections of the Member State they are residing in.[247] Shaw warns of the incompatibility of access to social welfare benefits and permanent residence with the absence of

[238] AO Hirschman, *Exit, Voice and Loyalty: Responses to Decline in Firms, Organisations and States* (Harvard University Press, 1970).

[239] G Davies, 'The Price of Letting Courts Value Solidarity: The Judicial Role in Liberalizing Welfare' in M Ross and Y Borgmann-Prebil, *Promoting Solidarity in the European Union* (Oxford University Press, 2010) 112–14.

[240] Case C-300/04 *Eman and Sevinger* ECLI:EU:C:2006:545, [2006] ECR I-8055 [52].

[241] Case C-145/04 *Spain v United Kingdom* ECLI:EU:C:2006:543, [2006] ECR I-7917 [94].

[242] LFM Besselink, 'Case C-145/04, Spain v. United Kingdom, judgment of the Grand Chamber of 12 September 2006; Case C-300/04, Eman and Sevinger, judgment of the Grand Chamber of 12 September 2006; ECtHR (Third Section), 6 September 2007, Applications Nos 17173/07 and 17180/07, Oslin Benito Sevinger and Michiel Godfried Eman v. the Netherlands (Sevinger and Eman)' (2008) 45 *Common Market Law Review* 787, 808.

[243] J Shaw, *The Transformation of Citizenship in the European Union: Electoral Rights and the Restructuring of Political Space* (Cambridge University Press, 2007) 122–67.

[244] Kochenov (n 21) 110.

[245] A European Commission public consultation found that 21% of respondents had faced difficulties in voting in European Parliament or local elections when living in another Member State. See V Jourová, 'Public Consultation on EU Citizenship 2015' (European Commission, November 2018).

[246] Shaw (n 248) 2557–58.

[247] Special Eurobarometer, 'Electoral Rights' (No 364, March 2013) 22.

national voting rights.[248] Being unable to vote in national elections in the Member State where a Union citizen actively chooses to reside is also identified, by Nic Shuibhne, as 'the most problematic gap in EU citizenship'.[249] To address growing interest, a European Parliament resolution in 2017 called for extending the electoral rights of EU citizens residing in a Member State of which they are not nationals 'to include all remaining elections' that were left out of Article 22 TFEU, including national elections.[250] However, as resolutions are not binding this has not yet resulted in the extension of voting rights for EU citizens.

The EU has also often been criticised for having a democratic deficit more generally and while it is not the intention of this book to discuss this at length, some elements of this criticism are important to the discussion on giving *all* EU citizens a voice, even when they do not exercise free movement. It is particularly important to reflect on issues of representation at the European Parliament level, including low turn-out in European elections,[251] and the indirect representation present in other EU institutions where roles are not directly elected.[252] However, the EU also operates a form of deliberative democracy which prioritises consultation with civil society organisations and experts on narrow agendas to inform policy choices. Through this, it aims to achieve 'consensus on the best policy rather than bargaining to reconcile competing interests'.[253] However, Bellamy and Castiglione point out that this approach cannot substitute the representation and transparency of the authorising and holding to account of decision-makers that is provided for by more traditional representative democracy models.[254] While claims concerning the EU's democratic deficit have been disputed,[255] it is likely a mixture of the issues above which influence 40 per cent of Eurobarometer respondents to express a feeling that that their voice did not count in the EU.[256]

The belief that the EU has a democratic deficit could be enough to deter some EU citizens from expressing allegiance to the EU. Efforts have been made to address

[248] J Shaw, 'EU citizenship and political rights in an evolving European Union' (2007) 75 *Fordham Law Review* 2549.

[249] Nic Shuibhne (n 1) 1622.

[250] European Parliament, 'Resolution of 16 February 2017 on possible evolutions of and adjustments to the current institutional set-up of the European Union' (2014/2248(INI)) 50.

[251] The 2019 elections produced an average turnout of 50.7%, a considerable increase from 42.6% from 2014: European Parliament, 'Final turnout data for 2019 European elections announced' (29 October 2019), europarl.europa.eu/news/en/press-room/20191029IPR65301/final-turnout-data-for-2019-european-elections-announced.

[252] S Hix and A Follesdal, 'Why is there a Democratic Deficit in the EU? A Response to Majone and Moravcsik' (2006) 44 *Journal of Common Market Studies* 533.

[253] R Bellamy and D Castiglione, 'Democracy by Delegation? Who Represents Whom and How in European Governance' (2011) 46 *Government and Opposition* 101, 118.

[254] ibid 114.

[255] K Lenaerts and JA Gutiérrez-Fons, 'Epilogue on EU Citizenship: Hopes and Fears' in D Kochenov (ed), *EU Citizenship and Federalism: The Role of Rights* (Cambridge University Press, 2017) 753–57.

[256] This Standard Eurobarometer was the first where an absolute majority (56%) of Europeans believed that their voice counts in the EU: Standard Eurobarometer, 'Public Opinion in the European Union' (No 91, June 2019) 148.

the feeling of detachment from the EU for all its citizens. An example of this can be seen in the European Citizens' Initiative (ECI) – a mechanism aimed at increasing direct democracy by inviting EU citizens to submit initiatives for consideration by the Commission once they have received one million signatures across seven Member States. However, Longo's analysis of the ECI identified the inaccessibility of 'e-democracy', difficulty in stimulating participation and the cumbersome role of the Commission's power of 'either hearing or not hearing the voice of the European people' as factors which hinder its success.[257] Awareness levels of this mechanism are also low[258] and despite running since May 2012 and attracting 98 registered initiatives, to date only five have been successful. Increasing the available routes of participation through the ECI is therefore unlikely.

If the EU does not foster an environment for political participation, including respecting the voting rights of citizens, addressing some concerns of the democratic deficit and potentially extending the right to vote, it cannot expect its citizens to feel included and loyal. The significance of this lies in the EU's potential to establish a supranational political community, that can draw on solidarity with fellow citizens to enhance the potential of free movement rights and social policies for all EU citizens.

EU citizenship's relationship with solidarity is one of its biggest challenges. As a supranational status, the difficulties faced in national contexts of constructing social solidarity are felt even more keenly. This is particularly noticeable when trying to construct solidarity through a shared identity or constitutional patriotism and through promoting the participation of citizens. The reframing of community to include those who demonstrate integration by choosing where they belong, live or work could offer a route through which solidarity can be fostered. However, setbacks in the CJEU's treatment of non-economic integration and the failure to protect political participation rights could in fact damage the construction of allegiance to the EU and any social solidarity that may be formed by that. While these challenges persist, solidarity in the EU may remain only between market actors based on 'interdependency and economic reciprocity between the migrant worker and the host state'.[259] In this conception of EU citizenship, those in atypical work must rely on being seen as economic actors to benefit from this solidarity, not as a Union citizen.

7.6. Summary

Overall, EU citizenship falls short of all the expectations of a social citizenship as set out in this chapter. The analysis identifies two main challenges for EU citizenship; the difficulty to develop beyond its market focus and the solidarity deficit in a supranational citizenship.

[257] E Longo, 'The European Citizens' initiative: too much democracy for EU polity?' (2019) 20 *German Law Journal* 181.

[258] D Hierlemann and C Huesmann, 'Policy Brief 2 / 2018 – More Initiative for Europe's Citizens' (Bertelsmann Stiftung, February 2018).

[259] F De Witte, 'Transnational Solidarity and Conflicts of Justice' (2012) 18 *European Law Journal* 705.

7.6.1. Beyond a Market Citizenship?

EU citizenship has not been freed 'from its market roots'.[260] The origins of EU citizenship are embedded in the achievement of an integrated market, and this is reflected in the foundations of Union citizenship. Instead of shifting its focus away from the market to a status which protects and enhances the values of rights, solidarity and political participation, EU citizenship continues to serve the economic interests of the market. While the status of EU citizenship has brought about some enhancements to the rights of those who hold this status, these are limited and often tangled up in the requirement for market credentials. These rights are therefore not always applied equally and universally among EU citizens. A reliance on the internal market as centrepiece around which many 'citizenship' rights have crystallised limits the scope of those who can enjoy it's benefits to those who are deemed to be engaged in the market. This results in the exclusion of individuals whose personal circumstances do not meet those of the model market citizen and solidifies atypical workers' reliance on worker status.

Such exclusions make it unsurprising that solidarity amongst EU citizens has struggled to develop. As Everson points out, market citizens are guided by their self-interest and as such allegiance or solidarity is difficult to foster.[261]

7.6.2. Solidarity Deficit

While some of the earlier case law cites solidarity as a justification to enhance the rights of Union citizens, it has not been enough to foster, either through a 'European identity' or constitutional patriotism, support and realisation of redistributive social policies for all EU citizens. Additionally, the level of political participation in EU citizenship is still quite low. Despite citizens' interest in extending these rights, the EU institutions have yet to deliver on this. Nor has the CJEU consistently asserted a route to citizenship rights through long periods of residence or other forms of integration. Without solidarity among EU citizens, any future detangling of citizenship rights from the internal market will be challenging.

7.6.3. EU Market Membership and Atypical Workers

Ultimately, EU citizenship has failed to meet the identified components of social citizenship. Instead, the two main shortfalls identified suggest that EU citizens cannot expect the rights and entitlements, equality or solidarity inherent in a social citizenship. It is a status where, to enjoy the fullest array of benefits of EU

[260] Spaventa (n 114) 207.
[261] Everson (n 6) 89.

law, a citizen must be involved with the market.[262] Therefore, theoretically and significantly in practical terms, Union citizenship appears to be an aspirational but erroneous misnomer and is, at best, no more than a form of market membership. Membership in this context allows EU nationals to choose to exercise free movement at their own risk. However, free movement and equal treatment rights are performance-related benefits attached to this membership. To access the fullest array of protection to ensure free movement can be exercised, an EU citizen must essentially pay their dues through market activity.

This chapter has raised an important question concerning the relationship between atypical workers and Union citizenship. As set out in the introduction to this chapter, EU citizenship could offer a potential route for atypical workers, who are not within the scope of Article 45 TFEU, to assert their right to free movement and protection from discrimination based on nationality. Therefore, this enquiry must ask whether the limitations of EU citizenship prevents the status from protecting the free movement and equal treatment rights of atypical migrant workers? This chapter suggests that status as a Union citizen is unlikely to provide solace from the market for those struggling to meet the restrictive 'worker status' conditions set by Member States.

Chapter eight will address this question by analysing the substance of EU citizenship in relation to free movement and unpick some of the consequences of its market construction through an examination of how the CJEU interprets free movement and equal treatment rights for all EU citizens. This will determine the extent to which status as an EU citizen can relieve atypical workers of having to contend with the difficulties of establishing worker status to be able to fully exercise freedom of movement.

[262] H Verschueren, 'Being Economically Active: How it Still Matters' in H Verschueren (ed), *Residence, Employment and Social Rights of Mobile Persons: On how EU Law defines where they belong* (Intersentia, 2016) 187.

8

To Each According to their Affluence: Atypical Workers and the Limits of Free Movement Rights

8.1. Introduction

Free movement, while considered 'the cornerstone of EU citizenship',[1] is not unconditional. EU citizens must fall within the scope of equal treatment rights to be protected from nationality discrimination by host Member States, without which free movement may not be a realistic prospect. Chapter seven established that EU citizenship is still very much constrained by the market. This has an impact on EU citizenship's capacity to provide rights and to establish solidarity, both of which are likely necessary to deliver free movement to all citizens, even when they are without market credentials. The focus on the market results in a conflict of two concepts that 'protect different values'; 'market integration' for the internal market and 'human dignity' for social citizenship.[2] It is, therefore, essential to examine the consequences of this, including its impact on individual citizens and their ability to enjoy free movement rights as a Union citizen, and specifically, the rights of atypical workers who fall outside the scope of Article 45 TFEU.

These rights appear to have gone through a phase of being enacted and enhanced with 'conscious attempt[s] to free citizenship … from its market roots',[3] but has since suffered from a reactionary phase retreating to 'minimalist interpretation' and a return to market citizenship.[4] This journey is worth examining in more detail to establish the limits of EU citizenship as a status from which to derive free movement rights. The role of this chapter is to determine the possibility

[1] 'Free Movement of Persons' (EU Parliament, October 2018), www.europarl.europa.eu/factsheets/en/sheet/147/free-movement-of-persons.

[2] PC de Sousa, 'Quest for the Holy Grail: Is a Unified Approach to the Market Freedoms and European Citizenship Justified?' (2014) 20 *European Law Journal* 499, 501; D Kochenov, 'On Tiles and Pillars: EU Citizenship as a Federal Denominator' in D Kochenov (ed), *EU Citizenship and Federalism: The Role of Rights* (Cambridge University Press, 2017) 43.

[3] E Spaventa, 'Earned Citizenship – understanding Union Citizenship through its scope' in D Kochenov (ed), *EU Citizenship and Federalism: the Role of Rights* (Cambridge University Press, 2017) 207.

[4] ibid 206–09.

for atypical workers to rely solely on their status as an EU citizen to access free movement and equal treatment rights in the UK, rather than relying on the limited scope of worker status.

This chapter analyses EU law concerning the free movement and equal treatment rights of all EU citizens. It will detail the transition of this law in EU legislation and in the Court of Justice of the European Union (CJEU) to analyse the terms, dictated by the Treaties and Directive 2004/38, by which mobile EU citizens can claim access to host Member States' national welfare systems. This will address whether the CJEU's interpretation of EU citizenship and free movement rights offers an adequate alternative for atypical migrant workers to access equal treatment. The chapter contributes to the literature on free movement and equal treatment rights in an EU citizenship undermined by its market focus through adopting the atypical worker as a focal point of these discussions. The limits of EU citizenship and transnational solidarity are therefore tested on the type of citizen who is both engaged in the market and may also depend on the protection of social rights to realistically exercise the freedom to move to another Member State. The previous chapters have shown how atypical workers are at risk of exclusion from Article 45, especially when their access to 'standard' employment is limited or they must balance work with informal care. The analysis in this chapter therefore examines the limited protection of EU citizenship to those who fall outside of the scope of Article 45 TFEU *even* when engaged in economic activity. Instead, Union citizenship emerges as an exclusive market membership, where those excluded from worker status are offered the opportunity to acquire membership status and more rights, should they take on more hours or get a pay-rise.

The chapter addresses this question by first analysing the relevant EU legislation in section 8.2, including the ambiguities and nuances introduced in EU secondary law. How the CJEU interpreted this legislation is then discussed in section 8.3. This section examines the case law by focusing on four different ways the Court has changed its approach to citizenship rights: the interpretation of the objectives of the relevant legislation to protect Member States from unreasonable burdens; the dismantling of an individualised approach to proportionality; and the reversal of residence documents as proof of lawful residence and permitting Member States to reclassify welfare benefits as social assistance to further restrict access. These changes have resulted in the restricting of free movement rights for EU citizens. Section 8.4 then considers the evidence behind the Court's 'reactionary approach', by looking to the potential political drivers behind this change and the correlation of the timing and response of the CJEU judgments. Finally, the chapter uses this analysis to examine the consequences for the free movement of EU citizens in section 8.5. This includes how Member States have used distinguishing facts to avoid compliance and how the more recent restrictive judgments permitting the discrimination of the 'economically inactive' reduces legal certainty and makes the exercise of free movement a less realistic option for atypical workers outside the scope of Article 45 TFEU.

Throughout this chapter, the term 'economically inactive' is adopted to describe EU citizens who would not be able to rely on their status as a worker, self-employed person and their family members under Article 7 Directive 2004/38. This term is used in its technical meaning and is therefore inclusive of many EU migrants who will, in fact, be engaged with economic activity including work. This echoes the findings of chapters three to six, where the boundaries of the definition of economic activity and how, in practice, this excludes many EU nationals who are working is explored. The examination of the rights of those deemed to 'economically inactive' is therefore an essential part of the story for atypical workers who are not covered by the definition of work.

8.2. The Free Movement of Persons in EU Legislation

In its design, the free movement of persons principally concerned workers and self-employed persons, perceived as essential to the furtherance of the European free market and improving the living standards of persons living in the Member States.[5] With the introduction of EU citizenship,[6] the freedom 'to move and reside freely within the territory of the Member States' was extended to all Union citizens in Article 21 TFEU,[7] albeit 'subject to the limitations and conditions laid down in the Treaties and by the measures adopted to give them effect'.[8]

Access to social rights in host Member States is essential for the freedom of movement to be feasible for many EU citizens. The introduction of EU citizenship therefore saw the CJEU, in *Martínez Sala*, extend the scope of protection from 'discrimination on the grounds of nationality' now provided for in Article 18 TFEU to mobile EU citizens.[9] It is from this provision that EU citizens can, in theory, claim equal treatment with Member State nationals in accessing welfare benefits, provided that the discrimination is not justified. In this regard, direct discrimination, or where a rule results in a decision being made on the basis of an applicant's nationality,[10] can only be justified on the strictly expressed and limited grounds of 'public policy, public security and public health'. Indirect discrimination, as defined in *O'Flynn*, concerns decisions based on criteria which, 'although applicable irrespective of nationality', is essentially more likely to affect EU migrants. This might be because the majority of those affected are EU migrants, the criteria can be more easily satisfied by nationals than EU migrants, or there is a

[5] 'The free movement of persons in the European Union: Salvaging the dream while explaining the nightmare' (2014) 51 *Common Market Law Review* 729 (Editorial Comments).

[6] Consolidated Version of the Treaty on European Union [1992] OJ C 325/5 Article 8 (Maastricht Treaty).

[7] Consolidated Version of the Treaty on the Functioning of the European Union [2012] OJ C326/47 (TFEU) Art 21.

[8] TFEU, Art 21(1).

[9] Case C-85/96 *Martínez Sala* ECLI:EU:C:1998:217, [1998] ECR I-2691; TFEU, Art 18.

[10] Case C-124/99 *Borawitz* ECLI:EU:C:2000:485, [2000] ECR I-7293 [24].

risk that it may operate to the particular detriment of EU migrants.[11] Instances of indirect discrimination can be justified where it is 'proportionate to the legitimate aim pursued'.[12] Where indirect discrimination is not justified, it will be prohibited. While aims that are determined to be 'purely economic' are not considered legitimate,[13] the Court has become more lenient where the protection of public finances from an 'unreasonable burden' from free movement or 'the financial balance of the social security system' is expressed as 'the pursuit of an objective in the public interest'.[14] Without an effective claim to equal treatment, EU citizens who are not financially self-sufficient or who cannot rely on rights through the status of a worker or self-employed person will face significant barriers to realistically moving to and residing in a new Member State.

The limitations and conditions expressed in Article 21(1) TFEU are shaped by secondary law. This includes, but is not limited to, what is now Directive 2004/38,[15] which was brought into force at the time of the 2004 enlargement amid concerns from existing Member States about the potential impact of differentiated economies joining the free movement regime.[16] Nic Shuibhne identified the creation of Directive 2004/38 as 'an opportunity to re-regulate free movement rights within the "new legal and political environment"'.[17]

Directive 2004/38 allows all Union citizens to reside in a Member State for three months without restriction.[18] Article 7 requires EU citizens to exercise a right to reside should they wish to stay in a Member State past three months. This includes residing as a worker or self-employed person[19] or, providing that they do not become a burden on the social assistance system of the host Member State and have comprehensive sickness insurance, as a self-sufficient person[20] or student.[21] Jobseekers may also have a continued right of residence providing they are continuing to seek employment.[22] After a reasonable period of time to find suitable employment has passed, jobseekers must then demonstrate that they have a 'genuine chance of being engaged'.[23] While the Treaties do confer 'competence on the legislature in the field of citizenship',[24] the TFEU provides that this should

[11] Case C-237/94 *O'Flynn* ECLI:EU:C:1996:206 [1996] ECR I-02617 [18].
[12] ibid [19].
[13] Case C-137/04 *Rockler* ECLI:EU:C:2006:106, [2006] ECR I-01441 [24].
[14] Case C-515/14 *Commission v Cyprus* ECLI:EU:C:2016:30 [53].
[15] Directive 2004/38/EC of the European Parliament and of the Council of 29 April 2004 on the right of citizens of the Union and their family members to move and reside freely within the territory of the Member States [2004] OJ L158/77 (Directive 2004/38).
[16] 'The 2004 Enlargement: the challenge of a 25 member EU' (Europa, updated 23 January 2007), europa.eu/scadplus/leg/en/lvb/e50017.
[17] N Nic Shuibhne, 'Limits Rising, Duties Ascending: The Changing Legal Shape of Union Citizenship' (2015) 52 *Common Market Law Review* 889, 895.
[18] Directive 2004/38, Art 6.
[19] ibid, Art 7(1)(a).
[20] ibid, Art 7(1)(b).
[21] ibid, Art 7(1)(c).
[22] ibid, Art 14(4)(b).
[23] Case C-710/19 *G.M.A.* ECLI:EU:C:2020:1037, [2021] 2 CMLR 13.
[24] Nic Shuibhne (n 17) 900.

be done 'with a view to facilitating the exercise of the rights' which enable the free movement of all Union citizens.[25] Yet, Article 7 Directive 2004/38 presents a watered down vision of the seemingly expansive right to free movement as expressed in the Treaty.

For EU atypical workers, the Treaty appears to provide a route through their status as an EU citizen to move and reside in another Member State. However, conditions in Directive 2004/38 may limit this, requiring them to exercise rights as a worker to gain *full access* to free movement and equal treatment rights. The exact meaning of becoming a 'burden' on the social assistance system of a Member State and the extent to which Article 18 TFEU can be relied on by those who do not meet the conditions of 'worker' status are therefore key questions in testing the boundaries of free movement for atypical workers. The next section explores how the CJEU has interpreted these rules.

8.3. Free Movement of EU Citizens in the CJEU

Different phases of the Court's judgments concerning the scope of Article 18 TFEU have been identified, with a transition to more expansive and pro-citizenship cases back to restrictive interpretations reinforcing the economic focus of EU citizenship rights.[26] Spaventa argues that this switch is a product of a 'reactionary phase', during which the CJEU responded to the political movement against EU migration with judgments permitting Member States to control free movement and restrict entitlement to national welfare systems.[27] However, Davies argues that rather than inconsistency, the recent judgments from the CJEU represent a change in the specific facts presented to them.[28] For Davies, this characterises a development of Member States' competence and subsequent assertiveness in bringing cases to the Court, only going to the CJEU when they are confident they can win.[29] Most importantly for atypical workers, the Court's delineation of citizenship rights is clear.

Rather than one exact 'turning point', there are several defining moments during the CJEU's citizenship judgments which represent a constraining of previous expansive approaches. For instance, in 2008 the CJEU in *Förster*, influenced by the adoption of Directive 2004/38,[30] approved national limitations on EU citizens' access to student maintenance grants from a host Member State for five years.[31]

[25] TFEU, Art 21(2).

[26] Spaventa (n 3) 204.

[27] ibid.

[28] G Davies, 'Migrant Union citizens and Social Assistance: Trying to Be Reasonable About Self-Sufficiency' (College of Europe Research Papers in Law No 2/2016) 7.

[29] ibid 25.

[30] Directive 2004/38, Art 24(2); although the Directive had been adopted it was not applicable to the facts of the case.

[31] Case C-158/07 *Förster* ECLI:EU:C:2008:630, [2008] ECR I-8507.

For O'Leary, this decision represented a potential 'end of an era' for the fundamental status of EU citizenship.[32] Similarly, the cases of *Dereci*[33] *and McCarthy*[34] saw a generally progressive approach to the substance of EU citizenship in relation to the rights of third-country-national family members be significantly limited.[35] While these shifts are both significant chapters in EU citizenship case law, they reflect – to use the language adopted by Thym – the 'battleground' of EU citizenship rights being drawn up either 'beyond the transnational market paradigm',[36] or for the rights specifically relating to students. Instead, this section focuses on the shift in approach seen in the cases of *Dano*, *Alimanovic*, *García-Nieto* and *Commission v UK*,[37] as they more directly impact the rights of EU citizens who are deemed to be 'economically inactive', the route most likely to be relied on by atypical workers excluded from worker status.

It must also be recognised that the trajectory of this case law is not a straightforward journey. There are outlying cases which enhance or reassert the rights of Union citizenship.[38] To discuss the 'reactionary phase' of the Court in this section deals with a degree of oversimplification. Nevertheless, it is argued that the overall trajectory of limiting the free movement rights for EU citizens exists and impacts the availability of free movement for atypical workers.

This section therefore analyses the CJEU judgments and identifying where the Court has been inconsistent, not just in the outcomes of the cases, but in the adopted reasoning and application of EU principles. It covers four main changes: the interpretive U-turn of the purpose and objective of the relevant legislation; the dismantling of the individual-centred approach to proportionality; the reversal of residence documents as proof of lawful status; and the permitting of reclassification of welfare benefits to social assistance so Member States could derogate from duties and exclude more people from entitlement. It is argued that these

[32] S O'Leary 'Equal treatment and EU citizens: A new chapter on cross-border educational mobility and access to student financial assistance' (2009) 34 *European Law Review* 612; M Dougan, 'The Bubble that Burst: Exploring the Legitimacy of the Case Law on the Free Movement of Union citizens' in M Adams, J Meeusen, G Straetmans and H de Waele (eds), *Judging Europe's Judges. The Legitimacy of the Case Law of the European Court of Justice* (Hart Publishing, 2013) 127.

[33] Case C-256/11 *Dereci and Others* ECLI:EU:C:2011:734, [2011] ECR I-11315.

[34] Case C-434/09 *McCarthy v SSHD* ECLI:EU:C:2011:277, [2011] ECR I-3375.

[35] N Nic Shuibhne, '(Some of) The kids are all right: comment on McCarthy and Dereci' (2012) 49 *Common Market Law Review* 349.

[36] D Thym, 'Towards "Real" Citizenship? The Judicial Construction of Union Citizenship and its Limits' in M Adams, J Meeusen, G Straetmans and H de Waele (eds), *Judging Europe's Judges. The Legitimacy of the Case Law of the European Court of Justice* (Hart, 2013) 155, 165.

[37] Case C-333/13 *Dano* ECLI:EU:C:2014:2358, [2014] ECR I-2358; Case C-67/14 *Alimanovic* ECLI:EU:C:2015:597, [2016] 1 CMLR 29; Case C-299/14 *García-Nieto* ECLI:EU:C:2016:114; Case C-308/14, *Commission v United Kingdom* ECLI:EU:C:2016:436, [2016] 3 CMLR 41.

[38] For example, the judgment in Case C-165/16 *Lounes* ECLI:EU:C:2017:862, [2018] 2 CMLR 9 saw the Court returning to EU citizenship as a status which grants free movement rights. This case concerned dual nationals who could not rely on Directive 2004/38 as they were residing in a Member State of nationality. However, they could rely on Art 21 TFEU and their status as EU citizens to provide derivative residence rights to a non-EU national family member as there had been prior exercise of free movement before the claimant had naturalised.

interpretative changes have contributed to Directive 2004/38 assuming the role of a ceiling to citizenship rights, leaving atypical workers with little to rely on should they fail to meet the requirements of worker status.

8.3.1. The Shifting Objectives of the Legislation

The CJEU's purposive interpretation of the relevant free movement legislation has shifted significantly overtime. From initialling viewing the residency Directives (which were repealed and consolidated into Directive 2004/38) as aiming to facilitate the free movement of EU nationals to it being necessary to protect Member States from unreasonable burdens. Nic Shuibhne identifies this shift, describing the CJEU judgments as retracting citizenship rights 'through prioritizing different or altered objectives'.[39]

An early sign of the Court's expansive interpretation can be found in the landmark case of *Martínez Sala*.[40] Here, the Court identified EU citizenship as a potential source of equal treatment rights.[41] Mrs Martínez Sala, a Spanish national, had previously worked in the host Member State (Germany – where she had resided since she was 12), and had been in possession of and had applied to renew a residence permit when her application for child-raising allowance was refused.[42] The case illustrates an opportunity taken by the CJEU to find that 'as a national of a Member State' and therefore an EU citizen 'lawfully residing in the territory of another Member State', Mrs Martínez Sala came within the scope of the Treaty and could rely on equal treatment rights.[43] At the time, O'Leary stated that this judgment did 'more for the status of Union Citizenship than legal commentators would have anticipated'.[44] While the Court did not expressly comment on the intention of legislation, *Martínez Sala* does act as the beginning of the expansive phase of EU citizenship with regard to free movement rights.

8.3.1.1. Facilitating Free Movement

Later cases saw the CJEU identify and act on the perceived intention of EU citizenship as a status which facilitates and strengthens free movement rights. In *Grzelyzck*, for example, the CJEU stated that EU citizenship is 'destined to be the fundamental status of nationals of the Member States, enabling those … to enjoy

[39] Nic Shuibhne (n 17) 909.
[40] Case C-85/96 *Martínez Sala* (n 9).
[41] C Tomuschat, 'Case C-85/96, *María Mar'ıa Martínez Sala v. Freistaat Bayern, Judgment of 12 May 1998, Full Court. [1998] ECR I-269*' (2000) 37 *Common Market Law Review* 449, 450.
[42] Case C-85/96 *Martínez Sala* (n 9) [37].
[43] ibid [61].
[44] S O'Leary, 'Putting flesh on the bones of European Union Citizenship' (1999) 24 *European Law Review* 68.

the same treatment in law irrespective of their nationality',[45] a sentiment that would be echoed in later cases, particularly to expand the use of proportionality in free movement cases.[46] The CJEU argued that since the introduction of EU citizenship, Mr Grzelzyck's right to equal treatment was derived directly from his status as an EU citizen and he could therefore be entitled to the minimum subsistence allowance without the requirement to prove a qualified residence status as a worker or self-sufficient person.[47] The Court also distinguished this judgment from previous precedent set in *Brown*,[48] due to the change in law since the introduction of EU citizenship.[49]

In reaching the conclusion in *Grzelyzck*, the CJEU also interpreted the requirement that EU migrants do not become an 'unreasonable burden' on a host Member State, found in the preamble of Directive 93/96 (now replaced with Directive 2004/38 with the same preamble language adopted), as indicative of the existence of 'a certain degree of financial solidarity' between EU citizens.[50] While it has been criticised as 'imaginatively interpreted' by Cousins,[51] it relies on an understanding that as an 'unreasonable burden' is prohibited, a *reasonable* burden must not be and should be expected and managed by host Member States.[52] Or, as Davies puts it, the language of an 'unreasonable burden' implies that an EU national 'can be at least a bit of a burden'.[53] The 'degree of financial solidarity' reasoning was also adopted in *Bidar* and *Brey*.[54] In *Bidar*, despite concerns of 'benefit tourism' being recognised as 'legitimate' in AG Geelhoed's opinion,[55] the CJEU relied on the proposed financial solidarity to ensure that student maintenance could not be withheld to lawfully resident EU citizens with a 'genuine link' with the host Member State.[56] *Brey* saw this reasoning used to require a proportionality assessment of individual circumstances when deciding whether granting access to pension credit would be an unreasonable burden.[57] In reaching this conclusion, the Court also identified the objective of Directive 2004/38 as being 'to facilitate and strengthen the exercise of Union citizens' primary right to move and reside

[45] Case C-184/99 *Grzelczyk* ECLI:EU:C:2001:458, [2001] ECR I-06193 [31].

[46] See Case C-413/99 *Baumbast* ECLI:EU:C:2002:493, [2002] ECR I-07091 [82]; Case C-224/98 *D'Hoop* ECLI:EU:C:2002:432, [2002] ECR I-6191 [28]; Case C-138/02 *Collins* ECLI:EU:C:2004:172, [2004] ECR I-2703 [61]; Case C-209/03 *Bidar* ECLI:EU:C:2005:169, [2005] ECR I-2119 [31].

[47] Case C-184/99 *Grzelczyk* (n 45) [29].

[48] Case C-197/86 *Brown* ECLI:EU:C:1988:323, [1988] ECR I-3205.

[49] Case C-184/99 *Grzelczyk* (n 45) [35].

[50] ibid [44].

[51] M Cousins, 'The baseless fabric of this vision" EU Citizenship, the right to reside and EU law' (2016) 1 *Journal of Social Security Law* 89, 90.

[52] M Blauberger, A Heindlmaier, D Kramer, D Sindbjerg Martinsen, J Sampson Thierry, A Schenk and B Werner, 'ECJ Judges read the morning papers. Explaining the turnaround of European citizenship jurisprudence' (2018) 25 *Journal of European Public Policy* 1423; Davies (n 28) 3.

[53] Davies (n 28) 3.

[54] Case C-209/03 *Bidar* (n 46) [56]; Case C-140/12 *Brey* ECLI:EU:C:2013:565, [2014] 1 CMLR 37 [72].

[55] Case C-209/03 *Bidar*, Opinion of AG Geelhoed [2005] ECR I-2119 [66].

[56] Case C-209/03 *Bidar* (n 46) [63].

[57] Case C-140/12 *Brey* (n 54) [72].

freely within the territory of the Member States'.[58] These expansive interpretations of the purpose of EU citizenship and relevant legislation opened up the possibility for EU citizens to be empowered simply by their status as an EU citizen, rather than relying on *enough* economic activity to meet the requirements of 'worker' status.[59]

This interpretation of the objective of Directive 2004/38 was also set out in *Lassal* as the facilitation and strengthening of 'the primary right to move and reside freely in the territory of the Member States'.[60] Further emphasis was bestowed upon Article 16, concerning the right to permanent residence,[61] which the Court identified as signifying a specific aim to 'promote social cohesion and strengthen the feeling of Union Citizenship'.[62] The Court found that this objective would be 'seriously compromised' if the five continuous years required for permanent residence could only be accrued after the Directive came into force.

The interpretation of EU citizenship as 'destined to be the fundamental status' of nationals in the Member States and of the legislation implying a level of 'financial solidarity' assisted the expansion of free movement rights to be enjoyed by some economically inactive EU citizens, even when they require access to financial support in a host Member State. More recently, the Court has altered its prioritisation of the purpose of these rules, often favouring the view that it intends to protect Member States from the threat of 'benefit tourism'. While this will inevitably involve the courts undertaking a balancing exercise between the two aims, the recent focus on the protection of Member States' finances has dismantled the ability of non-workers to rely on social assistance and overlooked their economic contribution through atypical work or informal care.

8.3.1.2. Protection from 'Unreasonable' Burdens

The shift in focus from facilitation of free movement to the protection from unreasonable burdens is perhaps most clear in *Dano*. Although, the CJEU did not hide from previous rulings by reflecting that it had been 'held on numerous occasions' that the status of EU citizenship is destined to be the fundamental status of nationals of the Member States,[63] the focus shifted from the Treaty rights of EU citizenship to the limitations and residency requirements found in Directive 2004/38. The requirement for EU citizens to demonstrate a right of residence as either a worker, self-employed person, student or those who could demonstrate self-sufficiency was elevated to a strict condition and became contingent to any expectation of equal treatment in regard to welfare benefits.[64] The Court's shift

[58] ibid [71].
[59] A Yong, *The Rise and Decline of Fundamental Rights in EU Citizenship* (Hart Publishing, 2019) 52.
[60] Case C-162/09 *Lassal* ECLI:EU:C:2010:592, [2010] ECR I-9217 [53].
[61] Directive 2004/38, Art 16.
[62] Case C-162/09 *Lassal* (n 60) [53].
[63] Case C-333/13 *Dano* (n 37) [58].
[64] Directive 2004/38, Art 7.

in focus is criticised by Nic Shuibhne as a failure to scrutinise 'the legitimacy of legislative limits vis-à-vis the Treaty and wider principles at both a general level and in the individual case'.[65] Besides the change of focus to secondary law, we also see the Court prioritising the protection of Member States from the burden of 'benefit tourism'.

The contrasting interpretations of the 'unreasonable burden' language in *Grzelczyk* and *Dano* indicates a change in approach. In *Dano*, the Court identifies the objective of Directive 2004/38 as the protection of Member States' social assistance systems from unreasonable burdens which could materialise from the free movement of EU citizens.[66] The CJEU relies on this to argue that granting access to welfare benefits to EU migrants with no qualified right to reside 'would run counter to an objective of the directive' as it would cause an unreasonable burden on the host Member State.[67] This contrasts with the reading in *Grzelcyk* of the identical language in the preamble of a preceding Directive,[68] where the Court identified the acceptance of reasonable burdens and an expectation of financial solidarity between Member States, as discussed above.[69] Thym argues that the judgment in *Dano* was 'founded upon an argumentative U-turn', where the 'shift of emphasis' sidelines constitutional arguments for welfare solidarity and equal treatment stemming from the Treaties which, if considered, could have justified a different outcome.[70]

Davies, on the other hand, argues that '*Dano* is as orthodox as can be, no more than an application of *Martínez Sala* or *Grzelczyk*'.[71] His argument relies on the recognition that the specific facts of *Dano* differ greatly from previous case law. While Mr Grzelczyk was a student with temporary financial problems, Ms Dano and her son were applying for a minimum subsistence benefit by relying on their status as jobseekers, but provided no evidence of looking for work. The CJEU noted that evidence of Ms Dano's circumstances suggested a lack of 'integration' in the host Member State.[72] The Court also acknowledged that the motives of an economically inactive citizen were potentially relevant where it reflected an intention to move 'solely in order to obtain another Member State's social assistance',[73] though no evidence was discussed to suggest this was the claimant's intention. The national court had also already declared that Ms Dano had no right of residence. The extent to which this judgment represented a change in interpretation, rather

[65] Nic Shuibhne (n 17) 910.

[66] Directive 2004/38, Preamble.

[67] Case C-333/13 *Dano* (n 37) [74].

[68] Council Directive 93/96/EEC of 29 October 1993 on the right of residence for students [1993] OJ L317/59.

[69] Case C-184/99 *Grzelczyk* (n 45) [44].

[70] D Thym, 'The Elusive Limits of Solidarity: Residence Rights of and Social Benefits for Economically Inactive Union citizens' (2015) 52 *Common Market Law Review* 17, 25.

[71] Davies (n 28) 19.

[72] Case C-333/13 *Dano* (n 37) [35]–[39].

[73] Case C-333/13 *Dano* (n 37) [78]; H Verschueren 'Preventing "Benefit Tourism" in the EU: A Narrow or Broad Interpretation of the possibilities offered by the ECJ in Dano' (2015) 52 *Common Market Law Review* 363, 374.

than an outcome determined by particular facts,[74] appears to be confirmed in the reasoning of subsequent cases.

Alimanovic, for example, concerned the rights of jobseeking EU citizens to receive social assistance after six months of retaining worker status under Article 7(3)(c) Directive 2004/38. This Article provides for worker status to be retained for a minimum period of six months for those who had become involuntarily unemployed from work lasting less than 12 months. In permitting the restriction to social assistance in this case, the CJEU referred to *Dano* to clarify that an EU migrant can only claim equal treatment with regards to accessing social welfare benefits 'if his residence in the territory of the host Member State complies with the conditions of Directive 2004/38'.[75] This case also replicated the reasoning in *Dano* where granting access to benefits to EU migrants with no qualified residence status was seen to be an 'unreasonable burden' which would 'run counter to an objective of the directive'.[76] Unlike in *Dano*, however, *Alimanovic* concerned a Union citizen who had work history in the host Member State. Her access to benefits represented a potentially temporary need before rejoining the labour market. A proportional approach could have been adopted to recognise these differing factual circumstances. Instead, the focus on protecting Member State finances resulted in the authorisation treating EEA nationals' ability to retain worker status for 'no less than six months' under Article 7(3)(c) as a maximum period of six months.

These two interpretations are replicated in *García-Nieto*, in which the Court permits the exclusion of economically inactive EU citizens from accessing welfare benefits in the first three months of residence.[77] Noticeably, any mention of financial solidarity between Member States or of EU citizenship as a fundamental status were absent from these judgments. Davies argues that these cases, rather than reflecting an overruling by the Court, demonstrates accuracy and consistency.[78] He regards *Alimanovic* and *García-Nieto*, like *Dano*, as exemplifying a change in the facts presented to the Court and that the law considered, which concerned the rights of jobseekers,[79] was more specific, 'uncompromising and non-contextual'.[80] Spaventa argues that these judgments show the Court departing 'from the fundamental status rhetoric' and interpreting that the citizenship provisions should protect host Member States from being held responsible for the unreasonable burdens of EU migrants, instead 're-allocating responsibility for the vulnerable Union citizen (solely) with the State of origin'.[81] While the facts in these cases might have been less favourable, the approach of the Court in the judgments

[74] Verschueren (n 73) 388.
[75] Case C-67/14 *Alimanovic* (n 37) [49].
[76] ibid [50].
[77] Case C-299/14 *García-Nieto* (n 37) [38]–[39].
[78] Davies (n 28) 20.
[79] Directive 2004/38, Art 24.
[80] Davies (n 28) 20.
[81] Spaventa (n 3) 205.

represents a shift from the expressed aims of facilitation and financial solidarity to the shielding of Member States from an alleged danger of 'benefit tourism', even if no such danger is evident from empirical studies.[82]

To provide greater clarity in the judgments, it would have been useful for the CJEU to have engaged with previous declarations of financial solidarity, detailing precisely how the circumstances and law should be differentiated. Without being clear on what aspects of previous judgments are still valid, Member States are left to try and operate a national welfare system which accommodates this piecemeal approach to sensitive residence and equal treatment rights. Member States may seek to cynically utilise this confusion to avoid responsibilities.[83] Consequences of this inconsistency has recently emerged in the UK, when determining the rights provided by EU Settlement Scheme status, the more generous interpretation of the residence rights in the Withdrawal Agreement. The CJEU in *CG* failed to engage with previous pro-citizenship case law on the relevance of domestic residence permits for lawful residence and access to equal treatment,[84] instead finding that those with presettled status were not entitled to protection from discrimination based on nationality.[85]

8.3.2. The Dismantling of Proportionality Assessments

As a general principle of Community law, any restriction on the right to free movement should be met with a consideration of proportionality.[86] The willingness of the CJEU to adopt the principle of the proportionality in its judgments has also seen a decline in recent citizenship case law.

8.3.2.1. Individual Circumstances and the Proportionality Principle

Grzelczyk saw the Court introduce the requirement for Member States to consider the specific individual circumstances of EU citizens when deciding whether provision of a welfare benefit would be an 'unreasonable' burden.[87] The Court argued that Mr Grzelcyzk's circumstances, as a student in his final year of study, meant that the burden on the host Member State would only be temporary and therefore

[82] See 8.4.
[83] See 8.3.3.
[84] Case C-456/02 Trojani ECLI:EU:C:2004:488, [2004] ECR I-7573 as successfully argued in the UK Court of Appeal in *Fratila v SSWP* [2020] EWCA Civ 1741, before being overturned by the UK Supreme Court following the CJEU judgment in *CG*.
[85] Case C-709/20 *CG* ECLI:EU:C:2021:602, [2022] 1 CMLR 26; see C O'Brien, 'The great EU citizenship illusion exposed: equal treatment rights evaporate for the vulnerable' (2021) 46 *European Law Review* 801.
[86] Case C-147/03 *Commission v Austria* ECLI:EU:C:2005:427, [2005] ECR I-5969 [63]; Case C-165/14 *Rendón Marín* ECLI:EU:C:2016:675 [45].
[87] Case C-184/99 *Grzelczyk* (n 45).

reasonable. Free movement and citizenship legislation was interpreted as establishing a 'certain degree of financial solidarity' between Member States and the union citizens who resided there.[88] This was further considered in *Baumbast*, where it was decided that the limitations and conditions to citizenship rights must be applied 'in accordance with the general principles of Union law, in particular the principle of proportionality'.[89] The strengthening of the proportionality assessment in these cases ensured that integration to the host Member State was recognised and valued beyond the requirement of economic activity. For example, this could include an EU migrant 'who has resided in the Member State for a number of years without reliance on social benefits and who required benefits for a specified temporary period'.[90]

Dougan and Spaventa recognised the requirement to look beyond the residence rules as creating an inverse relationship where 'the stronger the nexus of "belonging" between EU citizen and host state', the more disproportionate it is to consider them an unreasonable burden.[91] While there were concerns that the CJEU was overstepping its remit and using EU citizenship and proportionality to 're-write' the rules,[92] Dougan attributes this to the changing constitutional environment created by the introduction of Union citizenship. This, Dougan argues, 'furnished the Court with the opportunity' to review the appropriateness of all restrictions adopted by Member States to the residency and equal treatment rights of EU citizens, even where these restrictions are compliant with secondary EU law.[93]

By requiring all restrictions to be applied proportionately, EU citizens could demonstrate a 'real' or 'genuine' link with the host Member State to justify the protection of equal treatment rights, creating space for the consideration of individual circumstances. This test was introduced, and the link easily established, in *D'hoop* through nationality and a 'real link' with the 'geographic employment market concerned', as the claimant was a Belgian national who had been denied access to a Belgian welfare benefit which sought to facilitate transition from education to the employment market, due to having completed her secondary education in France.[94] This case law progressed in *Collins*[95] and *Bidar*,[96] where the CJEU identified a 'genuine link' in circumstances of non-national EU citizens access to welfare benefits, despite being considered economically inactive. In *Collins*, rights as a jobseeker, and access to 'a benefit of a financial nature intended to facilitate

[88] ibid [44].
[89] Case C-413/99 *Baumbast* (n 46).
[90] Cousins (n 51) 91.
[91] M Dougan and E Spaventa, 'Educating Rudy and the non-English patient: a double bill on residency rights under Article 18 EC' (2003) 28 *European Law Review* 699, 712.
[92] K Hailbronner, 'Union Citizenship and Access to Social Benefits' (2005) 42 *Common Market Law Review* 1245, 1251; Davies (n 28) 11.
[93] M Dougan, 'The constitutional dimension to the case law on Union Citizenship' (2006) 31 *European Law Review* 613.
[94] Case C-224/98 *D'Hoop* (n 46).
[95] Case C-138/02 *Collins* (n 46).
[96] Case C-209/03 *Bidar* (n 46).

access to employment', were interpreted in light of Mr Collins' status as an EU citizen.[97] This meant that any residence requirement adopted by the Member State must assess whether a genuine link to the employment market exists and must be applied in a proportionate and non-discriminatory way.[98] The judgment in *Bidar* also relied on the link forged through length of residence and attendance at secondary school in the host Member State to justify access to a student loan.[99] For Yong, this line of cases exhibits 'the true effectiveness of the Court in substantiating and legitimising the status of EU citizenship' as it established that status as an EU citizen under Article 20 TFEU was enough to engage consideration of the right to non-discrimination and proportionality.[100] Yet, rather than progress, O'Brien identified setbacks in the 'genuine link' criteria, as it retained national privilege and granted Member States considerable discretion in determining what defined a 'real link' and how it would be tested, only demanding that the assessment must not fall on a 'single binary condition'.[101] While these cases introduced a 'much more muted right' for EU citizens to have restrictions applied proportionately, as O'Brien argues,[102] they also illustrate that the CJEU was willing to treat almost any barrier to free movement as a potential breach of EU law and therefore requiring justification. Even where that justification rested on a proportionate restriction, it provided some basic protection and consideration of the personal circumstances in individual cases rather than the sweeping generalisations seen in more recent cases.

The introduction of Directive 2004/38, while formalising the limitations and conditions to the free movement of EU citizens, did not fully incorporate the CJEU case law on the need for Member States to adopt measures in accordance with the principle of proportionality. The principle of proportionality is only mentioned twice in the Directive, both in reference to the power of Member States to restrict the right of entry and residence to EU citizens in the preamble and Article 27.[103] This requires Member States to take into account, when considering expulsion of Union citizens, 'the degree of integration of the persons concerned, the length of their residence in the host Member State, their age, state of health, family and economic situation and the links with their country of origin'.[104]

While it includes no explicit mention of proportionality, Article 8(4) of the Directive includes a requirement for Member States to 'take into account the personal situation of the person concerned' when deciding if an EU citizen is self-sufficient. The language of Article 8(4),[105] alongside the need to view these

[97] Case C-138/02 *Collins* (n 46) [63].
[98] ibid [69]–[72].
[99] Case C-209/03 *Bidar* (n 46).
[100] Yong (n 59) 57–61.
[101] C O'Brien, 'Real links, abstract rights and false alarms: the relationship between the ECJ's "real link" case law and national solidarity' (2008) 33 *European Law Review* 643.
[102] C O'Brien, *Unity and Adversity: EU Citizenship, Social Justice and the Cautionary Tale of the UK* (Hart Publishing, 2017) 37.
[103] Directive 2004/38, Preamble.
[104] ibid.
[105] Case C-140/12 *Brey* (n 54) [67].

provisions in light of the Treaty,[106] was found in *Brey* to strengthen the need for a proportional approach to restrictions of equal treatment rights in relation to a pension credit benefit. The Court determined that Member States could not set a blanket rule or minimum income requirement to determine whether a claim for welfare benefits from an 'economically inactive' EU citizen would be an unreasonable burden.[107] Instead they must carry out 'an overall assessment of the specific burden' which granting the benefit would create. This should include a consideration of 'the personal circumstances characterising the individual situation of the person concerned',[108] whether the need for support is likely to be temporary,[109] the amount of aid granted to them,[110] if they have received a residence permit or certificate[111] or the duration of their residence.[112]

This expansive approach treats the residency requirements and limitations in the Directives as a 'framework' or 'the floor of rights available', with EU citizenship and treaty provisions providing for *some* protection for citizens who fall through the gaps.[113] The progress made by the CJEU in proportionality was limited yet provided for a way to assert free movement and equal treatment rights as Union citizens, rather than through economic credentials alone. For atypical workers, such flexibility and assessment of individual circumstances could assist with locating themselves within the scope of equal treatment rights. For example, an assessment which would consider links to the employment market, integration and an appreciation of the economic contribution made through informal care work could identify that the specific burden of many atypical workers is not 'unreasonable'. Such an approach to proportionality could licence access to social assistance during gaps in the availability of shifts or to temporarily top-up part-time wages where work is balanced with the care of young children. However, the trajectory of more recent cases, discussed below, limits the usefulness of proportionality to those who fall outside of the scope of 'worker' status.

A particular problem with this approach to proportionality was the scale of the test required by *Brey*, which was criticised as too onerous for Member States to realistically carry out. For Verschueren, it placed its own type of 'unreasonable burden' on Member States by requiring a proportionality assessment that is, in effect, twofold by requiring individual circumstances of the applicants and the overall burden to be considered.[114] Verschueren points out that the Court gave

[106] ibid [70].
[107] ibid [77].
[108] ibid [64].
[109] ibid [72].
[110] ibid [69].
[111] ibid [80].
[112] ibid [76].
[113] Spaventa (n 3) 219; Dougan (n 93); C O'Brien, 'Civis Capitalist Sum: Class as the new guiding principle of EU Free Movement Rights' (2016) 53 *Common Market Law Review* 937, 945.
[114] H Verschueren, 'Free Movement or Benefit Tourism: The Unreasonable Burden of Brey' (2014) 16 *European Journal of Migration and Law* 147.

no acknowledgement of the potential administrative cost and burden of this test, which could result in higher expenditure 'than the "profit" the Member State concerned could gain by refusing these benefits to a number of Union citizens'.[115] Thym argued that the test in *Brey* was unclear on whether it imposed an individual or systemic test, both of which would push 'the debate in opposite directions'.[116] An individual assessment of unreasonable burden alone could be viewed as insufficient as no individual could create a burden on a Member State's social assistance system. For Cousins, the unclear and administratively unworkable[117] individual assessment proposed in *Brey* required a closer inspection by the CJEU to determine how Member States should approach the proportionality test. The Court's clumsy handling of the proportionality principle created a confusing, burdensome and potentially contradictory test and set the path towards the prioritisation of convenience for Member States.

8.3.2.2. The 'Likely Overall Burden'-based Proportionality Test

When given the opportunity to review this test, in cases concerning the more politically sensitive topic of welfare benefit provision for those deemed economically inactive, the CJEU reversed its position on proportionality, unpicking the individual assessment language and instead opting for a more sweeping 'likely overall burden' test. In some cases, proportionality is ignored altogether.

The Court first appears to switch its approach in *Alimanovic*, where it found that individual assessments on the burden of granting a specific benefit cannot be viewed in terms of the single applicant as that 'can scarcely be described as an "unreasonable burden" for a Member State'.[118] The proposed new test required Member States to consider 'the accumulation of all the individual claims which would be submitted to it' if it granted the benefit in the specific situation of the case.[119] This exact wording was then repeated in *García-Nieto*.[120] Here, the Court established a 'likely overall burden' test where Member States are permitted to make a sweeping generalisation about the potential burden a type of claim could create.

Davies argues that this judgment reflects a clarification of the Court's position.[121] He argues 'the precedential effect' of *Brey* was addressed, clarified and simplified in *Alimanovic*.[122] In this light, *Brey* is considered a 'Janus-faced judgment' masquerading as 'migrant-friendly', while guided by the restrictive residence requirements in Directive 2004/38.[123] Even if the *Brey* judgment was not exactly

[115] ibid 174.
[116] Thym (n 70) 28.
[117] Cousins (n 51) 99–100.
[118] Case C-67/14 *Alimanovic* (n 37) [62].
[119] ibid.
[120] Case C-299/14 *García-Nieto* (n 37) [50].
[121] Davies (n 28).
[122] ibid 11.
[123] ibid 12.

'migrant-friendly', the judgment in *Alimanovic* goes further than clarification and instead produces a shift in the focus of the proportionality assessment. The CJEU specifically referred to and distances itself from the language in *Brey* on individual assessments, instead suggesting that individual circumstances should now be treated as largely irrelevant.[124] The reasonableness of the burden should instead be measured with 'the amount which would be awarded to some (undefined) broader group'.[125] This change can drastically alter the outcome of such an assessment. As seen in previous case law, a strong focus on personal circumstances can be essential to categorising the burden they present as 'reasonable'. In *Grzelzcyk*, the Court 'placed great emphasis on Mr Grzelczyk's successful efforts to "defray his own costs" during the first three years of his study'.[126] Additionally, in *Grzelzcyk* and *Brey*, the Court notably focused on the length of time which the Union citizen requires support and the amount of money they are requesting for that support.[127] The shift in *Alimanovic* therefore represents more than a mere clarification of language and instead alters the proportionality calculation significantly. Additionally, the Court also suggested that for some Union citizens, for example jobseekers, no proportionality test was required at all, as Directive 2004/38 had sufficient proportionality built into it.[128]

Cousins has called out the Court, suggesting that it should 'honestly acknowledge when it was distancing itself from earlier case law'.[129] As the CJEU is not bound by precedent, the subsequent pretence of consistency is unhelpful, particularly if the 'consistency' relies on a tenuous distinguishing of facts.[130] This can create unclear and conflicting rules for Member States to apply and result in the assertion that aspects of CJEU case law on citizenship rights do not apply to specific national administrative systems.[131] For example, a legitimate clarification that may have been addressed by the Court in *Alimanovic* is the unworkability of the individual assessment in *Brey*, discussed above. The demands of the *Brey* proportionality assessment appears to be unrealistic, which has led to the insistence that the Court must not have meant what it said. For example, in the UK Supreme Court, Lord Neuberger stressed that the rule taken in *Brey* would 'place a substantial burden on a host Member State if it had to carry out a proportionality exercise in every case' and therefore the reversal on this practice in *Alimanovic* seemed 'good sense'.[132] Based on these considerations, it would have been preferable for the CJEU to

[124] Case C-67/14 *Alimanovic* (n 37) [62].
[125] Cousins (n 51) 100.
[126] O'Brien (n 101).
[127] Case C-184/99 *Grzelczyk* (n 45) [44]; C-140/12 *Brey* (n 54) [72].
[128] Case C-67/14 *Alimanovic* (n 37) [60].
[129] Cousins (n 51) 100.
[130] See also 8.3.3.
[131] As seen in the UK Upper Tribunal, which found the ruling of *Brey* to not apply in the UK as they did not provide residence cards or assess levels of self-sufficiency; *VP v SSWP (JSA)* [2014] UKUT 32 (AAC); O'Brien (n 113) 946.
[132] *Mirga v SSWP, Samin v Westminster City Council* [2016] UKSC 1 [68]–[69].

follow the path set in previous cases by applying a proportionality test which safeguards the free movement rights of EU citizens, whose personal circumstances mean that the burden on a Member State would be limited or temporary.

While the need to address the cumbersome test formulated in *Brey* could go some way to rationalise the Court's change of direction, it does not necessarily justify its decision to replace it with the different but flawed 'overall burden' test. The 'likely overall burden' test proposed in *Alimanovic* is problematic as it requires the consideration of a theoretical number of claims which can much more easily demonstrate an unreasonable burden on the national welfare system as a whole. It is all too easy for Member States to dismiss claims for social assistance citing concerns for the 'unreasonable' burden of a subsequent rush of applications it could, in theory, inspire. The CJEU is also unclear on how exactly this overall burden should be calculated. Does the assumed overall burden include the number of EU migrants present in the Member State at the time, or an estimate of how many Union citizens might move to the Member State in the future? Does it include all Union citizens who would be eligible for the benefit or recognise that EU migrants may not choose to claim benefits or be aware of their entitlement to benefits in host Member States? Will it take into account the economic contribution of EU migrants in atypical work? Or will it include a calculation of the net financial benefit bestowed upon Member States by the free movement of EU citizens?[133] Unless individual circumstances are taken into account, an individual application for benefits may be assumed to create the burden of a total of all possible further applications by an immeasurable, and plausibly erroneous, number of EU citizens.[134] For O'Brien, the assumption in *Alimanovic* and *García-Nieto* that individual circumstances have little consequence on the burden placed on the host Member State 'relies heavily upon generalizations' and fails to recognise situations where the law disproportionately denies support.[135] Yet the administrative problems of the individual assessment are still pertinent. There is a risk that either approach will have overwhelmingly sweeping results. *Alimanovic* provided no fix to this dilemma and instead produced the new 'likely overall burden' test which now requires fresh clarification on how it should be operated. It therefore adds little improvement to the administrative confusion of the *Brey* test and instead reflects a shift in the focus of the test itself.

[133] Commission, 'Free movement of EU citizens and their families: Five actions to make a difference' (Communication) COM(2013)837 final; OECD 'Fiscal Impact of Migration' in OECD, *International Migration Outlook 2013*; ICF GHK Milieu, 'A fact finding analysis on the impact on the Member States' social security systems of the entitlements of non-active intra-EU migrants to special non-contributory cash benefits and healthcare granted on the basis of residence' (2013).

[134] The use of declaratory systems for free movement make estimates of the number of EU citizens resident in different states difficult to calculate. Such difficulties can be seen in the estimated number of EU citizens who had to register for the EU Settlement Scheme; see M Sumption, 'Not Settled Yet? Understanding the EU Settlement Scheme using the Available Data' (Migration Observatory, April 2020).

[135] O'Brien (n 113) 949.

The Court's apparent move to a restrictive approach has further extended to cases where the principle of proportionality seems to be forgotten entirely. In *Alokpa*,[136] the CJEU ruled that if an economically inactive citizen does not meet the residency requirements they will automatically fall outside the scope of Article 21 TFEU.[137] There is no mention of the need for Member States to conduct a proportionality assessment in this case. This omission is particularly problematic given the facts of this case. Ms Alokpa was a non-EU living in Luxembourg with her French national children. When seeking to establish a right to reside in Luxembourg for the purpose of accepting a job offer, the national court found that they did not meet the residence requirements in Article 7(1)(b) Directive 2004/38, as they did not have sufficient resources not to be a burden on the Member State.[138] Paradoxically, had an assessment of the personal circumstances been required and residence rights been granted to Ms Alokpa's children as self-sufficient EU citizens, Ms Alokpa could have used her right as an EEA national family member to receive a work permit and accept the job offer, thereby not being a 'burden' on the host Member States welfare system and instead being economically active. Spaventa argues that, by ignoring the need for proportionality in *Alokpa*, any flexibility to take account of individual circumstances from previous case law is deemed no longer relevant, with the limitations in Directive 2004/38 being treated as 'standard'.[139]

The rejection of the individual focus for proportionality assessments has tipped the balance in favour of identifying an unreasonable burden. It has therefore created a situation where any claim for benefits from citizens falling outside the scope of Article 7 Directive 2004/38 can automatically be declared a burden despite empirical evidence finding that the 'budgetary impact' of welfare claims by economically inactive EU migrants 'is very low'.[140] This current interpretation ensures that the Directive's residency requirements are the 'floor and ceiling of rights'[141] and are enough to 'sufficiently constitute "citizenship" in the eyes of the Court'.[142] The analysis in this section is also consistent with the argument that the Court adjusted judgments to appease Member States by providing a sweeping justification for limitations on EU migrants' rights; effectively allowing national authorities the final say on benefit claims. This leaves little room for the consideration of personal circumstances. Consistent and *enough* economic activity is therefore made even more vital for many Union citizens to access equal treatment rights.[143] For atypical workers who are not recognised as workers under Article 7

[136] Case C-86/12 *Alokpa* ECLI:EU:C:2013:645.
[137] ibid [31].
[138] ibid [30].
[139] Spaventa (n 3) 220.
[140] ICF GHK Milieu (n 133) 203.
[141] Spaventa (n 3) 220.
[142] O'Brien (n 113) 949.
[143] H Verschueren, 'Being Economically Active: How it Still Matters' in H Verschueren (ed), *Residence, Employment and Social Rights of Mobile Persons: On how EU Law defines where they belong* (Intersentia, 2016) 187, 191.

Directive 2004/38, personal circumstances and *actual* extent of burden are potentially irrelevant for their free movement rights to be safeguarded.

8.3.3. The Reversal of Residence Documents as Proof of Lawful Residence

Residence documents have also been subject to a change of approach by the CJEU. In the past, expansive citizenship case law had sometimes centred around the issuance of residence permits. As such, Member States diverted from the associated duty to provide equal treatment to those whose lawful residence had been confirmed, even domestically, by pointing to a lack of residence document. But more recently, the CJEU switched up its approach, relieving Member States of these duties by finding that a domestic confirmation of residence does not guarantee protection from discrimination. As such, EEA nationals in atypical work can no longer rely on having the explicit permission from a Member State to reside and work in that country to rely on equal treatment rights.

The early EU citizenship cases which are often cited as exemplars of the positive extension of EU citizenship rights, are instead argued by Davies to reflect the CJEU prescribing particular significance to the acquisition of a residence permit in a Member State as confirmation of lawful residence and therefore triggering equal treatment rights.[144] This interpretation views the claimants' free movement rights as stemming from national law, where a residence card operates as confirmation of a right of residence, rather than solely sourcing rights from the status of EU citizenship. The importance bestowed on residence permits left the increasingly limited equal treatment rights of economically inactive EU citizens dependent on Member States *accidental generosity* through the provision of residence permits, such as that found by Heindlemaier and Blauberger, where Member States were not effective at enforcing restrictive residence rules.[145] Equally, Member States which did not require registration for a residence document could distance themselves from this duty, relying on any lack of confirmation of lawful residence to deny an EU citizen's free movement rights.

Martínez Sala, as discussed above,[146] has been both celebrated as showing EU citizenship rights to 'have real teeth'[147] and criticised as too radical a concept of equal treatment, interfering with national welfare systems.[148] However, the specific

[144] Davies (n 28) 16.

[145] A Heindlemaier and M Blauberger, 'Enter at your own risk: free movement of EU citizens in practice' (2017) 40 *West European Politics* 1198.

[146] See 8.3.1.

[147] A Albors-Llorens, 'Case Comment: A broader construction of the EC Treaty provisions on citizenship?' (1998) 57 *Cambridge Law Journal* 461, 463.

[148] Tomuschat (n 41) 457.

facts of the case elicited concern from O'Leary that the judgment 'excite[d] as many questions as it provide[d] answers'.[149] This apprehension centres around the judgment's apparent reliance on Mrs Martínez Sala's acquisition of a residence permit in Germany as proof of her right to reside. The CJEU ruled that the German law requiring non-nationals to produce residence permits to access benefits was found to be directly discriminatory and could not be justified.[150] Firstly, the Court assumed that 'it is common ground' that Mrs Martínez Sala was lawfully resident in Germany as she has been authorised to reside there through consequent residence permits.[151] However, as the claimant did not have an extension of her residence permit – only 'documents certifying that the extension … had been applied for'[152] – the Court also suggested that Mrs Martínez Sala may have a right to benefits solely by virtue of her being a Union citizen.[153] Through these facts, Union citizenship rights might appear to be immediately limited to situations where the claimant has, or at least has had, permission from the host Member State to reside. The Court's discussion of equal treatment rights is not general and instead applied rigorously to the specific facts of the case, stating that a non-economically active citizen may rely on these in situations where Member States require a document which is not required of nationals to access benefits.[154] O'Leary views this reliance on residence permits as revealing of the limited nature of the Court's adoption of Union citizenship as a source of rights.[155]

Another expansive citizenship case, *Trojani*, saw a French volunteer apply for the minimum subsistence allowance in Belgium. While the Court declared that Mr Trojani had no right to reside, he was deemed lawfully resident under national law as 'attested by the residence permit',[156] which had been issued to him by the national administration.[157] Here, the Court appeared to expand on the meaning of lawful residence beyond the qualified residence statuses found in Directive 90/364 (now Directive 2004/38),[158] as a status which could be provided for through national legislation alone and in many cases confirmed by the issuing of a residence permit. Additionally, the Court in *Brey* ruled that EU law must be interpreted as precluding national legislation which automatically bars the grant of a benefit to a non-economically active EU migrant, 'despite having been issued with a certificate of residence'.[159] The Court also identified the issuing of a residence certificate confirming lawful residence as an indication that a burden may

[149] O'Leary (n 44) 77–78.
[150] Case C-85/96 *Martínez Sala* (n 9) [64].
[151] ibid [60].
[152] ibid [14].
[153] ibid [63].
[154] ibid [63].
[155] O'Leary (n 44) 77.
[156] Case C-456/02 *Trojani* (n 84) [37].
[157] RCA White, 'Residence, Benefit entitlement and Community Law' (2005) 12 *Journal of Social Security Law* 10, 16.
[158] Council Directive 90/364/EC of 28 June 1990 on the right of residence [1990] OJ L180/26.
[159] Case C-140/12 *Brey* (n 54) [80].

be reasonable.[160] Once again, the Court's specific reference to the ownership of a residence certificate suggests that the right to an individualised proportionality assessment was influenced, not purely by Union citizenship rights but, by the provision of nationally recognised lawful residence.

The focus on residence permits in these cases therefore puts into question how expansive these judgments were for EU citizenship rights. The CJEU's 'reactionary' approach in later cases may appear to be less dramatic when viewed through the residence card-specific facts. As discussed above, Davies argues that the behaviour of the Court in *Brey* is entirely predictable, and his view on this also extends to the judgment in *Trojani*.[161] He argues that a 'migrant's capacity to challenge decisions and enforce their rights' would be harmed if a Member State were to hypocritically provide a Union citizen with a residence permit confirming their right of residence and then deny access to welfare benefits on the grounds of lacking a right to reside.[162] It is from the distinction of earlier, often cited 'pro-citizenship', cases which include the possession of residence permits that Davies locates some of the CJEU's consistency, whereas more recent, so-called 'reactionary', cases present facts where the EU citizens involved had neither an EU nor national confirmation of a right of residence to rely on. In *Dano*, for example, the claimant was in possession of a residence certificate from the German authorities, which was provided automatically to all EEA nationals with unlimited duration and therefore not deemed to confirm a right of residence.[163] The Court decided that Ms Dano had no right of residence and was therefore not entitled to benefits and the residence certificate in this case was deemed to merely perform 'a declaratory function and did not change her status under EU law'.[164]

However, this analysis fails to recognise the importance bestowed on Union citizenship beyond the use of residence cards. The CJEU in *Trojani* drew on Mr Trojani's status purely as an EU citizen to bring him into the scope of the Treaty.[165] The Court gave effect to Union citizenship as a source of residence rights, where a citizen is 'lawfully resident in the host Member State for a certain time *or* possess[ing] a residence permit'.[166] While the permit was useful, Cousins argues that it was not necessarily the only source of these rights, as the claimant's long period of residence could also contribute to the finding of lawful residence.[167] White also views that Mr Trojani's lawful residence is identified on the basis of his long period of time in the country without 'fraud or improper purpose at the point of entry'.[168] As discussed above, non-economically active citizens have

[160] ibid [78].
[161] Davies (n 28) 16.
[162] ibid.
[163] Case C-333/13 *Dano* (n 37) [36].
[164] Thym (n 70) 41.
[165] Case C-456/02 *Trojani* (n 84) [31].
[166] ibid [43] (emphasis added).
[167] Cousins (n 51) 92.
[168] White (n 157) 892.

been granted access to welfare benefits in a range of cases and circumstances,[169] including through the use of proportionality to determine whether they are an unreasonable burden,[170] where they have a genuine link with the employment market[171] or have demonstrated integration into the society of the host Member State.[172] Nevertheless, the judgment's supposed reliance on Trojani's residence permit has been sufficient for Member States to utilise the absence of a permit as a reason to withhold access to benefits.

8.3.3.1. Domestic Residence Documents as a Tool to Sidestep Duties

While a residence document could provide important evidence of national recognition of lawful residence, holding a domestically issued document was not intended to be the determinative factor of examination into an economically inactive citizens' lawful residence, at least until the CJEU's later 'reactionary phase' in later cases such as *Dano*. Given that the resident permits held by the claimants in *Martínez Sala*, *Trojani* and *Brey* were granted on the basis of national rather than EU law, Tomuschat expressed concern that such an expansive approach to EU citizenship rights in *Martínez Sala* could 'stimulate negative state practices' and restrictive behaviour.[173] This could easily be achieved through a mere change of national law, ie removing the provision of residence documents.

Alternatively, the importance bestowed on residence permits has been utilised in national courts as a distinguishing fact, to separate their own national legislation, which does not provide such residence documents, from the more progressive CJEU case law. The result of this would be a sweeping dismissal of CJEU case law and subsequently restricting the scope of equal treatment for non-economically active citizens. An example of this practice can be seen in the UK, where national courts have directly referenced the residence permits in *Trojani* and *Brey* to withhold EU citizenship rights from migrants without a qualifying Directive right of residence. In *Abdirahman*, the Court of Appeal stated that 'Mr Trojani's possession of the residence permit made all the difference'[174] for the CJEU and that the right to reside 'was derived from the permit he obtained, in the nick of time',[175] without which he would have no right of residence.[176] As the UK did not provide residence permits to EU nationals, this judgment and the extension to EU citizenship and equal treatment rights to those with lawful residence was found not apply to the UK.

[169] See Verschueren (n 143) 191.
[170] Cases C-184/99 *Grzelczyk* (n 45); C-413/99 *Baumbast* (n 46); C-140/12 *Brey* (n 54); See 8.3.2.
[171] Case C-138/02 *Collins* (n 46); Joined Cases C-22 and 23/08 *Vatsouras and Koupatantze* ECLI:EU:C:2009:344, [2009] ECR I-4585.
[172] Cases C-456/02 *Trojani* (n 84); C-209/03 *Bidar* (n 46).
[173] Tomuschat (n 41) 456.
[174] *Abdirahman v SSWP* [2007] EWCA Civ 657 [32].
[175] ibid [68].
[176] ibid [32].

In *VP v SSWP*, the Upper Tribunal judge stated that the decision in *Brey* 'may have been influenced by the fact that Mr Brey had been granted a registration certificate' and that the repeated references to the certificate 'are a powerful indication that … the CJEU was not' trying to establish stand-alone rights for EU migrants falling outside Article 7 of Directive 2004/38.[177] Rather, the Upper Tribunal believed that the CJEU were 'concerned with what follows where a right of residence has arisen in the first place' through a residence permit.[178] The Upper Tribunal followed that, as the UK did not issue residence cards to EU migrants, the claimants had to demonstrate a current right of residence in accordance with Directive 2004/38. It is Member States' side-stepping of expansive citizenship case law that undermines much of the progress made and reduces access to equal treatment rights.

Allowing Member States to cynically seal off expansive judgments due to their reliance on residence permits has an overarching restrictive impact on EU citizens' free movement rights, which has only been intensified by the more recent patchwork of restrictive CJEU judgments. As O'Brien points out, the dismissive attitude towards these CJEU judgments in UK courts has meant that the UK 'has continued to treat the "economically inactive" as automatically not having sufficient resources at the point of claim'.[179] Such an approach has also been vindicated by recent CJEU case law that appears to overturn the judgments in *Trojani* and *Brey*.

8.3.3.2. Permission to Discriminate and the Irrelevance of a Domestic Residence Status

The CJEU in *CG* took a dramatic turn on the issue of domestically issued residence documents confirming lawful residence.[180] Here, an EU national in the UK had a residence document confirming her presettled status under the EU Settlement Scheme and issued, as stated on the document, in accordance with the Withdrawal Agreement, but it was found to be of limited use. Importantly, and unlike the residence certificate in *Dano*, presettled status is not declaratory, but constitutive. The status must be applied for, checks are conducted on the individual's residence in the UK, sufficient evidence must be supplied and the status was initially designed to expire after five years.[181] Article 18(1) of the Withdrawal Agreement states that where Member States require registration for a new post-Brexit residence status, this would *confer* the rights under the Withdrawal Agreement.[182] Nevertheless, the UK argued that the fact that presettled status is awarded on the basis of factual

[177] *VP v SSWP (JSA)* [2014] UKUT 32 (AAC) [79].
[178] ibid [79].
[179] O'Brien (n 113) 946.
[180] Case C-709/20 *CG* (n 85).
[181] The UK High Court determined that the five-year expiry on presettled status was not consistent with Art 18(1) of the Withdrawal Agreement, which requires one single application for a residence status: *R (Independent Monitoring Authority for the Citizens' Rights Agreements) v SSHD* [2022] EWHC 3274 (Admin).
[182] Agreement on the withdrawal of the United Kingdom of Great Britain and Northern Ireland from the European Union and the European Atomic Energy Community (2020) (Withdrawal Agreement), Art 18(1).

residence, rather than the more administratively costly task of checking residence under one of the conditions of Article 13 of the Withdrawal Agreement (largely the same conditions as Article 7 Directive 2004/38), meant that it was not a confirmation of lawful residence and subsequently did not provide equal treatment rights.

In the *CG* decision, the CJEU departed from its approach in *Trojani* and *Brey*. The Court found that the award of presettled status did not grant protection from discrimination under Article 18 TFEU.[183] It identified the rights in Article 18 TFEU as having been given specific, and seemingly sole, expression in Article 24 Directive 2004/38. As such, there was no protection from discrimination or equal treatment rights for those who are not residing on the basis of the Directive.[184] Nor did it require a proportionality test of the kind seen in *Brey*. While not expressly overturning the decision in *Trojani*,[185] the CJEU has seemingly shifted its position, finding that Member States have an overarching right to refuse economically inactive Union citizens access to benefits, regardless of whether they have a residence permit. Instead, the CJEU offered the conciliatory prize of requiring an assessment of the risk of violation of the fundamental right to live in dignity under the Charter for those who had a right to live in a Member State.[186]

This decision, while concerned with post-Brexit residence status, has repercussions for Union citizenship and exercising free movement more broadly. O'Brien points out that the Court's decision 'dismissed and marginalised primary non-discrimination rights' in Article 18 TFEU, finding it to be 'subordinate to, and displaced by, conditions attached to secondary law'.[187] As such, any EU migrant living in an EU Member State, even where they lawfully reside on the basis of domestic law, cannot expect protection from discrimination based on nationality under EU law. Instead, their only reliable option is to meet the conditions of Directive 2004/38. Ultimately, EEA nationals can be provided with the assurance and necessary proof that they have a rights to live, work, pay taxes and otherwise contribute to the host Member State, through a domestic immigration residence permit, but with no reciprocal duty on that Member State to provide support or equal access to the welfare system. This means that EU atypical workers, even when in possession of a domestic right of residence, are expected to demonstrate an additional and separate right of residence under the rules of the Directive to access equal treatment rights.

8.3.4. Inconsistent Categorising of Benefits

Another route through which EU citizens' equal treatment rights have been reduced is through the Court's failure to prevent Member States strategically

[183] Case C-709/20 *CG* (n 85) [67].
[184] ibid [66].
[185] The judgment does not discuss *Trojani* or *Brey* at all, only mentioning *Trojani* once to note that *CG* relies on it in their submissions: ibid [37].
[186] ibid [85]–[92]; Charter of Fundamental Rights of the European Union [2012] OJ C 326/02.
[187] O'Brien (n 85) 816.

miscategorising welfare benefits. This is apparent in two ways: firstly in the Court's treatment of jobseeking benefits being classified as social assistance, allowing Member States to withhold them from EU citizen jobseekers; and secondly, through subjecting benefits that cannot be categorised as social assistance to the same treatment as social assistance benefits.

8.3.4.1. Jobseeking Benefits and Social Assistance

Access to welfare benefits for work-seekers that aim to facilitate access to the labour market is protected by Article 45(2) TFEU,[188] particularly since the establishment of EU citizenship.[189] However, Article 24(2) Directive 2004/38 allows Member States to withhold entitlement to benefits classified as social assistance for the first three months of residence, unless the claimant is a worker, self-employed person or a family member under Article 7 Directive 2004/38.[190] The reclassifying of financial job-seeking welfare benefits as social assistance, as seen in *Alimanovic*, allows Member States to employ restrictive entitlement requirements while bypassing the need for the Court to address a potential change in approach.

The introduction of EU citizenship has seen the CJEU protect work-seekers' access to benefits that facilitate access to the labour market. In *Collins* the Court stated that the 'establishment of citizenship of the Union' was a development which must be reflected and distinguished from previous case law which had previously found that work-seekers could not rely on Article 45(2) for equal treatment rights.[191] In *Vatsouras*, the Court clarified this, stating that welfare benefits of a financial nature intending to facilitate a Union citizen's access to the labour market cannot be regarded as constituting 'social assistance', independently of the status given to it by national law.[192] Benefits which were considered to facilitate access to the labour market could therefore not be withheld from EU work-seekers under the rules intended for social assistance benefits in Article 24(2) Directive 2004/38. The Court also referenced AG Ruiz-Jarabo Colomer's argument that a benefit's objective 'must be analysed according to its results and not according to its formal structure', and therefore a requirement that the recipient be capable of earning a living 'could constitute an indication that the benefit is intended to facilitate access to employment'.[193]

In *Alimanovic*, the Court focused on the objectives of a benefit to give minimum subsistence to those looking for employment, finding that it should be classified as social assistance. The CJEU took note that the national authorities had 'characterised the benefits at issue as "special non-contributory cash benefits" … even

[188] TFEU, Art 45(2).
[189] Case C-138/02 *Collins* (n 46) [63].
[190] Directive 2004/38, Art 24(2).
[191] Case C-138/02 *Collins* (n 46) [63]–[64].
[192] Cases C-22/08 and C-23/08 *Vatsouras and Koupatantze* (n 171) [45].
[193] ibid [57].

if they form part of a scheme which also provides for benefits to facilitate the search for employment'.[194] It has already been established, in *Dano*, that a special non-contributory cash benefit was found to fit 'within the concept of "social assistance"'.[195] The Court in *Alimanovic* failed to consider the requirements of accessing the benefit, including that the recipient must be fit for work, or the relevance that it is one of two components to a benefit provided for by a job centre, described as 'entitlement to basic provision for job-seekers'.[196] Instead, they agreed with AG Wathelet's opinion, that the predominant function of the benefit must be regarded, which was determined to be the cover of 'subsistence costs necessary to lead a life in keeping with human dignity'.[197] The CJEU appears to have altered or at least stepped away from the guidance it provided in the earlier judgments of *Collins* and *Vatsouras*, which stressed the relevance of requiring recipients to be able to work or to seek employment in determining the objective of the benefit as the facilitation of access to employment. Instead, by singling out the 'human dignity' or means-testing aspect of the welfare benefit as the core objective, the CJEU has withheld access to financial support to would-be-worker EU citizens who would aim to contribute economically to the host Member State in the future. The ability to move to another Member State to seek employment is therefore only available to those who have savings, the low number of those who are aware of and can export their unemployment benefits under Regulation 883/2004[198] or those who are willing to live without the support 'necessary to lead a life in keeping with human dignity'.

8.3.4.2. *Social Security or Assistance*

The CJEU has also applied the rules relating to social assistance to benefits that are expressly identified as social security benefits, such as in *Commission v UK*.[199] Through this case, the CJEU extended the ability of Member States to require EU citizens to prove that they possess a right to reside to access social assistance to social security benefits. This extends the hurdles facing EU citizens when attempting to access financial support where they are not economically active.

Commission v UK concerned Child Benefit and Child Tax Credit which the CJEU identified as falling within the 'family benefit' category of social security benefits in Regulation 883/2004,[200] as they are 'granted automatically to families

[194] Case C-67/14 *Alimanovic* (n 37) [43].
[195] Case C-333/13 *Dano* (n 37) [63].
[196] Case C-67/14 *Alimanovic* (n 37) [13].
[197] Case C-67/14 *Alimanovic*, Opinion of AG Wathelet ECLI:EU:C:2015:210 [72].
[198] Regulation (EC) No 883/2004 of the European Parliament and of the Council of 29 April 2004 on the coordination of social security systems, [2004] OJ L200/1 (Regulation 883/2004). For an analysis of the low share of exportation of unemployment benefits, see C Grabbe, 'Free movement and access to social security in the EU: The challenge of exporting unemployment benefits' (2023) 25 *European Journal of Social Security* 20.
[199] Case C-308/14 *Commission v UK* (n 37).
[200] Regulation 883/2004.

meeting certain objective criteria, relating in particular to their size, income and capital resources'.[201] However, the Court agreed with the UK's submissions, finding that social security benefits should be applied with the same principles decided in *Brey*, namely 'that there is nothing to prevent … the granting of social benefits to Union citizens conditional upon those citizens meeting the necessary right to reside requirements' as economically active or financially independent EU citizens.[202] This argument relies on an overly expansive reading of the *Brey* judgment. The UK argued that the term 'social benefits', as seen in the original German and French language versions of the judgment, should be understood broadly and does not in any way indicate that the reasoning set out by the Court is confined exclusively to the type of benefits at issue in *Brey*.[203]

The UK argued, and the Court appeared to accept, that 'it is difficult to conceive' that Member States are not required to pay social assistance benefits, but are required to pay social security benefits when both 'have the potential to impose an unreasonable burden on the public finances of the host Member State'.[204] However, the benefits concerned in *Brey* were designated to be social assistance benefits rather than social security. O'Brien argues that the principle in *Brey* was seemingly applied, not as 'a standalone, catch-all principle' but was 'inextricably linked to the nature of the benefits'.[205] The CJEU found that the principle in *Brey* should be extended to cover special non-contributory benefits – a sub-category of social security benefits. In reaching this decision the Court did not explicitly agree with the UK or AG Cruz Villalón that the principle extended to social security benefits simply because the Court omitted to say that it did not.[206]

Davies sees the decision in *Commission v UK* as a continuation of previous judgments of *Dano*, *Alimanovic* and *García-Nieto*, which all followed the requirement of mobile EU citizens claiming benefits to have 'substantive compliance' with EU right of residence rules.[207] However, this doesn't consider the sleight of hand with which the CJEU intermingled principles for social assistance benefits with the theoretically better-protected category of social security benefits. O'Brien suggests that the *Commission v UK* judgment is 'very shaky', relying on the fact that the judgment in *Brey*, when determining that right to reside tests were permitted to grant access to 'social benefits',[208] omitted to specify that this was *not* the case for social security benefits. The judgment therefore relied on 'not only a single paragraph in a judgment, but on something the Court did not say in that paragraph'.[209] Additionally,

[201] Case C-308/14 *Commission v UK* (n 37) [60].
[202] Case C-140/12 *Brey* (n 54) [44].
[203] Case C-308/14 *Commission v UK* (n 37) [33].
[204] ibid [50].
[205] C O'Brien, 'The ECJ sacrifices EU Citizenship in vain: Commission v. United Kingdom' (2017) 54 *Common Market Law Review* 209, 219.
[206] Case C-308/14 *Commission v UK*, Opinion of AG Cruz Villalón ECLI:EU:C:2015:666.
[207] Davies (n 28) 15.
[208] Case C-140/12 *Brey* (n 54) [44].
[209] O'Brien (n 205) 220.

the CJEU ignored how social security and social assistance benefits should be treated differently. Had the Court identified the UK's right to reside test as direct discrimination rather than indirect discrimination, as it arguably should have done by considering how the right to reside test is intrinsically linked to nationality,[210] then it would need to locate specific exceptions in the legislation that allow for the derogation. Verschueren highlights that while exceptions to equal treatment are contained in Directive 2004/38 in relation to social assistance benefits and some benefits included in Regulation 883/2004, no such exceptions apply specifically to 'family benefits' in Regulation 883/2004.[211] These differences in restrictions should be respected. Merging the principles of social assistance regardless of the extra protections provided to social security benefits allows Member States to further restrict EU migrants' access to more types of financial support.

Overall, this section has analysed three ways in which the CJEU case law has transitioned from an expansive to restrictive approach when looking at EU citizenship free movement rights. In more recent judgments, the CJEU can be seen to ignore previous precedent or flexibly interpreting legislation and case law to allow Member States to restrict access to benefits. Given that the text of the Treaty and Directive has not been amended to warrant this departure from previous cases, it appears to be a change in approach for the Court. Examples of this change have been identified in the Court's language around EU citizenship rights and the objectives of the legislation to give them effect, the approach to applying the principle of proportionality, the relevance of a domestically issued residence permit and how the Court treats the reclassification of welfare benefits and the ability to restrict access to them. The change in the Court's reasoning and approach to core EU Treaty rights goes beyond the different and politically sensitive facts of these cases and improvement in Member State competence to defend their restrictions, as Davies has suggested.[212] The Court has been inconsistent in its handling of EU citizenship and free movement rights. For Nic Shuibhne, the CJEU is forgetting that, for now, citizenship rights are part of primary EU law and 'The Court should be responsible enough to guard the boundaries of existing primary rights' until it is altered by the legislature.[213] The switch in interpretation has resulted in restricting the scope of free movement and equal treatment rights to only those EU citizens who can evidence their right of residence according to Directive 2004/38. The implications of this for the free movement of EU citizens who are deemed economically inactive are discussed below.[214] In order to analyse the limitations

[210] As being a UK citizen automatically grants a right of residence in the UK. See also Case C-73/08 *Bressol* Opinion of AG Sharpston ECLI:EU:C:2009:396, [2009] ECR I-2735 [53],; H Verschueren, 'Recent case before the Court of Justice of the European Union: Case C-308/14, European Commission v United Kingdom, ECLI:EU:C:2016:436 (14 June 2016)' (2017) 19 *European Journal of Social Security* 71, 77; O'Brien (n 205) 225.

[211] Verschueren (n 210) 82.

[212] Davies (n 28) 25.

[213] Nic Shuibhne (n 17) 937.

[214] At 8.5.1.

to citizenship effectively, it is first useful to consider the potential drivers behind the Court's shift.

8.4. The Political Fragility of Free Movement

The shift in the Court's approach to free movement rights for EU citizens must be viewed within the relevant political context. Spaventa attributes the CJEU's reactionary phase to increased negative political focus on free movement and the desire of Member States to limit entitlement to their national welfare systems.[215] It is noticeable that the Court's approach to EU citizenship rights has progressively become more restrictive in recent years, with the CJEU's most restrictive judgments of *Dano*, *Alimanovic*, *García-Nieto* and *Commission v UK* occurring within a two-year period between 2014 and 2016. From the analysis above, the CJEU's switch in approach cannot be attributed to substantial legislative change as the text of the Treaty was not amended during this period. While Directive 2004/38 was introduced during the course of the cases analysed, judgments released after its implementation did not adopt the restrictive approach of the CJEU seen in more recent cases.[216] Instead, this section explores some of the potential political drivers of this reactionary phase, finding the Court and free movement rights to be vulnerable to political discourse, even when these discourses are not supported by the evidence.

8.4.1. EU Enlargement and Unfounded Fears of 'Benefit Tourism'

The question of who should be included in national welfare systems is a highly sensitive political topic. As discussed in section 8.2, the creation of Directive 2004/38 and optional transition measures were, at least in part, to soothe the concerns of 'mass migration' from new Member States joining the EU in 2004.[217] For Thym, the broad and sometimes vague construction of Directive 2004/38 suggests the EU has 'opted for deliberate ambiguity' to accommodate 'politically sensitive terrain'.[218] This ambiguity can be seen most notably in the language precluding EU citizens from becoming a 'burden' or an 'unreasonable burden', as discussed in section 8.3.2.

[215] (n 3).
[216] Blauberger et al (n 52) 1432.
[217] 'The UK, EU Citizenship and Free Movement of Persons' (The Migration Observatory, 2014), www.migrationobservatory.ox.ac.uk/resources/primers/the-uk-eu-citizenship-and-free-movement-of-persons.
[218] Thym (n 70) 26.

Given this reaction to new Member States joining the EU in 2004, it is not surprising that a 2014 report for the European Parliament identified the EU enlargement in 2007, alongside the 2008 economic crisis as catalysts to 'a sharper discourse against intra-EU immigration amid claims that it burdens national welfare systems'.[219] Alongside this, transition measures for Bulgarian and Romanian nationals ended in 2014,[220] sparking Member States' warnings against a possible '"flood" of immigration' and subsequent 'pressure on public budgets'.[221] This purported concern over free movement's role in enabling 'benefit tourism' was expressed in a joint letter sent from political leaders in Austria, Germany, the Netherlands and the UK to the EU in 2013. In the letter the four Member States detailed their concerns of EU migrants 'burdening the host countries' social welfare systems'.[222] The letter argued that EU free movement rules which provide access to welfare benefits were 'an affront to common sense' that 'ought to be reviewed urgently' to prevent any potential burden and to strengthen the actions that can be taken against those who, in their words, 'abuse' the right to free movement.[223] However, these concerns lack any substantial evidence. Poptcheva argues that the discussion of free movement and its potential burden on welfare systems 'has long gone beyond proof by numbers' with Member States instead relying on feelings of a loss of control over their welfare systems.[224]

On the contrary, evidence on the economic impacts of free movement tends to point to it as net benefit to the majority of Member States. A Communication from the Commission in 2013 refers to independent research showing that, in most Member States, EU citizens are net contributors providing more in tax than they receive in benefits or through use of public services.[225] They also provide evidence that no 'statistical relationship' has been identified between the generosity of welfare systems and the inflow of mobile EU citizens.[226] In response to the joint letter, foreign ministers from the Czech Republic, Hungary, Poland and Slovakia released a statement reminding the EU that free movement of people is vital for the success of the single market. The statement challenged the misconception of the burden of benefit tourism referring specifically to data on the impact of free movement in the UK which shows that migrants from Central and Eastern Europe 'have been hugely beneficial for the British economy'.[227]

[219] EM Poptcheva 'Freedom of movement and residence of EU citizens: Access to social benefits' (European Parliamentary Research Service, 2014) 1.

[220] L Andor, 'End of restrictions on free movement of workers from Bulgaria and Romania' (1 January 2014), europa.eu/rapid/press-release_MEMO-14-1_en.htm.

[221] Poptcheva (n 219) 3.

[222] Letter from Johanna Mikl-Leitner (Minister of the Interior, Austria), Hans Peter Friedrich (Minister of the Interior, Germany), Fred Teeven (Minister for Immigration, Netherlands) and Theresa May (Home Secretary, UK) to the EU Council Presidency and to Commissioners Viviane Reding, Cecilia Malmström and László Andor of April 2013, 2.

[223] ibid 4.

[224] Poptcheva (n 219) 4.

[225] Commission (n 133); OECD (n 133); ICF GHK Milieu (n 133) 203.

[226] Commission (n 133) 4.

[227] Joint Statement from the Foreign Ministers of the Visegrad countries of 4 December 2013.

Despite the evidence detailing the positive impact of free movement for most Member States, the politisation of free movement persisted. The European elections in 2014 saw a significant increase in support for Eurosceptic parties.[228] The issue of immigration came third in an assessment of voter concerns.[229] In the UK, this increase appeared to be related, at least in part, to the desire for stronger controls on immigration, a problem which was often attributed to membership of the EU and the free movement of people.[230] This was then followed by the 2015 UK general election, which saw the Conservative Party win a majority while promising a referendum on membership of the EU.[231] Before this referendum took place, David Cameron set out his demands to change the UK's membership with the EU, including relief from the 'pressures free movement can bring' by requiring EU migrants to reside in the UK for four years before they could 'qualify for in-work benefits or social housing'.[232] The EU agreed to a version of this provision, introducing the 'benefit-brake' mechanism. This would allow Member States to request, when experiencing exceptional pressure on their welfare system, labour market or public services as a result of free movement, the power to limit the access of newly arriving EU workers to in-work benefits until they had resided for a total period of up to four years.[233] The 'new settlement' made with the UK also provided Member States with a route to restricting the exportability of family benefits for EU workers.[234] Nic Shuibhne identified that neither of these restrictions 'could be defended against established principles constituting the integrated system of free movement and equal treatment law'.[235] Among issues such as fitting into the permitted derogations from equal treatment rights and ignoring the legal distinction of the treatment of those who are economically active and those who are not, Nic Shuibhne also identifies that these measures would struggle to meet 'the proportionality test and its demands for evidence-based decisions'.[236] A declaration from the Commission deemed that the circumstances in the UK demonstrated 'the type of exceptional situation that the proposed safeguard mechanism is intended to cover',[237] despite a lack of evidence supporting this finding published by either the Commission or reports by the UK Department of Work and Pensions.[238] The

[228] O Hawkins, V Miller and J Hardacre, 'European Parliament Elections 2014' (House of Commons Library Research Paper 14/32, 2014).

[229] European Parliament '2014 post-election survey, European elections 2014: Analytical overview, Directorate General for Communication, Public Opinion Monitoring Unit' (October 2014) 9.

[230] Hawkins et al (n 228) 2.

[231] David Cameron, 'EU speech at Bloomberg' (23 January 2013), www.gov.uk/government/speeches/eu-speech-at-bloomberg.

[232] Letter from David Cameron to Donald Tusk (10 November 2015).

[233] Decision of the Heads of State or Government, meeting within the European Council, concerning a new settlement for the United Kingdom within the European Union OJ C691/1 (New Settlement) Annex I, section D(2)(b).

[234] ibid Annex I, section D(2)(a).

[235] N Nic Shuibhne, 'Reconnecting free movement of workers and equal treatment in an unequal Europe' (2018) 43 *European Law Review* 477.

[236] ibid 496.

[237] New Settlement, Annex VI.

[238] O'Brien (n 102) 264; Nic Shuibhne (n 235) 495.

legal legitimacy of these restrictions are therefore put into question, particularly when it's implementation can rely on unsubstantiated predictions of the impact of free movement and equal treatment.

As the UK voted to leave the European Union in the 2016 referendum, the benefit-brake mechanism was never implemented. Nevertheless, it is telling of the extent to which the EU would tolerate and was prepared to contribute to the sacrifice of free movement rights for working EU citizens to placate Member States' desires to withhold access to national welfare systems. For Nic Shuibhne, the departure from equal treatment for a significant period of time, while not easing obligations on EU workers, such as tax payments, illustrates 'the degree of the inequality of treatment contemplated'.[239] If these measures had been adopted and implemented, EU migrant workers would have been expected to reside without the support provided by 'in-work benefits' for four years, regardless of their individual circumstances. Given the fragmentation of the labour market, discussed in chapter two, free movement under these requirements would not be a realistic possibility for many precarious, low-paid atypical workers. Such a limit would therefore have potentially reduced free movement rights beyond the pre-citizenship rules.

8.4.2. The EUs Sensitivity to Free Movement Concerns

This increase in political sensitivity surrounding free movement arose around the same period of time as the CJEU's most restrictive judgments in *Dano*, *Alimanovic*, *García-Nieto* and *Commission v UK*, and has therefore been highlighted as a potential driver for this change. Spaventa is not alone in her opinion that 'the Court is reflecting a change in the political appetite for citizenship'.[240] O'Brien also points to the judgment in *Dano*, stating that 'the Court was at pains to reassure Member States concerned about benefit tourism'.[241]

One of the most apparent examples of the CJEU reacting to political events is the judgment in *Commission v UK*, which was released just nine days before the UK's referendum on membership to the EU. Blauberger et al note that the decision not to postpone such a politically sensitive decision, which was a 'heated subject of campaigning', illustrates 'the Court's willingness not to avoid the impression of political intervention'.[242] The timing of this judgment may suggest the political intervention involved, while stark, was perhaps limited to the particular context of the UK and the upcoming referendum. For example, Costamagna described the judgment as an attempt 'to join in the efforts to defuse British voters' concerns with migration-related issues'.[243] Verschueren also criticises this judgment, suggesting

[239] Nic Shuibhne (n 235) 486–87.
[240] Spaventa (n 3).
[241] O'Brien (n 113) 946.
[242] Blauberger et al (n 52) 1437.
[243] F Costamagna, 'Restricting access to social benefits and the lasting legacy of the Brexit debate' (EuVisions, July 2016), www.euvisions.eu/restricting-access-to-social-benefits-and-the-lasting-legacy-of-the-brexit-debate.

that the referendum 'did not produce the result that the judges in Luxembourg probably had in mind'.[244] While the intention may have been limited to intervention in the UK referendum, the implications are far-reaching and speak to the growing politicising of free movement across Europe. For O'Brien, the 'sweeping acceptance of automatic exclusions of those falling foul' of the right to reside test and 'deference to the public finance trump card' provides a shining example of the Court dismantling EU Citizenship in an attempt to both 'placate the UK population sufficiently to tempt it to vote to stay in the Union' and 'accommodate Member States desires to discriminate'.[245]

By tracking the increase of both public discourse and media coverage of 'benefit tourism' or 'welfare migration', Blauberger et al identify a 'strong correlation' between increased public consternation and media attention to 'benefit tourism' and the more restrictive judgments of the CJEU such as *Dano*, *Alimanovic*, *García-Nieto* and *Commission v UK*.[246] In particular, Blauberger et al draw a comparison between public discourse around 'benefit tourism' and the Court's language in *Dano*,[247] where the Court referred to the motive of EU citizens to move 'solely in order to obtain another Member State's social assistance'.[248] Their research distinguishes the public mood from Member State opposition to free movement rules or threats of non-compliance, which they find has been present in many examples of expansive citizenship case law.[249] While this correlation does not automatically imply causation, it is important to recognise, as O'Brien states, that the Court does 'not operate in a vacuum'.[250] In fact, the CJEU was specifically drawn to the attention and interest given to 'benefit tourism' in the public sphere when it was noted by AG Wathelet in his opinion in *Alimanovic*.[251]

The ties between the Court's judgments and the political context suggests that the CJEU has been responsive to the political environment and may further suggest a politically motivated transition. While these decisions may be understandable and 'may even play a vital part in the preservation of harmonious EU relations overall', Nic Shuibhne argues that it represents 'a tainted compromise' where free movement rights, marketed to the public as rights for all EU citizens, are in fact restricted for only those who can afford them.[252] Given the indications that the EU is willing to restrict free movement rights further, as evidenced in the negotiated benefit-brake with the UK, it seems that concern around the future for these rights is entirely warranted. However, a response

[244] Verschueren (n 210) 82.
[245] O'Brien (n 205).
[246] Blauberger et al (n 52) 1436.
[247] ibid.
[248] Case C-333/13 *Dano* (n 37) [78].
[249] Blauberger et al (n 52) 1432.
[250] O'Brien (n 205).
[251] Case C-67/14 *Alimanovic*, Opinion of AG Wathelet (n 197) [4].
[252] Nic Shuibhne (n 17) 936.

to one political movement may be met with a backlash from another. Spaventa notes that by limiting free movement to an option only available to those who meet the residence requirements, while potentially aiming to comfort concerned populations, increases 'the sense of alienation from … a project that is exclusive rather than inclusive in nature'.[253] As a result, trust in the EU and perceived advantages of membership may be damaged. For EU citizens whose rights have been limited, and free movement no longer a realistic option, they may begin to question 'what has the EU ever done for us?'.

8.5. Uncertainty and Inequality in the Free Movement of EU Citizens

Given that citizenship rights were already limited, further squeezing of who counts as a worker could see the extinction of free movement as a realistic option available to many EU citizens. For example, before the Court's recent restrictive tendencies, Dougan identified the 'added value' of EU citizenship as merely 'a charitable fund for distressed gentlefolk to help them overcome temporary financial embarrassments' or to those who 'seem deserving of support because they are trying to better themselves in some orthodox economic sense'.[254] The Court's judgments in *Dano*, *Alimanovic*, *García-Nieto* and *Commission v UK* has further reduced this 'added value' by limiting the scope of rights. By making equal treatment contingent on fulfilling the residence criteria in the Directive, the Court has condensed citizenship 'rights' into an exclusive privilege. The Court's framing of free movement as a binary conflict of the 'market' interests of Member States against the 'social' interests of the citizen, ignores the need to balance multiple interests and 'subdues the complex reality' of the situations that arise.[255] Nic Shuibhne highlights where the 'balance between economic responsibility and protection of vulnerable citizens', are 'sidelined' and 'socially vulnerable EU citizens are not protected; and neither is their fate considered within the judicial discussion'.[256] The case studies discussed in previous chapters demonstrate that it may not just the more conventional idea of 'vulnerable' citizens who are at risk, but those who are in any kind of atypical or flexible employment.

This section will therefore examine some of the consequences of the Court's restrictive judgments, including the diminished ability for EU citizens to exercise free movement and what this means for the status of EU Citizenship and finally, the damage to legal certainty for EU citizens.

[253] Spaventa (n 3) 220.
[254] Dougan (n 93) 622–23.
[255] N Nic Shuibhne, 'The Social Market Economy and Restriction of Free Movement Rights: plus c'est la même chose?' (2019) 57 *Journal of Common Market Studies* 111.
[256] ibid.

8.5.1. The Reality of Limiting Free Movement to Directive 2004/38

By binding equal treatment to an EU citizens' ability to establish a right of residence under Article 7 Directive 2004/38, the full force of free movement rights are reserved for the economically active or those who have enough wealth or capital to be financially self-sufficient. The CJEU has even acknowledged that long-term free movement is severely restricted, with EU citizens having the luxury of not being required to demonstrate 'sufficient means of subsistence and personal medical cover' for the initial three-months in a Member State.[257] By singling out the ability to move with no restrictions for three months,[258] the Court recognises that after these three months, time is up on free movement, unless the residency requirements are met. As Davies puts it, this judgment confirms that 'even the poor are entitled to move for short periods'.[259] Additionally, *Alokpa*, discussed above, is illustrative of the Court's willingness to treat free movement rights differently depending on levels of affluence. The only notable difference between the individuals in *Alokpa* and the previous case of *Chen*, where a right of residence was identified,[260] is that self-sufficiency was established through pre-held resources in the latter whereas the former's self-sufficiency would have to be earned through work. Despite AG Mengozzi's wish to avoid 'individual situations of Union citizens and their family members being treated unfairly',[261] the CJEU found that Ms Alokpa could not rely on a derivative right of residence from her children as they did not have sufficient resources, despite Ms Alokpa's offer of employment which required a right of residence and permit to be granted.[262] Spaventa rightly calls this out as a 'form of hideous discrimination between those who have inherent resources … and those who have to earn their living'.[263]

Nic Shuibhne argues that the impact of the Court's restrictive approach raises important 'questions about the extent to which the existence and not just the exercise of free movement rights has been undermined'.[264] For Spaventa, free movement rules now only cater to 'the wealthy, healthy and good Union citizens', leaving out those who have a low income, disabilities and health conditions and those who have alternative lifestyles.[265] She further argues that the reactionary phase of the Court has returned EU citizenship to market-based rights as 'the European project helps those who can help themselves and solidarity is confined to those who have

[257] Case C-299/14 *García-Nieto* (n 37) [45].
[258] Under Directive 2004/38, Art 6.
[259] Davies (n 28) 22.
[260] Case 200/02 *Chen* ECLI:EU:C:2004:639, [2004] ECR I-9925.
[261] Case C-86/12 *Alokpa* (n 136) [29].
[262] ibid.
[263] Spaventa (n 3) 215.
[264] Nic Shuibhne (n 17) 892.
[265] Spaventa (n 3) 220.

proven their market credentials' fostering exclusion and discrimination.[266] Further to this argument and as seen in the case studies in previous chapters, clearly market credentials are not always enough to warrant solidarity. For atypical workers who do not earn enough or earn in the right way to be deemed economically active as a 'worker', EU citizenship as little to offer.

The limited added-value of EU citizenship also raises some serious concerns about the availability of free movement to all EU citizens. Unless a person is wealthy enough to reside in a Member State without accessing the welfare system, free movement is unlikely to be a viable option. Kochenov argues that these restrictions means that all citizens 'who fail to construct their lives along the lines enforced and endorsed by the economic project' are excluded from the rights and provisions that are supposed to go hand in hand with holding the status.[267] Spaventa contends that this exercise reduces the status of an economically inactive EU citizen to 'only one step above the "alien"'.[268] This may have a 'chilling effect' on EU nationals, who may be discouraged to take the gamble of free movement or who may choose to move and, due to the lack of clarity and mystification surrounding the rights EU citizenship, unwillingly expose themselves to the risks it entails. In this regard, three months' free movement, but with no entitlement to equal treatment,[269] is a poor consolation prize for a community of citizens – especially when the reliance on economic activity reinforces many of the inequalities present in the labour market, resulting in Union citizenship having even less value for women or Disabled people.

National welfare models are also becoming more unequal and increasingly reliant on conditionality, linking eligibility for welfare benefits to responsibilities and engagement with various sanctions for non-compliance,[270] a shift that is seemingly encouraged by the EU too.[271] In some circumstances, this has also been extended to previously exempt groups such as Disabled people, lone parents and low-income workers and their families.[272] The level of conditions relating to welfare benefits will differ greatly in different states, even within the territory of the EU. Nevertheless, the question here is not whether free movement fails to establish equality in welfare models, as many national welfare models are already unequal, but whether free movement, while inherently reducing the inequalities faced between *some* similar EU national workers and nationals of the Member

[266] ibid 222–23.

[267] Kochenov (n 2) 15.

[268] Spaventa (n 3) 220–21.

[269] Directive 2004/38, Art 24(2).

[270] P Dwyer, 'Final findings report: Welfare Conditionality Project 2013–2018' (June 2018).

[271] European Commission, 'Report from the Commission to the Council on the evaluation of the Council Recommendation on the integration of the long-term unemployed into the labour market' COM(2019) 169 final.

[272] P Dwyer, 'Citizenship, conduct and conditionality: sanction and support in the 21st century UK welfare state' in M Fenger, J Hudson, and C Needham (eds), *Social Policy Review 28: Analysis and Debate in Social Policy* (Policy Press, 2016) 41.

States they live in, also preserves and perpetuates existing inequalities or introduces further inequalities between its citizens. Spaventa warns against the 'link between rights and economic status', present in national systems, being 'reinforced and legitimised by its reiteration on a grander scale at the European level'.[273] The danger of this potential spiralling inequality is highlighted by O'Brien, who documents the utilisation of treating EU nationals as a menace to justify the restriction of their access to benefits resulting in the holding up of EU nationals as 'models' of personal responsibility, working around increased levels of conditionality.[274] Subsequently this inspires further conditionality for national citizens, who are expected to match the same level of individual responsibility.[275] With this in mind, it is no surprise that conditionality in the UK has been extended to in-work benefit claimants and that they are held to increasing demands on the earnings and hours they must work.[276]

To return to the use of Everson's distinction between entitlements and provisions, free movement rights' dependence on economic activity means that the status of EU citizenship merely offers the ability to choose to engage in the European internal market.[277] While, theoretically, any EU citizen could chose to exercise free movement as a worker, this choice is contingent on, among other variables, the available gaps in the market.[278] The expectation to choose to work is applied irrespective of the diversity in personal circumstances and fails to account for existing barriers to work and unequal opportunities.[279] More often than not, the requirement for economic activity 'perpetuates particularism and inequality' for marginalised groups already facing exclusion from the market because of these societal presumptions.[280] Alongside the disadvantage this places on women and ethnic minorities, as recognised by Hervey,[281] this also has a huge impact on Disabled people[282] and those in 'low paid, low status and low security jobs'.[283]

[273] Spaventa (n 3) 223.

[274] C O'Brien, 'From Safety Nets and Carrots to Trampolines and Sticks: National Uses of the EU as Both Menace and Model to Help Neoliberalize Welfare Policy' in D Schiek (ed), *The EU Economic and Social Model in Crisis: Interdisciplinary Perspectives* (Ashgate, 2013).

[275] ibid.

[276] Part-time workers were required to increase working hours or earnings if they earnt less than the equivalent of nine hours per week at national minimum wage. This was increased to 12 hours in September 2022 and 15 hours in January 2023. HM Treasury, 'The Growth Plan 2022' (CP 743, 2022) para 4.30.

[277] M Everson, 'The Legacy of the Market Citizen' in J Shaw and G More, *New Legal Dynamics of European Union* (Oxford University Press, 1995) 73, 87.

[278] ibid; see also ch 2.

[279] See ch 2 at 2.6 and ch 6 at 6.3.

[280] TK Hervey, 'Migrant workers and their families in the European Union: the pervasive market ideology of Community Law' in J Shaw and G More (eds), *New Legal Dynamics of European Union* (Oxford University Press, 1995) 91, 92.

[281] ibid.

[282] C O'Brien, 'Union Citizenship and Disability: Restricted access to Equality Rights and the Attitudinal Model of Disability in D Kochenov (ed), *EU Citizenship and Federalism: The Role of Rights* (Cambridge University Press, 2017) 509, 524–28.

[283] O'Brien (n 113) 953.

Ultimately, requiring a certain standard of economic activity[284] means that any migrant worker who fails to acquire worker status cannot fallback on their status as an EU citizen to access welfare support and secure their ability to continue to reside and work in a host Member State. As discussed in previous chapters, a focus on employment, rather than other forms of economic contribution, means that caring responsibilities are also ignored when assessing a union citizen's market credentials. Economic concerns alone cannot justify the strict approach to limiting lawful residence to residing in accordance with Directive 2004/28. The failure of EU citizenship to protect economic actors who are deemed to not work enough exposes the political choices that are made, not just about which Union citizens have economic credentials, but which have the right kind of economic credentials. While free movement gives the illusion of being available to all EU citizens, it is only practically achievable for a limited group of those who work *enough*.

8.5.2. The Uncertainty of the 'Legal' but Unlawful EU Citizen

Although permitted to move, reside and contribute to a host Member State, the economically inactive EU citizen cannot rely on that Member State for welfare support. Given that Member States do not always expel EU citizens who do not have a right of residence,[285] an EU citizen, while not treated as living in the Member State 'illegally', does not have lawful residence in the context of Directive 2004/38 and, after the restrictive turn in case law, equal treatment rights. Kramer argues that EU citizenship should be viewed as a double-edged sword, offering protection from removal and overt discrimination but, by limiting access to social security, exacerbating the split between workers and non-workers where people are expected to 'earn' social citizenship.[286] As Thym suggests, rather than actively removing these EU migrants, Member States may instead opt to 'starve them out'.[287] Equally a Member State may conveniently overlook these EU citizens, willingly accepting their labour and taxes while avoiding any duty to extend social solidarity to them.

The repercussions of the difference between lawful Directive residence and not illegal residence or presence also extends to the right of permanent residence, granted in Article 16 Directive 2004/38, in a host Member State for EU citizens who 'have resided legally for a continuous period of five years'.[288]

[284] See ch 3 at 3.3.

[285] See N Nic Shuibhne and J Shaw, 'General Report: Union Citizenship: Development, Impact and Challenges' in U Neergaard, C Jacqueson and N Holst-Christensen (eds), *Union Citizenship: Development, Impact and Challenges* (DJØF Publishing, 2014) 89–90; D Thym, 'When Union citizens turn into illegal migrants: the Dano case' (2015) 40 *European Law Review* 249, 259–60.

[286] D Kramer, 'EU Citizenship: a double-edged sword for European social secuirty' in F Pennings and G Vonk (eds), *Research Handbook on European Social Security Law* (Edward Elgar Publishing, 2023) 182.

[287] Thym (n 285) 259–60.

[288] Directive 2004/38, Art 16.

Despite permanent residence emerging in a Directive tasked with facilitating and strengthening the treaty rights of all EU citizens to free movement, the term 'residing legally' in this context is considered to link directly to the right of residence requirements in Article 7 Directive 2004/38.[289] Therefore, any period of time in the five continuous years relied on, where an EU citizen is deemed to be without a right of residence does not qualify, even if they have resided in a host Member State for well over the required five years. Long-term residents in a Member State who exercise their free movement rights in good faith and may not interact with their right of residence until it is needed will find out, at the point of need, that they do not meet the requirements. For those in irregular work, periods where their economic activity may drop below what is expected of 'genuine and effective' employment is at risk of having that period of residence disregarded and having the clock reset for building up five years of continuous residence under Directive 2004/38. Further to this, residing legally in this context has been interpreted by the CJEU to exclude time spent with derivative rights to reside that are not including in Article 7 Directive 2004/38,[290] such as through *Chen*,[291] *Teixeira*[292] and *Zambrano*[293] routes. The result of this leaves EU citizens who have a right to reside, and in the case of *Teixeira* carers have access to welfare benefits from this right to reside,[294] but find that they cannot use this time towards gaining the EU citizenship right of permanent residence. Despite the potential benefit of permanent residence as a method of recognising and awarding rights to EU citizens based on integration, the technical eligibility criteria limits this to only the *right kind* of integration.

Long-term residence rights are therefore limited to only those EU migrants who are sufficiently economically active or financially independent. The dichotomy between lawful and not illegal residence can cause significant uncertainty for EU citizens wishing to exercise their free movement rights. If the Citizen's Directive and subsequent case law visibly depart from the Treaty, the EU should seek to either correct this restrictive diversion or be responsible enough to, as Nic Shuibhne argues, alter the law to reflect these changes 'through the legitimate channels of legislative action and Treaty change where needed'.[295] This would require an honest recognition that free movement is not a right enjoyed by all Union citizens, and not even enjoyed by all economically active citizens. It should be clearly stated that where an EU citizen is not *sufficiently* economically active they may not have the right to access social security in other Member States.

[289] Joined cases C-424/10 and C-425/10 *Ziolkowski and Szeja* ECLI:EU:C:2011:866, [2011] ECR I-14035 [47].

[290] Case C-529/11 *Alarape and Tijani* ECLI:EU:C:2013:290, [2013] 3 CMLR 38 [40].

[291] Case C-200/02 *Chen* (n 260).

[292] Case C-480/08 *Teixeira* ECLI:EU:C:2010:83, [2010] ECR I-01107.

[293] Case C-34/09 *Zambrano* ECLI:EU:C:2011:124, [2011] ECR I-1177.

[294] Case C-480/08 *Teixeira* (n 292).

[295] Nic Shuibhne (n 17) 937.

8.6. Summary

The introduction of EU citizenship saw an extension of free movement rights from workers to citizens encompassed in EU primary law. These rights were not unconditional and instead were to be viewed in light of the limitations and conditions provided for in secondary law. It is through a restrictive lens to these limitations and conditions and treatment of secondary law as an almost overriding authority of the rights of EU citizens that has led to the dismantling of free movement for EU citizens who are not, or fail to maintain being, sufficiently economically active.

CJEU judgments on the free movement of EU citizens, while initially expansive, have since seen a shift to restrictive outcomes, limiting the ability of all EU citizens to claim equal treatment. Four changing aspects of the CJEU's judgments have been identified as signalling this shift. First, the Court has altered the perceived objective of the relevant legislation, from the facilitation of free movement to emphasising the aim to protect Member States from the burden of free movement. Second, the CJEU's re-examination of its approach to proportionality has seen a reversal of the previous individualised assessment, instead opting to implement ambiguous and potentially imaginary 'likely overall burden' assessments or ignoring proportionality altogether. Third, while previously expansive judgments were sometimes dismissed as merely concerning EU citizens who had their residence confirmed through a domestically issued permit, recent CJEU judgments have abandoned this protection, instead permitting Member States to discriminate against even those whose right to live and work in the country has been confirmed. Lastly, the Court has confirmed Member States' recategorising of both financial support for jobseekers and utilising the vague language concerning social assistance benefits to expand to social security benefits, both of which permit further restrictions to eligibility for EU citizens. The combination of these changes has altered the way the CJEU engages with the status of EU citizenship, giving overarching primacy to the residency requirements in Directive 2004/38.

The significant restrictions on EU citizens' free movement rights brought about by these cases were not triggered by an amendment to legislation and instead appear to be attributable to a change in political climate. Correlation can be drawn between an amplified, but unsubstantiated, concern of benefit tourism from Member States, the media and public discourse to the timing of the most restrictive judgments of the CJEU and the language used in them. The result of allowing free movement rights to be vulnerable to the political context they operate in leads to significant legal precarity and uncertainty. Through the authorising of sweeping discriminatory practices in more recent CJEU judgments, 'economically inactive' EU citizens have seen their free movement rights dismantled. Free movement must therefore be understood as a negative freedom as it requires activation triggered by enough or the right kind of economic activity.

This has implications for the fundamental status of EU citizenship. The journey of EU citizenship rights is significant here as it provides a glimpse into what the status of a supranational citizenship could have provided. While it is the case that many of the 'achievements' of EU citizenship are grounded in ties to economic integration, these limited achievements still offered a social safety net to some citizens who did not meet the residency requirements. Now, the deference to Directive 2004/38 as the full provision of a right of residence has meant that Member States can successfully restrict access to welfare benefits from those who need them, because they need them. The introduction of EU citizenship has therefore not released free movement from its market origins. EU citizens who are deemed to be economically inactive will not be able to enjoy freedom of movement without enduring great risk, if at all. As Nic Shuibhne puts it, market citizenship is not 'a construct of the distant past', but a continuing feature of Union citizenship.[296] Economic activity remains the key to unlocking the full range of free movement and equal treatment rights. By viewing EU citizenship as a membership, EU nationals can choose, through *enough* market activity, to opt-in or 'buy-in' to membership. Enough economic activity to meet the residency requirements acts as a subscription fee. Any EU national is welcome to try to move to and reside in a Member State, but if this fee cannot be paid they do not have full membership and therefore move at their own risk.

Where does this leave the EU atypical worker? With the definition of work or economic activity being left deliberately vague and where work that is irregular, temporary, or low-income regularly facing exclusion from Member State's narrowing interpretations of the 'genuine and effective' test, atypical workers may seek to rely on their status as an EU citizen to access equal treatment rights, especially where EU citizens face exclusion from the 'standard' labour market or must balance employment with informal and unpaid, albeit economically beneficial, care responsibilities. However, the rights of EU citizenship are now so limited as to be an inadequate and unreliable safety net. Atypical workers, if unable to establish worker status, are unlikely to find solace in their Union citizenship. This raises serious doubts about the extent to which atypical workers are protected in the EU's market 'citizenship' or membership. As a status that supposedly rewards rights to those based on market engagement, the automatic assumption is that citizens engaged with and participating in the market should be awarded access.[297] As flawed as market 'citizenship' or membership is, it still implies a collection of rights to those who can show their market credentials.

For those in atypical work, the question has become: are they economically active *enough and in the right way* to enjoy free movement and the rights associated with it?

[296] N Nic Shuibhne, 'The Resilience of EU Market Citizenship' (2010) 47 *Common Market Law Review* 1597, 1627.

[297] F De Witte, 'Transnational Solidarity and Conflicts of Justice' (2012) 18 *European Law Journal* 705.

9

Conclusion

This book has investigated the free movement rights of atypical workers as a way of analysing the credibility of EU citizenship's claim to 'fundamental status' in light of the changing labour market. I have argued that the EU concept of work and its national implementation can lead to the exclusion of atypical workers from equal treatment rights and the ability to exercise free movement. The position of atypical workers in free movement law has been examined with regard to the mobile EU worker, the EU migrant accessing rights in the UK and the Union citizen, to scrutinise the potential for free movement and equal treatment rights at each level.

9.1. Work as Defined or as Experienced

The first stage of this enquiry in chapters two and three examined the potential of Article 45 TFEU as a source of free movement and equal treatment rights for atypical workers. It considered whether the scope of economic activity under EU free movement law reflects the reality of work as experienced.

To examine the adequacy of the legal tests used to define economic activity, it is important to get a sense of how work in the EU and UK may be experienced. The labour market in Europe is fragmenting and work that is not full-time or permanent is increasing. New forms of work which sit in grey zones between employment and self-employment have emerged, particularly in the gig economy. Chapter two's examination of secondary data offers some insight into the increasing variety of employment circumstances present in the European labour market, and that analysis forms the premise for assessing the adequacy of the EU definition of work in later chapters. Taking on atypical work is also not always a free choice. Data on demographic representation in the atypical labour market has indicated the over-representation of workers who face barriers to the standard labour market, such as Disabled workers, lone parents, young workers and migrant workers. The EU's ability to provide free movement rights to atypical workers is relevant for a significant number of workers and will have an impact on the ability of marginalised workers who do not have the same opportunities as their comparators to engage in more standard employment.

Mobile EU citizens in the atypical labour market also face significant precarity in the form of underemployment, pay penalties, a lack of employment rights and risks to health. Access to welfare systems to offset or alleviate some of this precarity is therefore essential for those in atypical work to avoid the risks to personal wellbeing and falling into in-work poverty. Exclusion from equal access to social security systems *because* of a lack of economic activity is therefore no longer an accurate depiction of lived experience.[1] Those engaged in economic activity need access to welfare rights in a host Member State. This book has demonstrated that the rise and precarity of atypical work presents obstacles to free movement. Alongside this, the contested scope of worker status and the risk of losing access to welfare benefits can create significant barriers for atypical workers and makes the prospect of moving to another Member State to take up an employment opportunity unfeasible – a consequence that will entrench the exclusion already faced by marginalised groups from more 'typical' employment by limiting their ability to take advantage of the opportunities that free movement presents.

Chapter three asked to what extent EU free movement law ensures the protection of equal treatment rights for atypical migrant workers and identified gaps in this protection. The decision to keep the EU definition of work broad and vague may have the appearance of inclusivity, but (possibly deliberately)[2] devolves the responsibility to set the outer edges of worker status to Member States. The pivotal point in the definition – that work must be 'genuine and effective' and not 'on such a small scale as to be regarded as purely marginal and ancillary'[3] – has been used by the CJEU to incorporate a large variety of working situations including where work is conducted over relatively few hours per week, broad interpretations of remuneration and considerations of formal employment features. Despite this broad approach, the CJEU has not explicitly included other common characteristics of atypical work; some of these have instead been labelled as potential indicators of marginal and ancillary work.[4] Gaps in the vague definition mean that Member States can refine and distil it, such that atypical workers may face exclusion from free movement rights. A possibly inclusive approach taken in a few CJEU cases cannot without clear, consistent domestic implementation give confidence to atypical workers that their free movement rights will be protected.

Together, these chapters identify the disjuncture between how work is experienced in the atypical labour market and the fragility of protection offered in EU free movement law. This research makes the case for the explicit inclusion of atypical work in free movement rights at the EU level, and for the adoption of a more nuanced recognition of how expectations of 'genuine and effective' employment should differ where personal circumstances create barriers to 'typical' work. Leaving the outer edges of worker status to the discretion of individual Member States risks the separation of EU citizens in atypical work, including those in

[1] G Davies, 'Migrant Union Citizens and Social Assistance: Trying to Be Reasonable About Self-Sufficiency' (2016) College of Europe Research Papers in Law No 2/2016 5.

[2] AP van der Mei, *Free Movement of Persons within the European Community: Cross Border Access to Public Benefits* (Hart Publishing, 2003) 130.

[3] Case 53/81 *Levin* ECLI:EU:C:1982:105, [1982] ECR I-1035 [17].

[4] Case C-357/89 *Raulin* ECLI:EU:C:1992:87, [1992] ECR I-1027 [14].

already disadvantaged demographic groups, from the equal treatment rights, which are essential to mitigate precarity and make movement to another Member State for work feasible.

9.2. The Experience of Atypical Workers in the UK

Chapters four, five and six zoned in on the experience of atypical workers in the UK. Together these chapters contribute to the scrutiny of the UK definition of worker by evidencing how the test operates against common aspects of atypical working including low-income, inconsistent work, and overlapping or consecutive contracts. I have argued that this test infringes EU law, making the case for the EU to act on this incompatibility and for the UK Government to rethink the suitability of the MET considering the variety of work in the atypical labour market, especially as it has continuing relevance through the implementation of the Withdrawal Agreement.

Chapter four first took a doctrinal analysis of the MET and decision-maker guidance by examining materials introducing the MET, the rules themselves (including setting the MET at a considerably higher level than CJEU case law suggests is necessary for 'genuine and effective' work) and accompanying decision-maker guidance. This chapter argues that while, on the surface, these rules are technically compatible with EU law, they key is in the implementation. There are clear indications in press releases and guidance that the MET was introduced as a tool to restrict access to worker status.

Chapter five then combines these findings with empirical data collected from EU atypical worker interactions with the UK definition to argue that the MET is incompatible with EU law. In particular this chapter focuses on the ubiquitous reliance on earnings as an indicator of 'genuine and effective' economic activity. Empirical data gathered for this research has suggested two key sources of incompatibility. Firstly that the earnings threshold is frequently applied as determinative, withholding worker status on the basis of limited earnings, despite the CJEU declaring that limited remuneration does not have 'any consequence' for the determination of worker status.[5] Additionally, the level and requirement for consistency of earnings in the MET disadvantages those with low-income or irregular employment. As the guidance offers little by way of addressing atypical work characteristics, such as overlapping contracts, decision-makers can easily get lost when navigating these issues. This study found cases in which decision-makers demonstrated restrictive approaches, categorising work as marginal and ancillary on the grounds that it is atypical. Secondly, where work falling below the earnings threshold was assessed under the second tier, decision makers face steers in the guidance to reassert the importance of income and hours worked, establishing

[5] See ch 3 at 3.4.

what O'Brien calls a 'presumption of marginality' for work failing the earnings test.[6] Case studies also demonstrated instances where decision-makers had taken into consideration factors which have been explicitly excluded by the CJEU, such as asserting that earnings must meet a level of subsistence. Overall, this chapter identifies a concerning preoccupation with earnings that undermines the broad approach taken by the CJEU and risks the exclusion of many atypical workers.

Chapter six then analysed the empirical data to find that the MET not only infringes EU law, but also results in workers in the atypical labour market facing compounded discrimination through a combination of the EU definition, UK interpretation and decision-maker tendencies. Applying a uniform test, without expressly accommodating the personal circumstances of workers has a disproportionate impact, limiting free movement rights for those who face barriers to more standard employment, arising from disability, from care responsibilities (disproportionately borne by women), and from domestic abuse. The chapter also identifies misleading or incorrect guidance which appears to prompt decision-makers to consider a worker's motivation and physical capabilities – which could further hinder Disabled workers and encourages decision-makers to treat the motivations of those in low-income work as suspicious. In particular, the chapter makes an explicit case for protecting equal treatment rights for EEA nationals who provide informal care, drawing upon evidence of the problematic prevailing assumptions about care and work, and the requirement to balance both responsibilities to meet the standard of 'typical' worker status. The economic contribution of those balancing informal care with work is twofold but often ignored.

These discriminatory effects could be reduced with a more nuanced approach to these personal circumstances – either through EU-level instructions to explicitly recognise such variables as relevant factors for the consideration of 'genuine and effective' work or, where a Member State implements an hours or earnings threshold, through adopting a sliding threshold which appreciates barriers to work and constraints on time.

These two sections identify several flaws with the definition of worker status and its implementation at Member State level which risk the exclusion of atypical workers. The next step in this enquiry examines the potential of EU citizenship as an alternative source of equal treatment rights for those atypical workers who are deemed to be 'economically inactive'.

9.3. Atypical Workers as Citizens

Chapter seven questioned the fundamental status of EU citizenship through its theoretical and political contexts. The status of EU citizenship was assessed against

[6] C O'Brien, *Unity in Adversity: EU citizenship, Social Justice and the Cautionary Tale of the UK* (Hart Publishing, 2017) 156.

theoretical expectations of social citizenship, identifying that it has been unable to move past a market citizenship.[7] This analysis identified two main challenges to EU citizenship which could limit its effectiveness for atypical workers. Firstly, the market roots of the status have left many of the rights it offers, including those which facilitate free movement, conditional on a citizen's market credentials. Secondly, EU citizenship lacks the necessary affective components of solidarity to grow past its market confines. Seeking a shared identity is problematic, ineffective and unlikely in the EU context, while constitutional patriotism, though offering a viable route to solidarity, is too abstract and has not been fully embraced. Where solidarity exists, it is concentrated on reserving rights for those who can show their contribution to a host Member State. The full array of rights available under EU citizenship are therefore conditional on market activity. Yet the willingness to accept market activity or contribution beyond more orthodox expectations of secure and highly paid employment is limited. For citizens unable to demonstrate that they work *enough*, their status as EU citizens is of limited use.

Chapter eight then analysed the legal rights of EU citizenship in relation to free movement and equal treatment. Despite free movement and the protection from discrimination being theoretically available to all EU citizens on the basis of primary law, through Articles 21 and 18 TFEU,[8] these are subject to limitations provided in secondary law. The CJEU's recent restrictive interpretation of citizenship rights has elevated the residency requirements in Directive 2004/38 to supra-primary law status, effectively limiting primary law rights to only those with requisite levels of economic activity or self-sufficiency.[9] The focus of the CJEU has diverted from EU citizenship as a status to facilitate free movement to an overarching concern for the 'burden' on Member States' social security systems.[10] Thus the legal instruments that remove barriers to free movement must be activated by economic activity; the status of EU citizenship provides little benefit if this cannot be established.

The significance of this transition is drawn alongside the recently amplified, but unsubstantiated, concerns of benefit tourism from Member States. The political sensitivity of access to welfare echoes the concerns, identified in chapter seven, of the limits of solidarity in a supranational setting. Alongside the EU-sanctioned restrictions on the equal treatment of workers in the UK and EU's now defunct

[7] E Spaventa, 'Earned Citizenship – understanding Union citizenship through its scope' in D Kochenov (ed), *EU Citizenship and Federalism: the Role of Rights* (Cambridge University Press, 2017); N Nic Shuibhne, 'The Resilience of EU Market Citizenship' (2010) 47 *Common Market Law Review* 1597.

[8] Consolidated Version of the Treaty on the Functioning of the European Union [2012] OJ C326/47 (TFEU), Arts 18 and 21.

[9] Case C-333/13 *Dano* ECLI:EU:C:2014:2358, [2014] ECR I-2358; Case C-67/14 *Alimanovic* ECLI:EU:C:2015:597, [2016] 1 CMLR 29; Case C-299/14 *García-Nieto* ECLI:EU:C:2016:114; Case C-308/14, *Commission v. United Kingdom* ECLI:EU:C:2016:436, [2016] 3 CMLR 41.

[10] D Thym, 'The Elusive Limits of Solidarity: Residence Rights of and Social Benefits for Economically Inactive Union Citizens' (2015) 52 *Common Market Law Review* 17; Spaventa (n 1); C O'Brien, 'Civis Capitalist Sum: Class as the new guiding principle of EU Free Movement Rights' (2016) 53 *Common Market Law Review* 937.

2016 settlement, this chapter highlights the desire of Member States to reap the economic benefits of free movement, while curtailing the responsibility to support resident EU nationals – even when they are working. This places atypical workers, who are often both economically active and potentially dependent on welfare, in positions of considerable precarity.

Together these chapters illustrate the problematic entanglement of EU citizenship with the market. EU citizens who are deemed to be economically inactive cannot exercise freedom of movement without enduring great risk, if at all. For EU atypical migrant workers, being deemed economically active still matters.[11] From this, EU citizenship emerges as an aspirational misnomer and is, at best, no more than a form of market membership. Citizens are treated as potential members, who must pay their subscription by demonstrating *enough* market activity to attain the equal treatment rights attached to being a mobile citizen of the European Union. As a status that supposedly rewards market engagement with access to rights, the automatic assumption is that citizens engaging with and contributing to the market should be granted access.[12] However, for atypical workers, the question must be whether they meet the full requirements for membership.

This case study, analysing the impact of UK's MET on free movement and equal treatment rights in the changing labour market, lends support to two key arguments developed throughout the research. Firstly, it demonstrates how some of the EU's vague and imprecise definition can be manipulated in practice, and how it can become exclusionary. This reinforces the case for explicit inclusion of atypical forms of work and the recognition of personal circumstances at the EU level.

Secondly, in illustrating the exclusive nature of the test for economic activity alongside the limited rights available for those considered to be economically inactive, the research has contributed further evidence of EU citizenship's manifestation as a form of membership. This goes further than critiques of EU citizenship as market citizenship, to suggest that engagement in the labour market is not decisive. Alternatively, taking the model of EU citizenship as a membership, equal treatment rights and citizenship rights, such as permanent residence are reserved for those workers who are economically active *enough* and whose economic activity is conducted in the 'correct' consistent and regular way – subscriptions must be paid and club etiquette rules observed. An EU citizen's membership of the 'equal treatment' club is also constantly scrutinised. Unless and until they successfully prove five years of economically diligent membership, sufficient to attain the platinum membership card of permanent residence, even temporarily defaulting on the terms of membership can result in a complete loss of access to equal treatment. The limited conception of economic activity means that atypical workers may never be eligible for the perks of membership.

[11] H Verschueren, 'Being Economically Active: How it Still Matters' in H Verschueren (ed), *Residence, Employment and Social Rights of Mobile Persons: On how EU Law defines where they belong* (Intersentia, 2016) 187.

[12] F De Witte, 'Transnational Solidarity and Conflicts of Justice' (2012) 18 *European Law Journal* 705.

9.4. Beyond the UK and Future Challenges

For the UK, given the potential for the MET to exclude many atypical and vulnerable workers from free movement legislation, the transition out of the EU and the application of the Withdrawal Agreement must be scrutinised carefully to ensure that the rights of EU citizens are respected. As it stands, the MET still plays an important role for EU nationals in the UK. It is relevant for those who cannot evidence five years' residence with the EU Settlement Scheme. This cohort will need to pass the right to reside test to access many public services such as welfare benefits and housing. As the exact scope of the Withdrawal Agreement is still under dispute, including whether a right to reside under the EU free movement rights must have been evident on 31 December 2020,[13] it may also play an increasingly important role for all persons looking to seek to rely on their rights in the Agreement. Therefore, the inadequacies of the MET still limits the rights of EU atypical workers in the UK and is likely to continue to for many years to come.

Moving forward, it would be useful to expand this enquiry to the investigation of other EU rights associated with mobility, including experiences of cross-border claims, when residence and work are in different Member States, or where multiple work contracts are conducted across different Member States. While these factors did not appear in the cases examined for this study, a key theme throughout has been the recognition that lives, work and personal circumstances are rarely simple. Further research into these experiences of intra-EU mobility would be beneficial to flesh out the understanding of atypical workers experience with free movement.

It would also be beneficial to examine the free movement experience of EU migrant atypical workers in other Member States to see if their iterations of the definition of work present similar issues of exclusion. As mentioned in chapter four, restrictive applications of the worker status definition are not limited to the UK. Many Member States adopt thresholds using a mixture of earnings, hours or the two combined to assess worker status.[14] While this does not mean that countries operating a threshold interpret the overall assessment as restrictively as the UK, it does highlight some of the impact a threshold can have and offers caution to the use of thresholds as a device for this task, particularly where those thresholds reinforce the norms of more standard employment such as consistent and regular work. Further research into the impact of thresholds in these Member States would be necessary to determine if atypical workers are separated from their free movement rights more systemically across the EU.

An anachronistic model of work that excludes – or enables Member States to exclude – atypical workers from equal treatment rights disproportionately impacts

[13] See C O'Brien and A Welsh, 'Problems with the IMA's position on Art. 10 and 13 WA on the scope of the WA' (EU Rights and Brexit Hub, 18 March 2024), www.eurightshub.york.ac.uk/blog/problems-with-the-imas-position-on-art-10-and-13-wa-on-the-scope-of-the-wa.

[14] C O'Brien, E Spaventa and J De Coninck, 'Comparative Report 2015: The concept of worker under Article 45 TFEU and certain non-standard forms of employment' (FreSsco, 2016) 24–25.

Disabled workers, women and workers with caring responsibilities. In failing to keep pace with the changing labour market, the EU risks entrenching inequalities, deepening the disadvantage and exclusion faced by these groups. The model of market citizenship to justify the exclusion of economically active citizens is not logically sound. What EU citizenship, the UK case study, and the problematic positioning of carers show us is that sterile arguments about the economic or political origins or ambitions of the Union miss the point. The economic is political – how economic activity is defined is not a matter of 'fact'; it is a political choice. It is time to consider making a new one.

BIBLIOGRAPHY

Texts

Ackers L and Dwyer P, *Senior Citizenship?: Retirement, migration and welfare in the European Union* (Bristol University Press, 2002).
Anderson B, *Imagined Communities: Reflections on the Origin and Spread of Nationalism* (1987).
Barnard C, *The Substantive Law of the EU*, 6th edn (Oxford University Press 2019).
Bloodworth J, *Hired: Six Months Undercover in Low-Wage Britain* (Atlantic Books, 2018).
Commission on Social Justice, *Social Justice: Strategies for National Renewal* (Vintage, 1994).
Currie S, *Migration, Work and Citizenship in the Enlarged European Union* (Ashgate, 2008).
Delanty G, *Citizenship in a Global Age: Society, Culture, Politics* (Open University Press, 2010).
Esping-Anderson G, *The Three Worlds of Welfare Capitalism* (Cambridge, Polity Press 1990).
Etzioni A, *The Spirit of Community: rights, responsibilities and the communitarian agenda* (Fontana Press, 1995).
Habermas J, *The inclusion of the other: studies in political theory* (Cambridge, Polity Press 1998).
Hacker J, *The Great Risk Shift: The New Economic Insecurity and the Decline of the American Dream*, 2nd edn (Oxford University Press 2019).
Hirschman AO, *Exit, Voice and Loyalty: Responses to Decline in Firms, Organisations and States* (Harvard University Press, 1970).
Humpage L, *Policy change, public attitudes and social citizenship: Does neoliberalism matter?* (Policy Press, 2014).
Kellermann AE, de Witte B, Curtin DM, and Winter JA (eds), *Reforming the Treaty on European Union: The Legal Debate* (Kluwer Law International, 1996).
Kymlicka W, *Contemporary Political Philosophy*, 2nd edn (Oxford University Press, 2000).
Lister M and Pia E, *Citizenship in Contemporary Europe* (Edinburgh University Press, 2008).
Maas W, *Creating European Citizens* (Rowman and Littlefield Publishers, 2007).
—— 'Varieties of Multilevel Citizenship' in W Maas (ed), *Multilevel Citizenship* (Pennsylvania Press, 2013).
Marshall TH, *Citizenship and Social Class* ([1949] Pluto Press, 1992).
Molander A, *Discretion in the Welfare State: Social Rights and Professional Judgment* (Routledge, 2016).
O'Brien C, *Unity and Adversity: EU Citizenship, Social Justice and the Cautionary Tale of the UK* (Hart Publishing, 2017).
O'Leary S, *The Evolving Concept of Community Citizenship: From the Free Movement of Persons to Union Citizenship* (Kluwer Law International, 1996).
Paskalia V, *Free Movement, Social Security and Gender in the EU* (Hart Publishing, 2007).
Pettit P, *Republicanism: a theory of freedom and government* (Oxford, Clarendon Press, 1997).
Prassl J, *Humans as a Service: The promise and perils of work in the gig economy* (Oxford University Press, 2018).
Shaw J, *The Transformation of Citizenship in the European Union: Electoral Rights and the Restructuring of Political Space* (Cambridge University Press, 2007).
van der Mei AP, *Free Movement of Persons within the European Community. Cross Border Access to Public Benefits* (Hart Publishing, 2003).
Watts B and Fitzpatrick S, *Welfare Conditionality* (Routledge, 2018).
Weiler JHH, *Un'Europa cristiana: un saggio esplorativo* (Rizzoli, 2003).
Yong A, *The Rise and Decline of Fundamental Rights in EU Citizenship* (Hart Publishing 2019).

Chapters in Edited Collections

Bauböck R, 'Citizenship and Collective Identities as Political Sources of Solidarity in the European Union' in K Banting and W Kymlicka, *The Strains of Commitment: The Political Sources of Solidarity in Diverse Societies* (Oxford University Press, 2017) 80–106.

Bellamy R, 'Introduction: The Making of Modern Citizenship' in R Bellamy, D Castiglione and E Santoro (eds), *Lineages of European Citizenship* (Palgrave Macmillan, 2004) 1–21.

Berlin I, 'Two Concepts of Liberty' in H Hardy (ed), *Liberty* (Oxford University Press, 2002) 166–217.

Chung EA, 'Citizenship in Non-Western Contexts' in A Shachar, R Bauböck, I Bloemraad, and M Vink (eds), *The Oxford Handbook of Citizenship* (Open Univeristy Press 2017) 431–52.

Currie S, 'The Transformation of Union Citizenship' in M Dougan and S Currie (eds), *50 years of the European treaties: looking back and thinking forward* (Hart Publishing, 2009) 365–92.

Dagger R, 'Republican Citizenship' in EF Isin and BS Turner (eds), *Handbook of Citizenship Studies* (Sage, 2002) 145–57.

Davies G, 'The Price of Letting Courts Value Solidarity: The Judicial Role in Liberalizing Welfare' in M Ross and Y Borgmann-Prebil, *Promoting Solidarity in the European Union* (Oxford University Press, 2010) 106–22.

Deakin S, 'The "Capability" Concept and the Evolution of European Social Policy' in E Spaventa and M Dougan (ed), *Social Welfare and EU law* (Hart Publishing, 2005) 3–24.

Dougan M, 'The Bubble that Burst: Exploring the Legitimacy of the Case Law on the Free Movement of Union Citizens' in M Adams, J Meeusen, G Straetmans and H de Waele (eds), *Judging Europe's Judges. The Legitimacy of the Case Law of the European Court of Justice* (Oxford, 2013) 127–54.

Dougan M and Spaventa E, '"Wish you weren't here …" New Models of Social Solidarity in the European Union' in M Dougan and E Spaventa, *Social Welfare and EU Law* (Hart Publishing, 2005) 181–218.

Dwyer P, 'Citizenship, conduct and conditionality: sanction and support in the 21st century UK welfare state' in M Fenger, J Hudson and C Needham (ed), *Social Policy Review 28: Analysis and Debate in Social Policy* (Policy Press, 2016) 41–62.

—— 'Rewriting the contract? Conditionality, welfare reform and the rights and responsibilities of disabled people' in D Horsfall and J Hudson (eds), *Social Policy in an Era of Competition: from global to Local Perspectives* (Policy Press, 2017) 135–49.

Everson M, 'The Legacy of the Market Citizen' in J Shaw and G More, *New Legal Dynamics of European Union* (Oxford University Press, 1995) 73–89.

Ferrera M, 'Towards an "Open" Social Citizenship? The New Boundaries of Welfare in the European Union' in G de Búrca, *EU Law and the Welfare State: In Search of Solidarity* (Oxford University Press, 2005) 11–38.

Habermas J, 'Struggles for Recognition in the Democratic Constitutional State' in C Cronin and P De Greiff, *The Inclusion of the Other: Studies in Political Theory* (Cambridge, 1998) 203–38.

Hall PA, 'The Political Sources of Social Solidarity' in K Banting and W Kymlicka, *The Strains of Commitment: The Political Sources of Solidarity in Diverse Societies* (Oxford University Press, 2017) 201–32.

Hayward J, 'From Citizen Solidarity to Self-Serving Inequality: Social Solidarity, Market Economy and Welfare Statecraft' in J Connelly and JHayward (e ds), *The Withering of the Welfare State* (Palgrave Macmillan, 2012) 1–20.

Hervey TK, 'Migrant workers and their families in the European Union: the pervasive market ideology of Community Law' in J Shaw and G More, *New Legal Dynamics of European Union* (Oxford University Press, 1995) 91–110.

Honohan P, 'Liberal and Republican Conceptions of Citizenship in Contexts' in A Shachar, R Bauböck, I Bloemraad and M Vink (eds), *The Oxford Handbook of Citizenship* (Open Univeristy Press, 2017) 83–106.

Kochenov D, 'On Tiles and Pillars: EU Citizenship as a Federal Denominator' in D Kochenov, *EU Citizenship and Federalism: The Role of Rights* (Cambridge University Press, 2017) 3–82.

Kramer D, 'EU Citizenship: a double-edged sword for European social secuirty' in F Pennings F and G Vonk (eds), *Research Handbook on European Social Security Law* (Edward Elgar Publishing, 2023) 182–203.

Lamping W, 'Mission Impossible? Limits and perils of Institutionalizing Post-National Social Policy' in M Ross and Y Borgmann-Prebil (eds), *Promoting Solidarity in the European Union* (Oxford University Press, 2010) 46–72.

Lenaerts K and Gutiérrez-Fons JA, 'Epilogue on EU Citizenship: Hopes and Fears' in D Kochenov (ed), *EU Citizenship and Federalism: The Role of Rights* (Cambridge University Press, 2017) 751–81.

Maas W, 'Equality and the Free Movement of People: Citizenship and Internal Migration' in W Maas (ed), *Democratic Citizenship and the Free Movement of People* (Martinus Nijhoff Publishers, 2013) 9–30.

Mullally S, 'Children citizenship and constitutional change' in B Fanning (ed), *Immigration and Social Change in the Republic of Ireland* (Manchester University Press, 2007) 27–46.

Nic Shuibhne N, 'The European Union and Fundamental Rights: Well in Spirit but Considerably Rumpled in Body?' in P Beaumont, C Lyons and N Walker, *Convergence and Divergence in European Public Law* (Hart, 2002) 177–96.

Nic Shuibhne N and Shaw J, 'General Report: Union Citizenship: Development, Impact and Challenges' in U Neergaard, C Jacqueson and N Holst-Christensen, *Union Citizenship: Development, Impact and Challenges* (DJØF Publishing, 2014) 37–224.

O'Brien C, 'From Safety Nets and Carrots to Trampolines and Sticks: National Uses of the EU as Both Menace and Model to Help Neoliberalize Welfare Policy' in D Schiek (ed), *The EU Economic and Social Model in Crisis: Interdisciplinary Perspectives* (Ashgate, 2013) 93–114.

—— 'Union Citizenship and Disability: Restricted access to Equality Rights and the Attitudinal Model of Disability' in D Kochenov (eds), *EU Citizenship and Federalism: The Role of Rights* (Cambridge University Press, 2017) 509–39.

Passerini L, 'From the Ironies of Identity to the Identity of Irony' in A Pagden (ed), *The Idea of Europe: From Antiquity to the European Union* (Cambridge University Press, 2002) 191–208.

Roulstone A, 'Disability, work and welfare' in C Grover and L Pignott, *Disabled people, work and welfare: Is employment really the answer?* (Policy Press, 2015) 257–74.

Sadiq K, 'Postcolonial Citizenship' in A Shachar, R Bauböck, L Bloemraad and M Vink(eds), *The Oxford Handbook of Citizenship* (Open Univeristy Press 2017) 178–99.

Schwab C, Bouckaert G and Kuhlmann S, 'Conclusion: Lessons and Advice for Future Local Government in Europe' in C Schwab, G Bouckaer and S Kuhlmann (eds), *The Future of Local Government in Europe Lessons from Research and Practice in 31 Countries* (Nomos, 2017) 101–12.

Shaw S, 'Comparative Welfare' in P Dwyer and S Shaw (eds), *An Introduction to Social Policy* (Sage, 2013) 144–55.

Spaventa E, 'Earned Citizenship – Understanding Union Citizenship through Its Scope' in D Kochenov (ed), *EU Citizenship and Federalism: The Role of Rights* (Cambridge University Press, 2017) 204–25.

Stinson H, 'Supporting people? Universal Credit, conditionality and the recalibration of vulnerability' in P Dwyer, *Dealing with welfare conditionality* (Policy Press, 2019) 15–40.

Thym D, 'Towards "Real" Citizenship? The Judicial Construction of Union Citizenship and its Limits' in M Adams, H de Waele, J Meeusen and G Straetman (eds), *Judging Europe's Judges: The Legitimacy of the Case Law of the European Court of Justice Examined* (Hart, 2013) 155–74.

—— 'The Judicial Deconstruction of Union Citizenship' in D Thym (ed), *Questioning EU Citizenship: Judges and the limits of free movement and solidarity in the EU* (Bloomsbury, 2017) 1–16.

—— 'The Evolution of Citizens' Rights in Light of the European Union's Constitutional Development' in D Thym (ed), *Questioning EU Citizenship: Judges and the limits of free movement and solidarity in the EU* (Bloomsbury, 2017) 111–34.

van Riemsdijk M, 'Politics of Free Movement in the European Union: Recognition and Transfer of Professional Qualifications' in W Maas (ed), *Democratic Citizenship and the Free Movement of People* (Martinus Nijhoff Publishers, 2013) 115–41.

Verschueren H, 'Being Economically Active: How it Still Matters' in H Verschueren (ed), *Residence, Employment and Social Rights of Mobile Persons: On how EU Law defines where they belong* (Intersentia, 2016) 187–214.

Journal Articles

– 'The free movement of persons in the European Union: Salvaging the dream while explaining the nightmare' (2014) 51 *Common Market Law Review* 729 (Editorial Comments).

Ackers L, 'Women, Citizenship and European Community Law: The Gender Implications of the Free Movement Provisions' (1994) 16 *Journal of Social Welfare and Family Law* 391.

Albors-Llorens A, 'Case Comment: A broader construction of the EC Treaty provisions on citizenship?' (1998) 57 *Cambridge Law Journal* 461.

Azoulai L, '"Euro-bonds": The Ruiz Zambrano judgment or the real invention of EU citizenship' (2011) 3 *Perspectives on Federalism* E-31.

Bambra C, Lunau T, Van der Wel K A, Eikemo TA and Dragano N, 'Work, Health, and Welfare: The Association between Working Conditions, Welfare States, and Self-Reported General Health in Europe' (2014) 44 *International Journal of Health Services* 113.

Bartle I, 'Political Participation and Market Citizenship in a Global Economy: The European Union in Comparative Perspective' (2006) 29 *International Journal of Public Administration* 415.

Bauböck R, 'Why European Citizenship? Normative Approaches to Supranational Union' (2007) 8 *Theoretical Inquiries in Law* 453.

Bell M, 'Disability, rehabilitation and the status of worker in EU Law: *Fenoll*' (2016) 53 *Common Market Law Review* 197.

Bellamy R, 'Evaluating Union citizenship: belonging, rights and participation within the EU' (2008) 12 *Citizenship Studies* 597.

Bellamy R and Castiglione D, 'Democracy by Delegation? Who Represents Whom and How in European Governance' (2011) 46 *Government and Opposition* 101.

Besselink LFM, 'Case C-145/04, Spain v. United Kingdom, judgment of the Grand Chamber of 12 September 2006; Case C-300/04, Eman and Sevinger, judgment of the Grand Chamber of 12 September 2006; ECtHR (Third Section), 6 September 2007, Applications Nos. 17173/07 and 17180/07, Oslin Benito Sevinger and Michiel Godfried Eman v. the Netherlands (Sevinger and Eman)' (2008) 45 *Common Market Law Review* 787.

Blauberger M, Heindlmaier A, Kramer D, Martinsen DS, Thierry JS, Schenk A and Werner B, 'ECJ Judges read the morning papers. Explaining the turnaround of European citizenship jurisprudence' (2018) 25 *Journal of European Public Policy* 1423.

Carens JH, 'Aliens and Citizens: The Case for Open Borders' (1987) 49 *The Review of Politics* 251.

Cherry MA, 'Beyond Misclassification: The digital transformation of work' (2017) 37 *Comparative Labor Law and Policy Journal* 577.

Cousins M, 'The baseless fabric of this vision" EU citizenship, the right to reside and EU law' (2016) 1 *Journal of Social Security Law* 89.

Cvijic S and Zucca L, 'Does the European Constitution Need Christian Values? A review of Un'Europa cristiana: un saggio esplorativo by J. H. H. Weiler' (2004) 24 *Oxford Journal of Legal Studies* 739.

de Swaan A, 'Perspectives for Transnational Social Policy' (1992) 27 *Government and Opposition* 33.

De Witte F, 'Transnational Solidarity and Conflicts of Justice' (2012) 18 *European Law Journal* 705.

Dougan M, 'The constitutional dimension to the case law on Union citizenship' (2006) 31 *European Law Review* 613.

—— 'So Long, Farewell, Auf Wiedersehen, Goodbye: The UK's Withdrawal Package' (2020) 57 *Common Market Law Review* 631.

Dougan M and Spaventa E, 'Educating Rudy and the non-English patient: a double bill on residency rights under Article 18 EC' (2003) 28 *European Law Review* 699.

Dwyer P and Wright S, 'Universal Credit, ubiquitous conditionality and its implications for social citizenship' (2014) 22 *Journal of Poverty and Social Justice* 27.

Elsmore MJ and Starup P, 'Union Citizenship – Background, Jurisprudence, and Perspective: The Past, Present, and Future of Law and Policy' (2007) 26 *Yearbook of European Law* 57.

Etzioni A, 'Citizenship Tests: A Comparative, Communitarian Perspective' (2007) 78 *The Political Quarterly* 353.

Evans M, 'EU migrants, abuse and access to welfare' (2015) 29 *Journal of Immigration, Asylum and Nationality Law* 273.

Faist T, 'Social Citizenship in the European Union: Nested Membership' (2001) 39 *Journal of Common Market Studies* 37.

Featherstone D, Ince A, Mackinnon D, Strauss K and Cumbers A, 'Progressive localism and the construction of political alternatives' (2012) 37 *Transactions of the Institute of British Geographers* 177.

Ferri D, 'The Unorthodox Relationship between the EU Charter of Fundamental Rights, the UN Convention on the Rights of Persons with Disabilities and Secondary Rights in the Court of Justice Case Law on Disability Discrimination' (2020) 16 *European Constitutional Law Review* 275.

Fudge J, 'After Industrial Citizenship: Market Citizenship Or Citizenship at Work?' (2005) 60 *Industrial Relations* 631.

Giubboni S, 'Being a worker in EU law' (2018) 9 *European Labour Law Journal* 223.

Goodman SW, 'Integration Requirements for Integration's Sake? Identifying, Categorising and Comparing Civic Integration Policies' (2010) 36 *Journal of Ethnic and Migration Studies* 753.

Gorham E, 'Social Citizenship and its Fetters' (1995) 28 *Polity* 25.

Grabbe C, 'Free movement and access to social security in the EU: The challenge of exporting unemployment benefits' (2023) 25 *European Journal of Social Security* 20.

Gregory M and Connolly S, 'The Price of Reconciliation: Part-Time Work, Families and Women's Satisfaction' (2008) 118 *The Economic Journa*l F1.

Hailbronner K, 'Union Citizenship and Access to Social Benefits' (2005) 42 *Common Market Law Review* 1245.

Heindlmaier A, '"Social Citizenship" at the Street Level? EU Member State Administrations Setting a Firewall' (2020) 58 *Journal of Common Market Studies* 1252.

Heindlemaier A and Blauberger M, 'Enter at your own risk: free movement of EU citizens in practice' (2017) 40 *West European Politics* 1198.

Hix S and Follesdal A, 'Why is there a Democratic Deficit in the EU? A Response to Majone and Moravcsik' (2006) 44 *Journal of Common Market Studies* 533.

Horton R, 'Caring for adults in the EU: Work–life balance and challenges for EU law' (2015) 37 *Journal of Social Welfare and Family law* 356.

Johnston R, Banting K, Kymlicka W and Soroka S. 'National Identity and Support for the Welfare State' (2010) 43 *Canadian Journal of Political Science* 349.

Kochenov D, 'Free movement and participation in the parliamentary elections in the Member State of nationality: An ignored link?' (2009) 16 *Maastricht Journal of European and Comparative Law* 197.

—— 'The Essence of EU Citizenship Emerging From the Last Ten Years of Academic Debate: Beyond the Cherry Blossoms and the Moon' (2013) 62 *International and Comparative Law Quarterly* 97.

Kostakopoulou D, 'The Anatomy of Civic Integration' (2001) 73 *Modern Law Review* 933.

Lock T, 'Rights and principles in the EU Charter of Fundamental Rights' (2019) 56 *Common Market Law Review* 1201.

Longo E, 'The European Citizens' initiative: too much democracy for EU polity?' (2019) 20 *German Law Journal* 181.

Lowndes V and Pratchett L, 'Local Governance under the Coalition Government: Austerity, Localism and the 'Big Society'' (2012) 38 *Local Government Studies* 21.
Maas W, 'Unrespected, Unequal, Hollow? Contingent Citizenship and Reversible Rights in the European Union' (2009) 15 *The Columbia Journal of European Law* 265.
—— 'Boundaries of Political Community in Europe, the US, and Canada' (2017) 39 *Journal of European Integration* 575.
MacDonald R and Giazitzoglu A, 'Youth, enterprise, and precarity: or, what is, and what is wrong with, the 'gig economy'?' (2019) 55 *Journal of Sociology* 724.
Magnussen AM and Nilssen E, 'Juridification and the Construction of Social Citizenship' (2013) 40 *Journal of Law and Society* 228.
Martinsen DS, Blauberger M, Heindlmaier A and Thierry JS, 'Implementing European case law at the bureaucratic frontline: How domestic signalling influences the outcomes of EU law' (2018) 97 *Public Administration* 814.
Milani TM, 'Language Testing and Citizenship: A Language Ideological Debate in Sweden' (2008) 37 *Language in Society* 27.
Müller JW, 'A general theory of constitutional patriotism' (2008) 6 *International Journal of Constitutional Law* 72.
Nic Shuibhne N, 'The Resilience of EU Market Citizenship' (2010) 47 *Common Market Law Review* 1597.
—— '(Some of) The kids are all right: comment on McCarthy and Dereci' (2012) 49 *Common Market Law Review* 349.
—— 'Limits Rising, Duties Ascending: The Changing Legal Shape of Union Citizenship' (2015) 52 *Common Market Law Review* 889.
—— 'Reconnecting free movement of workers and equal treatment in an unequal Europe' (2018) 43 *European Law Review* 477.
—— 'The Social Market Economy and Restriction of Free Movement Rights: plus c'est la même chose?' (2019) 57 *Journal of Common Market Studies* 111.
O'Brien C, 'Real links, abstract rights and false alarms: the relationship between the ECJ's "real link" case law and national solidarity' (2008) 33 *European Law Review* 643.
—— 'Social blind spots and monocular policy making: the ECJ's migrant worker model' (2009) 46 *Common Market Law Review* 1107.
—— 'I Trade Therefore I am: Legal Personhood in the European Union' (2013) 50 *Common Market Law Review* 1643.
—— 'Driving Down Disability Equality' (2014) 21 *Maastricht Journal of European and Comparative Law* 723.
—— 'The pillory, the precipice and the slippery slope: the profound effects of the UK's legal reform programme targeting EU migrants' (2015) 37 *Journal of Social Welfare and Family Law* 111.
—— 'Civis Capitalist Sum: Class as the New Guiding Principle of EU Free Movement Law' (2016) 53 *Common Market Law Review* 937.
—— 'The ECJ sacrifices EU citizenship in vain: Commission v. United Kingdom' (2017) 54 *Common Market Law Review* 209.
—— 'Acte cryptique? Zambrano, welfare rights, and underclass citizenship in the tale of the missing preliminary reference' (2019) 56 *Common Market Law Review* 1697.
—— 'Between the devil and the deep blue sea: Vulnerable EU citizens cast adrift in the UK post-Brexit' (2021) 58 *Common Market Law Review* 431.
—— 'The great EU citizenship illusion exposed: equal treatment rights evaporate for the vulnerable' (2021) 46 *European Law Review* 801.
O'Leary S, 'Putting flesh on the bones of European Union citizenship' (1999) 24 *European Law Review* 68.
—— 'Developing an Ever Closer Union between the Peoples of Europe? A Reappraisal of the Case Law of the Court of Justice on the Free Movement of Persons and EU Citizenship' (2008) 27 *Yearbook of European Law* 167.

—— 'Equal treatment and EU citizens: A new chapter on cross-border educational mobility and access to student financial assistance' (2009) 34 *European Law Review* 612.

Pickard L, 'A growing care gap? The supply of unpaid care for older people by their adult children in England to 2032' (2015) 35 *Ageing and Society* 96.

Rennuy N, 'The Trilemma of EU Social Benefits Law: Seeing the Wood and the Trees' (2019) 56 *Common Market Law Review* 1549.

Reynolds S, 'Exploring the "intrinsic connection" between free movement and the genuine enjoyment test: reflections on EU citizenship after *Iida*' (2013) 38 *European Law Review* 376.

—— 'Explaining the constitutional drivers behind the perceived judicial preference for free movement over fundamental rights' (2016) 53 *Common Market Law Review* 643.

Schauer F, 'The Convergence of Rules and Standards' (2003) 3 *New Zealand Law Review* 303.

Scheiwe K, 'EC Law's Unequal Treatment of the Family: The Case Law of the European Court of Justice on Rulings Prohibiting Discrimination on Grounds of Sex and Nationality' (1994) 3 *Social and Legal Studies* 243.

Schutze R, 'On "Federal Ground": The European Union as an (Inter)National Phenomenon' (2009) 46 *Common Market Law Review* 1069.

Shaw J, 'EU citizenship and political rights in an evolving European Union' (2007) 75 *Fordham Law Review* 2549.

Shayo M, 'A Model of Social Identity with an Application to Political Economy, Nation, Class and Redistribution' (2009) 103 *American Political Science Review* 147.

Shultz V, 'Life's Work' (2000) 100 *Columbia Law Review* 1881.

Sibley E and Collins R, 'Benefits for EEA migrants' (2014) 22 *Journal of Poverty and Social Justice* 165.

Sousa PC, 'Quest for the Holy Grail: Is a Unified Approach to the Market Freedoms and European Citizenship Justified?' (2014) 20 *European Law Journal* 499.

Spaventa E, 'Seeing the Wood Despite the Trees? On the Scope of Union Citizenship and its Constitutional Effects' (2008) 45 *Common Market Law Review* 13.

Teodorowski P, Woods R and Catriona K, 'The Mental Health and Wellbeing of EU Citizens in the UK: A Systematic Review of the Qualitative Literature' (2020) 10 *Border Crossing* 43.

Thierry JS and Martinsen DS, 'Lost in translation: how street-level bureaucrats condition Union solidarity' (2018) 40 *Journal of European Integration* 819.

Thym D, 'The Elusive Limits of Solidarity: Residence Rights of and Social Benefits for Economically Inactive Union Citizens' (2015) 52 *Common Market Law Review* 17.

—— 'When Union citizens turn into illegal migrants: the Dano case' (2015) 40 *European Law Review* 249.

Tomuschat C, 'Case C-85/96, *María Martínez Sala v. Freistaat Bayern, Judgment of 12 May 1998, Full Court. [1998] ECR I-269*' (2000) 37 *Common Market Law Review* 449.

Tryfonidou A, 'In Search of the Aim of the EC Free Movement of Persons Provisions: Has the Court of Justice Missed the Point?' (2009) 46 *Common Market Law Review* 1591.

Verschueren H, 'Free Movement or Benefit Tourism: The Unreasonable Burden of Brey' (2014) 16 *European Journal of Migration and Law* 147.

—— 'Free Movement of EU Citizens: Including for the Poor?' (2015) 22 *Maastricht Journal of European and Comparative Law* 10.

—— 'Preventing "Benefit Tourism" in the EU: A Narrow or Broad Interpretation of the possibilities offered by the ECJ in Dano' (2015) 52 *Common Market Law Review* 363.

—— 'Recent case before the Court of Justice of the European Union: Case C-308/14, European Commission v United Kingdom, ECLI:EU:C:2016:436 (14 June 2016)' (2017) 19 *European Journal of Social Security* 71.

Walby S, 'Is Citizenship Gendered' (1994) 28 *Sociology* 379.

Webster J, 'Micro-workers of the Gig Economy: Separate and Precarious' (2016) 25 *New Labor Forum* 56.

Weiler JHH, 'Bread and Circus: The State of European Union' (1998) 4 *The Columbia Journal of European Law* 223.

Welsh A, 'Permission to discriminate – EU nationals, pre-settled status and access to social assistance' (2022) 44 *Journal of Social Welfare and Family Law* 133.
White RCA, 'Residence, Benefit entitlement and Community Law' (2005) 12 *Journal of Social Security Law* 10.

Other Resources

European Institutional Documents

European Commission, 'Proposal for a Directive of the European Parliament and of the Council concerning certain aspects of the organisation of working time' COM(2002) 0336 final.
—— 'Free movement of EU citizens and their families: Five actions to make a difference' (Communication) COM(2013) 837 final.
—— 'First phase consultation of Social Partners under Article 154 TFEU on a possible action addressing the challenges of access to social protection for people in all forms of employment in the framework of the European Pillar of Social Rights' SWD(2017) 205.
—— 'Impact Assessment Accompanying the document Proposal for a Directive of the European Parliament and of the Council on transparent and predictable working conditions in the European Union' SWD(2017) 478 final.
—— 'Proposal for a Directive of the European Parliament and of the Council on transparent and predictable working conditions in the European Union' COM(2017) 797 final.
—— 'Proposal for a Council Recommendation on access to social protection for workers and the self-employed' COM(2018) 0132 final.
—— 'Proposal for a Directive of the European Parliament and of the Council on improving working conditions in platform work' SWD(2021) 395 final.
European Economic and Social Committee, 'Resolution addressed to the European Convention' (CES 1069/2002).
European Parliament '2014 post-election survey, European elections 2014: Analytical overview, Directorate General for Communication, Public Opinion Monitoring Unit' (October 2014).
—— 'Motion for a Parliament Resolution on Women Domestic Workers and Carers in the EU' (2015/2094(INI)) OJ C-66/30.
—— 'Resolution of 16 February 2017 on possible evolutions of and adjustments to the current institutional set-up of the European Union' (2014/2248(INI)).

Working Papers and Reports

ATLEU 'Legal aid and immigration advice for victims of modern slavery' (April 2018).
Belfield C, Cribb J, Hood A and Joyce R, 'Two decades of income inequality in Britain: the role of wages, household earnings and redistribution' (Institute for Fiscal Studies, 2017).
Benton M and Patuzzi L, 'Jobs in 2028: How will changing labour markets affect immigrant integration in Europe?' (Migration Policy Institute Europe, October 2018).
Benton M, Sumption M, Alsvik K, Fratzke S, Kuptsch C and Papademetriou DG, 'Aiming Higher: Policies to Get Immigrants into Middle-Skilled Work in Europe' (Migration Policy Institute Europe, November 2014).
Berger T, Frey CB, Levin G, Danda SR, 'Uber Happy? Work and Wellbeing in the "Gig Economy"' (Working Paper for the 68th Panel Meeting of Economic Policy, October 2018).

Berrington A, Tammes P, Roberts S, McGowan T and West G, 'Measuring Economic Precarity among UK Youth during the Recession' (University of Southampton, ESRC Centre for Population Change Briefing Paper, 2014).

Bourquin P, Cribb J, Waters T and Xu X, 'Why has in-work poverty risen in Britain?' (Institute for Fiscal Studies Working Paper W19/12, 2019).

Brewer M, McCurdy C and Slaughter H, 'Begin Again? Assessing the permanent implications of Covid-19 for the UK's labour market' (The Economy 2030 enquiry, May 2021).

British Red Cross, 'Hope for the future: Support for survivors of trafficking after the National Referral Mechanism' (July 2019).

Broughton A, Biletta I and Kullander M, 'Flexible forms of work: "very atypical contractual arrangements' (Eurofound, 4 March 2010).

Broughton A, Green M, Rickard C and Swift S, 'Precarious employment in Europe part 1: patterns, trends and policy strategy' (European Parliament Committee on Employment and Social Affairs, July 2016).

Buckner L and Yeandle S, 'Valuing Carers 2015: The Rising Value of Carers' Support' (Carers UK, November 2015).

Carers UK, 'The Importance of Carers Allowance: Recognising and supporting family care' (July 2015).

—— 'Juggling work and unpaid care A growing issue' (February 2019).

CIPD, 'To gig or not to gig? Stories from the modern economy' (March 2017).

Clarke S and Cominetti N, 'Setting the record straight: How record employment has changed the UK' (Resolution Foundation, January 2019).

Codagnone C, Abadie F and Biagi F, 'The Future of Work in the "Sharing Economy": Market Efficiency and Equitable Opportunities or Unfair Precarisation?' (European Commission, Joint Research Centre, 2016).

Confederation of British Industry, 'Submission to the Taylor review: Work that Works For All: Building a fair and flexible labour market that benefits everyone' (2017).

Countouris N, Deakin S, Freedland M, Koukiadaki A and Prassl J, 'Report on temporary employment agencies and temporary agency work' (ILO Governance and Tripartism working paper series, 2017).

Davies G, 'Services, Citizenship, and the Country of Origin Principle' (Mitchell Working Paper (Edinburgh) No 2/2007).

—— 'The Entirely Conventional Supremacy of Union Citizenship and Rights' in J Shaw (ed), 'Has the European Court of Justice Challenged Member State Sovereignty in Nationality Law?' (Working Papers, EUI RSCAS, 2011/62, EUDO Citizenship Observatory 2011).

—— 'Migrant Union Citizens and Social Assistance: Trying to Be Reasonable About Self-Sufficiency' (College of Europe Research Papers in Law No 2/2016).

Degryse C, 'Digitalisation of the economy and its impact on labour markets' (European Trade Union Institute Working Paper, 2016).

Dewar L and Ben-Galim D, 'An impossible bind: Requirements to work under Universal Credit' (Gingerbread, November 2017).

Dias MC, Joyce R and Parodi F, 'Wage progression and the gender wage gap: the causal impact of hours of work' (The Institute of Fiscal Studies Briefing note BN223, 2018).

Dougan M, 'Some comments on Rottmann and the "personal circumstances" assessment in the Union citizenship case law' in J Shaw (ed), 'Has the European Court of Justice Challenged Member State Sovereignty in Nationality Law?' (Working Papers, EUI RSCAS, 2011/62, EUDO Citizenship Observatory 2011).

Dunstan R and Anderson D, 'Vulnerable workers: preliminary findings from the Citizens Advice client research' (Department for Business, Enterprise and Regulatory Reform, 2008).

Dwyer P, 'Final findings report: Welfare Conditionality Project 2013–2018' (June 2018).

Eichhorst W et al, 'Social protection rights of economically dependent self-employed workers' (European Parliament 2013).

Eurofound, 'Aspects of non-standard employment in Europe' (Publications Office of the European Union, 2017).
Fernández-Reino M and Rienzo C, 'Migrants in the UK Labour Market: An Overview' (Migration Observatory, 15 July 2019).
Ferrant G, Pesando LM and Nowacka K, 'Unpaid Care Work: The missing link in the analysis of gender gaps in labour outcomes' (OECD Development Centre, December 2014).
Ferrell-Schweppenstedde S, 'Day 46: Is there life after the Safe House for Survivors of Modern Slavery?' (Human Trafficking Foundation, October 2016).
Field F and Forsey A, 'Delivering Justice: A report on the pay and working conditions of Deliveroo riders' (July 2018).
Fihel A, Janicka A, Kaczmarczyk P and Nestorowicz J, 'Free movement of workers and transitional arrangements: lessons from the 2004 and 2007 enlargements' (Centre of Migration Research, University of Warsaw, 2015).
Forde C, Slater G and Green F, 'Agency Work in the UK: What do we know?' (Centre for Employment Relations Innovation and Change, 2008).
Francis-Devine B and Pyper D, 'The Gender Pay Gap' (House of Commons Library Briefing Paper 7068, 2020).
Fujisawa R and Colombo F, 'The long-term care workforce: Overview and strategies to adapt supply to a growing demand' (OECD Health Working Papers no 44, 2009).
Gardiner L and Slaughter H, 'The effects of the coronavirus crisis on workers: Flash findings from the Resolution Foundation's coronavirus survey' (The Resolution Foundation, May 2020).
Golynker O, 'The correlation between the status of Union Citizenship, the rights attached to it and nationality in Rottmann' in J Shaw (ed), *Has the European Court of Justice Challenged the Member State Sovereignty in Nationality Law?* (EUI Robert Schuman Centre for Advanced Studies Paper No 62, 2011).
Hardy G and Lane J, 'Walking on thin ice: The cost of financial insecurity' (Citizens Advice, February 2018).
Harris SD and Kreuger AB, 'A Proposal for Modernizing Labor Laws for Twenty-First-Century Work: The "Independent Worker"' (The Hamilton Project, 2015).
Hawkins O, Miller V and Hardacre J, 'European Parliament Elections 2014' (House of Commons Library Research Paper 14/32, 2014).
Hierlemann D and Huesmann C, 'Policy Brief 2 / 2018 – More Initiative for Europe's Citizens' (Bertelsmann Stiftung, February 2018).
House of Commons Work and Pensions Committee, *Self-employment and the gig economy* (HC 2016-17, HC 847).
Hunt A and Machingura F, 'A good gig? The rise of on-demand domestic work' (Development Progress Working Paper 07, 2016).
Hunt A and Samman E, 'Gender and the gig economy: Critical steps for evidence-based policy' (ODI Working Paper 546, 2019).
Huws U and Joyce S, 'Crowd Working Survey: Size of the UK's gig economy revealed for the first time' (Foundation for European Progressive Studies, February 2016).
Huws U, Spencer NH, Syrdal DS and Holts K, 'Work in the European Gig Economy: Research results from the UK, Sweden, Germany, Austria, The Netherlands, Switzerland and Italy' (Foundation for European Progressive Studies, November 2017).
ICF GHK Milieu, 'A fact finding analysis on the impact on the Member States' social security systems of the entitlements of non-active intra-EU migrants to special non-contributory cash benefits and healthcare granted on the basis of residence' (2013).
Innes D, 'What has driven the rise of in-work poverty?' (Joseph Rowntree Foundation, February 2020).
Joint Research Centre 'The Changing Nature of Work: and skills in the digital age' (Publications Office of the European Union, 2019).
Jones L, 'Women's Progression in the Workplace' (Government Equalities Office, October 2019).
Jourová V, 'Public Consultation on EU Citizenship 2015' (European Commission, November 2018).

Joseph Rowntree Foundation, 'Budget 2018: tackling the rising tide of in-work poverty' (Joseph Rowntree Foundation, 2018).

Judge L and Tomlinson D, 'Secret Agents: agency workers in the new world of work' (The Resolution Foundation, 2016).

Kennedy S and Gheera M, 'Carer's Allowance' (House of Commons Briefing Paper, Number 00846, 9 January 2020).

Kochenov D, 'Citizenship without Respect: The EU's Troubled Equality Ideal' (2010) Jean Monnet Working Paper (NYU Law School 08/10).

Lipsky M, 'Toward a Theory of Street-Level Bureaucracy' (IRP Discussion Paper No 48–69, Institute for Research on Poverty, 1969).

Longhi S, 'The disability pay gap' (Equality and Human Rights Commission: Research report 107, 2017).

Lucas S, 'Flexible working solid facts: A summary review of the socio-economic benefits of flexible working in 16 countries' (Regus, July 2018).

Matthew Taylor et al, 'Good Work: The Taylor Review of Modern Working Practices' (July 2017).

Migration Advisory Committee 'EEA migration in the UK: Final report' (September 2018).

Migration Observatory 'Young People and Migration in the UK: An Overview' (December 2016).

O'Brien C, Spaventa S and De Coninck J, 'Comparative Report 2015: The concept of worker under Article 45 TFEU and certain non-standard forms of employment' (FreSsco, European Commission, 2016).

OECD, 'Fiscal Impact of Migration' in OECD, *International Migration Outlook 2013.*

—— 'OECD Employment Outlook 2014' (3 September 2014).

Oxford Economics 'The Fiscal Impact of Immigration on the UK: A report for the Migration Advisory Committee' (June 2018).

Papademetriou D and Benton M, 'Towards a Whole-of-Society Approach to Receiving and Settling Newcomers in Europe' (Migration Policy Institute Europe, November 2016).

Poptcheva E, 'Freedom of movement and residence of EU citizens: Access to social benefits' (European Parliamentary Research Service, 2014).

Powell A, 'People with disabilities in employment' (House of Commons Library, Number 7540, 2020).

Powell A, Francis-Devine B and Clark H, 'Coronavirus: Impact on the labour market' (House of Commons Library Briefing CBP8898, 9 August 2022).

Risak M and Dullinger T, 'The concept of 'worker' in EU law: status quo and potential for change' (European Trade Union Institute Report 140, 2018).

Sayce L, 'Switching Focus: Whose responsibility to improve disabled people's employment and pay' (London School of Economics, November 2018).

Sehmi R and Slaughter H, 'Double trouble, Exploring the labour market and mental health impact of Covid-19 on young people' (Resolution Foundation, 13 May 2021).

Shaw J, 'Setting the Scene: the Rottmann case introduced' in J Shaw (ed), 'Has the European Court of Justice Challenged Member State Sovereignty in Nationality Law?' (Working Papers, EUI RSCAS, 2011/62, EUDO Citizenship Observatory 2011).

Social Protection Committee and European Commission, 'Adequate social protection for long-term care needs in an ageing society' (Luxembourg: Publications Office of the European Union, 2014).

Special Eurobarometer, 'Electoral Rights' (No 364, March 2013).

Standard Eurobarometer, 'Public Opinion in the European Union' (No 89 March 2018).

—— 'European Citizenship' (No 91, June 2019).

—— 'Public Opinion in the European Union' (No 91, June 2019).

—— 'European Citizenship' (No 97, June 2022).

Statistical Services and Consultancy Unit, 'Platform Work in the UK 2016–2019' (Foundation for European Progressive Studies, 26 June 2019).

Sumption M, 'Not Settled Yet? Understanding the EU Settlement Scheme using the Available Data' (The Migration Observatory, April 2020).

Sumption M and Allen W, 'Election 2015 Briefing – Migration and Welfare Benefits' (Migration Observatory, May 2015).
Tinsley M, 'Parenting Alone: Work and welfare in single parent households' (Policy Exchange 2014).
TUC, 'Great Jobs with Guaranteed Hours: What do workers really think about "flexible" zero-hours contracts?' (4 December 2017).
Vacas-Soriano C, 'Recent developments in temporary employment: Employment growth, wages and transitions' (Eurofound, 2015).
Vargas-Silva C and Fernández-Reino M, 'Briefing: EU Migration to and from the UK' (The Migration Observatory, September 2019).
Verashchagina A and Bettio F, 'Long term care for the elderly: Provisions and providers in 33 countries' (European Commission, 2012).
Wadsworth J, Dhingra S, Ottaviano G and Van Reenen J, 'Brexit and the Impact of Immigration on the UK' (Centre for Economic Performance, London School of Economics, 2016).
Weber T, Hurley J, Adăscăliţei D, 'COVID-19: Implications for employment and working life' (Eurofound, COVID-19 series, Publications Office of the European Union, 2021).
Williams M, 'Kapow to GPOW: The "Genuine Prospect of Work Test"' (Child Poverty Action Group, November 2015).
Work and Pensions Committee, *Valuing and Supporting Carers* (HC 2007-08, 485-I).

Miscellaneous

Cameron D, 'EU speech at Bloomberg' (Bloomberg, 23 January 2013).
'Carers deserve a liveable income' Letter, *Guardian* (31 March 2015).
'Conclusions of the Presidency' (Edinburgh Summit, 1992).
'Dublin European Council 13 and 14 December 1996 Presidency Conclusions: Annexes' (European Parliament, December 1996).
Green D MP, 'Keynote Speech: A Welfare System that Works for All' (Reform Welfare Conference, 16 November 2016).
Hansard (HC Deb) Vol 671, Col 175 (4 February 2020).
Joint Statement from the Foreign Ministers of the Visegrad countries of 4 December 2013.
Letter from Andrew Byrne (Uber Head of Public Policy) to Rachel Reeves MP (Chair of Business, Energy and Industrial Strategy Committee) (08 November 2017).
Letter from Chris Comely, Benefits and Awards Team Manager at Sandwell Metropolitan Borough Council to Ranjit Bains (26 May 2017).
Letter from David Cameron to Donald Tusk (10 November 2015).
Letter from Johanna Mikl-Leitner (Minister of the Interior, Austria), Hans Peter Friedrich (Minister of the Interior, Germany), Fred Teeven (Minister for Immigration, Netherlands) and Theresa May (Home Secretary, UK) to the EU Council Presidency and to Commissioners Viviane Reding, Cecilia Malmström and László Andor of April 2013.

INDEX

www.ingramcontent.com/pod-product-compliance
Ingram Content Group UK Ltd.
Pitfield, Milton Keynes, MK11 3LW, UK
UKHW021904150926
475560UK00004B/342

9 781509 966608